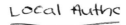

A JOURNEY THROUGH PARTITION AND BEYOND

Volume 2 – Living in United Kingdom

Om Khurana

A Journey Through Partition and Beyond.

Copyright © 2018 by Om Khurana.

All rights reserved. No part of this book may be reproduced in any form or by any electronic or mechanical means including information storage and retrieval systems, without permission in writing from the author. The only exception is by a reviewer, who may quote short excerpts in a review.

First edition, March 2019
Republished with minor changes, June 2019

Cover designed by David Skipper

Edited by Keith Ougden www.the-ancient-editor.yolasite.com

Om Khurana. Visit my website at www.omkhurana.com

CONTENTS

Chapter 1: Passage to Britain 1

Chapter 2: Enter Britain...17

Chapter 3: Journey to India for Marriage 122

Chapter 4: Married and Graduated 168

Chapter 5: Employment after Graduation...............................210

Chapter 6: USA, the Land of Opportunity...............................249

Chapter 7: Back to Britain..287

Chapter 8: Hello to a New Business Venture...........................338

Chapter 9: Health Issues...370

Chapter 10: Two Burglaries 382

Chapter 11: The Conclusion 397

Appendix 1: Insulting Correspondence....................................400

Appendix 2: The Babbles...407

CHAPTER 1: PASSAGE TO BRITAIN

Journey to Cochin

Around 16th April 1958, we boarded the train from Ratlam on our way to Cochin from where I was catching my ship to sail in style to Europe. Accompanying me to Cochin on this historic journey of my life were my parents, my sister, my classmate friend, and my niece V.

For V to accompany me, I went to see her head teacher of the Christian school at Ratlam. I asked her to allow my niece a week off to accompany me to Cochin. She asked the reason and I said I was going to UK and she was coming to see me off. She was very happy for me and showed her Christian gesture of displaying a cross with her fingers. Then she bowed as if she was saluting to the queen of England. That gesture surprised me. She lived in India, worked in India, she was a citizen of India, and yet her loyalty and allegiance were to a British Crown. Why? I just cannot fathom it till today. However, she permitted my niece to accompany me.

My only deep regret was that I could not see my brother Pritam. I was told that he was not well, but I did not know the details. Nobody had told me. But I had failed in my duty to see him before leaving India and I can never forgive myself for that. He must have scolded me for my unforgivable behaviour. It was very stupid to trust in life that one is going to live forever. He died in the summer of 1959 and that increased my agony more. I do not remember the pressing reasons that failed me to do my duty. I could not see my younger brother Ved too as he then had a job to construct border roads in the Kashmir area and could not manage to come.

On the day, we all boarded a train at Ratlam and reached Mumbai in the morning from where we changed for the train going to Chennai. This was my first trip to the south of India. I found a lot of cultural differences between the North and the South. At mid-day at a junction station, I noticed that all the passengers were lining up along the railway line and getting ready for their lunch by holding a banana leaf as a plate for their meal. Soon the rice and curry were being served and the passengers were enjoying their lunch with their fingers. Everyone was speeding up and swallowing the food in a hurry so that they did not miss the train. They were used to this kind of break for lunch. As soon as the lunch was finished, they ran to board the train and we sped towards Chennai. We got to Chennai at midnight and stayed at the station. Next morning, we were on our way to see the sandy beach. The sun was bright as ever. The cool breeze, laden with the salty moisture of the Indian Ocean was giving a false impression of coolness in the air, thus making the body feel comfortable. The beautiful beach was reflecting the sunrays as if a million stars had landed there. But this reflection was marred by the excretions of the morning visits of the Chennai citizens. The rising waves of the mighty Indian oceans were pounding on the Indian soil as if they were trying to swallow the whole of India. It was like a love affair between the Ocean and the soil, trying to meet its beloved. It was a billion years' old battle between the two mighty forces of the planet. It was a no-win situation between the two. This situation was further aggravated by the frustration and the anger of the devastating waves which were given a dirty job of cleaning the beaches. But the Ocean forgot that human dirt was also a nutritional meal for its inhabitants, living in the total darkness of its depth. By swallowing that it was feeding its own population of fish. The same fish was then eaten by the inhabitants who had soiled its shores with excretions in the first place. The nature was at work to educate me that someone's waste was the food for the others.

The Ocean was noisy, and the soil was calm, peaceful, and collected. It was taking all that pounding and erosion in tranquillity and with dignity. It was challenging the mighty waves to come and grab it from its lofty safe heights. But the Ocean had never been successful. It is a continuous tug of war between the two. The land mass has been laughing at Ocean's mighty powers and its repeated attempts to malign its nature of peaceful co-existence. It has been demeaning its force. But the Ocean, while not accepting the defeat, has been feeling 'the grapes are sour'. It has been retreating with every attack like a fox walking away after standing under a fruit tree with greedy eyes, unsuccessful in reaching the juicy fruits.

In the evening we caught a train and we were on our way to Cochin. We ventured into the town and found a place to stay in a wayside hotel. The tempting reason to stay there was that they promised to serve Punjabi chapattis to us instead of rice, the staple food of South India.

We went sight-seeing, riding on local buses, and boat trips. We came to know that there was another ship coming from Australia at the Cochin harbour en-route to Italy. We took the opportunity to go and see what the ship would look like. It was evening by the time the ship anchored. It was quite an experience to see

A JOURNEY THROUGH PARTITION AND BEYOND

some passengers disembarking while others were boarding for their long sea journey. The passengers were nearly all Italians, very few British or Americans. The Italians, settled in Australia, were on their way to Italy for their holidays.

I was busy watching that fascinating scene, the disembarkation of the passengers with their baggage, and the huge size of the floating steel monster on the ocean waves. I knew I was going to wave the same way in a couple of days' time as the Italian passengers were doing to the Indian crowds on the shore. I was thus lost in my own dreams of travelling in a similar monster. Suddenly I noticed a coin rolling down near my foot. I looked up. Some Italian passengers were not just looking at the Indians and waving but were throwing coins at them too. Then I saw some people in the crowd near me running to grab them. I looked up again at the deck of the ship; the Italians were giggling and enjoying this game of fights between the Indians to wrestle for a pittance Lira. I saw another one throwing a coin towards the other begging crowd nearby and the pulling and pushing among the beggars to grab the coin amused the Italians even more. More coins were thrown at different locations and more fights to grab them gave more fun for the throwers. Even some Italians were taking photographs to show to their media barons and to their relations at home to prove the poverty of the begging Indians. Obviously, the Italians were displaying their arrogance to humiliate the entire Indian nation for their hospitality to allow their ship to anchor to drop their passengers on the Indian shore, to pick up some more, and to procure some more fresh foods and vegetables for those gigglers. I felt very humbled and insulted. I swallowed my little pride, even though the ego was protesting at my cowardice and timidity. I could not tell my fellow citizens that what they were doing was utterly wrong and insulting to all their fellow beings in India. I also could not protest to the Italians to stop this game of exploitation of the poor in the Indian society. The Europeans had plundered the whole world and made their lives comfortable and now they were enjoying the game of coin throwing to the same people from whom only a few years earlier they had snatched the same coins away. But now the world had woken up. The times of looting had disappeared forever from the history books but those who were reduced to destitution by colonialism had no opportunity left to rob any to get richer. The world was now, rather than being colonised and exploited, entering another form of exploitation – the migration of job seekers on economic grounds. I was one of them to be exploited by selling my skills to those who had robbed my nation in the first place. But I was no one to interfere and lecture for the human behaviour. Also, I was part of the Indian culture and its environment and I did not appreciate its implications at the time. I too was feeling guilty to a certain extent. I lived in that poverty myself, I was part of it, and I never questioned its existence. I never took an initiative to alleviate it. Now I was lucky that I was getting away from it all. For a moment my dreams evaporated, and I questioned my emigration to the west and then sharing my life with that kind of people. In that moment of agony, I was shattered, apprehensive, scared, and angry at why my own country was incapable of providing me with the opportunity to higher education and employment. But I had forgotten that only eleven years ago my country had thrown away the yoke of colonialism, exploitation, and plunder of a thousand years. Whom could I blame? Maybe the timing of my birth! Maybe my stupid, timid forefathers whose vision extended only up to the tip of their nose? They are now reduced to ashes and have left no history or legacy for the living to know their part of the story. The question of why would never be answered to eternity.

On 27th/28th April, my ship, belonging to Lauro Lines, finally arrived at the Cochin harbour and the time had come to say goodbye to my country, its citizens, and my relations who were so kind to come to say goodbye to me. I had mixed feelings of sadness to leave the shores of my country, which nurtured me up to the age of 27 years, gave me my basic education, and now when I was able to serve it as a young man, I was dumping it and walking away from its woes. But there were millions like me who were looking for the same opportunity to achieve something in their short life time but, alas, opportunities were few and far between. The colonial powers of all kinds had sucked the country dry to its bones and whatever was left there the new corrupt brown rulers were exploiting to fill up their own pockets and those of their cronies and supporters. I, as one of the millions of destitute refugees, was right at the end of the queue to collect the leftover crumbs if there were any. But at last with the opportunity in hand, I had beaten that oppressive corrupt brown regime. For that, I was grateful to my Lord and my generous and kind brother. The fear of going to a totally alien country with a different culture, different language, and totally uncharted territory was boggling the mind. But when my feelings were tormented with a mixture of better or worse future, it must have been equally a nightmare for my parents and sister who came to see me off. They had not done anything wrong to deserve this separation. Any mother, who would go extra miles to protect her child, would now become totally helpless to rescue her son in trouble, thousands of miles away because of her financial constraints. From now onwards I was going to be on my own, in thick and thin, in heaven and hell, all alone. I bowed my head and touched the feet of my brave parents in reverence that they must be bleeding in their hearts and yet did not show it. They sent me off with smiles but visible tears on their cheeks with a long list of do's and don'ts.

So, with tears running, with instructions to 'take care', 'keep on writing regularly', 'stay away from bad company', and so on, I took courage to climb up the steps with my suitcase, full of the bare minimum requirements of life. I stayed on the deck to continue to see my nearest ones until they had disappeared from sight. With tears welling from my eyes, I continued the survey of the shores of my country. Would I ever come back to it? Would I ever be able to manage to see my relations? Who would be gone by the time I could afford to visit them? Such questions had no answers. The communications were very poor in those days. An air letter would take three weeks to reach home. The telephone would cost £1/minute and even then, very few people had the phones.

The fear of landing in a new country and its treatment to my brown skin had never entered my head until I saw the behaviour of the coin throwing Italians on the ship. I was already labelled as 'refugee' in my own country, and that the British would call me a brown immigrant with all its connotations had never dawned in my head. Those behaviours would create an inferiority complex and push me into my own little mental shell I had never imagined. The host countries never recognise the sacrifices and mental tortures of those who leave their land of origin and their kith and kin. But when their own expatriates left their shores a few centuries earlier to exploit, plunder, and build colonies, they call them explorers, adventurers, and pioneers. Why do people on this planet have double standards? Why?

Crossing the Indian Ocean

The ship was an old navy-rejected ship turned into a passenger ship with poor amenities for even our type of passengers. The Italians who were going back on holidays back home were also working people, employed by various Australian factories. Being whites they had better living facilities and better foods, although we ate in the same dining hall. I shared my cabin, one deck below the top deck, with three other Indians. We had proper beds and common toilet and bath facilities which became very unhygienic as we Indians on board misused them and made them very dirty. Our civic sense was very poor. A lot of the Indian passengers were from the villages. Some were even easing themselves in the shower trays, as they were not used to sitting on the toilet seats.

Some passengers were housed in the bottom deck. They did not have proper beds but hammocks hanging from the ceiling. We called those dormitories 'cattle sheds'. Their fares were cheaper, but they ate the same food as we did. In fact, the ship was converted from a naval battleship. While the upper berths of the ship were modernised to carry passengers in comfort with modern toilets, showers, cinemas, dining halls, entertainment areas etc., the lowest deck in which the soldier sailors used to sleep, remained the same.

Friends of Convenience on the Deck

As soon as the beautiful shores of India disappeared from the scene, we hurried to our allotted cabins, deposited our baggage, and began to get to know the fellow travellers with whom we were now to share the cabin for the next two weeks. Then we went to see the dining areas, the bursar office, the dance hall, and the other entertainment areas. Finally, we were on the top deck to view the mighty Ocean waves, lit by the night sky. The huge movements of the waves were going up and down. The Blue Mountains were being made for a moment and disappearing the next. The ship followed the pattern of those waves by moving up and then down. I stood on the front deck, looked at the moving waves, and I became a part of those waves. I was moving up and down as the waves were doing. It was the most fascinating experience of my life. The silvery shining fish were jumping through the blue waves as if they were ruling over the waves that we were making. Maybe in their small way, they were protesting at our intrusion of their habitats. I could not make it out. We left those Oceans millions of years ago to become another species called humans. We had forgotten our ancestor's language a long time ago. The seagulls flying in the sky were the other living creatures, reminding us that we were still on the living planet. Occasionally the gulls would dive down to catch their prey, swallow it without a hitch, and would continue to fly alongside the ship. They had an enormous stamina for a long flight. The ocean water was blue, the sky without the sun was blue, and in that surrounding blueness the white gulls and the silvery grey fish made a spectrum of colours, touching my tender heart. They were unforgettable scenes to witness in that solitude of the nights.

Western people have their own habits of making friends. They are very reserved and individualistic - appearing to be selfish. Someone pointed out to me in London on my arrival that in trains, buses, or coaches no one talks to anyone. Everyone has his head buried in a book or a newspaper. They would not even share or allow you to read from their newspapers. This is west but, in the East, we are accustomed to sharing the pages of the same newspaper. If not this, then we co-travellers would engage in some gossip to know the background of others to start a conversation. We would like to find out where they were coming from, where they were going, how many family members they had, their caste, their marital status, and their education and so on. This may appear to be intrusion and nosiness into strangers' lives. But this is the way we break the ice in human relationships and create familiarity with whom we would be travelling. Then they would find some common topic of interest and exchange views on it. If not that, then politics is the easy subject to argue on. We are all travellers on this land. We are all travelling together. Then why not know who your co-travellers are and what their interests are? I am not criticising those who would like to travel quietly to their dreamland and not gossip but I am only explaining the different culture that we have in the East.

A JOURNEY THROUGH PARTITION AND BEYOND

Humans are very discriminatory in choosing their acquaintances. The selection process is very quick. The mind would look at the subject, survey the body appearance, attire, the way of talking, the style of walking, the expressions on the face, the body language, the vibes between the two, and give its decision of nay and yeah in just moments. If it is yeah, one moves forward to introduce oneself, otherwise walks away. What makes it tick is mysterious. It is a very complicated process of the mind and one would never know how it reaches to that conclusion and on what basis it decides. Maybe the other half of our bodies plays a part in reaching the conclusion. Man's feminine half may be playing a role in selecting a woman he would fall in love with. We do not fall in love or friendship with anyone we see or meet in life. In that process we soon begin to find with whom we would comfortably float on the same wavelength and with whom we would not. The process of elimination works unconsciously in our minds. The process of falling in love is a mysterious gift to humans only. No one can predict when and with whom one would fall in love. So, we roamed around the deck, chatted with some, took our pick, and then decided to stick together with those few for the rest of the journey.

Shortly the bell tolled, and we were on our way to the dining hall to face the Italian pastas and a bottle of red wine on the table to be shared by six of us. On my table, there was one elderly Sikh gentleman, and five others. No one else would take the wine except this gentleman. The issue of who would drink the wine and how much was settled. This gentleman would drink the whole bottle at lunchtime and the whole bottle at dinner time. He would then be tipsy in the afternoon and drunk after the dinner. He would retire to his dormitory and would go straight away to dreamland. He was visiting to see his sons who were living in Britain and perhaps stay there for good and work. I don't know the other four who shared the table, but it used to be good fun. The Italian waiters would speak to us in Italian of which we had no knowledge. The waiters did not speak English. The conversation would be in sign language – good fun.

The major problem was getting a vegetarian meal. No waiter would commit that the food being served was vegetarian. To avoid the issue, we vegetarians only took mashed potatoes, carrots, beans etc. and we always believed that the desserts would be vegetarian although we were never sure whether the fat content of pastries or ice cream was made with butter or came from animal sources. These issues became more apparent after we came to live in UK.

One person with whom I had developed closeness was again a Sikh gentleman who was going to Nottingham to work. We used to be together on the deck, in the dining hall, literally everywhere. We never went to the canteens for a drink, coffee or fruit machines. We had only a few pounds in our pockets (I think

I had about £50 in all) and we wanted to conserve our resources for the rainy days in UK

The Altercation at Port Suez, the Tail End of the Suez Canal

We reached Port Suez just after dinnertime. It must have been around 10pm. We had not retired to our cabins yet. It was pitch dark outside and on the deck except for those twinkling lights on the shores of Port Suez. We assembled on the deck to see those shining lights. We were to anchor there for a day or two until the canal was free from the ships arriving from the other side. It was single lane traffic in the canal. Every ship was boarded by an Egyptian Master who knew the depths of the canal at various places. They would manoeuvre the ship through the exact route. If they did not follow the charted course, the ship could capsize, closing the canal for days for the vital commercial traffic. These masters were very well paid. Before the nationalisation of the canal, the same job was being done by British and French nationals.

The ships normally conducted sight-seeing tours for their passengers. The passage through the canal was to take 3-4 days. We had a choice of taking a short trip, a long trip, or simply staying on the ship. A short trip was offered to go for the day to Port Suez on a boat for sight-seeing, returning in the evening. A longer tour was offered to go to Cairo for 3, 4 days, depending upon the length of the time the ship would take to reach the other side to Port Said, and stay in the hotels and look around the capital. The tourists would spend the last day in Port Said to see around and then catch the ship at the Port. I opted for none of these trips in order to conserve my resources. Also, I was happy with my lot.

While viewing those twinkling lights, we noticed some boats, anchored near the ship, laden with Egyptian art work, souvenirs, watches, electronic goods, and other merchandise. People in the boats installed rope ladders to the deck and started climbing up them to ferry their wares to the top deck. They were very aggressive in their approach to reach the deck to display their merchandise. The ship employees resisted their attempts to climb up but failed. We witnessed the bitter struggle between them. The Egyptians would not understand the Italians and the Italians would not understand the Arabic. But both parties were determined to achieve their goal. The Egyptians were angry, and we could see that they were shouting and calling names to the Italians in their language. I ventured to ask a passing waiter who used to serve us in the dining hall, and who knew broken English, about the commotion. He said, 'The Arabs in boats, down there, want to come up on to the top deck.'

'Why?'

'Well, they want to sell their goods to the passengers. It is not only one. There are so many. They all have plenty of merchandise to display. There are many boats full up with Arabs and their merchandise. We cannot cope with so many. Therefore, we are resisting their efforts to come up.'

'Well they are quite aggressive. Aren't you scared of them?'

'No, we get this every time we cross the canal. We are used to their threats. It is not only the verbal threats; some of them are criminals as well. They loiter around the ship in boats and have been known to steal passengers' goods. They also demand free meals; use of toilets and leave them in a state, and finally when they leave they leave behind a lot of rubbish to be cleared.'

I could hear a lot of noise down there in the boats, anchored near the ship. It was dark, and we could only hear the noise and glimpse the reflections of their white robes and the turbans but nothing else.

However, during those lengthy commotions, it was getting quite late and I went to my cabin to have some sleep. The ones who were going to Cairo for sight-seeing had already left.

Next morning as we went for breakfast, we saw a lot of activity on the top deck. The Arab merchants had finally managed to climb up the rope ladders to the deck. They had all kinds of merchandise to sell - electronic goods, watches, carpets, clothes, and other fancy goods. The selling techniques were very revealing and a new experience. They were chasing us with goods, offering to sell us a watch say for £10, and would continue to haggle the prices. If they failed they would offer another product, and finally be ready to sell the same goods at a throwaway price of £2-£3. It was very high-pressure salesmanship mixed with abuse and aggression. If we were a simple trusting people, we would be nicked many times more. I did not have much money and so I went there just to gain the experience.

The Trouble

Sometimes visiting such risky places can land you into difficulties. I got friendly with one young British student who was returning to his country after a short stay in India. As we moved from one stall to the other, the Arabs showed more interest towards the British or any other white Europeans rather than to us. We Asians were clever and trained buyers. We knew how to haggle and negotiate prices. We knew their selling techniques, harassment, intimidation, and coercion and therefore we would not become their easy prey. They stayed away from us and instead displayed their hatred towards us. But the whites were more trusting people. They would pay what they were asked. This I discovered when I arrived in Britain. All products were marked with prices in the shops and they would pay what was displayed on the price tag of the product.

I noticed that despite their-five-times-day prayers to their God, they were mere exploiters. Money was their God. It was a disgusting experience. Furthermore, the Arabs knew that the Asians were not that rich and would not spend as much as the whites. Therefore, the whites were chased more to buy their wares at exorbitant prices.

When I found that every stallholder Arab was intimidating my white co-traveller, I could not resist protesting to one of the stallholders.

'Why don't you just leave him alone when he does not wish to buy your watch?'

'He will when we put enough pressure. We do it every day.'

'But he said to you "no" so many times that you should respect his wishes.'

'I am surprised. You Indies,' as they called us, 'are our brothers, coming from a Nehru country who helped us to regain the control of our precious national resource, our pride and joy – the Suez Canal - a couple of years ago, and yet you are supporting this white British man. This is our time to take the money from their pockets and we are doing it legitimately and not by exploitation as they did to us.' He was right. He had not forgotten the exploitation by the British, while we Indians had in India. But we should not live in the past. We should learn from the past, its tragedies, its mishaps, and its cruelties to fellow humans, its joys, its creations but not stay there and demand revenge for the past misdeeds.

I knew I was now getting into hot water. He visibly showed his anger towards me. If I had persisted further, I knew we were in their territory and at their mercy to cross through the canal. I could also now see why the Italian boat managers were reluctant to confront them. It was time for me to quit the unpleasant scene. I said, 'I do understand your reasoning, but you know this guy is a student. He went to India for a few days on a study trip. He has no money to buy anything from you. I was only trying to tell you that there is no point in chasing this guy because he just cannot afford to buy.'

With this statement we quickly walked away. My co-traveller thanked me and told me that I should be careful in future in dealing with such situations. He said he did not mind this intimidation as you find a lot of this high-pressure salesmanship when you travel around the world. Mine was the first international travel and I had no such experience. He was right as we experienced later in Italy the same kind of high-pressure salesmanship.

Next morning around 11am the caravan of ships started moving towards the canal. The journey was slow. An experienced Egyptian navigator was provided on every ship. He knew the terrain of the canal at various places to steer the ship safely so that it did not get grounded in the shallow mires of the canal. It was a single file of ships that sailed, as the canal was not wide enough for two-way traffic. If I remember correctly it took us around 15 hours to reach the other side of the canal, Port Said.

A JOURNEY THROUGH PARTITION AND BEYOND

The canal was re-opened only a year earlier (April 1957). As far as we knew it had been closed by the sinking of the ships by the treacherous collusion of the three air forces of the GB, France, and Israel. It was a huge political drama of the time. The canal was finally declared to be an integral part of Egypt by the resolution passed by the UN. The political and economic pressure exerted by the American administration forced all the three attacking powers to withdraw their forces from the Canal Zone. As we sailed through the Canal we could see the damage caused to the Canal by the three air forces' strikes, and saw some sunken ships still in the Great Bitter Lake.

From Port Said, we continued to sail to Malta, our first landing on European soil. At that time, the very small island was under British control. I admired the global strategic genius of the British. They were controlling Singapore, Hong Kong, the Maldives, the Suez Canal, desolate Malta, Cyprus, and then Gibraltar. We reached Malta in the morning. There was nothing to do there. In Malta we felt a little bored. You could walk from one end to the other in a couple of hours. There was no sight-seeing on offer. The population was small and there was nothing else to do. Soon the evening came, and we set sail to Messina.

Messina

We reached Messina in the morning. The ship was to stay there for the whole day and was to set sail for Naples in the evening. We had our usual good breakfast. Mr Singh and I went out sight-seeing. As we came out of the ship and on to the streets of Messina, Mr Singh became the VIP of the Italian crowds. The Italians had never seen before a handsome and majestically looking Sikh, with his nicely tucked-in beard, moustache, and well-groomed long hair tucked under his colourful turban. Or maybe they had read some stories about the bravery of the Sikh soldiers in the 2nd World War. Whatever the reasons, we never discovered them because of the language difficulties. They considered him as if the Maharaja of India had landed for the first time on their shores. People would stop, wave, smile and follow us wherever we went. We sat in the open upper deck of the tourist bus; the shoppers would look towards us on the bus. It became a memorable scene. Nobody gave me a damn or noticed my presence. Around noon we ended up in a park. It so happened that on that day, some pretty, young school girls were having an open day in the park. The moment they saw Mr Singh, they went bizarre. They followed him wherever he went. They would ask questions in their language and with their body language to know what he was hiding under his turban, is he a maharaja? where does he come from? is he going to stay in Messina? They queued up for his autograph, they wanted to have his address so that they could correspond with him. Mr Singh was enjoying every moment of being the centre of attention, especially from the young white-skinned girls. Who would not? - coming from the continent where contact between the opposite sexes was frowned upon. Even to talk to a strange girl would invite immediate hostility from the passers-by. Any un-intentional advances towards a girl would invite immediate retribution and even some girls may rain blows on you with their sandals with added verbal abuse. So, to find ourselves mingling freely with the opposite sex was a great experience. We boys were accepted as equal without any distinctions. The girls in India were quite happy to sleep with you after marriage but they displayed their nastiest hostility at other times. They never showed any affection or respect towards the boys in their prime age. In one word they were hypocrites. This attitude is now changing. Young people now have girlfriends and boyfriends as in the West. However, it was a great day for Mr Singh and for me too but to a lesser extent.

On the way back from the park to the ship, we rode on the open top deck of a bus. As we reached near the harbour, where most of the offices were located, Mr Singh attracted a lot more attention from the milling crowds on the footpaths. They were waving to him very enthusiastically. Some were sending their flying kisses. I saw him blushing with that kind of attention. Maybe it was the time when offices had closed, and the people were returning home with a bit of shopping. We thought we were the tourists and were out for sight-seeing but instead we became the centre of their curiosity.

As we finished our evening dinner the ship was ready to sail for Naples where we anchored again in the morning. After breakfast we were out for sight-seeing again. There were no excitements here, maybe because Naples was a cosmopolitan city. The citizens of this city had seen Sikh soldiers during WW2. Mr Singh was reduced to my level of popularity, that is - no attention; just another brown sight-seer except that he had a turban and I had black hair, blown around by the cool breeze.

Naples is a big city with all kinds of amenities. Some of our co-travellers went to the post office to post letters to their parents and friends. As they came back, we heard strange stories. They compared the cost of postage stamps. Everyone paid different postage for their letters even though all those letters were posted to Delhi. We could not figure it out how a government-run postal service would charge different rates for the same weight letter going to the same city in India. We just gave up on it. It was not that we were penny-pinchers that led us to compare the postage costs but because we were given very little foreign exchange by our Indian government and we were prudent. Also, all of us did not belong to rich families and we had only limited money. After the bad experience of the Arabs' high-pressure salesmanship, we expected a better deal in Europe. But alas this was not true. The hagglers on the streets were also selling some merchandise, like watches, cameras etc. with again exorbitant opening prices and then coming down by 90%, shattering our confidence about the quality of the goods they were selling.

We sailed from Naples late that night for Genoa and we reached there not next morning, but the morning after.

Genoa

The sea journey was well planned and as usual we reached our destination, Genoa, in the early morning. It was a sad moment in a way. The ship journey provided us the safety, tranquillity, peace of mind, entertainments, food, and many other benefits. Come what may, we would get our twice-daily meals, breakfast, lounging on the deck, some entertainment in the evenings and finally a well-made bed for the relaxation in the night. We were totally free from all the chores of life which we must accomplish for daily living. We had built an association with our living quarters, the dining hall, and the service providers. We lived there as posh maharajas. But now the sad day had come when we would be thrown out from that security which we had been enjoying for the last thirteen days. From now onwards, we had to fend for ourselves. We would be on our own. The friendships and kinships which we had made with other fellow travellers in the ship would be all gone. It was a relationship of convenience, which was imposed upon us being the co-travellers and was now going to disappear. Everyone had to find their own way to his/her destination for which they had started their journey and had left their loved ones in their homelands. We had already packed our meagre baggage, had our usual heavy breakfasts, and were ready to disembark. As we came out on the streets to find a taxi to go to the Genoa Railway Station, we found no taxi would be willing to serve us. We flagged them to stop, but they would move onto the other passengers with white skin. We were four and we decided to hire a taxi together to save costs and to look after each other until we reached Britain to be met by our respective minders. Finally, some decent taxi driver had a pity on our plight and took us to the station. As we reached there, the baggage handlers at the station who were to provide a free service to the passengers to carry their baggage to the platform would not even look at us. The slogan, 'Welcome to the great racism of Europe, O brownie Indians,' was showered upon us. It was an undeclared hatred for us. We had some heavy suitcases and we needed help to move them but, no, they would rather run towards the whites. This was the moment when the wake-up time dawned on us. We now realised that this colour hatred, racialism was deeply rooted in Europe. The co-traveller Italians on the ship did not mix with us either because we were brownish. Even those working-class whites felt that they were superior to us. They suffered from a complex, a mental disease only found amongst humans. We now realised that that was also the reason that they were taking the mickey out of the poor

Indians at Cochin by throwing pennies and then taking photographs to show those pictures to their compatriots. We were beginning to feel inferior and insulted. Our ego as proud Indians with so much history and philosophy behind us had melted and had no meaning for these people. We thought that only the Arabs had money as their god, but it appeared that money was the supreme god of the entire world, without any religious or national boundaries. Our soldiers who had fought their wars and shed their blood on their soils for their politics had no meaning to them. We now knew that our coming to Europe for earning our living and making ourselves better would be an uphill task and the roads to make ourselves better would be full of thorns. They did not wish to read or like to know the history of their plunder, the exploitation, and the systematic stealing of our wealth from our lands. Their memory had gone short and their mental faculties were short-circuited. Today we Indians were only trying legitimately to earn some crumbs from their countries which they had industrialised with our looted wealth. We could only blame our hapless forefathers who, with their short-sightedness, reduced their future generations to destitute levels.

Soon we realised that the baggage handlers preferred to move the baggage of those who were Americans. Americans would give them a good tip and so it was the greed that attracted them to the ones who paid them handsome tips. Some may call it 'tips' but to me it is another form of begging. Salute those who drop a bigger coin in their box and walk away from those who looked poorer. The irony of the situation was, we came to know later, that the baggage handlers were paid by the railway stations. However, with some effort and being young we moved our own baggage to the platform. It was true that we did not have enough spare money on us to tip.

The Cup of Coffee

We settled down at the platform and found out the departure time of the train to London. It was to leave late in the evening; we had some time to look around while sharing the times between us to look after the baggage. We two of us sat with the baggage and the other one went to have a cup of coffee at a café down the road, just outside the station. He came back after a while and then the other one went. When he came back these two compared the cost of the cup of coffee each had paid. One of them paid more than the other. Both had only coffee and ate nothing. So, we had to solve the puzzle. Both were of the same colour, look-alike Asians, both were young boys, then why had one paid more than the other. We debated among ourselves and two of us decided to ignore it but the third was not a quitter. He wanted to satisfy his curiosity - why? So, he ventured back to the shop. He discussed the matter by using sign language and came back to announce that the one who paid more had his coffee by sitting down in the café and was therefore charged more. We were learning fast the European way of conducting a business. In Naples we had paid more postage for the same letters but here we were paying more for the same coffee for the privilege of sitting down. Rob man rob but first find the reasons how to rob.

Again, I did not go for the coffee. I was mean. I wanted to conserve my resources.

Train Journey to UK

The train left on time and we were on our way to UK. I do not remember whether we ate that evening, or we observed a convenient fast. Being vegetarian I was always reluctant to try food outside. It was a big handicap. It was not imposed by anyone from my family, but it was within me. I would not eat anything which was non-vegetarian.

As we travelled through Italy, we found some way to sleep on our seats. It was cold in the night and we were covered with some woollies. As the train crossed through the borders of one country to the other, the ticket collector would wake us up, sometimes violently by pulling our blankets or shaking our toes. He would demand in his native language to see the tickets, the travel documents, and passports. I remember that at some border crossings when I did not wake up, the ticket collector pinched my big toe to wake me up and I sheepishly enquired what he wanted. He rudely demanded to see my documents. This was the norm in those days when Europe was divided into so many small independent countries and the border control was maintained aggressively with arrogance.

We reached Calais in the morning via Milan and Paris. Here we were to disembark and board a ferry to cross the English Channel to Dover. It was nearly afternoon when we got to Dover. As we were waiting for the train for London, one of us, strolling on the platform, wanted to smoke but found he had no matches. We thought we were in UK where we would have no problems in communications but how wrong we could be. So, he saw a man smoking. He walked down to him and asked, 'May I have fire from you?'

The man was puzzled and surprised. He looked at him closely but could not figure out what he wanted. Eventually, he noticed that he had a cigarette in his hand and said, 'Oh, you want a light for your cigarette.' Now this guy did not understand what a light was going to do to his cigarette. But nevertheless, he nodded. The man took out the matchbox from his pocket and gave it to him to light his cigarette.

The dilemma of lighting a cigarette was over amicably.

Finally, the train arrived to disembark its passengers who were on their way to Europe. As soon as it emptied, we started to find a compartment to suit us on the way to London.

Hi, welcome on board to Britain. Let us see what more was stored there for us. Keep patience and read on. I won't disappoint your curiosity for more details.

CHAPTER 2: ENTER BRITAIN

I wanted to come to Britain not to make it my permanent abode but a temporary residence to get an engineering degree and go back. Returning to India was not only my dream but a dream of lots of others who later became our family friends. They wanted to earn a bit of money, save, and then go back to their roots in India. Britain was only a springboard to make ourselves financially a bit better off. But we were all caught in some kind of vicious circumstances, beyond our control, that caused us to be stuck here for life, an immigrant for life. Lord Ram was sentenced to live in forests and was banned to return to his kingdom for only fourteen years and when he went back to his kingdom he was given a hero's welcome with millions of candles lighted in his honour in the streets of his capital. The people showered their love and affection with music and dances all over the kingdom. Perhaps he was a prince and not an ordinary soul like us. But here we have been thrown out for the whole life. We neither have any hope of returning back to our country nor have our countrymen understood our predicament. We have been declared pariahs of the country. We are now known as Non Returnable Indians (NRI, in fact 'non-resident-Indians'). We have been written off for life, not of our making but by being caught by our own circumstances as well as by the negligence and the cruel attitude of the ruling classes of India. For them the brain drain has no meaning. Perhaps the following episode which happened only recently in 2012 and some others you will read later will make it clear. We are not settled here in UK voluntarily or by choice but we find no way of returning home. Maybe the hierarchy feels threatened with our presence there now. It is opposite to what once Macmillan had said about a trouble-maker colleague while reshuffling his cabinet, 'I prefer to let him piss out rather than piss in.' So we NRI are forced to piss in.

On 5th January 2012, I made an enquiry through Alibaba for a Stick Pack machine from Uflex in India. They replied to me by email, giving me a brief description of the machine. They also attached a machine picture with their terms and conditions. That picture, when viewed closely, caught my attention. It was an old rusted machine. Being a man of Indian origin, I was disturbed at how such a big reputable company could send such old pictures to their would-be buyers. I wrote a letter asking 'Is that the machine in the picture' you were selling me. From that letter, their Vice President got so much annoyed that he wrote me very rude and impertinent letters, accusing me of lack of integrity and disloyalty to the country I come from. Please see the email correspondence in Appendix 1 and decide for yourself.

It was Saturday, 17th May 1958 when I landed on British soil at Dover. We reached King's Cross station in the evening. It was a bit nippy and dark that evening. Mr A was at the station to receive me. It was really great. First he had helped me get the passport by sending me a letter and now once again he was here at the station to receive me. I salute him, adore him, and thank him a million times for showing that compassion towards me. Without his help, I would not be here in UK and would not be able to get the education I have received so far. After my elder brother, A was my other mentor. My brother laid the foundations of my early education and helped me to wear the tiny toddler shoes. A made me grow bigger to wear the shoes of adulthood. And that without any strings or conditions attached. Such people are found rarely on this planet.

Any newcomer from the subcontinent brought new problems to UK. Firstly they never had enough money on them because they came from working and middle-class families. Secondly they had poor food and civic habits. Thirdly they had typically annoying habits of gazing at the love-making young couples for hugging and kissing each other. Fourthly they spoke very loudly as they walked on footpaths in their own language – something very annoying to the British in those days. Fifthly some had the habit of spitting on the roads; they had no manners to use the toilet and bathroom facilities; had poor or non-existent table manners; and never had a habit of saying 'thank you'. So it was a total shock to both - for the entrant to adjust to a world of ethics and the recipients who by nature are very tolerant but if annoyed at times they never showed it on their faces. In fact it was a complete cultural shock to us as well as to the people of the host country. It was not only the locals who were uneasy with the newcomers but also those who had already settled here and had adopted and adjusted well in the country. They felt embarrassed to walk with the newly arrived ones. I remember a number of instances, after only a few months of my settling down here, when I felt quite humiliated. Once I was taking a visitor from India for sight-seeing through St James's Park to Buckingham Palace. As we were walking past a young couple, lying on the lawn embracing and kissing each other, this visitor pointed out that scene to me.

'Hey Om, look at that. What they are doing?'

A JOURNEY THROUGH PARTITION AND BEYOND

I looked and was not as surprised as he was; because to me they were the daily scenes on the British streets and I had seen some even more open displays at Hyde Park Corner. However I advised him not to pay any attention to them and let them get on with their lives, otherwise they would be quite abusive and aggressive towards us. But his eyes were not satisfied and he wanted to see more of it to know how far they would go with their love-making in that public park. So rather than accepting my advice, as we continued to walk past, he continued to turn around to see and enjoy that scene. To me it was a childish behaviour and could have potentially landed us both into trouble. So there you are. What can one do in such situations? Nothing really except to wait till wisdom dawns on the inquisitive soul. I do not blame him as he had come from India, that was sexually repressed, to visit a country with an open society.

However, going back - After getting my baggage I went to customs to clear it where I got into an argument with the customs officer over a leather briefcase I had brought for A as a present. It cost only a couple of Pounds in Indian Rupees but the duty charged was more than 100% of the cost because, the officer said, it was a luxury good and was not an essential part of life. It appeared the charge was imposed at the discretion of the officer. He also objected to the price of the case I gave him. The following dialogue ensued between us.

'You are giving me a deflated buying price. Have you got a receipt to prove that your buying price is £2?'

'I do not have a receipt. You do not carry receipts for the essentials you buy in life.'

'Well this item, if you bought it in shops here, would cost you around £4.'

'It does not follow that the Indian price would be around yours. It is a poor country with a lower standard of living. The prices have to be cheaper there. I am sorry I will not pay for this exorbitant 100% duty.'

'But it is a luxury item and not an essential item to have. Also you have brought two.'

'Yes, one is a present for my friend who is going to look after me when I am in the country and the second one is for me. I need it to carry my books when going to college. I have arrived here to study. It is not a luxury item for me but an essential part of my studies.'

'Are they new?'

'Yes. I cannot give a second-hand item as a gift. They have to be new. I am also going to use it for four years for my studies. I cannot just bring a second-hand one that would not last me at least four years.'

'Anyway, that is the duty you have to pay before you are allowed to bring it into the country.'

'What if I refused to pay?'

'I will keep it here and it will be auctioned into the open market with other similar goods. The country cannot afford to lose the revenue as we are still paying our war debt to USA.'

'That is not my fault. We in India did not ask you to go to war. It was your war not ours. In fact we too are paying the debt imposed on us by Britain for the war you fought, in kind as well as in blood.' I rebuffed his argument.

The heated argument was now leading us to an emotional nationalism where he was digging his heels deeper into his British soil and I, being young and hot-headed, was not prepared to give up my rights. So I walked away and narrated the story to A. He persuaded me to be practical. It would still be cheaper to pay the duty rather than buying from local shops. So I went back and said, 'Ok officer I will pay the duty you are asking me to pay, not willingly but under duress. It is your country and you are imposing this unnecessary burden on my purse which I am trying to save from such raids for my future studies.'

'Ok please pay £5 for the two and I will give you a receipt.'

I handed over a fiver grudgingly, took the receipt and walked away to freedom to roam around on London streets as a free man until death.

On the way to A's house, he briefed me that he had rented a separate room for me. Before I expressed my uneasiness he hastily added that the room was in the same house where he was staying. He explained that it was better to be in two separate rooms and be independent. I agreed. I asked A if the job for which he sent me an appointment letter was still available and when I would be able to join it.

'No that job is not there. It was only arranged to get you an appointment letter so that you could get your passport.'

'Oh! That means I will be on the road until I find another job.'

'Yes. It should not be difficult. You will get one soon. It is only a matter of time. I tried in my office but there is no vacancy at the moment.'

It was a shock. I now had the problem of finding another job, and soon. If I didn't get one soon, my dream of saving some money for my further education would turn into a pipe dream. To a certain extent I was prepared for it because I had arrived in UK one year after receiving that letter. For any new venture, uncertainty is always part of a game. The past experience of finding a job in India in 1953 was a good guide. But one has to steel oneself for all eventualities and face the music of life with courage and determination. I was ready for that. I had not left my loved ones for a joke.

We took the underground to Westbourne Grove station. His house was just five minutes' walk from there. This area is now famous for the yearly Notting Hill London Carnival. We went inside the house. A showed me my room on the

A JOURNEY THROUGH PARTITION AND BEYOND

ground floor. A had his room on the first floor. We put the baggage in my room and then he showed me the bathroom with toilet. He explained to me how to light and use the hot water gas geyser in the bath. The gas flame lights itself automatically, he said, when the water is turned on. I could fill the tub to take a bath or fill a bucket and use a jug to pour the water on the body as we were doing in India. He also showed me the common kitchen to use for cooking. We then went to his room to talk about my journey and India. The time came to go to bed and I went to my room to allow him to have his privacy and rest.

We spent next Sunday together. He enlightened me on how to manage the cooking facility in the kitchen. He showed me how the kitchen appliances, the gas cooker, and the iron were used. He also explained how to clean and tidy the kitchen, the bathrooms, and make our own beds in the morning. In the evening he took me out to some parts of London. While travelling in the underground, he explained how to use the maps, how to go from place A to B by using buses and the underground and come back home safely. In short, it was a comprehensive introduction to living in a modern cosmopolitan city and adjusting to the British way of life.

Gas Explosion

Learning any skill is slow and never easy. One has to experience, experiment, and use initiatives. On Monday I got up as usual early, went to toilet, and got ready to have a bath. Everyone staying at the house had already gone to work, including the middle-aged, friendly, and well-spoken English landlord. I decided to take a bath in the traditional Indian way, with a bucket and a jug. To take a bath with cold water even in May in those days was impossible, especially for me coming from a hot country. Furthermore, the cold and damp British weather in those days could create joint problems.

As I turned the gas water heater tap on, the cold water continued to come. On close inspection I found that the gas was not turning on to warm the water because the pilot light was off. On Sunday when we were cooking in the kitchen, A explained to me how to light the gas burners with a mechanical spark generator. I had no matches even though I used to smoke. So I dressed again, went to the kitchen, got the friendly invention of the spark generator. First I tried to ignite the pilot light with the spark generator without the water tap on. I attempted a few times, but without any success. Ah, is it possible that the gas was not being released to the pilot and that was why it was not being lit? So the clever thought came that I should open the water first to allow the gas to flow from the burners and then ignite the gas with the spark generator. So I turned on the water, inserted the spark generator inside through the small opening near the pilot, and stroked repeatedly to produce the sparks. No luck. Then I tried again. No success again. I turned the water off. After a little deliberation, I decided to have a go again. This time the gas burners ignited but with a frighteningly big bang. The accumulated gas inside the boiler had exploded. I was badly shaken, nervous, and my whole body was shaking and trembling with fear. When I mentioned the experience to A in the evening, he explained that the heater did not light as the pilot light might have gone out. It was working in the morning when he took a bath but as the heater is connected to the outside environment to clear the un-burnt gases, the air might have blown in to turn the pilot out. It does happen sometimes, he said. The procedure was that if the pilot was out, I should have lit the pilot first with a match and then turned the water on. But when I opened the water first the gas also opened and accumulated in the small space in the heater and exploded as the spark lit the gas inside. So the learning curve to use the modern technology of the advanced nation started with a big bang, just a day after my arrival.

During the week, I wrote a few letters for jobs. One of the addresses was given to me by A. I also went out but it was too scary. I was feeling terribly homesick. I was like a fish thrown out of the water, struggling for some breath to survive and live. It was a huge cultural shock and I just wanted to be amongst my own kind of people who spoke my language, ate like I did, and talked about a subject that would be common between us. Britain looked horrible. I felt very insecure while sitting behind those four walls of the room. In the evening, I found out from A about other Indian places where I could go and talk to our people. He said that there was an Indian High Commission office at Aldwych, and a commercial procurement office at Acton. I wanted to go to the Indian High Commission to see someone in the commercial section who lived at Cricklewood with his family. I had a parcel to give to him. I also had a message to hand over to someone at the Acton office. The Acton place was very local, so next day I went to that office. The peon at reception asked me to wait for an hour as the officer was busy. I suspect he was probably late to report for work. As I was waiting in the peons' office, I became friendly with a couple of them. They were very nice people and asked me the purpose of my visit to UK. They offered me a cup of tea. I felt at home amongst them.

They were both in and out to provide the service to their clerical staff. Lunch break came and one of them asked me to accompany him to the shops in the street below. He said he was also going to a betting shop to stake some money on horses and dogs. In between serving his bosses, he would nip down to the shop to hear the commentary about the winners and losers. When he came back after betting, he explained to me in detail how the betting worked in the country. A lot of working people were addicted to gambling, he said. Betting was one of their hobbies. He asked me if I would like to bet. I politely refused. To me it was a waste of money and time. I had no wish to move away from my chosen goal of getting

A JOURNEY THROUGH PARTITION AND BEYOND

higher education for which I had come here. I had not come here all the way from India for betting.

I met the man after a couple of hours, handed over his parcel but stayed on with the peons in their little office. Soon it was time to close their office. I went back home after seeking their permission to come back again to sit in their office, to kill my loneliness and homesickness. They were nice and allowed me. I went back there again a couple of times.

During these visits I became closer to one of them. He kept up his acquaintance with me for a very long time. When later in the year I moved to Muswell Hill, he used to come on some Sundays to see me there. He was not married and had no friends. His loneliness was too much for his mental health. A lot of times I noticed that he would lose coherence in his thoughts. He would get totally confused. While talking on some subject, suddenly I would find him talking about some angels and souls floating around in the sky. Whenever he would phone me to visit me in the weekend, I started dreading his visits but I could not refuse him. I knew that it was all because of his loneliness. If I also had refused him to visit me, he might have a mental breakdown. So this association continued. I could not find much about his background as the conversation was always erratic and confusing. However this association ended because I stopped getting his calls and I did not know where he lived.

Soon the working days of the first week passed and the weekend arrived.

The Exposure to London Life

A had good friends, settled in London and Luton. They were his classmates and acquaintances from India. They were coming on Friday and Saturday and spending the weekend with him. They had also come from Delhi to live and work in UK. They were going to have lunch at his place, then go to a movie and after that to a pub at Shepherds Bush.

One of them B was living in the Acton area; the other C was living in Luton and was working for the Vauxhall motor company.

B was working in some factory. He was short with fair complexion and wore some pink lipstick on his cheeks to enhance his facial appearance. He was quite clever, money-minded, and used to have a jewellery stall at the local marketplace. I went with him twice to his stall. He would get up 4am on Sundays to prepare to go to the stall, set it up with his wares by 7am before the appearance of customers. He explained that the business was very lucrative, especially from the tax point of view. Whatever he made – and he made a good kill – it would all go into his pocket. The taxman would never be able to find his sales and profits. He offered me to be a partner in his business. He insisted that one Sunday I should go to his stall to see him in action. I accompanied him one sunny Sunday and was with him all day.

Next to his stall was a Mr Singh. He was selling shoes and sandals. One day he came with his six-year-old boy. The boy was asking his father to give him a couple of shillings to buy something from a shop. But father refused. The boy was persistent and kept on crying but father would not budge a bit. All the passers-by were looking at the father with disgust and were walking away. Finally B offered to give the money to the boy. Mr Singh had created a shameful scene. He had a full-time job, and he also earned good profit at the stall, so why he was so mean was beyond my comprehension.

The behaviour of Mr Singh towards his son, the exploitation of customers, fiddling the taxes, and the taunting of the young girls passing by, was enough experience for me to make a decision. I refused to join him.

C was the only son of his parents who were settled in Delhi. His father was a doctor. Obviously it must have been a heart-breaking experience for the parents to let their only child go to UK, especially for the mother. He told me that his parents permitted him to go to UK only because he said to them that he was going for higher education. He was tall, handsome, a bit skinny with thinning hair, and cultured. The parents had some expectations from their son. He was still unmarried, as we all were. Very quickly we became close friends and began to share and discuss views on personal matters.

A, B, C and others invited me to join them in their Saturday fun: for a lunch at an Indian restaurant, to a movie, and then to a pub. They all had jobs and they could afford to spend for the evening. I had no income and so I declined. Besides I was not keen to go to the pub. I had never been a society boy. Their culture would have been totally alien to me. I would have found myself out of place there. I was poor in society babbles. I was a serious introvert man. If there was nothing for me to share on some interesting topic, I would get bored and uncomfortable. I would become a bad companion. I had another problem too - that I was a vegetarian. Even if I had a job I would still not join them as my aim was to save up, and then go for full-time education.

Next morning on Sunday, A & C both got up late because they had come back late from the pub. They were still tipsy. They said they had had a good time at the pub. They talked about their encounters with some girls. A was busy somewhere, C and I got the opportunity to share our views. C explained the purpose of his visit to UK, about his family, the expectations of his father and all that. He also asked me the purpose of my visit to UK. Having known that I had come to study too and my determination to pursue it with vigour, he felt a bit uneasy in my company. He had done nothing so far to keep his promise to his father. He was deceiving him. He was breaking his trust. I had already seen that

A JOURNEY THROUGH PARTITION AND BEYOND

attitude in Mohan and Vohra at Gwalior and now him. I will narrate later that I met some more similar people who had done the same to their elders, cheating those who supported them. Why do they do it?

We continued. 'If you have come to study, why don't you pursue it?' I asked.

'I would like to but have no money.'

'Why don't you save some rather than spend on drinks?'

'I know but if I tell you how much money I have wasted on drinks, you would be amazed. Don't ask me how many bottles I have drunk since coming to this country, ask me how many cars and houses I have drunk so far.'

'So you know it and yet keep on doing it?'

'Yes! I was also getting engaged before coming to this country. My father wanted me to marry before coming here.'

How could I imagine about the drinking? I had hardly touched the damn thing while in India except for a couple of times with K at his Air Force canteen in New Delhi. It was not my job to humble another intelligent being. Why was he doing what he was doing? Was that due to his company? Was he addicted to it? It was not my business to project my image as 'holier than thou'. I had seen it all before when Vohra had ruined his whole life the same way as this man was now doing. You cannot interfere. It is their birthright to be free. You can never tell the drowning souls that you are holier than them. Everyone has to find his own way, but for me the lessons were written on the wall that if I ever continued in this type of company, the ruination of my career was not that far off. I'd had the opportunity to come to UK. All avenues were wide open to me. One door was leading me to riches, cars, houses, and plenty of women and wine. The other one was taking me through the future promised land to achieve something worthwhile – the good education, later a good standard of living, and a nice comfortable home with a well-groomed partner, service to my country and my parents, brothers, and sisters who had all sacrificed to send me here. This route was not a bed of roses but was full of hardships and that was worth a journey. The choice was always mine and obviously I chose the latter and never regretted it.

I had seen the sadness in the eyes of C. He knew that he was on the wrong track and yet I noticed that he seemed helpless to do anything to turn the tide around to his advantage. Till this day I have not found the answer, why was he doing that?

Another week started on Monday.

During the week, I went to India House, the Indian High Commission at Aldwych. Here nearly all visiting Indians to London used to come for lunch. The canteen would serve rice with curries and it used to be always full. It was cheap also. It would only cost 1-2 shillings. This had also become a meeting place for us.

25

Surprise, Surprise! One day at India House Canteen I bumped into a young handsome fellow Kapoor who was working with me at NPL at Delhi as a glass blower technician. When in India, he once mentioned that he was trying to go to Britain but I never told him that I too was trying to quit India. I must admit I was secretive. So the meeting at India House was a big surprise to both of us.

Kapoor was smart, well dressed, handsome, smiling and happy, well spoken, believed in the best of the world, and ready for fun and enjoyment even if it happened to be unethical. He belonged to the generation of young people who believed in showing off. He was egotistic, proud, and walked elegantly in a suit and colourful neckties on the meticulously clean white shirts. He always had well-shined shoes. But had no money to buy a cup of coffee for girlfriends. We were never friends at NPL. I hardly knew him. I would always shy away from people of that type. Maybe I was suffering from a complex. Maybe my early childhood conditioning was a handicap. Maybe it was my meagre monthly pay packet that I wanted to use to serve my family members rather than on show-off outfits. Maybe I was not a selfish, self-centred, egotistic man. Maybe I was a dedicated son to meet my social responsibilities. Maybe I was a simple soul and had no stomach for show-off youths of the day. Whatever the reasons I always avoided people like him. I did not know anything about his background. But his way of dressing, his manners, his way of talking, and his rich friends whom I met in London at a later stage, all pointed me to believe that he belonged to a good family.

Meeting him became a blessing in disguise. We talked about the little experiences we had so far in London. We both were in the same situation except that he had arrived in London a couple of weeks earlier by air. Like me, he too was unemployed and was looking for a job. In his case his money was running out, he had more financial worries, and was desperate to find a job. We talked about the discrimination in the work places, discrimination in renting rooms, and discrimination in the underground. We both had experienced that if we sat next to someone who didn't like our company, they would get up and move away. When we walked on the road, we would be scrutinised with dirty looks. Whenever we did manage to get something, it would always be the rejects of the society. That included housing, the menial type jobs, and the rejected women. We were considered as the scum who had managed to enter the country. As we continued our dialogue, he said, 'You know it is a strange society. When you travel in the underground, no one talks to anyone. They all buy their newspaper and bury their heads in them.'

'Do they talk among themselves?'

'No, they don't. If you try to read their newspaper, they feel offended. They would move their paper away from you or they would give you a dirty look.'

A JOURNEY THROUGH PARTITION AND BEYOND

In India we did the opposite. When people travelled in trains or buses they would start conversations by asking your backgrounds, the place you live, your parents, your education, what you do for a living, and so on. The introduction then may turn into a kinship to share views on social and political affairs, exchange the pages of the newspapers to read when fed up with chattering. The relationship may even advance further quickly to a stage that we might even share our foods, buy things for their children, pay for cups of tea and so on. So to us the British attitude was totally alien and very selfish.

We had shared so much information and the local experiences that we decided to plan our future together in London. While A helped me to come to London, Kapoor boosted my morale to fight out our circumstances together and make our living in London a success.

I was lonely, so was he. We were dying to talk to someone in our own language and share our daily routines. We were both unemployed and both new to a strange country. So we decided to find a common flat where we could live together. He also had some friends from rich families; the friends were here on the pretext of doing further study.

One of them was the son of a jeweller at old Delhi. His family was very rich and he was the only son. He was married but came alone without his wife. Rather than joining the family business, he had a craze for photography. He left with differences with his family to pursue his interests in UK. He bought a very expensive German camera in London. He could have bought much cheaper in Germany but the import duty on such luxury goods was 300%, thus making it very expensive. He was going to college to study photography. Later he brought his wife here. After a couple of years he went back to India to join his family business.

Another one was also a son of a jeweller. Their business was located at Karol Bagh Delhi. He too came to study but never went to college. He was roaming around the streets of London aimlessly, indulging in women and wine.

The third one also belonged to a rich refugee family. His father had set up a machine shop a few miles out of Delhi where he took me when I went to Delhi in 1961 to marry. The place was managed by his father and his other brother. I discovered that his contribution towards managing the business was nearly zero although he attended his office every day. They were doing some lathe turning jobs on contract for big companies. He too came to study but never went to college. When I met him, he was sharing a flat with someone in North London.

All of them must be bored to death, as they had nothing to do all day. They were rich but spoilt and had no experience of the hardships in life. I was reminded of the experiences of Vohra again. They just did not know what they were doing. They had never understood the importance of life and its gifts bestowed upon them by God. They hated to work for their living. It was below their dignity. They would wait for the money to arrive from India. If late, beg, borrow, and live was their motto.

I came across another young fellow Malik. He had a heart of a lion and was very generous. He was studying for a degree in Metallurgy at Cass College London University as an external student. His help and guidance about how to pursue a degree course at London University became very valuable to me. He also invited me to share his flat. He loved sports. On the weekends when I moved away from A, we would go to his flat, play tennis, and watch sports on TV. He was very fond of watching boxing and wrestling, the games I detested to see. To me they were cruel games - to hit, to punch, and twist each other's bodies - but, to be polite, I would join him. He later moved to Germany and was married there to a German girl. I never met him after 1961.

Through Kapoor I met some more people. We used to go quite often at weekends to a flat at Belsize Park where two friends D and Sharma-junior were living. This flat belonged to a German lady. D used to be quiet, reserved, was single and was working for a company repairing TVs. He gave us an impression that he did not wish us to visit them. While we would all chip in to cook in the kitchen, he would be glued to his TV to watch the programmes of his interest. He would have no time to talk to us. He behaved just like the British. Maybe he was already anglicised. However, later on after his marriage we became quite good friends.

Sharma-junior was friendlier. He would show interest in us and suggest ways we could find jobs in London. Later on his older brother also joined him from India. The older one had worked for the Indian Air Force and had arrived as we did, as a British subject. He had a wife and young children, but they were all staying in India until he had a job. So we, Kapoor, Sharma-senior and I used to go together to hunt jobs in the industrialised areas of London.

A Taste of British Beer

Next weekend was with an extra bank holiday. A had planned to go to Luton. We left home early on Saturday and reached Luton in the afternoon. We were going to stay there for two nights and were to be back on Monday.

On Sunday afternoon we all, six of us, walked down to a local pub for lunch. We settled down on the two opposite benches with a table in the middle in the front lawn of the pub. The group followed a British rota tradition of buying beers. First one took the order from everyone of the type of beer he would drink and would it be a pint or half pint. Armed with that information, he dashed down to the pub and came back with six pints of beer in glasses brim full with overflowing froth. He dished out the glasses so each could quench their thirst on that hot summer day. 'Hey, cheers and bottoms up', they cried loudly to finish off

A JOURNEY THROUGH PARTITION AND BEYOND

their pint. Soon another one got up to bring another round of six as his contribution to the binge-drinking session. I never could see the bottom of my first one before the second one arrived right in front of me. My first glass was still nearly full. I had managed to have a couple of sips only. It was very bitter in taste. How do they gulp this bitter liquid so fast? It was beyond me. Did I really belong to this type of world? I questioned myself.

So now I had two to finish.

They were chatting, joking, laughing, and were deeply engrossed in their subjects of interest. The session of drinking their favourite drink continued with full vigour. As the intoxication level increased the proportion of noise level also increased and the depth of the discussion deepened. Luckily we were sitting outside and the level of noise generated in a foreign dialect did not penetrate to the locals. The pub landlord was only interested in the shillings (we used to call it Shiv-ling) adding to his till.

It was a beautiful day, with sunshine and a warm fresh breeze, a rare phenomenon for the British weather in those days. So who would not indulge in quenching his/her thirst in that hot summer? In that jovial mood and congenial environment, while everyone was enjoying, I was getting more and more worried. What would happen when a third pint is lodged firmly in front of me? An idea struck that as they were all busy in drinking, chatting, and getting tipsy, I should quietly move my pint in front of my neighbour on my left. It worked and nobody noticed it, so I thought. I felt relieved that I was successful in deceiving the tipsy crowd around me. When everyone's glasses were nearly empty, I got up fifth in turn to bring my share of the round but I brought five without bringing my pint. B who was sitting opposite to me, noticed and commented:

'Hey, where is your share?'

'I don't need it as my glass is still full.'

'No, that is not the rule of the game. When you bring the round, you bring for everyone including yourself.'

'Ok but you know I am not used to drinking. So I cannot take any more until I get used to the system in this country.'

He did not pursue the matter any further and I thought I had convinced him. The drinking and chatting continued with passion and vigour. Soon the bottoms were visible and came the turn of the next round. I had now two plus. Again, I was trying to find the opportunity to pass on the third to someone. This time I pushed it opposite towards B. No comments and I felt relieved that I was successful again in my cheating game. Everyone now had five pints of beer in their belly and they were enjoying and getting tipsy. Their conversation showed signs of erratic speech. B appeared a bit tipsier than others. His cheeks were getting rosier. He became more courageous and bold. He was losing the grip on his wits.

His behaviour became erratic and unpredictable. Suddenly he jumped up to announce:

'Hey boys, listen to me. Om is not drinking his share of the pints as is expected in mate drinking rules. I have seen him pushing his beer glasses to his neighbours. He also did not bring his own glass when he went to bring his round. It is now my turn to fetch the finishing round. It is nearly half an hour before closing time. I will now bring two for him. He will have to finish those two and the one sitting in front of him within this half hour.'

I protested, 'No, please listen to me. I know I have been doing what you have just said but I cannot drink. I am not used to it. The beer is so bitter for me to swallow. This is the first time I am drinking since a couple of years ago when I had two bottles of beer at a club with one of my friends in Delhi.'

'I don't care. You have to drink the three points within half an hour.'

'Please don't insist. It would just go to waste.'

'No, I will make sure that you finish them before the pub closes.'

A supported me and asked him to mellow and not to insist. But B was adamant. His ego was at the highest peak because of him being tipsy. He was feeling aggrieved that he was being hoodwinked in broad daylight by a recent arrival from the subcontinent. It was unbearable for him to take that insult. The six pints of beer was making him aggressive and arrogant. He was ready for a revenge and showdown. Also in such a company no one tolerates the other person who happens not to be like them. Therefore the odd one must either follow suit or get out of the company. Otherwise the mob would feel that you are showing the attitude of 'holier than thou'. That is never acceptable to them. So his attitude towards me was understandable.

He got up in a huff, rushed to the pub, brought the round with two for me and one each for the others. He dumped two of them right in front of me and said, 'Now mate, I am sitting right in front of you, finish them all.'

He looked at his watch and reminded me that I had only twenty minutes to finish as the pub landlord was very strict in his timings.

I had no way to deceive or cheat now. I was under observation. All the eyes were focussed on me. The chatting and fun drinking was over. I had not a chance in hell not to obey. The closing minutes turned into watching minutes; a cheat was on the line for revenge. I was coaxed and reminded of the minutes left to bottom up my glasses. It was like a racing game in a stadium. Everyone was, it appeared, tired of their chatting; they found it amusing to see me through those three pints of beer. So I started, gulping one mouthful after another to beat the clock. It was a bitter taste; every mouthful would put a shiver in my spine. I could hear the rumbling in my stomach. It was protesting that I am treating it like a dumping ground under duress. It was also saying that I was a damn coward and was not strong enough to say no, no, no. All these tricks of pushing the beer round to others were played by the mind but the punishment was thrust upon the poor stomach, the feeder, the nutrient supplier to the body. Was it fair to the stomach? No, but that is how the mind works. It enjoys itself by inflicting the pains and sufferings on other limbs and organs of the body.

I had just about managed to finish in time. We all got up and started walking towards the house. The slow drinking for those regular drinkers was already intoxicating their heads and they were enjoying its addiction. But mine had not had the time to go to my head yet but it was bursting the limits of my colon. It was sending urgent signals to the head to be watchful for the consequences of it accepting the threat of a mouthy idiot. Some went ahead of us but there was one who was with me. We must have walked only a couple of hundred yards and I started throwing up. The belly has its own brain. It is trained to throw out if some food does not suit it or it cannot be digested. Throwing out was its protest and its final defence. Having thrown out some, I felt relieved. But I must have walked only a few hundred feet more before I threw up again. This time the stomach had really shown its determination to clear all the garbage which should not have been swallowed. It chucked out whatever it felt was an unnecessary burden. I looked around in shame in case some people on the street were watching my bad behaviour. It was a horrible experience. Some people will never learn to leave others alone to enjoy their lives the way they think is fit for them. B was walking way ahead of me. He had no idea of my plight. He walked staggeringly on the road, his legs showed a lack of coordination, and he talked erroneously. The intoxication of the six pints plus one of my beers had taken its toll even on a very experienced drinker. He reached home and slumped on the bed and soon he was asleep with the loud snoring of a giant. That was the evening that was of 'fun'.

Shortly after, I saw another experienced drinker, throwing up near the curb. What a shame. The hard-earned shillings spent on the drinks were now finding their way into the gutters of the streets of Britain. The culture and the name of our nation India, written all over our brown faces, were so visible for the locals to frown upon us. We had not only degraded ourselves but had also brought our country down, thus providing the ammunition to the racist elements of the British society. Britain was already infested with such elements in those days and people like Enoch Powell were in the making.

The beer was bad, the drinking habit was bad, but to combine it with a company of those who do not match to your expectations of life is worse. Never compromise on that.

Hope for a Girlfriend

I am a shy person by nature. I was a coward and was always scared to make advances to a lady in case she rebuked me. I was a damn egotist and I was never ready to take rejection. I had no knowledge of their nature and I never cared to learn or find out their tastes, their likes and dislikes, and their emotional needs. I was of a very different male species. I do not have that natural talent of a male to chase or play a flute to the ears of the females as the snake charmers do to the snakes. I do not believe in weaving the webs around the ladies as the spiders do. I believe in equal rights and the ladies should play an equal role in the lovemaking as the men do but this is totally alien to a woman's nature. I will never chase them to satisfy my lust to go to bed with them. I am a great lover but it must be mutual and must be reciprocated. I am not a 'hunter' and would not go for procreation to please the gods. Therefore it was so lonely for me for all those years of approaching twenty-seven. If there was no system of arranged marriages by parents, I am certain I would have remained a bachelor all my life. I would never go out to pester and propose.

So when A suggested that we have 'to find a girlfriend for you here' it sounded a god-sent opportunity. I did not show any outward emotions but inside me, I felt happy. At last, in UK, I would be able to win over this handicap of not making friends with a female. I would be able to throw away those oppressive taboos instilled in me by the Indian society. It was considered a sin to touch, to chatter, to adore, or to look at a beautiful lady. It was just like saying to a poet or a painter that if he comes across a well laid-out garden, full with dancing fragrant flowers with shades and colours, he should walk away from that experience without writing and painting their beauty to enlighten his heart. God would turn upside down at this behaviour by insulting his greatest invention on this planet – love. We adults all know what goes on in the darkness of the bedroom, a temple of God. There is nothing wrong in it. After all, this is where the two godly energies meet to create a new energy – the new being. We are all born out of it. Why should all the religions condemn and fuss about its practice and create guilt among the mortals? Do they wish to banish the gods' future creation after us? I would agree with the priests if these energies are consumed to satisfy the lust of the individuals. But if these energies meet in love and harmony, then the practice must be welcomed and encouraged. So far in the East it has never happened, while the West is enjoying the freedom of making love openly, in parks, in streets, on beaches, and under the trees. You name it and it is witnessed in every nook and corner of the available places.

Sorry I went off the track.

A JOURNEY THROUGH PARTITION AND BEYOND

A had a German girlfriend who was learning English at a London college. As the weekend was approaching, he said to me that his girlfriend was coming at the weekend.

'I have asked her to bring another girl this time to introduce her to you. After all, you have come to live in this country where everyone has a girlfriend. So why not you?'

'Yeah, but I have no clue how to handle the girls, how to talk to them, entertain them. I am just dumb in that relationship. My early childhood teachings at Gurukul would create a big handicap. My spoken English is poor too.'

'Don't worry, all these aspects of handling a female come automatically and naturally. She is a girl from western culture. She will be able to make you smarter. She is German and learning English, so your English would be better than hers.'

'So after you introduce me, what do I do?'

'Take her to a picture or a pub. These girls like evenings out. She would love that.'

So the weekend arrived. I planned in my head how to address the girl and what to talk about. I had no job, a totally free mind and it was planning castles already. His girlfriend came with another girlfriend. She was a bit plump and attractive to some but not to me. If I had a choice, I would have walked away. We are all prejudiced people. It is the mind which accepts or rejects. But still I was ready for the experience as I knew that I would never be able to find any on my own.

We all had our lunch together with some of his old chums who had come for the weekend. After lunch we went for a walk on the streets of the local shopping areas. The shops were closed as it was Sunday but window shopping was welcome rather than sit within the four walls of the house. In those days no one was allowed to sell on Sundays as it was God's day to join the congregations of the church. A lot of churches had big banners and posters posted on the walls, saying 'COME IN- ATTEND A SUNDAY SERVICE. HOT COFFEE IS BEING SERVED.' Even with the serving of coffees, the churches were empty but the pubs were full in the evening. God had run away from these centres of worship. The godliness was absent. The congregation was shedding its fear of death. They were more interested in fun, food, fights, and f***, the four f's of life, I call them. The priest had lost his respect and charm.

Walking all those streets and during the lunchtime, A had plenty of time to introduce me to that new girl but he did not. Rather he was taking more interest in the new girl himself while his previous girlfriend walked on her own. I knew the omens were not that good. He fancied the new girl and dumped his previous. There was no loyalty. New is always more interesting and attractive. He had used the old and was now ready to dump her. It was an affair of convenience. However the Sunday passed. I asked A what happened to my introduction to the girl. He said, 'Well the girl was new in the country and I thought it was not advisable to introduce her to you in the first meeting.' A few weeks later I saw that girl became his girlfriend and he dumped the old one.

Was I disappointed? Yes, because I was looking for an opportunity to have some experience of handling the opposite sex. But no, it was a big relief that I did not have the embarrassment of moving with a white woman. My arms around her waist could have brought some jealousies and fights with other young locals in a racist country. A woman is always a bone of contention and I was neither trained nor ready to take a challenge. It was not that the grapes were sour. I know my nature. Who knows - I might have got hooked to marry her and be ready for a divorce in a couple of years with a broken heart. I am not a dumper but a sincere and loyal person. I never make relationships for rainy days alone but for life. I am grateful to God that He never allowed it to happen although I wanted it to happen.

Marrying a New Couple

A's Indian friend was getting married to an Indian girl in A's flat. There were no priests (Pundit) available to conduct Indian marriages. A tried his best to find one but without any success. So we all assembled at his house on a Sunday morning, bought the clarified butter and some other bits required for the holy fire to conduct the marriage. We decided to have a go ourselves with our rudimentary knowledge of the ceremony. Before the marriage ceremony started, A asked, 'When we go around the holy fire, do the couple go around six times or seven times?' Nobody was sure. Also he wanted to know if the couple go around in the clockwise direction or anti-clockwise. Again none of us knew. We were all bachelors. They asked me because they knew I had studied at Gurukul so I should be more up to date. But no, I was not sure either. I had studied there as a kid but I never conducted marriages. So we decided to conduct the marriage with six rounds in the anti-clockwise direction. A few weeks later we found out our mistake but it was too late. The couple were married and remained married. The marriage and its commitment always come from our hearts and not from the ceremonies conducted by the priests.

House Buying and Renting

A began to have more confidence in my sincerity and loyalty than with his other classmate chums. We were having a dinner one evening; he said, 'When you get a job, I would like to buy a house in our joint names in Acton with a view to renting it. Once successful, we could then add more to our portfolio, thus creating a business of buying and renting the houses.' With hindsight it was a very

A JOURNEY THROUGH PARTITION AND BEYOND

good proposal. He was very far-sighted as far as the financials were concerned. We would have been multi-millionaires within ten years and rolling in money. But I had my reservations. I said, 'I have come to study here. That is my main goal. To achieve that, I have to save every penny in the bank to support my education.'

'What is there in education? At the end of the day you wish to earn money. You are 27 years old. The time for education is over. So let us do this business.'

I was a bit upset by his comments. To get the higher education was my aim and my biggest priority. I had many slips so far on my path to become a full-fledged engineer. I had prayed for this opportunity. Now it was within my reach and how could I let go? I had not chosen to go to Gurukul where four precious years of my childhood were gone. I had no control over the partition of India. I had taken the right subjects in my high school – English, Physics, and Chemistry – to pursue the engineering degree. After the partition, again I took a job and studied part-time to pass my BA but without Science subjects. For those subjects I had to be a full-time student. My parents had lost everything at the time of partition so there was no financial support. All these years I had been dreaming, planning, and working to get a degree in engineering. Now I just could not let go the opportunity. I could not say all that to A as I was so much under his obligations but I was not very happy. If age had caught up with me, nothing I could do. I had to move on to fulfil my dreams without any diversions. To succeed or achieve something in life - God had never set a 'best before date' for that.

So I said, 'Ok let us see how the things develop and we will decide.'

From then onwards, I faced a tremendous pressure in my mind to make a decision on his suggestion. The dilemma was, should I stay on in the company I had acquired by chance and not by choice or should I move out now rather than regret later? The issues were, after I got a job at New Barnet (see later):

1.   How should I commute from Acton to New Barnet? New Barnet was a very long way from Acton. There were so many changes from underground trains to British Rail and then buses. A further problem was that the bus drivers were on strike and the buses were not operational. So I decided to move to somewhere nearer to my work place. I talked to Kapoor. We both agreed that we would rent a flat together when we found one. But it still left some other following issues. My purpose of coming to Britain was different to those of A's companions

2.   I was not built for booze and womanising. My rearing was different, my ambitions were diverse, and my interests were dissimilar. I had come for the opportunity to meet the goals I had set for myself. This country had all kinds of facilities. It provided the alternative to make something of yourself or destroy yourself. I could choose to drown myself in booze, visit the casinos and

gambling houses, or find the women and flirt with them. Booze and boobs is the worst cocktail for the integrity of a man. The biggest tragedy of humans is that we have the opportunity to move between hells to heavens, from sinners to saints. I could have chosen any of those routes. I was young, free, had a reasonable job with good income, and there were plenty of pretty women around looking for a good bloke to provide them security and get settled down. That also included the girls from India. These choices were very tempting but corruptive. There could never be a right answer to all these choices. I was not built for booze and womanising. Sometimes the doubts do come in your head. Is that creation not meant to be enjoyed? Is that youth going to be there forever? Then why not make the best of it when the opportunity is available to indulge. There can never be a right answer to it. One has to decide for one's fate in that given moment and not look back. If the decision happened to be wrong, so be it.

3.   If I decided to move, I would have the advice, the guidance for a degree and help from people like Malik. Also none of these people were indulging in drinks and womanising. They would bring some beer home on Fridays to drink socially. If I did not wish to drink, they would not impose their opinions on me.

All the above ideas were making me to move but the only issue which was persuading me to stay with them was that A had helped me to come to this country and I did not wish to be seen as a cheater and ungrateful. Because my focus was on my goal of getting the education and not to waste my life in boozing, I decided to cheat and deceive and leave that company for good. And I did when the right moment came. If I had done wrong, I beg to be forgiven. It is not practical to live two types of lives at the same time to find out which one was better. As far as I am concerned I believe I made the right choice. Other people would differ and would make their choices according to their training and their ambitions of life. That is their prerogative

Dracula – The Horrible Monster Film

A huge advertisement campaign was in full swing for the Dracula film in London cinemas. The big posters on the walls read,

"MUST WATCH THE MOVIE, DO NOT GO ALONE"

'Do not go alone', I thought that it was some kind of a sexy film and therefore one must find a partner to go with or with a girlfriend. I had none. A lonely soul, caught in an alien culture, and homesick. So I asked B, 'What is the meaning of this ad "do not go alone"?'

'It is a horror movie. So they are asking you to go with a friend in case you get frightened.'

'Oh, ok. Have you seen it?'

'No, but I would like to see it. I like horror movies.'

'Should we go together one day?'

So one day we went to the Hammersmith cinema to watch this movie. It was a horrible movie. I regretted going there. A scene, in which a killer lodged his teeth into the neck of a beautiful woman was just frightening. It reminded me of the scenes of burning bodies at funeral pyres when I was at Gurukul. It also reminded me of the horrific scenes of murder and stabbing I had witnessed during the Indian partition era. I lost my sleep once again. I would keep awake all night. There was nobody to share that experience with. It took nearly a year to recover from those frightening scenes. A few months later I landed up in hospital in a psychiatrist's chair. The psychiatrist diagnosed that I was suffering from anxiety and homesickness. He prescribed Valium capsules to make my brain nerves dull. Since then I never watch such movies.

Visit to Cambridge, the Centre of English Language

Kapoor was looking for a job in the glass blowing area, in which the glass is heated to melting point, then air is blown from the operator's mouth to shape the glass into various elaborate shapes required for the science laboratory. He was quite good in that skill which he acquired at NPL. He applied for a job at Cambridge Instruments at Cambridge and he was called for an interview. As I had no job at the time, I accompanied him. The company was located only a couple of minutes' walk from the railway station. As we got there he asked me to look around, while he attended his interview.

I wanted to go to the toilet after a long journey from London. I did not find any at the station. I came out of the station; I noticed big lawns in front of it. Beyond the lawns I saw a row of houses where some builders were working. I walked towards them, hoping that they would be able to guide me to find one. With the time the urge was getting more and more acute and I was becoming more desperate. I reached there and enquired from one of them. From the conversation, I gathered that he was an Irish worker. Most of the workers engaged on the building sites were Irish. Here in the heart of an English country town, an Indian foreigner confronted another Irish foreigner. Both were not that literate in English. They only knew that much to get by. I was speaking to him with my limited command of the English language and with a broken Indian accent, and he was trying his best to help me with his own Irish brogue. He knew who I was because of my colour but to me he was an Englishman. He knew his colloquial language better, like any other working-class person, while I was trying to communicate my best by finding the suitable words in my limited vocabulary. So the dialogue started as below:

'Can you please tell me where is the Gentlemen?'

'"Gentlemen"? What is that? I don't know.' I did not understand him but I threw another question nevertheless.

'Do you know where the toilets are?'

'No.'

'Is there any lavatory around?' He shook his head.

'Is there any public bathroom around which I can use?' His face showed that he was trying to find the answer to what I was asking. I was now in dire need to relieve myself.

In desperation to make him understand what I needed, I threw at him the last word in my armoury.

'Is there a place for urination?'

Once again he communicated 'no' with his body language. But he had figured out that I was asking for something for which I am very desperate. We were both frustrated. In disgust, I walked away cursing that here was a seat of English learning where leaders of the other nations came and studied and yet the people of the town cannot understand the word toilets, urination etc. Rather than those words, they had invented a new word in their dictionary for the easing facilities - 'Gentlemen'. Not knowing what to do next and there were no more bodies around to seek help, I had walked only a couple of hundred feet when I heard yelling from him.

'Hey, do you mean loo?'

I had never heard of that colloquial word before and did not know its meaning either. But nevertheless I nodded my head. So he pointed his finger towards a little manmade shack and asked me to go there. I went in. There was a small dug-out hole in the ground, just like you would find in India except that it was more respectful to provide me some kind of privacy to ease myself. In India we had to meet nature's calls by exposing our bottoms in the open, not only men but the womenfolk too. It was a great relief in the end. I thought of becoming a pupil at the university to learn the English language.

After this long ordeal, I rushed back to the station where Kapoor was waiting for me. He did not get the job. We found our way back to London.

It was a great experience to have at the famous seat of learning.

Finally A Job

To get a professional job in any civilised country you must look for the advertisements of interest in the newspapers or go to job centres, register your name, and then hope for the best. You may also try to find vacancies in the workplaces where your friends and relations are employed. It is normally a very tough game and very frustrating in a new country where the employers have their own prejudices about hiring foreigners. As we were in a foreign land and new, the only chance was to go from factory to factory, armed with our CV and certificates, and also by responding to any suitable advertised vacancies.

The friends we had made suggested, with their experience, that we should go in the heavily industrialised areas of London from door to door. Ask the receptionists if there was any job going to suit our education and experience. The same tactics are now being used by the new arrivals from Poland and other East European countries. Our friends knew London better than us and they had adopted the same techniques to get a job. They guided us to go to Angel Road Industrial area, near Tottenham in North London. In those days there were many manufacturing industries located there. British Oxygen was one where many immigrants were already working. So one day I, with another friend Sharma-senior, took my briefcase, full with testimonials, picked up a train and headed to Angel Road British Rail station. It was just around 10am. We did not go together from one factory gate to another as we had different backgrounds. Sharma-senior had been working in India in IAF on aircraft maintenance while I was looking for a job in the design office. There were better chances of Sharma-senior getting a job than me. He could fit in any engineering workshop producing components and there were many, from small, medium, and to very large ones such as BOC. We also split in case the receptionist would be frightened that a large number of workers had invaded the area. There were more chances of an individual getting a job than two together. We spent all morning going from one gate to the other without any luck. In between, if we bumped into each other, we shared our notes in case there was a suitable vacancy for the other. We had our lunch break together at a café and tried our luck all afternoon as well but without any success. On these factory doors we had a mixed reception as you would expect. Some would treat us well and show an understanding of our desperate needs in a new country while others would be abrupt and rude. In general, at most gates we were treated well.

In the evening we reported the outcome to our job minder friends. They were surprised as this was one of the biggest industrial areas in London. However, not to give up we tried some other industrial areas of London. It was a great experience. A lot of people got jobs by this method but we were not that lucky.

I had also applied for a job in a contract design office as a senior jigs and tools designer located at New Barnet.

One fine morning I got a letter from New Barnet inviting me to attend an interview for the vacancy I had applied for. The company was designing jigs, fixtures, and tools under contract for the production of Ford cars, tractor engines, and Rolls Royce Aero Engines. I planned my journey and attended for interview.

They liked my credentials and my experience. After the interview they said they would write to me. After a week I received a letter of appointment offering me the job with a weekly wage of £17-10-0 (£17.50 today) for 37½ hours, starting the week after. I was offered the job with a trial period of four weeks. I was over the moon with the offer. I was told that very few are offered that kind of wage. I was also offered overtime if and when available after the trial period. I was getting a wage just under ten shillings an hour when the factory workers were paid two shillings six pence an hour. I showed the letter to A. He was very happy for me and congratulated me.

So my mind was set to move and in fact I had already talked about it with Kapoor. We both agreed to rent a flat together when it was available. The only stumbling block was to convince A that I was moving simply because commuting to my job was more convenient. I was also very careful not to offend A in case he felt that I was a damn selfish fellow and I had used him for coming over here. So I made a decision to move and let A know. He accepted my reasoning. I was grateful for his understanding of the difficulty of travelling to work daily from his residence.

Racism in Room Renting

Renting a room for an immigrant was a huge problem in those days. There were very few people of my colour here. I remember when we used to go window shopping in Oxford Street, if we would see a person of our colour we would point out to one another, 'Hey look, our countryman is going along there.' There were perhaps more in the Southall area but in other areas of London there were hardly any. Very few Asians owned the houses as we were very recent arrivals in the country. Very few English people would rent the rooms. If some did they were very choosy and racist. Their ads in the shop windows would always say 'sorry no coloureds.' The other minority communities such as Cypriots, Greeks and the Jewish would rent the room but again they were also very strict and put a lot of conditions on the tenants. Their main aim was to grab the tax-free cash in their pockets. As the Finsbury Park area was quite suitable for me to commute to my workplace and also it was nearer to the West End and Stamford Hill where Malik lived, we were looking for a room or a flat around there. In the evenings and weekends we would go to Finsbury Park underground station, look at the 'Room to Rent' billboard and then go to view. A typical ad would read as

Room to Rent

Single room with cooking and bathroom facilities (note: bathroom facilities were not always included)

A JOURNEY THROUGH PARTITION AND BEYOND

Must be single or married with no children

Rent £2-10-0/week in advance (some may even demand 3-4 weeks rent as a deposit)

There would always be all or some of the following conditions attached for renting.

SORRY NO COLOUREDS OR BLACKS
This condition was always attached by the English and other white people. We would never go there as either they would not open the door or would slam the door in your face saying angrily, 'Sorry it is gone,' or 'Sorry no vacancy.'

NO CHILDREN, NO COOKING FACILITIES, NO BATHROOM FACILITIES. Or, if allowed, it would be restricted to certain times and days of the week.

Out of thirty, forty ads, there would be hardly one or two for us where we could go with some hopes. So it took us weeks to find a suitable room and that too with many restrictions and conditions.

<u>At last I got a Room</u>
On one Saturday, I was scanning the room-to-let board at Finsbury Park. I saw an ad for a room near Manor House underground. It was only two hundred feet from the main traffic light junction on the main road. I walked down and knocked at the door. A lady came out. From her looks and spoken language, I could guess that she was a foreigner like me except that she was of a fairer skin. I blurted fearfully but ready for the regret.
'Hello, I have come to see the room you have advertised at Finsbury Park Station.'
'Oh, yes come in.'
Then she asked me a number of questions to know my background. Was I married, did I have a job, and how long had I been in the country? I answered them all. Then she moved on to dig out more about my personal life.
'Have you got many friends?'
'No'
'Have you got a girlfriend?'
'No, I haven't.'

Having satisfied her terms and conditions, she led me to the room on the first floor in the front of the house. The room looked ok, with bare minimum furnishings. It had a single bed with blankets, a table lamp on a side table, and a chair but without any cooking facilities. It was a nice room to hide for a solitary homesick soul to get bored to death after a day's work. There was no heating in the room and no other soul permitted to give me her body heat to warm me during the winter months. There was no radio and no TV. It was a room you enter stealthily; change the dress, and away you move on to dreamland. It was bare existence with plenty of noise and free polluted air to breathe from the car engines' exhausts. It had notorious French sash windows that allowed all kinds of fumes and traffic noise to filter in.

Then she showed me the shared bathroom and toilet. She warned me that I would be only allowed to take a bath on Saturdays between 2-4pm and if I missed those hours, I missed my week's bath. Imagine if the humans could control their daily secretions to weekly secretions; the lady would have not hesitated to impose that condition on me too. This dilemma was faced by a Gurukul man who was trained to take a bath every day and he was denied that facility. But one has to be prepared for all kinds of terms and conditions imposed by the haves onto the have-nots, simply because the haves have been lucky to own some possessions. Have-nots are always treated like pariahs, a burden on this earth. The haves forget that those who are pariahs today and have been denied the opportunity to own the goodies and necessities of life, can also shoot up to fame one day and may reach to the highest peaks of the society and compete with the elites in their own game. It is these elites who have deprived them the opportunity to climb up the higher rungs of the ladder. Who knows that one day many of them may join the rich list of millionaires, may become doctors, scientists, and philosophers of repute. They may also become mystics, sages, saints, and even Buddha and Christ. Nature does not discriminate when it starts showering its gifts onto the mortals. We are all His creations.

Then she laid down more conditions for the usage of the bathroom.

'You will leave the bathroom in meticulously clean condition after you finish.'

'Yes, ok that is fine.'

'The rent is £3-10s/week, with one week deposit.'

'Ok, you got it.'

'You are not allowed to bring in any friends or girlfriends. Nobody else is allowed to sleep in the room except you.'

'I will try to stick to that condition but please allow some exception to that. I have a friend and sometimes we go to watch a movie in the area. If he gets

A JOURNEY THROUGH PARTITION AND BEYOND

late he may not be able to find a bus or tube to go back. In those circumstances will you allow me to let him sleep.'

'No, if that happens, you will have to leave before the weekend.'

I had no choice and I nodded. The beggars don't have choices in life anyway. They have to do what they are told. I told Kapoor the whole conversation and he said that as we were looking for a flat to move to together, let them put their conditions, put up with it, and hopefully I'd be out of there soon.

I paid the £7 cash and moved in next Sunday evening with the help of K.

The memories of staying in that house are not that great. They are full of frustrations, bad treatment by the landlord, and loneliness. In the night I had to just enter the house as a thief would enter. Every step in the corridors had to be placed carefully, and every stair had to be climbed in total silence, sometimes after removing shoes. There were no cooking facilities so that meant I had to hunt around for a vegetarian meal somewhere out in restaurants. The traffic noise and fumes were keeping me awake. I would go home to my room late and spend most of my time with Kapoor.

The first night I had a very drowsy sleep. I put that down to being in a new place with some new house odours. The second night the same and I thought I would soon get used to it. They were the lonely nights of life. By the time I would get to the room it would be around 8-9pm. The night was still young but there was nothing to do - no TV, no Radio, and no books to read. It was a horrible life, or should I say, just existence. In addition, the cars, trucks and motorcycles would come to a stop at the traffic light junction and as they waited for the green light, the vehicles would continue to pollute the environment with fumes. Eventually the fumes would filter into the room through the sash windows. Also when the lights would go green, the vehicles, especially the motorcycles, would accelerate with a deafening engine noise. I had to sleep in that polluted room without any fresh air. I remember I used to sleep with a blanket covering my whole body, including my head, something I had not done in my whole life. Life turned into a nightmare. We doubled our efforts to find a flat.

About three weeks later, one Sunday, Kapoor and I went to a restaurant and then to a movie. Kapoor got late and could not find a bus to go back to his residence. So we decided that he should sleep with me. We opened the outside door and went in very quietly so that we wouldn't disturb the landlords of the house. We observed the pin-drop silence right up to the time we entered into my room. We changed and went to bed. Next morning Kapoor woke up early, got ready, and left for his work. The whole landlord's family was still in bed and were enjoying their early morning dreams. I also got ready and found my way to the office. When I came back in the evening, as I reached my door, the landlord followed me.

'Was anybody else sleeping in your room last night?' I was surprised. I thought we had managed to keep it all secret, then how on earth had they sussed it out? Maybe the guy was a bad sleeper? So I replied, 'Yes, it was my friend. He could not get the train to his residence, as it was not safe to travel at that time of the night. So I asked him to stay with me.'

'Are you sure it was your friend and not a girlfriend?'

'Yes I am sure because I do not have a girlfriend.'

He disputed that what I was saying was the truth. He became a bit agitated and threatened me to be evicted if it ever happened again. Obviously I felt insulted at his accusations. I knew that there were conditions that no one should stay for the night in my room but to impose those rules so rigidly was hurtful. I just could not tell the landlord to get lost. He continued his babble, 'However this was one of the conditions that no visitor would sleep here. You have broken that condition. Therefore you have to vacate this room by Friday.'

'But sir, you have to look at the circumstances under which my friend had no choice but to sleep here. As a friend I just could not ask him to go away.'

'Well, you have to leave this room by Friday or else.'

'If that is what you want, OK, I will leave.'

Next day I told Kapoor. We phoned Malik and he kindly agreed to allow me to move to his flat on Friday. My eviction was a blessing in disguise. Malik's flat was located in a residential area and was miles away from the main roads and therefore was much more peaceful. I came home on Friday, took my baggage with the help of Kapoor and moved out without asking the landlord to refund my deposit. The instinct of owning a house of my own one day had begun in earnest.

A Flat

A few weeks after staying with Malik we managed to find a flat on Clapton Common, Stamford Hill. The house belonged to a Jewish family. It was a self-contained flat. It had two rooms with a kitchen, toilet/bathroom on the first floor. The rent was £7/week. We hardly saw the landlord family. The man was working and the wife would mostly stay within her quarters downstairs.

One winter Friday when I arrived from work, when the days were much shorter, the whole house was plunged into darkness. The lovely, polite, and very gentle landlady came dashing to the door and asked me to switch on the lights for her.

'Where is the switch?' I asked.

'Oh! Here.'

She guided me to it in the dark. I switched the lights on. She thanked me and I went upstairs to my room. When Kapoor came from work, I asked him why

A JOURNEY THROUGH PARTITION AND BEYOND

this lady asked me to switch on the lights for her. She knew exactly where the switch was and yet she would not switch on the lights herself.

'You know Om, they are orthodox Jews. They are not allowed to touch the electric after the sunset on Fridays.'

Another day Kapoor brought a cracked egg. It had a blood clot in it. The lady had given it to him to eat as they were not allowed to eat an egg in such a condition.

'But they do eat meat. Then why fuss about a drop of blood in it?' I asked.

'Well, their religion does not allow them to eat that type of egg as it is not kosher.'

So I was learning fast about the intricacies of other religions I hardly knew.

Stamford Hill is a Jewish area. You could see their dresses with long black coats, with long flowing beards. They look elegant, smart, serene, and very religious and saintly. I feel like bowing to them. They look as humble and innocent as if the God abides in their souls. Their bodies are the temple of God. They are a small community, living as minorities in the various parts of the world and have made a tremendous contribution to science, arts, music, and education. God has bestowed upon them the title, 'the cream of humanity'.

Hyde Park, the Tourist Attraction

Malik's flat was only four minutes' walk from ours. The two P's were staying with him in his flat. They were freelance people, nothing to do all day and living in London by the mercy of the hand-out from their rich parents in India.

One P asked one day, 'Have you seen Hyde Park?'

'No not yet. Where is it?'

'Wait until we take you around one night.'

The P's knew that we were the new birds in London and had not seen much of it. For them it was added fun to impress the newcomers with their knowledge of the famous city of London. It was a great opportunity to boost their ego from their fledging daily life. Either they were stupid or just plain idiots who were refusing to see the daylight that they were wasting away the precious times of their lives by whiling away their time on an aimless existence. However who was I to interfere in their personal affairs.

So one afternoon on Sunday, we went to see Hyde Park. We walked around the Park. We first went to the Speakers' Corner where some cronies were standing high and above and the crowd was gathered around them. They were all twisting and manipulating their words on a theme of their choice. The listeners were equally good at arguing with the speaker and putting forward their views on

45

the subjects. In fact they were all trying to satisfy their egos and showing off the bookish knowledge they had gained. Some were speaking loudly, aimlessly, blowing their trumpets to attract the listeners. They were allowed to say any babble to their listeners except that they were not permitted to criticise the reigning monarch. We could move around to listen to any speaker and if we did not like his/her views we moved on to another one. We could ask questions; interrogate, and challenge the speaker for his crony ideas. I had seen the same kind of a discussion in a small park at Karol Bagh Delhi but on a very small scale.

From there we moved on to the other parts of the park and ended up, as one would expect, at the major area of attraction, The Serpentine Lake. There were a lot of people moving around, hugging, kissing, and gossiping. It was getting a bit dark because of winter. We had already spent nearly a couple of hours. Suddenly we spotted a group of young people, milling around near a tree. Curiously, we approached to see what that loud hooting and whistling was all about. It became a real eye opener scene. There were a girl and a boy in the centre and a few more jostling and moving around them slowly in a circle as if to catch a view of something special. The boy and the girl were embracing one another and kissing very passionately. Then the girl raised her skirt and the boy took the penetrating position. Soon the sexual act was in full swing in a standing position, right under the lustful and envious eyes of the other youngsters surrounding them. Some were booing and the others were making their own sexual scenes without a partner. Wow, so that was London of the late 50's, the great city of the world. A young man like me, coming from the early Gurukul culture, was now thrown right in the middle of open sex for everyone to watch. As I see it there was nothing wrong in it. This is how God creates everything - the vegetations, the beautiful flowers, the fruits, and the whole animal world, including humans. If the Bible says that Adam and Eve were punished because they ate the forbidden fruit from the Garden of Eden, then so be it. It is only said and written by the humans. If God had written that then he would not bribe all its creation to enjoy the joy of the sexual ejaculations. At the peak of the act, every cell and every organ of the human body vibrates and participates in having the biggest joy of their life.

Coming from a country where to touch a girl would bring a shower of abuse and beating, this whole scene appeared interesting. Thousands of years ago we had written Kamasutra with all the possible sexual postures. We had chiselled those scenes of the Kamasutra on solid rocks of Ajanta Caves for the whole world to see. We have built monuments of love. We have read of the playing of the flute by Lord Krishna to charm his Gopies. We also know that we adults play bed polo in the darkness of the night. The growing population of the world is the clear indication. With all that evidence available to us, why are we frowned upon by society for a little intimate conversation with the opposite sex? We in the East only

A JOURNEY THROUGH PARTITION AND BEYOND

preach and write books but in the practical day-to-day life we suppress our emotions. Love and sex is a natural way of life bestowed upon the whole creation by God. This country does not write such wonderful books and yet practices openly what we have written. I think that is how we all should lead our lives. The West is more practical and the East is full of hypocrites.

First Encounter with a Naked Lady

Hyde Park also has some other memories. One of them is the following experience I faced.

When I came here, prostitution was in full swing. All around the Park, Park Lane and Soho were known as the red-light district. They were no-go areas for the timid, the sages, the moralists, the preachers, and the godly. All along the streets, young girls were soliciting for customers. In India prostitution is ugly, socially unacceptable, unwelcoming, dirty, infested with criminals, and full of diseases. Venture into those areas and sooner or later you are bound to get venereal disease with its horrible consequences. But over in UK, the girls were smarter, well dressed, conscious about their physical body and its health, willing to go to your residence, and were cheap. They considered what they did to be a profession. They were there to provide a service to meet its ultimate goal – their client's satisfaction. Why were they doing it? I don't know. I am not an expert on this subject. Money was certainly a consideration. It is possible that the girls had the freedom to do what they liked. They had no parental controls and no family ties or interference. It is possible that they had chosen that profession because of the shortages of men due to WW2 and they had lost their way in the brutal system managed by some wicked men who were ready to sell someone else's body to make some bucks. They had laid so many attractions for these simple girls coming from an average background. There were many open bars in the West End areas, openly enticing, inviting, and coaxing the tourists to sit down in the laps of these beautiful, sparsely dressed young ladies and have drinks and chatter. They would talk over their love tales and might even negotiate to sell their bodies for the whole evening and night if you were rich enough to pay them handsomely for the services they were going to provide. It was a place to be drowned with women and wine. It was the biggest scandal to witness in a civilised society. The choices were wide open to me. But they did not interest me. I was free to participate or not in those vulgarities; I was neither asked nor had I given any vows to my mother to remain vegetarian or to stay away from women and wine as Gandhi had to give. But the route I was planning to move into was my personal choice. The guidance always came from the core of my heart and not from my wicked head. It came with some convictions. I knew that I was new in the Western liberal society and was surrounded by all kinds of cronies wherever I went. Their interests were to drag me down to their way of living and thinking. But I wanted to be a lotus, staying above the muddy waters of the ponds I was staying in. Many opportunities were thrown my way, they gave me good experiences and thus leave lasting memories

One day again we all went to Hyde Park. It was a lovely summer day. That was a place young people would meet, and have fun. After roaming around for a couple of hours, we hired a taxi to go home. As we drove past on Park Lane, P noticed some young girls standing on the curbs to sell their bodies. How had he sussed out that they were there for that purpose? The devil must have the devil's eyes to recognise its prey. He must have been expert in it. He immediately instructed the driver to slow down. He was now examining their sexy appearances, their bodies, and their attractiveness to satisfy his lust for the evening. As soon as he spotted one to meet his requirements, he ordered the driver to stop. He got out and went back to negotiate his terms with the young lady. He came back with that young beauty in her late teens. He told us in our language that he would be taking her to our flat. We had never done such things in our flat before. I was concerned in case the orthodox lords found out, they might kick us out. But I never protested nor did Kapoor. After arriving at our flat, P ushered the lady into my bedroom and we all others huddled together in Kapoor's adjacent bedroom.

After depositing her on my bed P came in and announced, 'Om, this girl is for you,'

'What! I did not ask for it.'

'I know. But you have never been in bed with a woman before. So she is your prize to have the experience in tackling a woman tonight. This is Britain, not India. Here no one is allowed to be virgin. So get up and go.' That was quite an unexpected tall order.

'No I have no clue what to do with her. I have no experience. I never asked for this.'

'Look man, she has been picked up for you. She knows all about sex as she is White and experienced in the sex trade. She will teach you what to do to her. She will guide you.'

Cheers went up in the room. Everyone supported him. None of them was interested in my plea and what I was trying to say. It was gang rule. The young crowd all over the world are of that type. They just see a young sexy lady and are ready to jump into bed with her. It was like an animal male meeting with a female. No hello, no love making, no introduction, not knowing who the lady is. Just open up and be ready for action. It was not my cup of tea. It was just impossible to be aroused with looks and a nude body. So I begged again to be forgiven.

'Tell me, have you got any problem as a man?'

'No, that is not the case but since I have never done such things, I just cannot.'

'Look, everyone has agreed here. She is your girl and she is waiting for you. She knows you are the man going to go to her. She has already been paid £2, and if you don't go that would be a sheer waste. When you finish I will also have a go.'

'But then why don't you go now and I will see it later.'

'No, first she is reserved for you.' How nice it was to know. A man hunter was handing over his prey to another man as a gift. I must admire his sacrifice. Very few people would have this quality that they would select a lady for you, pay for her, and then hand her over without polluting her first. That was the most admirable character of that friend. Why I was chosen for his favour from the whole lot of others is a mystery. He had closer friends than me. I had known him only for a couple months.

He held my hand firmly and led me to my bedroom and left me there to face the music. I had already left my previous companions exactly for the same reasons and now I was caught among the same type of people once more. Is that how all the young ones behave?

I was nervous. I did not know what to do and how to tackle the situation. As I opened my bedroom, she was sitting on my bed and waiting for my initiative.

'I am sorry; I am totally new in this game. They arranged all this without my knowledge. I haven't a clue what to do with a young lady,' I blurted hesitantly.

'How do you want me?'

'What?'

'Do you want me to undress all over or just remove my panties?'

'I don't know, I cannot tell you.'

She started to undress her body. As she was doing that, I felt embarrassed to keep on looking at her. So I turned towards the door and started removing my shirt and the vest. I had no guts to take my trousers off, never mind the panties. I was sinking below the ground in shame. I had an awful feeling to be naked in front of a lady in that brightly lit room with a 100w bulb. It was impossible to expose myself in front of a total stranger and especially a woman. I could not bear this ordeal of inner conflict any more. As I turned around to say that I am quitting all this dirty business, I saw her naked lying in my bed and waiting for my initiative. She was looking eagerly at me for my next response. She was an experienced girl because of this adopted profession. She had tackled all kinds of men in her tender young age. She never blushed. For her it was another client, another thrust, another partner, another sexual intercourse, and another ordeal to last for a couple of minutes and soon be over. She must have thought that, like many before me, I was another invader to her privacy, and it would end up in the history of her encounters.

Embarrassingly I said, 'I know my friends would hate me for this but I cannot go through this ordeal for which I know nothing. You may dress and go.'

'Are you sure? I can wait until you are ready.' She was very kindly allowing me to take my time.

'No thanks. Please get dressed and you keep your £2 which my friend has paid you. I will pay him back.'

'But I cannot go until your friend says. He is the one who hired me.'

'Ok, I will go and tell him.'

So I left her there, put my shirt on, and walked back to Kapoor's room. They all looked at me with a cheeky smile.

'Did everything go OK?' P asked

'Nothing happened. I had no idea what to do.' Boos were raised in the room. I was blushing. I felt low. My failure was challenging for my manhood. But sex and sleep are beyond human controls and they don't just happen when you want. Love always precedes the sexual act and it is the ultimate consequence that happens naturally. Every cell of the body participates in the sexual act. Love and laughter are nature's gifts to the humans only. Sex only results in animals without love. That is why all religions are against it and call it an 'animal instinct'. But who could enlighten that idiotic crowd who had never learnt the art of loving? I was stuck in that sort of company. I gathered courage and said, 'But I never asked for her. I have no experience of women and I do not know what to do with them. That is not my childhood training. She was being imposed on me by you, P. You brought her and you deal with her the way it suits you.'

'No Om, you have to go back right now and do what a man does to a woman in bed.' They all shouted in one voice.

I was caught in a no-win situation and they were all ganging up on me. It was a mob rule being imposed right at my residence. So I protested again, 'No I will not go back and insult the lady again. P, it is your problem and you deal with it and I am through with it.' P noticed my determination and said, 'Ok, I'll have a go. After all, I have to settle the accounts for the money I have paid.' P boasted and rushed out towards my bedroom.

All the chattering in the room stopped, followed by a pin drop silence. All the ears were glued to the partitioning wall to hear any signs of activity. After all, he was an experienced bull and they wanted to see how he would act. They must have done the same when I was pushed into that room. Time passed on. The clock kept on ticking. Shortly P appeared before the inquisitive crowd about half an hour later.

'Hey, you had a good time?' his very close chum enquired.

'No, I also did not do anything to her.'

'Why?'

A JOURNEY THROUGH PARTITION AND BEYOND

'I was not in the mood. I just could not manage the erection. So I asked her to dress. I then walked with her to the bus stop. I asked for my money back but she refused. It was around 8pm and it was turning dark. I gave her the bus fare and left her there to go home.'

'Isn't it too late to go home alone by bus for a young girl? You should have sent her back in a taxi,' I said.

'That is her bloody problem,' (in fact he called a bad name in our language). 'She must be used to these kinds of encounters. She did threaten me that she would call the police when I insisted on her paying back my £2 for the service she never rendered. She said it was not her fault - she was available if only you people had performed.'

She was right.

You may conclude what you like, but I believe that I saved my virginity. I am aware that it is only the woman's virginity which is considered paramount and pure by society, but, to me, my virginity was important, and I don't give two hoots for society's rules. Why should a man be a vagabond roaming around like a free bull to continue to pollute any woman he can get hold of? I know nobody would give a damn to my thinking. In society's eyes a man's virginity carries no value anyway as it does for a woman's. But for me, I feel that I did the right thing to walk away from a lady without sucking any juices out of her beautiful body and without robbing her self-respect for a mere couple of £s to satisfy my animal needs. Her dignity and honour can never be evaluated with £s. I am grateful to God and very much relieved that I did not violate her privacy to satisfy my humanly lust. God only permits that violation if one is in love with the other partner; otherwise it is an animal behaviour in His eyes. That is what I believe. I am aware that she was selling her body but it might be that she needed the money desperately. But my 'friend' exploited her needs and hired her because he could afford to blow away a couple of £s for me. I kept my virginity till I got married. I was still an innocent, inexperienced, and ignorant young man and did not know the ropes of tackling a lady even after marrying my wife.

The whole show was manipulated by very experienced and cunning hands. At the end of the day, what the gathered companions thought - I don't give a damn to their thinking. I am only concerned with my feelings. I have heard many times similar kinds of chauvinistic statements from these erring men about how would I answer to my maker when he would question me why I had failed to enjoy the beauties of the world he had created. This world is dialectical. There is always an opposite to such thoughts. So on the day of judgement when I stand up in front of my Creator, I can bravely say, with an eye-to-eye contact with Him, 'Sir, I am not guilty to any of the charges you would lay at me. If as a human, I have ever erred, then it was done innocently.'

If my Maker is not happy with my reply, then tough, and I will willingly accept his verdict whatever that verdict would be.

That night I felt great.

A lot of you readers would have opinions about my behaviour on that day. Some would condemn it while others would support it. Still others may have some other funny ideas. I did what my conscience said I should. I do not regret it and I am happy that I did not play bed polo on that day. If by chance I had done that, my conscience would continue to prick me till today. So I don't care what others might think of my behaviour. I believe that sex should be between the two lovers and not between the two strangers, especially when the stranger is being forced to sell her body for some financial gains. That young lady would also have a tale to tell about her encounter with two Asian youths on that night. What that tale would be is only guesswork. Of course she would judge me either harshly or kindly, depending upon her attitudes towards this beautiful life we have been endowed, free, by our Maker.

A Rich Businessman's Visit

I had been in Britain only for 4 months. I had a letter from my father informing me that a rich businessman from Ratlam was coming with his wife to London on a sightseeing trip. He was staying in a hotel around Tottenham Court Road. I went to see them. They were a middle-aged couple, very courteous, friendly, and down to earth. I never felt uneasy in their company. Wherever we went, they made sure they spent their own money. I did not have the money anyway. What they wanted was the company of someone who was in London. They had already chalked out their programme for sightseeing and whenever I could accompany them, they bought my tickets too. We visited the following places together:

1. To a Cinema: One evening we went to watch a movie. When the first show finished, we walked to our chairs on the balcony. As we were settling down, RM spotted ten newly minted, crispy one-pound notes, dropped on the floor. He picked them up and said, 'Om, I have found this bundle of notes on the floor. What do we do?'

'I don't really know. Should I go and give them to the manager and ask him to announce on the intercom to claim the money if someone has lost them?'

They agreed. So I hurriedly went downstairs, hunting for the manager to give him that bundle. He was sitting in his little, dark, dingy, one chair room on the ground floor. I was excited and feeling very proud, egotistic, and elated that I was an honest decent bloke who was doing a great service to humanity by giving up this little fortune we had found.

'Hello, Mr Manager, we have found this bundle of £1 notes on the floor. I am handing it over to you because they have been found on your premises.' And I put the bundle on his desk.

'Yeah, ok thank you.'

'May I please know how are you going to give it back to a rightful owner?'

'I don't know how to find the person who dropped it. You may keep it if you want, as you found it.'

'No, it is not mine. But why don't you announce it on the mike at the interval or put a little billboard under "Lost and Found" in case someone may come and claim the money.'

'Yeah, ok I will do that.'

So with that assurance I returned back to my seat to watch the movie, which had already started. I told RM what had been agreed and the announcement would come on the intercom during the interval break. We waited for the announcement during the interval. Nothing happened. I was now feeling a bit uncomfortable. My worry was in case RM might be thinking that I had pocketed the money and given them a story. So after the movie was over, I narrated for them the whole conversation I had with the manager, often repeating to prove that I had done exactly what I was telling them. It was the manager who had pocketed the money and we were stupid enough to hand it over to him. But the whole episode left a bitter memory till today.

I thought that it was right to hand over the money, and I still believe that.

2. <u>Visit to a Striptease</u>: One day when I went to see them in the evening, they said that they had booked three seats in a striptease in Soho. I was amazed. I'd heard of such places where a woman would undress herself in the open to entertain the menfolk. It was such degrading and disturbing news to me. Have we also got a place where men expose themselves for the benefit and amusement of women? Would they be eager enough to show their manly prowess to the women so that they can see whether the man is manly enough to interest them? But here it was not the man only but his wife too who had no qualms about watching her own kind getting naked on the stage. She was also encouraging her man to be a pornographer. This was pure, simple exploitation of the simple, innocent, and motherly women. The middle-age also did not bother the couple. They seemed to be still young at heart. I am not trying to be holier-than-thou but I did feel uncomfortable. So I said, 'You please go. I do not wish to visit such places.'

'Don't worry, we are not going to tell your father that we took you to a striptease, if that is the reason you are saying no.'

'No, no it is not that. I just don't feel comfortable to see the women being stripped.'

They insisted and I accompanied them. I saw them watching very closely how different women each arrived at the stage and did her act by stripping her clothes one by one. They did not all strip themselves to be naked. Some stripped to the waist, one or two went naked. I had to turn my face away. I could not see that scene.

I confronted a similar situation in Wales where I was teaching. Christmas came and the annual celebration was being conducted in a big hall, all arranged by the top brass. Mira and I went into the hall with one of my colleagues who became our good friend later. After some speeches, the entertainment programme started. Finally, to wind up the evening, a woman came on stage. At that moment my colleague whispered in my ear, 'Let us go out. She is now going to strip, a horrible and insulting act to all the womenfolk. I can never see such scenes but the Principal insists on displaying such filth on the stage despite so many protests. You won't like it either I know. So let us get out.'

I said, 'But the principal is not a young man and he still enjoys such scenes?'

'He not only enjoys it but he would gaze around her body very closely as if he is trying to see something special. It is very stupid and disgusting!' he replied.

And we walked out and stayed in the open veranda in the bitter cold of a December night.

3. Visit to a Maharaja's 'London Palace': The guests were friendly with the Maharaja who had no power base in India anymore. All their rights had been curtailed in 1948 and their princely states were merged to form different provinces. These royal families were in bewilderment and were looking for shelters wherever they could find any. This young maharaja was living with his young wife in a posh area of London. When he walked on the streets of London, he would be just like me, 'a damn brown Asian immigrant' looking for some crumbs in London. At least in his old kingdom people still respected them as maharajas. They also had their property and a circle of admirers. However, it was his decision. But it appeared to me totally stupid to come and live here.

We had a cup of tea and some biscuits. Then the maharaja and RM went out to sit in the porch to talk about their private matters. Most of the time, it was the Maharaja who was talking. We were there nearly two hours. After their long discourse we hired a taxi and we were on our way back to their hotel. RM's wife and I asked RM what they were discussing. He said that it was all about their family feud. Someone is spending more money, another one had taken more of the property and so on. The Maharaja had wanted RM to intervene and help sort out the problems. Maharajas derive so much respect and love from their subjects and yet they are also not free from the daily grinds of life, I thought. They have the same problems as we have; they sit on the same loo as we do except ours may be made from common materials while they might sit on golden seats. They have all the same humanly characteristics as we have. Then why do we bow our heads to them? Are we commoners not stupid?

On another occasion, we hired a taxi to go to Oxford Street. In those days the taxi fare was 2 shillings and 6 pence in old currency. As we were getting out, RM asked me what tip he should give to the driver. I whispered in my language to give him six pence tip (6d coin). So he did. As we dismounted, the driver made some typical scene. He shouted at us, called us some names, without giving due respect to the lady. He came out of the taxi and threw the coin on to the footpath. Even the coin did not like his rejection and insult. It rolled away with speed and no one knew where it had disappeared. I shouted back, 'You don't deserve it; we should not have given you. For a fare of 2/6, how much tip could one expect?' And we walked away in disgust. RM commented, 'These taxi drivers are very rude here.' I nodded. The tip we gave was 20% of the fare the taxi driver had asked.

A Cheeky Kiss and the First One

You might wonder why do I remember the first kiss on my cheeks by a young pretty girl. Don't you remember it? If you don't then it may be that you were in your teens and for you it carried not much importance. But when it happened to me I was edging to be twenty-eight years old. I had never touched a lady, saving my sisters and mother. We know that we all enter into puberty at the age of fourteen years. It is said that we reach our prime at the age of twenty-five and then start declining. If that is true then my youth had already started declining and at that age, if a lady kissed me, it became an unforgettable experience. But that kiss did not have the warmth that happens between two lovers meeting for the first time. But it was a muted one as it was between two strangers of opposite poles. And yet I remember it and I like sharing the experience with you all.

Just a few weeks after joining the design office, my first place of work, a young colleague started giving me a ride to a Tube station on his motorbike. The buses were on strike in those days and travelling to and from the office was a big problem. The winter used to be quite severe in those days. Pollution in London was also a big problem. There was no central heating and people were warming their homes by burning coal. You could see nothing but smoke belching out of the home chimneys everywhere. The smoke mixed with wintry fog was named as smog. When that happened the visibility would go down to just a few feet. Although there were very few cars on the roads there used to be a lot of accidents as the drivers could not see where they were going. The best driving guide was the reflection of the light from the buried glass pyramids and the white lines in the middle of the road. I remember whenever we could not see the tree from our office window on the main road, my colleagues used to shout, 'We can't see the tree out there, we want to go home.' With that repetitive shouting, sometimes the management would allow us to go home earlier, even though there were still a few hours left to work.

As the travelling was difficult in the winter, plus the bus strikes, it was a great help to get a lift to the underground station. It was my first experience of riding on the back of someone's motorbike. He taught me to lean my body at bends in the road to stabilise the bike. It was scary in the beginning but later I got used to it.

Soon the Christmas season was on the horizon. I noticed a lot more activity on the roads, in-home decorations, lighting, Christmas trees, and holly tree branches displayed in the rooms and the entrance halls. I began to know the importance of Christmas and its celebrations. I also came to know that the annual Christmas dinner was being arranged by the company I was working for. It was a great experience to participate in the Celebrations and to have first-hand knowledge of how the Christians enjoyed the festival with their families, with drinks and well-planned foods, and be merry. But it was a totally unknown territory for me. While I was very happy to join in, I was also anxious about how I would adjust with so much change within such a short period without offending the host community.

There was just about a week left before the Christmas break. As usual I hopped on the back of the bike and away we cruised towards the station. Shortly my colleague blurted, 'Om, on our way to the station, do you mind if I break the journey at my friend's house just for a couple of minutes?'

'No, that is fine. Suit yourself.'

When we arrived, he parked the bike in front of the house, and said, 'Come on Om let us go in.' I hesitated as it was his personal matter and who was I to listen to their personal conversation. But he insisted for me to join in. So I followed. A young pretty girl opened the door. I was behind him. He greeted her with a very warm hug and a kiss on both her cheeks. She also reciprocated. Their meeting suggested that they were quite close and knew one another very well. They were in the mid hallway near the staircase and I was still at the door. He looked back and said, 'Come on Om, give her a kiss.'

'No, no.'

'Yes, come on in. give her a kiss. It is Christmas season. She will not mind.'

I could see the girl blushing from a kiss coming from one of the very few brownish Asians in the country but my blush was in fact even more than hers.

'No, I just cannot kiss her as I have never kissed a lady before. It is not in my blood. I have no training for it.'

'Om, if you are worried that she would hit you or bite you, I will hold her face for you. Come on Om, we have to go soon. Please come and kiss her.'

He held her smiling face while insisting on me to move forward to kiss her on the cheek. I inched my way forward apprehensively. As I reached there he pulled my head with his strong arms and pushed my lips on her right cheek saying, 'Come on Om, give her a kiss, this is Christmas.' She was giggling and he made her land her lips on my left cheek. The strong grip was loosened. We both were blushing. I was new in that game and she had never seen and kissed a real-life gollywog.

I moved out and he followed after wishing her well. We rode away. On the way he said, 'I can understand that in your culture, you do not kiss the girls in public. But over here, if you don't kiss the girl, she would feel insulted. She would feel that she is not beautiful and that is why you hesitated to kiss her. She would feel rejected.'

Now, what answer could I give him? He did not know how I had been brought up. I did understand that it was a normal thing to do in the Western world. There was nothing wrong with kissing the lady on her cheek. But at that time I was timid, scared, with no initiative and also I could not get rid of my brainwashing at Gurukul which was diametrically opposite to the western culture. I just could not forget for a moment my childhood teachings that it is only one woman in life that would be my wife and the rest would always be my mothers and sisters. The dialogue was between two people – one was conditioned in the Eastern philosophy and the other was brought up in the liberal Western world. Both would resist changes in their convictions. There was no way of compromise between us. Both were right. The present world is moving fast towards a melting pot when such barriers would be broken and the Eastern would be thinking like a Western and vice versa. This change will be brought about in the not too far distant future because of the modern communication systems.

I also learnt a lesson that the way I was showing my hesitancy to kiss was offensive to the young lady. My friend's advice was taken on board that one should avoid such offences because of cultural differences.

The Knife & Fork Question

Soon Christmas had come and gone. Then came the following Saturday the 27th December, when the Christmas party was arranged by the company at a hotel. I had to overcome many cultural hurdles before the party. The hurdles were

1. How to use fork & knife at the dinner table. I had used them when eating in the dining rooms of the ship. But I was not perfect. I was sharing the table with all the Indians. So it did not matter how cumbersomely and bad mannerly I ate.

2. But here I was surrounded by the English colleagues who had probably invented the table manners and etiquette of eating in the dining halls. The crowd present there had learnt the eating techniques from their parents in early childhood. For me it was all new. I was also very conscious of the fact that I was the only one of my brown-skinned kind present for the dinner there. So I asked for guidance from Kapoor who was smart and had moved in the higher, sophisticated society of Delhi. He trained me on our dining table at home but he could not help me change my nature of being self-conscious in the company of the western people.

3. I had another problem too. I was the only vegetarian amongst those meat eaters. How I would ask for only vegetables and not the meat dishes, especially at Christmas dinner. Kapoor said I should only ask for vegetable dishes. In those days the vegetables in the menu were peas, potato chips fried in animal fat or mash, green beans, cauliflower, and carrots. Later on, I came to know that even the bread we were eating had animal fat; ice cream also had animal fat. All the pastries contained animal fats. Oh God, was there anything without any animal fats?! It makes me shiver when I remember those old days. It is not the religion that made me vegetarian. A lot of Indians of my faith do eat meat and a lot of it. But I do not eat because I do not believe in killing the innocent animals for my food. The sheer sight of meat makes me bleed. How humans, having so many choices of vegetarian foods can systematically murder those poor animals to eat is beyond my comprehension. Perhaps they just close their minds and do not wish to think about it. They just eat to satisfy the taste buds of their tongue. Or they are just trained to think that these animals were made to be eaten.

4. Another problem was what conversation I should have with those who would be sitting next to me? Impossible task! I could not discuss politics, religion, or philosophies which are sensitive issues to discuss with strangers. I am not a sports fan and I do not know the rules of any popular games. I did not know their tastes, their backgrounds, and their cultural outlook. These subjects are only meant for whom you know a bit intimately.

So finally we sat down for the Christmas dinner, they were all having turkey, ordering various types of alcohol. I had never heard of any except beer or whisky. Before my turn came I took the advice of my colleague Roy who was next to me. He was a quietly spoken, helpful, friendly young fellow. We shared the same room at the office.

'Will I be able to get only the vegetables?'

'Why? Don't you like meat?'

'No. I don't eat meat.'

'What about turkey? That is not meat.'

'No, I am a vegetarian. I do not eat any meat.'

'You should try some meat. It is Christmas dinner.'

'No, sorry I just cannot eat it. If there are no vegetables available, I would just sit to give company to you people but I would not eat. It does not worry me if I don't get anything to eat. I can always share sweets with you people.'

'Ok. Let us try to order vegetables,' he said.

So he looked at the menu and ordered ½ pint of lager, peas, mashed potatoes, Brussels sprouts, and a bread roll with tomato soup. Lo! I had plenty to eat and drink. How can one go hungry on Christmas day in Britain? Impossible!

Shortly the speeches started, praising some people here and there for their contributions for the well-being of the company. Every speaker was massaging the egos of each other. The drinks were served and the food came. So with shivering hands and conscious of being surrounded by so many strange and unknown faces, I took the knife and fork delicately in my inexperienced hands, and I started to eat my meal. I first finished my soup with bread roll. I then sprinkled salt and shook a generous helping of black pepper powder to make the vegetables a bit hotter. I chopped the easy vegetables and gulped one by one. Roy was keeping an eye on me and suggested that I could mix and match the portions of veggies together to improve the taste. I did and he was right. He had the experience of munching this type of food. However, when the easily eaten veggies had gone, I was now left with delicate round peas. I left them to the last as I was not sure how to tackle them. As I pricked them individually they would roll away like a football on the playground. I tried to prick each one into a heap of three or four and then get them into my mouth. With this attempt sometimes I dropped one or two; another time nearly all; or sometimes I could only manage to get one into my mouth. It was a game of hit and miss. The dining plate had become a playground with about sixty or seventy green balls running around here there and everywhere. The futile exercise turned into a nightmare. God knew how many eyes were glued on me. As I was attempting to tackle them, I was also looking at Roy to see if he was watching me. He was. So he politely came to rescue me.

'Om, how is the meal? Are you enjoying it?'

'Yes, no problem. It is nice.' A straight, damn lie coming from the lips, what else could I say.

'Is it enough for you or do you need more?'

'No, it is plenty, thanks.'

I continued the fight with the peas to fork them individually and eat. It was frustrating. I have the habit of not leaving any food on the plate, I like to clear it. I was worried that when everyone had finished, their forks and knives would stop the chinking sounds, and they would put them together on the dining plates while mine would continue to send the cracking music to their ears. Then everyone would focus on my eating activity. That was the worry that was. Roy knew my plight but being a polite British gentleman did not wish to show his awareness of my problem. But there comes a time in life when you do put etiquette into cold storage and come out of your shell. He could not resist suggesting to me how to eat the peas. He suggested,

'Om, if you cannot eat that way, you may use your fork as a spoon to eat them.'

'Is that acceptable to eat that way?'

'Yah, I eat them that way. You cannot eat those tiny rolling stone monsters any other way.'

'Oh. Ok, thanks.'

Life became so easy and soon I saw all the peas disappear from the plate, sent into the grinding wheels of the stomach, and on their way to be well-digested. I became an expert in munching them. So this was my first Christmas Dinner in Britain. Another milestone of learning to eat veggies was achieved on that night that helped me in settling down in a strange and alien country.

Taste Of Delicatessen Cheese

The same kind of a situation arose when Martin my colleague and his young wife invited me to their home for a lunch. At the dining table his wife served a lovely vegetarian meal for which she had to struggle to find a good menu. She prepared all kinds of vegetables, boiled them with delicacy, and served them with a variety of cheeses, which they knew I loved to eat. In the middle of the meal, Martin suggested that I should try a mature green cheese but I declined. I was already getting a hell of a repulsive odour from it. As Martin took a big chunk of it again, he insisted that I should try a little as it was very nice and I would love it. That was quite un-British but he felt that he was now becoming a friend and he took the liberty to persuade me. Knowing that I was a guest and it would have been rude to keep on declining, I plunged to take a small piece into my plate. The horrible smell became even stronger as the morsel was now on my plate and I was finding it more difficult to bear it. So to hasten my ordeal, I took that little piece, added a portion of a chip, and swallowed it immediately. As I did it, I immediately felt like throwing up. That smell was strong, repulsive, and awful for the stomach to accept. The stomach is managed by its own brain and it was beyond my control.

I resisted throwing up. Within me the struggle had ensued. The stomach did not want to have anything to do with etiquettes and table manners. If it refused to have something it just would not budge. But the mind was struggling to convince the stomach to let go this time and it would not permit any more to come on the plate. Eventually the mind won the battle. The stomach accepted the persuasion this time under duress. Martin did not know my inner battles. He was enjoying the cheese as he always had done. However he wanted to know my reaction to the cheese. He asked, 'How was it? Did you like it?'

'Yah, it was ok.' a lie again. What do you do with these etiquettes?

'Have some more.'

'No, I would not try any more as it was the first time I have eaten it. I have to get used to it.'

'Yah, you are right. It took me some time to develop the taste for it and now I love it.'

So Martin and his wife took another big chunk to satisfy their taste buds for that cheese. I thanked my stars that they let me off this time.

Hey, readers would you like to experience it? Go ahead, be my guest and have fun.

I also felt in those days that I was eating a vegetarian cheese but later in life when Tesco and other supermarkets started writing on cheese and yogurts 'suitable for vegetarians' I was horrified to discover that the milk was split with rennin, a by-product of calf stomach, rather than with vinegar or lemon. There was no way for me to protest or riot on the British roads as once happened in India in 1857 when Indian soldiers of the British Raj declared a mutiny on Indian roads when they were given cartridges, greased with pig and cow fats, to be bitten before use. History can be painful but it has to be managed sensibly.

The Life around Trafalgar Square

The square is a tourist attraction. It has its good points and the bad ones. It depends upon the nationality of the visitor. It has all kinds of memorials to boost the ego of the British. It has statues of Nelson and some other great generals who waged wars on this planet to humble the other mortals. When I visited the Square for the first time at some weekend, I mingled with the other tourists and some local love makers.

After visiting the square, we walked down to Piccadilly Circus, Leicester Square, China Town, and the Soho areas where we were tempted to go into the local pubs spread out on the pavements. As we walked past them, the lovely bunny waitresses in their sexy dresses would coax us to go in and have drinks with them, sitting on their laps. What a despicable way to earn a few bob for the pimps, dressed respectably as pub owners. The pub owners were indulging in:

'Come in sir, here is the girl who is going to look after you.'

I looked at Kapoor and asked, 'What does he mean, "she will look after you"? Would she be happy to go to bed with us once we finish our drinks?'

'Don't be silly. These girls do not go with anyone who comes for a drink. They might go with those who are rolling in money and that too if they want to.'

'Oh! But how come there is no colour discrimination here.'

'Well, money is the god here. They are only interested in the tinkling sounds of the coins in your pocket.'

'Oh!'

How true that was.

But we just moved on. We had neither the money nor the courage to let them slip into our arms. We also went to some of these cafes in the evening. They used to be full of young people where the boys were looking for girls and the girls for boys for the night and maybe for a long-term relationship. It was a meeting place for the young to find their suitors. They hated arranged marriages and even made a mockery of our system in India. I agree. It is a system which is now breaking down. The western influence is reaching there too through modern electronic communications. The whole world is in a melting pot and changing very fast. That is one of the reasons that the orthodox preachers and fanatics are chucking bombs to stop the infiltration of new ideas into their decadent society. They like to keep their centuries-old world backward in the name of religion and the people of the world are paying a heavy price for it.

Trafalgar Square is a romantic place too where the young ones would like to mess around in the darkness of the statues with some beautiful bird in their arms. It is also an exciting place to feed the birds who would lodge themselves on our shoulders, on our heads to see if we had some seeds to feed them. They are fearless, friendly, and very demanding. Their nature and habits are just like the young ladies. No wonder the ladies are also called 'birds' and it is very appropriate. The ladies would assess the weight of your wallet and would be willing to go with you anywhere – in a hotel room or even to your residence provided you could afford their indulgences. The birds have a very little demand. Just a handful of seeds would lure them on your head for a decent photograph for your memory. They might jump on your hand, snatch a couple of seeds and whoop; then fly away onto the top of a statue to munch on their loot. Once they had munched, they would be looking for another victim with a handful of seeds. They too are choosy like the young ladies. Some may be trying desperately to get the attention of a bird to have them on their arms for a photograph but without any success. The same goes for the ladies. You may be very smart and charming; you may have plenty of dough in your pocket to spoil them, and yet they are quite capable of ignoring you. You may try desperately to get their attention and you would still fail. What makes

A JOURNEY THROUGH PARTITION AND BEYOND

them tick for some but not for others is an interesting research topic for the psychologists. They have given some theories but without any evidence. It is your nature which plays a domineering role in selecting your partners in bed. No one can predict their moods except a man's inner woman. Maybe that inner woman decides whether you are worthy to be their bedfellows or to be left on a scrapheap. And that inner woman is no stranger but part of your mother that nourished you for nine months in the darkness of the inner walls of her tummy. Otherwise, if you look around the various couples walking around arm-in-arm, you will find a strange combination. If the man is aggressive the woman is good-natured and sober. And so on. They would always be of opposite characters. If the woman is fat the man is slim or vice versa. It is always the opposites which attract, but after a little familiarity the attraction turns to hatred and fighting. That is the law of nature.

When I visited the Square for the first time, I was fascinated by the number of statues there. So I went to see every one of them and read the captions on them. When I went to read the captions written on General Havelock's statue, my Indian sentiments revolted in me. This man had suppressed the 1st Indian War of Independence in 1857 (as Indians call it) and his statue was being displayed proudly at a prominent place of the Square. I would not be exaggerating if I say that inside me I was very angry. How can they dare to show such a man who brutally murdered so many Indians in their aspiration to be free about 150 years earlier? Here was the golden opportunity provided to the colonial power to quit from its immoral deeds of keeping another nation in bondage but he, out of his short-sightedness, blew it away. He could not see into the crystal ball that the future generations would spit on those nations which had colonised the other people for exploitation and denied them their basic human rights to be free. It is the birthright of every human on this planet to be free and live in dignity. For the British he was a hero but for us Indians he was a villain. I have always been haunted to find the answer to how on earth such a small country – 1/13th part of India in area and with a population of thirty million - could rule so successfully a nation so big with a population of three hundred million that was a hell of a lot superior in culture and the home of so many religions. This clearly shows the deterioration of the type of citizens who lived in India in the past few centuries. They had reached to such a low level that they had allowed their rich country to be plundered, looted, and enslaved by so many foreigners, even coming from such small neighbours like Afghanistan. The Indians must be very cowardly people and have no stomach to match their opponents in the skill of warfare. Or maybe they cared more about their inner world and neglected the dangers of the outer world which surrounded them. But it was the shameful history of India and I feel it was reprehensible for me to be born as a 'slave' in my own country.

In disgust I just walked away from the statue.

The Intentions of a Lady?

In 1958 I was living with Kapoor at the Stamford Hill flat. Malik recommended that I register with his Indian lady doctor. It was only a two pence bus ride and a bit of a walk to reach her surgery. She had allocated two rooms from her residential home for her practice, a very convenient and economical way to run the surgery. In those days, it was essential to register with a doctor in case one needed some assistance for some medical emergency. The surgery was also not very far from my evening college.

It was the summer when the days were long and warm. It was my second visit to the surgery. When I reached there, it was just about closing time. I was the last patient to be seen. When my turn came I went inside the doc's room. It was only some minor ailment of a cold or cough. However she told me not to worry and did not give me any medication. As I got up to leave, she said, 'Would you like to have a cup of tea?'

'No, thank you. I don't drink tea that often.'

'No, have some. I'll make one for you and give you company.'

I did not say 'no' again. I thought it would be rude to keep on saying no to a lady. After all, she was my GP, and I had to be on good terms with her. In India we are taught to be respectful to the doctor profession and especially to a lady doctor. She must have been about fifteen years older than me. So as we came out of the doc's room, she offered me a chair in the open waiting area and asked me the type of tea I would like to drink, and went away to make the tea. I settled down in my chair and wondered how I would keep the conversation going on my own with a lady older in age and well settled in her profession. I hate to be alone with the ladies. One can never predict the behaviour of either party. Soon she came back with a cup of tea for me.

'I'll go and fetch my tea and my chair and I'll sit down with you.'

She brought her chair, placed it next to me, then got her cup of tea and settled down on her chair. She started the conversation, 'I have a young son. He has gone to the evening college and he will be late today.'

'What is he studying?'

'He is attending some course to help him to get into University. We came from India a few years ago.'

'That is good. So you are well settled here. You have the surgery in your house you own and the young son is also settling down well.'

'Yes. My husband works for the Indian High Commission as a security man. He is on late night duty today. He will be back around 10pm.'

'Oh, India House is a good sheltering place for the new arrivals from India like me. I love to go there whenever I can to have a rice and vegetable curry. It is very cheap. You can fill up your tummy for two shillings, including some Indian sweets. I also go there some Saturdays to read Indian newspapers just to keep abreast of what is happening back home.'

'Yes, would you like to have another cuppa?'

'No thanks. I must go. My flatmate might get worried about what happened to me that I am so late.'

So I hurried off to catch my bus for the flat. Kapoor was waiting for dinner. So we settled down to do justice to our meals which he had so nicely prepared. During our dining, he enquired what the doc said about my cold. I narrated him the whole story. He started his sermon, 'You know Om, you are just stupid.'

'What have I done?'

'Can't you see that she insisted on you to have a cup tea when all the patients had gone, she locked the surgery, then sat next to you on another chair and not in front of you, then she told you about her son and her husband that they both were going to be late today. This all leads to the conclusion that she wanted you to make advances towards her and finally leading you to her bedroom. You just did not understand her message which she was clearly trying to convey to you.'

'Is that what you think?'

'She just wanted to go to bed with you and you missed that opportunity.'

'But how can you go to bed with someone who is unknown to you, older than you, has grown up children, and her husband is away on duty somewhere? It would have been violating the privacy of her husband.'

'You know Om; you are in Britain where such moral issues carry no values. Here everyone is out there to quench the thirst of their body needs. Everyone is out there to get what you need and it is all in the open and is never swept under the carpet.'

These ideas never entered into my mind. I would have never interpreted the intentions of the lady that way. However, I accept that according to Kapoor I might have been stupid and I have no quarrel with his opinion, but I just could not have done it. That was not in my blood. It was not my cup of tea. If I had done it, I would have suffered all my life with guilt of using someone's property in his absence. Anything and everything you do in life always comes from your inner being. If the being does not agree then I feel the selfish mind must be controlled.

You reader, what do you think?

<u>A New Year Kiss</u>

It was Wednesday 31st December 1958. I had been in UK for only just over seven months and was still trying to find my way. Friends had been making noises about going to Trafalgar Square for New Year's Eve. They said it was one of the best places in UK to see the New Year celebrations. Temptations were aroused and I started to wait eagerly for the event.

We set out by bus and reached there just before the crush started. I was with Kapoor and the two P's. We had gone there by public transport but there were no means to return back as all the undergrounds and buses were going to be terminated just before midnight. Nevertheless we did not bother about the return journey as long as we were there to see my first New Year celebrations. We loitered around Piccadilly, Soho, and finally, around 11.30 we reached the Square. We mingled around to see all kinds of celebrations, to get the experience of how the various groups of people of the country step into the New Year with shouts of joy, hugging, and kissing. They were all happy to let the old year pass into history and witness the ushering of the new. As the hour of midnight approached, our attention was caught by a group of 8-10 people who were holding their hands and were dancing and singing in a merry-go-round circle. With my poor knowledge of English, I could not understand a word of their songs. I even don't understand them today. It is a colloquial music language, which has to be mastered to decode the words. This group looked quite fascinating and they were really enjoying themselves. We, like many others around them, were watching and enjoying their body movements, their chorus singing, and their smiling. It was the experience I did not wish to miss. When you move into another circle, into another society, or another country, the mind always gets busy in drawing comparisons. I felt that this kind of spirit of joy was missing in India. The British, although looking serious and reserved when in foreign lands, in their own country they do have fun, they do love jokes. As I was deeply engrossed in those thoughts, suddenly a young girl broke out of the circle and advanced towards me. Before I could realise what was happening, she grabbed my hand and shoved me in the circle and took her position right opposite to me. She was singing and dancing very joyfully and was encouraging me with her body language to participate and to join in the singing and dancing the way she was. How could I? I could not sing in the English language, I did not know how to dance. I was shy, blushing, and was sweating with embarrassment in that cold wintry month of December. Many people around, including my friends, were watching me and were expecting me to blend into something alien I had never done before. Soon the clock at the Square tolled midnight and declared that a new year had arrived. The singing and dancing stopped, and the young lady ran towards me. She hugged me, embraced me with a great force and started kissing me on my mouth. I was stunned. I just stood there motionlessly, without even putting my arms around her. I did not know how to react to her advances and the spontaneous warmth of her body. I did not respond to the affection she was showering at me. I just stood there like a dead statue, like a robot motionless and emotionless. Inside me my Gurukul was wide awake. It was controlling all my reactions with the deeply buried teachings in the unconscious mind of my early childhood.

That reminds me of a story I was told by my brother in my early days.

A man from India was visiting Britain. He stayed with a family where he got friendly with a young lady. The intimacy reached to such closeness that one night they went to bed together but they were separated with a cushion in the middle. The whole night passed and nothing happened between the two souls. The cushion acted as an unconquerable Himalayan wall. Next morning they had breakfast, chatted and shared their views to pass the time. In the afternoon they went to play tennis in the garden. One shot, the ball went over the fence. The boy rushed to climb the fence to fetch the ball. The lady shouted, 'Hey, I will get the ball. You cannot climb that fence. You could not climb a cushion last night, how could you climb this high fence.'

So that was me, just like that fellow. I did not know how to climb the cushion that night.

The lady, having found no warm response from me, must have felt silly, humiliated, insulted, and let down and she just walked away disappointedly. She went to kiss others in the circle. I had hurt her feelings and her self-respect. I sheepishly moved out of the circle towards my friends who were ready to give me a good rebuke.

'What the hell Om, why could you not embrace her. You just insulted her. It is shame on you. She was waiting to be kissed. She liked you and that is why she pulled you away from us to join the dance.'

'But I did not know why she did what she did. I am not that smart.'

'She fancied you, you stupid.'

A good hiding is always welcome as long its intentions are genuine.

Soon it was time to find our way home. We hired a taxi and were on our way to our flat by 2-3 in the morning.

That was the first ever New Year celebration of my life and that too happened in Britain. Indians do celebrate New Year's Eve in style but I had never joined such high society celebrations. I had always shied away.

Mugged in the Car

It was December 1961; I was married and was living at Leytonstone. It was Mira's first New Year's Eve in the country. So it was for Bhalla who sailed with us in the same ship from Mumbai. He was also living in the same area. We used to meet together quite often. So we decided to go to Trafalgar Square for New Year's Eve.

I was still a full-time student and without any job. Bhalla too had no job yet. We roamed around in the square to see the fun. This time I was with a lady bodyguard with no chance of being hijacked by another one. However, as usual, the New Year bell tolled, and we saw all the fun of kissing and hugging, and after loitering around an hour more, we decided to find our way back to the flat. We spotted a couple of guys sitting in a car who also appeared to be leaving the Square. Bhalla approached them and asked which direction they were heading. Luck had its own agenda. They were also heading towards the East side of London. Bhalla asked for a ride and offered to share the cost of petrol. They agreed. We were happy that we got the lift and felt safer too. On the way they were talking to us with civilised manners. Bhalla, Mira, and I were on the back seat and they both in the front. They asked where we came from and what were we doing in London. As we approached Stratford junction where one route was going towards Leytonstone and the other towards Forest Gate, they stopped the car. They asked us to give them the money we had, any watches, or any other valuables. We protested that we agreed to share the petrol costs but not this. The guy on the front passenger seat started abusing us and turned around to Bhalla and demanded to be given his watch. Bhalla protested and refused. The man came out of the car, opened the car back door, and, shouting and abusing, he asked us to get out of the car. Bhalla came out first as he was sitting next to the door and we followed. He manhandled Bhalla and pulled his jacket off. Bhalla threatened that he would call the police, but the man got in the car with his jacket and they sped off. Bhalla had lost some valuables but we were spared the violence that was so common in those days against the immigrants. From Stratford, three of us walked to Leytonstone in the cold wet dark night of the new year, fearing for our safety at that time of the night. After reaching home we thanked our stars. It could have been a lot worse incident. It was a 'lovely' unforgettable first Happy New Year present from London to Mira. She had also got away without being kissed or molested by some young, drunk stranger on her first New Year's Eve visit to the Square.

Visit to the Senate House

Kapoor knew that my main objective to come to London was to get education in engineering. So I asked him to take me to the Senate House at Russell Square. He had already mastered the way of travelling in London, to find the places on the map, and then get there by using the various public transport systems available. On one summer Saturday in 1959, we set out to visit the Senate House. We got down at Russell Square Tube station, walked across the memorial park, and within 5 minutes we stood in front of the new Senate House tall building.

'Om, that building is the Senate House. It is not a college but a central administrative office for the University of London. All the University Colleges are independent but are affiliated to give the University's internal degrees.'

'Can we go in?'

'No, it is Saturday. All the offices are closed and there is nothing to see inside.'

I stood on the lawn in front of the building. Kapoor walked away to see if there was any entrance to go inside the building. In those solitary moments, I stood in silence in a sombre mood, saying prayers in my mind. In that aloneness, I prayed to my God to give me enough courage and help me to fulfil my dreams for which I had left my country, my relations, and had travelled thousands of miles. Those moments made me a bit emotional.

As I was saying those prayers with eyes closed, the tears were rolling down my cheeks. I had been dreaming for this day since 1947 when everything was shattered by the disruption of my education because of the partition. A damn struggle had started to achieve this lifetime goal. The dream was now so near and yet there were so many hurdles to cross before its realisation. And yet I was wrong. God had already heard my prayers a long time ago; otherwise he would not bring me to British shores. It was only I who was short-sighted and was lacking to recognise that fact.

Soon Kapoor came back. He could not find any entrance. All the doors were locked to keep crazy people like me out. 'One day you should come and see it,' he said.

'Yes, I would certainly come when I have joined one of its colleges for an engineering degree.'

That was a brief brush with the history in making. And we retreated back to Russell Square and were on our way to the real world to spend our Saturday.

Preparing the Groundwork for Admission

I had already started making enquiries about the Colleges of engineering. Malik was a good source as he was already a 2nd-year student for his degree in Metallurgy. He found out what were my Indian qualifications and explained that I would have to pass Chemistry at O-level and Physics at A-level.

Chemistry was not a problem, as I did not have to attend the college for the O-level course. It was just a case of memorising the various chemical formulations from the book like a parrot and spit it out correctly on the examination paper.

But for the Physics at A-level, I had to attend a local college, learn the theory as well doing the numerous practical experiments at some college. These practical experiments were the part of a curriculum and had to be submitted on the day of the A-level practical examination to show that I had been doing these experiments at a recognised college.

Our location of the flat was ideal. The local Tottenham College of Technology was just two miles from Stamford Hill and was running evening classes for Physics A and Chemistry O. There were two handicaps. One, I had to attend the classes in the evening regularly and, second, the course for Physics was for two years but the Tutor at the college told me that I could appear for the examination earlier if I had done enough experiments to pass the practical examination. But he was sceptical that it would be achievable. Alternatively, he suggested that I should join a part-time course. I should attend one full day and one evening per week to do the course in a year. I could not do that as I needed a full-time job to save up the money for full-time study for three years. I decided to join the course for two evenings a week. One evening was fixed for Physics theory classes and the second evening for the practical.

Life now became quite hard. I was spending a lot of time in travelling from Stamford Hill to New Barnet, work 7½ hours a day, back home, cook and eat, and then go to college. The routine for studying three days was to be on the road at 6.30am and back home around 10pm. The other two days I had to study Chemistry and Physics at home. However, I managed it well with all the odds against me.

A Sad Story of a Disillusioned Student

Before 1961, coming to Britain and settling down was very easy provided you had managed to obtain a passport from your Government with or without some connections; were able-bodied, had a few Pounds in your pocket, were willing to work, and were ready to live as a second-class citizen. For the middle classes, with support from the bureaucrats of Delhi, it was a piece of cake, but for others like me it was a nightmare. Being a commonwealth citizen there were no restrictions to enter and work in Britain. No visas were required and once you landed in UK, you were considered a British citizen with all the citizen rights of voting, health benefits, and access to jobs and social security services. Britain called itself 'the mother country'. It was the greatest honour bestowed by Britain on every citizen of the Commonwealth.

But to settle and to live in a totally western alien culture, especially for those coming from Indian villages that had no exposure of living in even cosmopolitan cities like Delhi, it was a passport to end up in a nightmare. I heard a story about a couple of young Sikhs who came from Delhi. They both had the admission at Faraday House, Holborn to study engineering. The following is the story of one of them, I'll call him 'X'.

A JOURNEY THROUGH PARTITION AND BEYOND

The father of X was a simple, ambitious, hardworking father who had a dream of educating his son in England. He was, like a million others, a refugee from Pakistan who had reached India on a bullock cart and on donkey rides. That age of donkeys and bullock carts was fast changing into the cycle age as the industrial revolution was moving in full swing. Thousands of bureaucrats were riding every day on bikes to their offices. The buses' queues were getting longer and the waiting times were becoming more unbearable. I had seen such queues on Pusa Road when I used to bike to NPL from the old Rajinder Nagar. Pusa Road was leading the bureaucrats to the central offices through a rocky hill. There is a steep hill to climb and everyone would dismount and walk up that part of the road from Rajinder Nagar. All the civil servants living right up to East and West Patel Nagar had to ride through this route.

The father had a roadside stall just on the top of the hill for repairing punctures and pumping air in the bikes for these daily riders. For this service he sweated all day under the burning sun, collected pennies, and saved them to fulfil his dream of getting his son educated in UK. The family also believed in some religious ethics. The day before X was to fly out to UK, the mother made her son sit down with her and made him honour the following vows:

1.   That he would not touch and drink any alcohol as long as he was in UK.
2.   That he would not smoke.
3.   That he would not eat meat. He would remain a vegetarian.
4.   That he would neither make any girlfriend nor would he have sex. He would also not marry a foreigner.
5.   He would read daily his religious scriptures without fail.

It was a very daunting commitment the boy had to make to his mother's demands. Effectively she had robbed him of all his freedom of social mixing with the locals in UK. However these were not the issues which worried him. There were a lot worse problems to cope with here than the food habits. I too had to struggle to find vegetarian foods. Nearly everything, even the basic foods needed for sheer survival, was contaminated with non-vegetarian ingredients. For instance the loaf of bread contained animal lard; the potato chips were fried in lard; mashed potatoes contained lard to make them a bit greasy; all the pastries had lard in them; even the ice cream had added lard rather than milk fats. None of these ingredients were listed on the labels in those days. These revelations came slowly with the time as we were settling down. The information had trickled out of the bakeries and from the other food processors where more and more Asians were being employed. I ate all those products, thinking that the products would be vegetarian.

Now how on earth the ice cream manufacturer was adding lard to their products was beyond comprehension except to earn more profits at the cost of a citizen's wellbeing. But the British businessmen have never been ethical in conducting their businesses throughout the ages. To me, by creating all these weights and measures in pounds and the currencies in pennies and shillings, not based on the decimal system, was to hoodwink their not very literate consumers. It was brazenly open cheating on the name of nationalism. It is only recently when the age of electronic calculators has arrived on the scene that they have changed the system to decimal.

But X did not know these facts, like so many others who were arriving in the country as students and cheap labour. However his settling down was a cultural shock and he was finding it difficult to accept the sudden change. I survived this shock by sheltering in India House and meeting with other Indians there during the early days. Also, with a bit of luck, I weathered the storm by having met people like Kapoor, Malik, and many others. X probably was not that lucky. In my case I had no choice but to make it a success as I had no return ticket and money to go back. On the other hand, X had the return ticket in his wallet to use if and when he wanted to. I had a lot to lose as a self-supporting person. I had burnt all my boats in India before coming here. I had no job to go back to and I would find it difficult to find financial support to find me another job. Therefore for me it was a one-way ticket and no chance of even contemplating to think of returning. I had burnt those options for good. I also had the ambition and a goal for higher education to fulfil. Those were my dreams and not of my parents. I had to achieve them and there was no turning back. I had to survive and live here come what may. The thoughts of returning back to India had never entered into my head. I would have never entertained them. I had to move forward. I had to make a success of it. I was not going to blow up the opportunity now which had come in my way from Heavens.

I heard X flew back within 2 weeks of his arrival. The shock of financial loss to his parents would be unimaginable. His family must have been heartbroken and shaken. His father would have to work many long hours and for many more years to recoup the losses inflicted by his stupid son. I was lucky that way that I had no restrictions imposed by my family and also I had only a one-way ticket. But the story was a sad one and the lessons had to be learnt.

Seeking Admission

I had no clue about which University college was better than the others. Once again Malik guided me. He encouraged me to apply to Imperial College in London. This college is world famous and the degrees gained in that college are respected all over the world. At the time I was not aware of the reputation of this college. If that was the case, then why not aim for the best, I thought.

A JOURNEY THROUGH PARTITION AND BEYOND

I applied and I was called for the interview with the admission tutor who was very kind and showed a lot of understanding. He looked at my qualifications, which I had already mentioned in my application form.

'Which type of engineering are you interested in?'

'Sir, I would like to go for the Mechanical Engineering. That is where my heart throbs.'

'Do you know that presently you do not have qualifications to meet the entrance requirements? You have a degree from India in English and Mathematics and that gives you exemption in English and Mathematics but you need to have Physics at A-level and Chemistry at O-level to join the course.'

'Yes sir, I do. I am addressing that problem already. I am attending an evening college to study Physics at A-level and Chemistry at O-level. As the examination is twice a year, I will appear for them and pass if I get the admission at the college.'

'The full-time education at the Imperial is expensive. The fees are higher. We also expect students to live in digs, participate in all the social activities of the college, and do not expect the students to work in those three years study, even during summer vacations. Have you got enough savings, resources or income from India to support yourself?'

'Yes sir, I would be able to get financial support from parents in India.'

I bluffed boldly without any hesitation but I knew in my heart that I had no such support and if the chips were down I would be on the road within a year without a degree and not a penny in the pocket. My savings from my job would last me just under two years. Without working during summer and Christmas breaks, my third-year studies would be in doubt. I had no rich uncle with a merciful heart in India who would support me. There were millions like me trying their best to fulfil their dreams on this planet. Who would care about my studies and dreams?

He pondered on my papers for a while as I looked on nervously to know his decision.

'Hum, I am prepared to give you the admission subject to the following conditions:

1.   Your passing of the Physics at A-level and
2.   Chemistry at O-level.
3.   Also we would need a 'no objection certificate' from the Indian High Commission.'

'Thank you, sir. I assure you that I will work hard to pass those examinations. I will also go to the Indian High Commission and ask them to send you the "no objection" certificate.'

With that note, I departed. You can imagine my joy. I was ecstatic. I was over the moon. I was on the way back home.

I was literally surprised that I got the admission in such a well-known college. Malik had his reservations that I would ever get the admission in that college, especially when I was still trying to pass the two main entry subjects. He was also doubtful about my admission because I was a recent arrival to the country with no connection with any Indian elite family and had no financial support. I was just a son of a retired refugee who himself was struggling to survive the economic hardships of India. When Malik heard about the news, he was surprised but very happy. He congratulated me and encouraged me to do my best to pass those examinations.

A Battle for a Letter from the Indian High Commission

So far, so good, but now it was time to address more urgent issues. While passing the examinations was within my capabilities and my hard work, getting a letter from the Indian High Commission was beyond me. I had a recent experience of how the Indian Bureaucracy worked. It was full of people who were corrupt, jealous, and infested with the ideas of 'whom you know'. However I had to try my luck.

One day I took a day off from my office and went to the Indian High Commission's office at Aldwych. At the reception, they sent me to the Education Department on the 2nd floor where I met an official. I explained to him that I had been given admission at Imperial College subject to a no objection certificate from his department. I informed him that I would be grateful if he could send this letter as soon as possible to the College so that my admission could be confirmed.

He decided to give me a good grilling. He asked me a number of questions. How and when did I arrive in this country? Did I report my arrival to the High Commission? How did I get my passport? Is it genuine and who issued it in India? I satisfied all his questions. I showed him my passport. I also said that I was not aware that I was supposed to report to them about my arrival into UK. But the official was determined to be awkward and I could not understand any reason for that.

'You got this admission directly from the college without submitting your application through us. So we cannot give you a 'no objection' certificate.'

'But I was not aware that I am supposed to apply for the admission through you.'

'Yes, that is the procedure. All candidates from India are to apply for studies in UK through us.'

A JOURNEY THROUGH PARTITION AND BEYOND

'But I was not applying from India. I now live here and work here. It is because I am an Indian citizen that it is a formality that you write to the college that you would have no objection for me studying there.'

'Who is funding your education here?'

'I am now working here and saving enough from my weekly wages and that will see me through my three years education. We are refugees from Pakistan and my education was disrupted due to partition. I have come here to complete my education, which was not possible in India because of my age discrimination and lack of engineering education facilities. So please I need your help to support my application to the college.'

Pleading to a hard-hearted man who could not care less was like hitting my head onto a brick wall. It was not only discouraging but was also insulting to plead my case to a dumb officer who was probably power drunk. However, he finally agreed to talk to his boss and see what could be done. With that assurance, I departed but I was not very hopeful. I never knew that this nut would be that much harder to crack. Even today when I look back, I cannot understand why it was so difficult for him to write a letter to the College. My status in Britain in those days was that I, being a de-facto Commonwealth Citizen, was a British Citizen. I just had to go and surrender my passport to the British Home Office and get a British passport. But to surrender my nationality was an emotive issue. No good person in his right mind would surrender his nationality so easily. We always love the land of our birth. It is a natural affinity with that piece of soil which nurtured us, where we were born, and where we had grown up.

Quite a few days had gone by and the Indian High Commission had still not sent the letter. I had a reminder from the College that they still had not received a 'no objection' certificate from the IHC. So I took another day off from the office and presented myself to the boss in the Education Department of the Commission. I explained once more about my requirements to him, hoping that he would show better understanding of my problem. This man was even nuttier than his subordinate.

The conversation started amicably and in a good mood. But as the discussion progressed, it became more difficult and acrimonious. He maintained his position that as the application had not gone through his office, he was not prepared to give any letters to support my application to the college. I was young, haughty, and a bloke who would accept no nonsense, so it turned into a nasty heated argument.

'We will not give the letter as the admission has not gone through our department.'

'This is only academic. I am an Indian citizen and it is your duty to help me whichever way you can rather than finding petty excuses.'

'No, we just cannot help in this case.'

We both paused for a few seconds and then he commented:

'I don't know why people like you come out of the country without any education and then ask for help.'

'How dare you say I have not got the education? I am a graduate from Punjab University in English and mathematics and you call me uneducated? I now wish to pursue the engineering education and for that I need to pass some more subjects to meet the entry requirement. How can you conclude that I am not educated? My parents and I did not choose to become refugees. Fate had imposed its will on my future destiny.'

When I went in, I was sheepish with a begging bowl in my hand. His remarks about me being not educated made me aggrieved and depressed. I was in no mood to plead for mercy and help anymore. I had become frustrated, angry, disillusioned, and aggressive. I marched out of his office like a hurting, wounded lion. His outbursts were too much and insulting to bear. As I stormed out, the uncontrollable tears were rolling down my cheeks. It was too much to take, I was frustrated. Why could he just not understand my predicament? I did not make this journey from India to Britain in futility. I was just seeking a small mercy, help, and understanding. But I don't know how and why; something touched the inner cores of his heart. He realised his mistake. As I was sobbing in the open yard to his office, suddenly I found a warm embrace of his arms behind my body, saying: 'I am very sorry. I did not mean to hurt you Khurana Sahib. I was just carried away and I should not have said those words to you. I have changed my mind and I will send a letter of "no objection" to the college today.'

With his embrace and genuine display of understanding, I melted too. I thanked him for his generosity. There was nothing more to be said. The issue was amicably settled in the end. The mission accomplished, and I was on my way home. I was sad with the whole affair but a ray of hope and happiness was appearing in the horizon to console me. That is life.

Time to Move On

On the Financial Front:

Everything was under control now. I was managing my living expenses to a bare minimum. My basic wage/week was £17.10s, a very good wage for 37½ hours. Whenever I was allowed, I did overtime about an hour every day and 4 hours on Saturdays to boost my income. This was bringing me another £4-£5/week. So the weekly take-home pay, after all deductions, was on average £15/week. My expenses in those days were

A JOURNEY THROUGH PARTITION AND BEYOND

£3.10s/week........Rent
£2.0/week..........Food
£2.0/week..........Travel
£0.3s/week.........Weekly cinema
£1.15s/week........Other sundry weekly
£7.0/month.........To parents. Later it was increased to £10/m

I was saving nearly £6+/week in the post office savings account.

I was quite pleased with my savings and I knew I would be able to save enough to see me through for three years college with some hardship if I was going to study at Imperial. So by the time I left my job and joined my college at West Ham College of Technology in September 1960, I had saved up an impressive £700 in the post office. From today's standard it is peanuts but in those days with that cash I could buy a good three-bedroom house in Forest Gate with still some cash left over in the bank.

Attendance at the Evening College and the Exams

To attend three nights at the college was quite demanding with a full-time job, travelling to work, and then fending for the food. I was missing quite a few lessons. The tutor, a very nice and caring person, would warn me about attendance. He said to me that the theory I may be able to cram from the books at home and may pass with a bit of luck, but to master the experiments without attending would be quite daunting. He was right but I was more confident in tackling the practical examination than he was. That was very short-sighted thinking on my part.

In May 1959, I appeared for the Chemistry at O-levels and Physics at A. The practical examination was to take place at the Physics Department of the Imperial College. I passed the Chemistry examination and the Physics theory, but alas I failed in the Physics practical examination. I was given two practical experiments. One of them was to find the focal point of a lens by immersing it into castor oil. I had read in the practical books how it should be done but I had not done it in practice. Many attempts and drawing from the memories of some of my experiments in my 9th class did not help. I just could not get the reading. So I bungled it. The examiner was nice and gave me an alternative practical examination to do but for that test I had no clue at all. So I had messed up my practical examination and when the results came, I had failed in the practical.

I had failed for the first time ever in my life. I had many successes so far but now it was time to taste being a failure. It was a setback but it was not a disaster. I had lost a battle but not the war. Failures are also a part of life. They are the other side of the coin. Then why are they not accepted in grace? It is society which makes you feel guilty as if a sin has been committed. Those who do not ride horses would never fall but then they would not enjoy the horse ride either. If there is no failure, we would never enjoy the fruits of success. We would never know the meaning of the success.

In one way it was a blessing in disguise and I am not saying that with sour grapes. Let us assume that I had passed my examination. In that scenario, I would have worked only for a year + and during this period I would not be able to save enough funds to support my three years full-time education, without some outside support and that support never existed. I was also warned by the admission tutor at the time of interview that the college would not want me to work during the summer and Christmas holidays. Furthermore, the yearly fee of the college was a lot more and was not affordable. In those circumstances I would have had no choice but to pack up my studies in the middle of the 2nd year. The big advantage of a degree from Imperial was that it would have opened a bright future, not only in Britain but nearly all over the world. But it was not to happen. I had to lose something to gain the other. So I consoled myself with my first failure and swallowed the bitter pill of pride.

When I went see the teacher at the Tech College, he immediately said before I uttered a word, 'Hey, I am sorry to know that you did not make it in the practical exam.'

'How did you know, sir?'

'The examiners knew that you were a student at this college. So they sent your results to us.'

'Oh! You were right to warn me and encourage me to attend the classes regularly to do the practical.'

'Well, what I was saying was the experience I had.'

'Yes, thanks for that. But where do I go from here?'

'Well, try again. The examination is every six months. Go and see the admission tutor at Imperial and ask him to let you start the degree course on a condition that you will pass it in the next examination after six months. If you don't then you would leave the course. They can only say no!'

'Thank you, sir, and good idea. I will try.'

'You can come back and join the course again. But this time make sure that you are attending the lessons regularly.'

Malik and Thambaya, Malik's friend from Sri Lanka, were also disappointed to know my results. They knew the education game more than I did. To get the education without any financial backing and moral support was not a joke. Both of them had seen such failures. Malik never shared with me his mishaps but Thambaya told me about his own tales and Malik's.

A JOURNEY THROUGH PARTITION AND BEYOND

I sent my exam results immediately to the Imperial and begged the admission tutor to allow me to start the course on a condition that if I did not pass the exam in the next sitting, I should be chucked out. But alas the trick did not work. I had a rejection letter, saying that the admission was granted on the condition that I would pass those two examinations before I would be allowed to join the college. That condition was not met.

I did not give up. I made an appointment with the tutor to convince him, face-to-face. He did not budge but said that if I had failed in Chemistry, he would have allowed me to join with a condition to pass the Chemistry exam within a year but Physics being at A-level, he could not bend the college rules. So finally and sadly, the chance to get the engineering degree from the Imperial had just evaporated.

Back to Planning

I went to see Malik, my experienced mentor. After some discussion, we reached a conclusion that the route open to me was to join a college which did external degrees of the London University (LU). The external degrees have a lot of disadvantages for the future career prospects.

1. The colleges are totally unknown to the interviewers of the well-known employers.

2. These interviewers studied at the nationally well-known colleges, and had their own prejudices. They preferred to take candidates from well-known colleges or from the colleges they had studied. It is a well-known fact that nearly all the cabinet ministers have been appointed from the two universities only – Cambridge and Oxford. Therefore one will either not get a job or, if offered, it will be at a lower level. The whole system is loaded with corruption and nepotism, although it is not as much visible here as in India.

3. Each internal college of the university is independent to grant their degrees with the grades they think is right. The lecturers will only teach the topics from which they will set the exams. Their students will have no difficulty in passing and getting good grades. By following such practices, the reputation of the tutors will also be bolstered. It will also enhance the popularity of the university. The students know their tutors personally and that was the greatest advantage they had in getting the final grade. The readers may be sceptics about what I am saying but I have experienced such practices when I was teaching. I will give two examples:

A. A student ('Y') of Physics at one London internal college was living with us as a tenant. I had done my degree and was teaching at a local Polytechnic.

I was home because it was my day off from the college. A call came from Y's tutor around 11am. 'Is Y there at home?' someone enquired. 'I don't know I will have a look.' 'I am his tutor, his exam started at 10am and he has not turned up yet. If you find him please ask him to come to the college immediately to take his exam. I will keep his exam paper up until 3pm. He can report any time during this period to take his exam. I am not supposed to do that as the exam has already started but I have the authority to bend the rules to allow him to sit in his exam.' So I went to Y's room. He was fast asleep and my knock woke him up. 'Hey, your tutor called that you were to be taking the exam and you are sleeping.' 'Oh damn! What did he say?' I relayed the message. He got ready, took a bus and reached the examination hall around 1pm. He took his exam and you guess what? He got Lower Second in Physics. He eventually got a PhD and went for a teaching post at another University.

B. As we were allowed to give degrees at Polytechnics, once a principal lecturer confided to me that there were a couple of students in his class who did not deserve to be given degrees. I asked what he was going to do. He said, 'I have two choices. Don't give them the degrees now and let them repeat for another year. Then if they still don't come to the required level, give them the degrees. The instructions from the higher authorities are that it was a waste of national resources to keep on failing someone for more than two years whether they deserve the degree or not. The other choice was to grant them the degrees now and kick them in the unemployment pool. I don't believe they deserve degrees even after two years. They should not have been allowed to start a degree course. It is too late. So if I have to give them a degree in two years, I might as well grant them the degrees now.' So they got their degrees. I bet they would not get their degrees if they were studying at the external colleges of the university.

4. On the other hand, the external colleges would teach to cover a very comprehensive curriculum of the subject as they would not know from which areas of the subject the questions would be set. So the teachers and the students both have to work harder. The exams were set and marked by the internal university tutors. We always bet that whatever the grade an external student was getting, he would get at least one grade higher if he/she was an internal candidate.

5. The social life of the externals is poor. In fact there is none. There are no students' unions, which give a lot of help to overseas students at the internal colleges.

6. The welfare organisations at the external colleges are non-existent. These organisations are very supportive to the overseas students. They make their life more comfortable.

A JOURNEY THROUGH PARTITION AND BEYOND

The external colleges are far and few. There was one college in East London which was preparing students for the LU external degrees – The West Ham College of Technology. It was expanding and growing in status as the demand from the overseas students for such colleges was increasing. I applied for a place and was granted without any fuss or interviews. I accepted. The course was to start in Sept 1960. I had plenty of time to save the money and also pass the Physics practical examination. I think the college fee in those days was only £100 per year, to be paid in three quarters. This was affordable.

The time passed on and the year had gone very quickly. I passed my practical in Physics in the next examination. Another six months passed and I was ready to join the college full-time.

Tension With Kapoor

Time takes its own way to solve the problems of the world. The three musketeers stayed in the country, whiling away their precious times and achieving nothing and went back. I met two of them in Delhi when I went for my marriage in 1961. Since then I am not in touch with them.

As I lived in the room next to Kapoor's in the flat, I was beginning to know more about him. He was lovely company. He was very sincere and a good friend. We would go to cinemas, play tennis with Malik and one of the Sharma brothers at the weekends at a park about five minutes' walk from where we lived. He used to sing a lovely, touching morning song in the kitchen while shaving. I learnt that from him. He was a good bathroom singer with a lovely voice.

Being young, he would make girlfriends, have fun, and then dump them, or the girls would dump him. Well, that was the British culture too. There was no sincerity in love or love making. Just have fun for a few days and then find another one. Just like changing to a new garment when soiled.

One day when I came home from work, he was in his bedroom.

'Hey, what happened, you are early home today.'

'No, I did not go to work today. I took a day off sick.'

'But you look ok to me.'

'Yeah, in fact I made a girlfriend and I had asked her to come to my room today during the day to have some fun. You were working so that helped in having some privacy.'

'Who is she?'

'Oh, she is an Anglo-Indian girl, living not very far from here. She is quite nice. When she was here we had a bit of a drink and lunch together. Then we kept on gossiping and fooling around. She was with me for about 4 hours. I asked her to go with me in the bed.'

'Did she?'

'She hesitated and said that she would not like to sleep with anyone until he was ready to marry her.'

'Then?'

'She said it is our second meeting and "I hardly know you". She continued to object and showed her reluctance. Finally I had to throw in my trump card.'

'What was that?'

'I said don't worry if you do get pregnant with our love-making today, I promise I will marry you. And on that note she relented and we made love.'

'Suppose she becomes pregnant, would you really marry her?'

'No, no way. She is not my type to marry but she is fine for a couple of bed trips. Sometimes in life, you have to tell stories and give false assurances to get the girls in bed. Otherwise they would not let you make love.'

'Oh, that is quite interesting.'

One Saturday as we were shopping, he waved to a young lady. She smiled back at him. That was his girlfriend with whom he had slept the other day, he confided. She was a plump, typical Asian girl. To me she was not attractive but then who am I to comment on her attractiveness or her beauty.

A few weeks later he left that girl for good. When I asked what happened, 'Oh she refused to come to my room until I promised that I was courting her seriously with an aim to marry her. Otherwise her parents would be very upset. So I decided to dump her.'

Soon he moved on to find another girl. He knew all the ropes of the British boys how to fish out a young lady to satisfy his manly lusts. Maybe it was also prevalent in his type of society in India too where he came from and he was quite at ease with it. He had no bad feelings or morality of changing girls. For him it was just a routine.

This second girl was Jewish. She did not live with her parents and no one knew her background. She already had another boyfriend. Later I began to know a bit more about her. She always kept two boyfriends. When one dumped her or she dumped him, soon she would replace him with another one. So she would come to Kapoor's bedroom in the nights whenever he wanted her. Being a common dividing wall between our bedrooms, I could hear her giggles in the middle of the night and that would wake me up. I was young too; sometimes it became unbearable to go to sleep. My job was quite demanding, being a contract design office and I had to travel a long distance every morning. This was having its toll on my wellbeing. Either I had to follow his way of life by doing what he was doing or go my separate ways and live my life my way. But temporarily I had no choice but to shut up and put up with it.

A JOURNEY THROUGH PARTITION AND BEYOND

One day Kapoor asked me to take his girlfriend out. I asked where? He said it did not matter. Just take her to a pub, offer her a drink and just chat with her about anything to have an experience of dealing with girls. You cannot be on your own as a young man. You've got to learn these tricks of chatting with the girls. You have to learn the techniques to manipulate the girls. You are in Britain and not in India. 'Yes, but what have I to talk about? You are asking me to talk to her for hours – all through the journey to and from the West End, then a couple of hours in the pub. I have not got that much material to talk about. I am not used to it. I do not know the topics to talk about with strangers whom I do not know intimately. I am not a lady's man.'

I knew he was trying to change me, with his good intentions, but I was too mature to learn all those hunting tricks. My suppression in my early childhood was complete and total and to forget those teachings, it needed a phenomenal effort. It was impossible to wipe out the old memories from my head. Or was it that he, being with her for so many months, was getting fed up with her old charms and wanted to unload the old bag on to me so that he moved on with someone new, fresh with a new face to keep him entertained? The human mind is so devious that even the trained psychologists cannot fathom its depths.

However, one Sunday I took her out. Kapoor had already asked her and she had consented that she was willing to go with me to a pub in the West End. Both were well experienced in handling their love preys. While he was looking for a change, she too was ready to dump him for a new suitor. They were both well-experienced poker players. Kapoor told me the pub I should take her to. We had been together to that pub a couple of times. So we travelled in a double-decker bus and went to a pub at Tottenham Court Road. We walked as boy and girl, without any arms around the waists, went into a pub, ordered the drink she wanted and lager for me, talked what we thought was right for us. I do not remember any of the conversation we had. We were in the pub for about an hour. She had a couple more drinks, and we came back the way we went, by bus. So that was it – an experience of an outing with a young girl who was someone else's property. Kapoor was at the flat. I thanked him for allowing me to go out with her, and handed over his possession back intact, in one piece, untouched.

As the visits of the young lady were becoming more frequent and even sometimes she stayed at Kapoor's room for the night, I was getting a bit concerned. I was worried in case she became pregnant, or she reported to the police, or what the landlord would do if he came to know. I was also concerned that in case of any problem I too would be involved because I was sharing a flat with Kapoor. Life runs very smooth as long as nothing untoward happens, but if something does go wrong, it can create nightmares for everyone known to the person. So I reminded Kapoor about his responsibilities towards the lady in case of pregnancy. I also came to know from a source that she was also meeting another boy. It added more problems. Now if she did get pregnant, how would Kapoor prove whose child it was. There was no DNA scanning in those days to determine the parenthood. I did not wish to tell Kapoor that she was going with another young fellow but I was concerned about Kapoor's future and his wellbeing. He was a good friend. I adored him; I respected him; and I admired his qualities. He came from a good family in India and I did not wish him to land himself in marrying a girl who was not suitable for him. She had a dual personality and had no loyalty or integrity towards anyone. We had no clue about her background. My protests and warnings had no effect on him. In the end I gave up and left him to face the consequences himself. I decided to rent a double bedroom at a house in Muswell Hill. There, two brothers also had a one bedroom flat with kitchen facility. I shared with them their kitchen. This place was also nearer to New Barnet where I worked. Obviously Kapoor was not very happy. He stayed on in the same flat, perhaps paying rent only for a room and the kitchen.

A few weeks later I heard that Kapoor had left the country and had gone to Germany. The girlfriend he was going with became pregnant and he left the country in panic. He could not face up to the situation to marry her. The girl decided to bear the child. She continued to keep the same lifestyle of going with two boyfriends. I saw her visiting another man named Tiwari who was also living at Malik's flat where I also moved in 1960 to follow my full-time education at West Ham College of Technology. I never saw the child but Tiwari told me that she was a mother now and was looking after that child herself. What a cock-up, first those two lives who never married and later the third innocent, born out of the misadventure of the two irresponsible adults.

Life At Muswell Hill

In one word, life was just lonely, very lonely, and very boring.

The Sharma brothers had a car. At weekends we would play tennis. We would go for a walk to Alexandra Park, which was about ten minutes walk from my residence. I had no TV and no other entertainment. Every Sunday I would walk down to the local cinema to watch an English movie. It did not matter whether it was a good one or a bad one but it helped me to understand the colloquial English. The brothers had their own TV in their room. Although I could watch it, I felt I was intruding in their personal lives, so I would stay in my room. I did not know of a library around to borrow books and also I did not have the habit of reading in those days. Sometimes a lonely Scot, who lived in a room above mine, would knock at the door uninvited for a chat. He would not understand my Indian colloquial English and I would not understand a single word of his. But out of politeness I would always nod my head in response. It was boring and later I started

A JOURNEY THROUGH PARTITION AND BEYOND

dreading his company. There was nothing in common between us to talk about but because of my Indian rearing I always put up with it.

The Death of my Eldest Brother

One evening as I came in from the office, I had a letter from my mother. It had devastating news. My eldest brother, Pritam, had died a few weeks earlier. I knew he was not well as my uncle from Delhi wrote to me now and then, but his information used to be sketchy. I sat on my bed and cried, cried, and cried a lot. The man, who supported me all my life, helped me to achieve so much, was no more. He had gone for ever. I could not see him while on my way to Britain. My younger brother Ved told me that Pritam been travelling on a railway touring trolley. This is a 10-feet long platform, only as wide as the railway track, with seats for 4-6 people – engineers, surveyors and the like. It was pushed at running speed by two workers. There were no protective rails, and Pritam had fallen, damaging his back. He never recovered. My only regret is that my family failed to write to me about his condition. I could have sent some medicine from here provided they had shared his ailment with me. My thinking towards life had totally changed. I was ready to find solutions to problems rather than surrender to nature. But it appears that my family, finding no answers to his medical problems, must have just given up. I hated that. They had not given me the opportunity to help him. They kept everything secret from me, resulting in the loss of a young life. He was survived by his wife, two daughters and a son, all young.

But, as it must, life continued.

The landlady at Muswell Hill was a Greek old lady, very active but fat. She would clean the bedrooms, tidy them up and change the linen every week and I was paying her £3 rent every Friday. We had never been inside her ground floor flat. She had an English husband, very stern, and never friendly, just the opposite of his wife. They lived with the rental income coming from the rooms in that big house.

I used to sit in my bedroom window to see the different passers-by on the road. I spotted a young Asian girl who used to pass by to her home from work or a shopping trip. She was a pretty, attractive, slim, and well-dressed girl. Loneliness always tries to find a solution for itself. I felt some attraction towards her. It was natural. I was young, lonely, no one to give me company to go to the cinema or to share other crazy chats of two young foolish heads. But as usual I lacked the skill of a woman charmer. So one day I collected my courage to ask my landlady if she could introduce me to that girl. I gave her the timings when she passed that way. She said she knew the girl and she would try. I waited eagerly for

85

her reply. Days passed and no reply from the landlady. I gave up hope. However one day, when I went to give her rent, she said 'You know the girl you were talking about, I have spoken to her. She has a boyfriend. I asked her if she would like to meet another boy. She said she had a boyfriend and was going with him quite seriously. However she wouldn't mind seeing this person.'

'That is good. I don't mind seeing her too.' I said

The landlady found a date from her. The young lady told her that she would see me on one Saturday. She would talk to me for a few minutes in the landlady's sitting room. So we met. We had a brief chat, nothing specific. Just the same parrot talk, 'I have a boyfriend and I'm not looking to go with another.' I don't blame her. I had nothing much to offer her. Was I foolish to meet her? Maybe, but that is all what being young can do.

The time passed and the year had gone too quickly in that routine life of travelling to work, back home, cook, sleep, and play tennis with a bunch of known friends at the weekend. Soon the time had come to join the college.

Moved to Malik's Flat

I moved back to Malik's flat. He was a lovely man and offered me a room in his flat. He had a first floor flat at Stamford Hill with four rooms, a kitchen, and a toilet/bathroom. He had some more people living there as well. Most of the time, he did not stay there. Where he was going and staying we did not know.

In September 1960 I left my job as a designer. I had saved up enough money to see me through my three years full-time course.

Life at the College

On my first day I travelled by changing buses from Stamford Hill to West Ham College. It was a great day for me. I was very excited and jubilant. I had toiled for so many years to fulfil my dream, to study for an engineering degree from London University. I reached there in the morning. There were a lot of students milling near the office, gossiping and introducing themselves. Then all we new recruits moved into the assembly hall, near the office. This hall was later turned into a library, and then into a computer room a year after I left the college.

A senior lecturer of the Mechanical Engineering Department stood on the dais with no microphone to welcome us all. He had to shout at the top of his voice to make us hear him. His welcome address was drowned in the hall in the presence of so many bodies and was hardly audible. So the Sir blurred, 'This college welcomes you all in the first year of the engineering course. I can see a sea of faces, deep down in the hall. There are 120 students in all. Before I ask which country of origin you all are from, and as I hardly see any white faces here, let me rather ask how many English students are here. Please raise your hands.'

A JOURNEY THROUGH PARTITION AND BEYOND

Guess what - there were only seven British students from a crowd of 120. Sir was shocked. He continued, 'That shows that the people of Britain are not interested in the higher education. As most of the faces are Asian, it means the people from that part of the world are on the way to development and it also means the downfall of Britain in the years to come, a very sad day for us.' He was very disappointed. But it was nothing to do with us. The dreams of higher education instilled in me were because of the social pressures imposed on me and others like me by society. We were expected to shine, compete, and achieve more than our peers. The people of this country never valued education because of the government policies. They were only trained to be craftsmen, labourers, and the fodder for the army. That is what the elite ruling classes wanted. They never wanted the general mass of the people as intellectuals, poets, scientists or philosophers to compete with their offspring. They just wanted to preserve those professions for the sons of lords, and the other hierarchy of the rich classes. The whole society was riddled with a class system. Even the political system was infested with the class system. The Tories were representing the rich industrialists and businessmen while Labour was supported by the unions drawing their power from the working classes. It is only very recently the expansion of education is taking place because of the economic pressures from the Chinese and the Indians who have thousands of well trained and educated graduates to man their industry. That was a wake-up call for the ruling classes of this country.

We were also surprised and became conscious of the fact that soon after our graduation, we would be in the job market to change the employment scene of the country. Here in the education system there was no discrimination because it was a necessity to have the students of any colour or nationality to keep the wheels of the colleges turning, but the real test had to come in the job market, and it did. One day the Evening Standard had headlines on its paper saying that the locals working for the Birmingham city bus company went on strike because an Asian had been promoted from a bus conductor to an Inspector to monitor the timekeeping of the buses. This was not one odd case of a storm in a teacup and there were a lot to come later on.

At least one thing was great about the British Educational Institutions - there was no discrimination on the basis of age for pursuing higher education. India was totally lacking in that and was throwing its matured youth on to a scrap heap. I was one of the examples. Instead the institutions here encouraged the mature students to go for higher education by offering them scholarships. When I joined the college I was told by a fellow student that after the age of 30 you were considered a mature student. The Greater London Council used to give mature students a scholarship of £270 per year, paid £90 every quarter of the year plus the college fee. I was 29 years old when I joined the college. So I applied when I came to know about it and I got it. That was a great financial help. If I had known of the existence of such a scheme I would have certainly tried to go for an internal degree in some other University college. I don't think even Malik was aware of it otherwise he would have applied for it himself.

So after a brief introduction from Sir, we dispersed, went to the central office, filled out forms, paid our fees, got registration numbers, prospectus, timetable, and the date to attend the classes. Hey, I was now on the road of no-return, with only one way to go - forward.

Soon I made some friends. There was one from Delhi, another from Mumbai, two from Punjab. We would go for lunch in the canteen together, we would visit each other's rooms, share home-work problems and exchange classroom notes. I also made friends with a 2nd-year student ('Z').

Lesson in Etiquette
Once it happened. I was attending an engineering drawing lesson. This lesson used to be in a big room on the third floor of the building. The lecturer would dish out the assignments and disappear, thus leaving us alone to get on with our assignments. These assignments were part of the course work, which we were to submit at the end of the year. So the drawings had to be clean, accurate, and submitted in a well-presented format. The building was centrally heated and the room temperature used to be set high. The sweat on the hands and arms, combined with the pencil's black carbon, would mess up the drawing's finish. To avoid that, I used to remove my jacket and hang it on my chair.

One day I felt thirsty. I was dashing down the stairs to the ground floor where the dining room was and Z was going up.

'Hey, where do you think you are going?'

'Oh, I am going downstairs to the canteen to drink some water.'

'Where is your jacket?'

'Upstairs, in my classroom.'

'You know in this country we do not go out in front of the ladies without a jacket. It is considered as disrespectful to the ladies.'

'But there are no ladies in sight right now.'

'That is no excuse. You may find one around somewhere in the building. Please go back to your room, wear your jacket, and then go down to the canteen.'

I just obeyed without any further ado. This used to be the social taboos in those days. One could go to the striptease to see a women undressing right under your nose; you could bring a prostitute into your room and ask her to become naked to satisfy your natural urges; you could also see couples engaged in intimacy in open parks, and yet you do not appear without a jacket in front of a lady. Who is a lady and who is a woman, and what is the distinction between them I wondered? The one who spreads these etiquettes must be bonkers.

Thirsty! Drink tea

In the canteen, I went to the serving table and asked the assistant, 'May I please have a glass of water?'

'What do you want with a glass of water?'

'I am thirsty. I went to the dining hall to see if there was any jug of water and glass but there was none. None of the tables had water on them.'

'We do not serve water in this country in the dining halls.'

'What you do if you are thirsty?'

'You drink a cup of tea, coke, or beer in the pub. Nobody drinks water.'

'I do not wish to drink tea. I just want a glass of water if you can give me one please.'

She obliged grudgingly. A week later, we found all the tables in the dining hall had a jug, full of water with empty glasses to drink the water if you wished to. The feedback to change the system was swift and immediate, a great quality of the British.

Indian Welfare Society

As the college life began in earnest, I found it necessary to have an Indian students union where we could meet socially, to know 'who is who', and which part of the continent we had come from. We had no such platform where we could get together to discuss and debate the political and economic issues confronting our country. We also needed a pressure group to approach the Indian High Commission to provide us the protection we needed from everyday racist attacks and insults on the streets of London. It was a fact too that Asians were the largest group among the first-year students. So it was time that we did something about it.

One day I took courage to go and talk to another Indian student who used to sit just behind me in the engineering drawing lessons. This lesson was the best time to discuss such things as most of the time the lecturer was never there. It was a practical tutorial and the students could move about in a big classroom from one seat to the other. Even if the lecturer was around he would only think that we might be discussing the problems of our given assignments. Before I began, I had to establish that this guy was from India. I started,

'Hi! Are you settling down well in your studies?'

'Yeah!'

Then I asked some other relevant questions to continue the dialogue, such as, what was his name, where he came from, where he was staying, and so on. With this introductory conversation, I established that he was from India, he came from the state of Bengal, and was attending the 1st year civil engineering course. Having established a rapport, I was now ready to know his views on setting up an 'Association of Indian Students'.

'You know that Indian students are the largest single community in this college, should we set up an Association? Would you support the idea?'

'I believe it is not going to work. Who cares about such associations? No, I am not for the association and I would not support the idea.'

'But we should try at least. Let us go to some more Indian students and have their views.'

'No, I don't think it would work and nobody is going to come to the meetings.'

'You know you are just writing off the idea. Why don't you come with me to some more students? Let us try to convince them that the association is good for all of us. We can get our association affiliated with the college students union as a pressure group. We can at least get some help on social welfare for our students.'

'No. I am not joining you to convince others.'

This time his 'no' was blunt, emphatic, and rude. I got the message. Disappointedly, I went back to my seat. I thought that I had some opportunity now to do something for all of us. I knew with my little experience of dealing with the Indian High Commission that they were the most useless and arrogant bunch of bureaucrats to deal with. They got their appointments here with supports and recommendations of their crony relatives. In a way, they were already retired on a pension, supported by the poor Indian masses. To enjoy their holidays, and get the education for their children in UK was an added bonus. With his no, I felt a bit disappointed and gave him the benefit of the doubt that he might be right. I gave up the idea of trying it again.

A couple of months later, I saw an announcement on the students' notice board, asking all the Indian students at the college to attend a meeting. The ad said,

"A GENERAL MEETING IS CALLED FOR THE

ASSOCIATION OF THE INDIAN STUDENTS

IN THE ROOM NO? PLEASE ATTEND."

The date, the time, the name of the president, the general secretary was given on the bottom. I went to attend the meeting on the day. To my surprise, the general secretary was the same person whom I had tried to convince to form the association. A stab in the back; well, he was a good politician and he knew how to manoeuvre somebody else's idea to gain the limelight for himself. I felt sad at human behaviour, but I forgot that that was the meaning of the name - politics. I never had the intention that I wanted to gain some position or fame to my advantage. My motto was only the service to the community. In that meeting we exchanged our views only by a couple of eye contacts. I noticed an embarrassment on his face with our first eye contact. He blushed but very courageously gave a cheeky smile at his success of assembling that many Indian faces in that room. He never came to me to talk to me. I stayed in the meeting for half an hour with a fellow student friend and then went home, wishing him luck in my mind. The union was formed but never made much headway. The success of an organisation obviously depends upon who leads it and what kind of imagination and qualities of leadership one has. It is not a cup of tea for the feeble and the copycats or for those who live on borrowed ideas.

Thrown Out of a House

A fellow immigrant, N, a young fellow from the Caribbean, was living next door to Malik's flat. On occasions we had exchanged greetings outside the house when entering to our homes. He was quite pleasant and polite to talk to. As I was getting more and more assignments in the college it became imperative for me to spend more time on my studies. As the world enjoyed, I used to be glued to my chair and the desk.

It was a fine and lovely Saturday. The sun was shining to its glorious heights to keep the Londoners in a chirpy mood, a rare occasion in those wintry days. I was at my desk, as usual with head down to work on my assignment of the week. It needed some concentration. All of a sudden, a loud music went in the air from the next-door flat. For a little while I took it but it went on and on. Desperately I decided to knock next door to ask if it would be possible to reduce the sound a little. As I knocked, the young N appeared on the door.

'Hello, I would like to talk to someone who lives upstairs.'

'Hello, I do. Please come on in.'

So he led me to his room upstairs and offered me a chair. We exchanged some generalities for a few minutes such as what he does and what I do. However, after setting the right environment, I decided to throw a question and test the depth of the water.

'As I just mentioned that I am a student. I sometimes have to do my assignments that need concentration. Is it possible for you to reduce your music sound a bit so that I can do my homework more effectively?'

'Is that why you came here?'

'Yeah, I thought I can request you to do that.'

'I love my music and I like to listen to it with a louder pitch. I am not going to give up my music for your studies.'

'I am not saying that you shouldn't listen to your music. I am just saying that you tone it down.'

'Hey, you just get up and get the hell out of my room and don't you ever come here with such nonsense interference in my affairs.'

I realised that I was in hot water and if I didn't obey, he might physically throw me out. Sheepishly I got up, hurried downstairs and left the house. As I came back to my room, I found the music was a lot louder. The ego had touched his raw nerves to be revengeful. I regretted that I ever went with that kind of a request to another immigrant. It left quite a nasty memory till today and also that scene of greetings in the beginning and changing of the moods from pleasantness to nastiness keeps on jogging my memory now and then. Instead of showing some understanding for my predicament the guy was aggressive and arrogant. He was ready to show his muscle power if I had not left him in peace.

New People in Life

There were always different people who lived at the flat temporarily as visitors or a stop gap stay for a few weeks or months and then moved on. Some came and stayed free in the flat, ate out in restaurants, went out sightseeing and enjoyed London life, and spent their nights in bed. This was Malik's hospitality, generosity, and broad-mindedness and I never heard him moaning about those.

Being a resident there I had the privilege of meeting these people. The memory of meeting some still lingers on.

An Anglo-Indian angry chap lived there with his girlfriend and a child. He was very un-sociable and bad-tempered to his girlfriend and us. On Fridays he would cook some good meal, open bottles of Guinness, drink with his girlfriend, get tipsy, and retire to his bedroom without even offering to share. He would never engage in some friendly chat. He would never discuss his background, where he came from, and what he did for his living. The whole environment in the kitchen used to be filled with tension. Perhaps he suffered from some complex or he had some personality problems.

Tiwari was from India and came to live here. He was a quite jolly and happy fellow. We cooked together, ate together, and discussed a lot of subjects of common interest. He also got hooked with Kapoor's old girlfriend. She would come now and then at the flat to relieve him from his manly needs. I could hear a lot of giggles from his room when she used to be with him, then a complete silence as if the world had gone to a deep sleep, followed by some changing activities, and then the thumping sound of steps on the staircase. I knew the lady was on the way out after satisfying his and her own urges. The fun was over until the next meeting.

A JOURNEY THROUGH PARTITION AND BEYOND

One day Tiwari was not at home and I was busy studying in my room. The young lady knocked at the door. I went downstairs to open the door and there was Tiwari's girlfriend.

'Sorry, he is not at home.'

'It does not matter. I will sit with you and chatter.' Before I could react she barged in and went straight upstairs into my room.

So, nervously I accepted her presence in my room, as there was no one else in the house except me. I never feel comfortable with a lady in aloneness. This is my nature and I cannot help it. Also I do worry in case I am accused of any inappropriate behaviour towards the lady. In that scenario it would be my word against hers. The ladies are always right. They never make advances, so it is believed. It is always the men who are hunters. However she settled down on my bed and I sat on my chair. My room was study-cum-bedroom. That was the furniture I had in the room. With some chats, she asked, 'Come and sit next to me. I am not going to eat you.'

'I know you won't eat me but I'd rather sit where I am. I am comfortable here.'

'Come on Om, we've known one another for a very long time,' she insisted. I did.

Within minutes, the closeness of the two young bodies, the warmth of that sharing breath in a cold winter night, the meetings of the two souls, made us slowly move towards intimacy. It was a natural phenomenon between two young people of opposite sex. Here was a young lady, very experienced in seducing and manipulating the boys. Tiwari was the third guy I knew with whom she was flirting. She always kept more than one to play with. She would visit them between intervals to keep in touch. If one left her she would replace him with another. That was her game. There was never sincerity towards anyone. She already had a child from Kapoor who had deserted her and left the country. It was not a new game for her. She was used to it. She had made it her profession in deception and cheating. This was her style of life. Now was it my turn to be entrapped? Was she making me her next prey to play with? Read on.

On the other hand it was me, a total novice in the playful games of deception and hoodwinking between the two opposite sexes. I believed in more sincerity, honesty, and true love. I was not there for the physical intimacy, where the two so-called 'lovers' breathe each other's breath; suck each other's germ-infested spit in the name of love making. In fact, they were both using each other for satisfying their selfish motives of sexual gratification. This endless game of 'love making' was not for me. However just about that time when the things were moving fast in the wrong direction, and the moments of touch and go were fast moving to the peak of humanly lust, the downstairs door swung open with a bang.

The rightful 'owner' of her body was entering into the hall. I knew it was Tiwari because he entered the house by loudly singing a Hindi song. Oh, God saved me once again and nothing happened between us. Being young and alone with a known lady who would never say 'no' to an able-bodied male was a big fishing net to be caught in. She was a big manhunter and she had a habit to never let go and accept defeat. Time was always in her favour and her clutches were powerful and calculated. She was a type that was always on the lookout for some sexual gratification from another untested man. I would not like to predict what could have happened if Tiwari had not arrived on the scene just in time. I still believe that it was a divine intervention that saved my virginity on that day once more.

Tiwari came into my room. He was pleased to see her. He commented in Hindi, 'I never asked her to come and I did not know she was coming.' However he took her to his room, had his fun, and shunted her out. In Tiwari she had found her equal - have fun and walk out. The world admires such people.

T's Sense of Humour

In some ways Tiwari could act as stupid. One 31st March night it was around 1am and I was still doing my college homework. He entered my room, giggling and laughing.

'Hey what happened? What is making you laugh that hilariously?'

'No, that is ok. I was just having some fun before I came home.'

'What fun? Tell me.'

'You know today it is 1st April.'

'Oh, I did not realise that.'

'I was making an April fool to a lot of people.'

'How did you do that?'

'From the telephone booth, I would dial a number; as soon as the receiver was picked up I would put the phone down. So I called nearly 20-30 people. I was just waking them up to attend the phone.'

'That was very childish Tiwari. You were disturbing them from their sleep and worrying them with no reason. They would be wondering who would be calling them at this time of the night. Who knows they may be busy in making love after a hard day's slog.'

'That is what I wanted, to wake them up, to make them stay awake, and to worry them.'

'I think it was a very stupid thing to do to have fun at the misery of others and also waste your money too. Where did you get that many coins in the night to phone?'

A JOURNEY THROUGH PARTITION AND BEYOND

'No you don't need coins. I found a trick to phone without coins. You tap the ring tone as many times as the number and you get yourself connected. So no money was spent but a lot of free fun.'

'You are very stupid Tiwari that is all I can say.'

As he was going upstairs to retire to his bed for the night, I could hear his loud giggling as if he had achieved something spectacular on that night. You come across all kinds of people on this planet and that is why God's creation is so great. No one gets bored. There is an entertainment for everyone. Great dramas are in the making. Then why are some bored and fed up with this great life?

Bajaj, Tully and their Friends:

Before I came to Britain, I met a fun-loving person, Sapra, at Delhi. He worked for the foreign affairs department at Delhi. He was appointed to Pakistan for a brief period of 2 years. I visited his house a couple of times in the evenings. He narrated his experiences when employed at Lahore embassy very eloquently. He spent two evenings in telling us his sexual conquest of two women – the mother and the daughter – related to some army officer. The scary part was the risks he was taking. Firstly he was having an affair with the women of an army officer; both the women were in the same family with such wide difference in age; he was a hated Indian living in a hostile country; he was a Hindu and the girls were Muslims; he was an 'infidel' who would be killed to protect the honour of a middle-class family; he was employed by the hated Indian Embassy; and he could have been blackmailed into passing on the secrets of his own country. He was taking so many risks in bragging about his conquests so openly to all of us present. During his narrations we were keen to find out whether he was aware of his personal safety or not. Was he not scared that he might be caught or even murdered? We never got the right answers. He was so happy about his conquests that when he was boasting about it his face would light up as if he had achieved the impossible. He always maintained that both the women were in love with him and were ready to run away with him to India if he was ready to face the family music himself. His story was so fascinating that we were just glued to his talking even when his mother was telling us that the food was served.

So that is how I came to know Sapra. He also had a cousin. The cousin had worked with Bajaj at the government offices. Bajaj got my address from Sapra. Bajaj reached London Victoria on 8th October 1960. He had sailed with Tully and a couple of others from Bombay by the SS Roma of Lauro Lines. I was at Victoria station to receive him. Bajaj introduced me to Tully and another friend of theirs as D. Bajaj had some luggage which needed to be custom cleared. One of them was a leather handbag, which he brought for me as a present. We went to the customs office to declare the duty payable goods. They said they would charge

100% duty on the handbag as it was made of leather. Made of leather! The tax imposing bureaucrats had gone bonkers. Tax them but be truthful and open about it. Do not test the intelligence of the commoners. They pay because they are law abiding citizens. They are not dumb. How else would you make handbags in those days anyway, with cotton or silk fabric? Manmade fibres were rare. The officer was talking baloney. The truth was revealed later. I did not like it. The cost of the bag was much less than the duty being collected. So I went into an argument with the officer that he was charging the duty un-reasonably. He persisted on charging that amount. With memory I think the figure was £5 for one bag and Bajaj had two, one for himself. Here the history was being repeated from when I arrived here in 1958 with a similar kind of leather handbags. The world had remained the same. The arguments with the duty officer were the same as in my case only the actors were different.

'Sorry officer we are not paying that sum.'

'Well, that is the duty to be paid.'

'How did you work out that duty? It costs much less to buy in India where he bought it from.'

'The duty is charged on the price he would pay to buy in this country and not what he paid in India. It is also new and so the duty has to be maximum – 100%.'

'Officer be reasonable, we cannot pay that much. I am a student and it is not a luxury item but an essential item to carry the books to my college.'

'No, all leather goods are considered as luxury items in UK and are charged at 100%.'

'You are the only country charging so much duty to visitors and students. You are penalising people like us who come from India here to study.'

'Because we are paying a lot of war debt to America, which you, in India, don't have to pay.'

'Oh, yes we Indians too are paying the debt for the war you fought. It was not a war India wanted to fight in Europe and for what reasons. So don't give me that crap of war debts.'

The argument went on for a few minutes and eventually we accepted defeat and decided to pay. On parting I said to the officer, 'Ok, we will pay the duty but not with pleasure but under duress.' With that note we paid the duty and came back to where Tully was waiting for us.

The problem arose how to accommodate three people at my place. I was living with Malik and there was no vacancy there. I apologised to Bajaj that I couldn't put them all up at Malik's flat, as there was no vacant room there. I said to Bajaj that he could stay at my place that night and we would find an accommodation for him next day. But how do we accommodate the other two? I

A JOURNEY THROUGH PARTITION AND BEYOND

apologised to Tully and D that they would have to stay in a bed and breakfast that night in the Finsbury Park area. And we will see what we do next day. So we came to Finsbury Park by underground and hunted around for a room for them for the night. They paid for a double room 12s 6d for the two of them for the night with breakfast. Not a bad bargain! Bajaj and I went to my place at Stamford Hill.

Next day we went out and found a room for Bajaj at a Jewish house. I helped him with whatever guidance I could give to find a job and settle down. We became good friends. He is a very sincere, down-to-earth, happy, honest, and decent person. You could rely upon him as a friend. Shortly his other friends C and H came to UK. He knew them as he worked with them in Delhi.

Soon with his own efforts and campaign, Bajaj got a job in a design office, earning good money.

My Friend Tully's Plight and his Friend D

Everyone's circumstances and problems of life make them adventurers and bigger than their shoes. Tully was no exception. He took the challenges of life with whatever odds were against him to succeed and make himself and his family better and secure for their future. From that one night stay with D at Finsbury Park in a bed and breakfast hotel, his immediate requirement was to find a job as soon as possible. The Government of India had generously put £5 in his pocket and gave him a big kick that landed him safely at London Victoria station with no hope in hell to return.

Next morning they both moved to the West of London looking for a room and a job. He went to Southall Rubber factory where some Asians had jobs. He asked the security guard there if he knew if there was any job available as he was desperate to have one. The security officer rebuffed his advances and shunted him away. Disappointed, he was roaming around on the streets of Southall. By chance he met a Mr Singh walking along the road window-shopping. Tully asked 'Do you know English?' A cheeky question, but in those days a lot of us did not know the language.

'Yes a little! I am new here and trying to find a job to survive. Who are you?'

'I am also looking for any job around here if you know any. I am very desperate.' What a coincidence the beggar meets the beggar. Both were desperate to keep hunger at bay. When that happens something positive must follow.

'Try the Rubber Factory,' Singh suggested.

'I have tried but the security guard said that they don't have any.'

'You know the guard takes bribe to let you in to see someone. He takes a pound. If you had given him a pound he would have allowed you to meet the boss, who would have given you a job.'

97

'Well I did not know that,' Tully admitted.

'Anyway buy a local gazette; it will have the local vacancies and the rooms to rent. For jobs, go to Uxbridge where there are a lot of factories. Go from factory to factory and ask for a job. Now can you telephone for me and give them a message on my behalf?' Singh asked.

He took Tully to a coin-operated telephone booth. Tully did not know how to use them. Singh explained to him. Tully phoned and passed on his message and they parted.

Tully bought the gazette, looked through it and found a room above a shop to view. He phoned, got the appointment, and went to see. It was raining. Desperate, soaked with rain by walking from the station to the parade of shops, he reached there a half an hour earlier than the appointment. He stood outside a hair salon in the rain with his innocent baby face. The girls at the hair salon shop thought that he was waiting for the bus and just ignored his plight. Buses came and went but Tully was still there in the wet cold weather. The landlord was late to see him for the appointment. He had nowhere else to stay for the night until he had seen the room and rented it. It was a desperate situation for a man coming from a Kashmiri family and thrown penniless in the middle of an unknown foreign land. He did not wish to be a vagabond for the next night. The girls in the shop somehow sussed out that he was not waiting for the bus but he had some other problem, as he was staying there for such a long time. A young lady ventured out to talk to him. Tully told her that he was waiting for a lady to come and show him a room above the shop across the road. She was a kind and compassionate young lady and invited him into their shop and asked him to wait there rather in the rain. They gave him a towel to dry himself, and put a fan heater next to him to warm him. The room lady came, showed him the room, and he agreed to rent it. So that was how he found his room. One problem of sheltering in the night was solved.

Next he went to hunt for a job in the Uxbridge industrial area of London. By this time after paying rent and other travelling expenses, he had only 10s (50p) left in his pocket. Again it was raining. British rain was so kind to him and accompanied him wherever he went. He spent the whole day in that industrial area. He went factory to factory for soliciting any job but without any luck. By the evening, drenched, soaked, hungry, thirsty, tired, fed up, and disheartened he gave up. He walked towards the station to return back to his rented room.

When all the hopes are dashed, when all the rays of hope have faded, when the dazzling turns into darkness, when there is nothing except the ugly head of despair, God steps in. He, hiding somewhere in the Universe, checks one's perseverance, forbearance and stamina, reveals himself and showers his grace that protects the suffering soul. When the final call from the inner being comes to give up, it also means a gift of the creation is on the way. The creation always tests your patience, your determination, and how deep you can go into the water before ending up in an abyss. It happened to Lord Buddha too. After six years of wandering in the forests, trying to find some Guru to guide him to achieve Nirvana, it is said that he too gave up. Tired, hungry, weak, and fed up he went to sleep in the late morning under the Bodhi tree. It is there when he woke up that suddenly he found that he was enlightened. I am not comparing the poor sinning soul of Tully with that of the first ever-enlightened soul of Buddha on this planet but just saying that this is how the nature operates. First it exhausts you to the core and then it showers you with its blessings. The same thing was happening to Tully. He was going back to the station, frustrated, beaten, and drenched and soaked with rain when he saw a factory on the way, housed in a dilapidated building. Conflicting thoughts came to his mind. One, the negative mind, said, 'Why bother? You have gone to so many good factories and had no luck, how you would succeed here in a rundown factory.' The positive mind woke up to challenge it. 'Never mind what happened in those factories. You are here right in front of it. Try it.' The positive side won. And he went in. The factory was being run by a one-man-band show. The owner greeted him. He inspected Tully from top to bottom. Tully blurted out with his well-rehearsed dialogue, 'Sir, I am looking for a job, in fact any job you have. I need it desperately. I am running short of money.'

'What job can you do?' the owner asked.

'Any, it does not matter. I am not a chooser right now.'

'Can you work on a drilling machine?'

'What is that?'

The owner smiled. He took Tully to the machine to show him what kind of beast it was.

'If you show me how it works, no problem I would be happy to drill the holes for you.'

'Yeah, I will train you how to operate the machine and drill holes. You can start work next Monday. Just come at the door at 7am sharp like anybody else. I will pay you 4s3d per hour.'

Tully was over the moon. At last he too got his 'enlightenment' when he never expected it. That is how the Divine operated in his case. If the Divine has brought us on the planet he already had made sure our daily grind was available.

The mind is always dual and a doubter. Having got the job, now Tully's mind went into a thinking mode, 'Oh, isn't he paying me too much? Has he given me the job because I was drenched, cold, and he pitied me for my plight? How will I live on 10s till I get my wage?' Just then, suddenly an idea struck Tully. Why not ask the boss to let him start the job tomorrow? He turned to the owner, 'Sir, can I start tomorrow if you don't mind?'

Perplexed and amused, the owner knew that such a request could only come from a desperate man. Tully was a foreigner and was not aware of the British culture. So with a smile and a little thought, he said, 'Ok come tomorrow. But be here at 7am and no later.'

Tully walked back home that evening with a job and with a good weekly wage. But he did not realise that no company would give a job for the sake of sympathy. The owner must have been looking desperately for someone to operate his drilling machine. It was only by chance that Tully happened to be at the right spot at the right time and got the job.

This was the beginning for Tully in this country. From that humble beginning, he then went on to study for HNC in engineering in the evenings, changed jobs, got married, had a son and a daughter, went into a clothing business to earn some good money, built shops with some flats above near the area of Finsbury Park where he had stayed on his first night on arrival in London, bought a lovely house in a sought-after area, threw lovely parties at his residence, retired, and now enjoys his life to the full. Quietly he has made a history for himself and his family in this country.

Like many thousands of immigrants who landed penniless on the British shores, this is one of the success stories amongst so many more.

With the colonies, some gone and some in the process of going, the British factories were busy in meeting the demands for industrial goods for its previous colonies. German industry was still in its infancy due to the systematic bombardment by the Allied forces to destroy its industrial infrastructure. During the war Britain also lost its young human resources. They had become the war fodder. As the demands for industrial goods started growing, the shortage of labour became more severe. Big advertisements were being placed in the Caribbean islands to tempt the inhabitants to come and work as conductors, drivers, cleaners in the buses, underground railways, and many other menial industrial jobs which the locals would not like to have. Most of the available jobs were of low level. Furthermore there were jobs which were shift work and the locals would not like them either. These jobs were available in foundries, steel mills, bakeries, rubber factories, garment factories, transport, and at airports.

Most of the Asian migrants were from the Indian subcontinent, especially from the Punjab villages. There was a lot of discrimination at every level of the society. At the factories nobody would talk to you, communicate with you, and socialise with you. The only communication we would have was what was essential for doing our jobs. No locals would rent their rooms to us. It was only the earlier arrived immigrants who were settled and had houses who were willing to rent a room or a flat to earn some extra tax-free cash.

A JOURNEY THROUGH PARTITION AND BEYOND

Because of this rampant discrimination and racism in the housing areas, our people started to flock to and live in the areas where their compatriots had already settled. Southall became the hub of the people coming from Punjab because it had an airport with big employment opportunities for all kinds of skilled and unskilled people. It had cheap houses to rent and also it is at an easy commuting distance from the airport. When a few of the Punjabis settled there and got the jobs, they invited more of their friends and relations to come to Britain to live and work. In those days there was no restriction to entry for the commonwealth citizens. There was no visa system in place to regulate the entry to the 'mother' country.

The Punjabis are very enterprising, resourceful, and are very community-minded, hard-working people. They are scattered all over the world - in USA, Canada, Australia, Europe, and Africa. They have an ability to survive in any adverse circumstances and they live happily as a close-knit community in any part of the world. They are known for being good soldiers, farmers, taxi drivers, hosiery and garment manufacturers, and engineers. They are good workers, honest, loyal employees and have the qualities of entrepreneurs in running enterprises both small and large. The town also had a rubber factory and some bakeries as a further bonus to the newcomers where no British had the stomach to work. Having seen the good times during colonial rule and after fighting the exhausting WW2, they were now tired and had no stamina to man those hot, dirty factories. They were now looking for an easy life to indulge in women and wine.

As the Asians started moving in the British were moving out. They could not bear an Asian next-door neighbour. The British would not accept that they were racist and that is why they were moving out but they cried the well-known 'wolf' that the Asians were bringing down the house prices. The ratio of Asian to British was increasing by the days and weeks and soon the area was being called 'Little India'. The Asians became the locals in the town and the British became the foreigners. It took time but the writings were on the wall for everyone to see.

In the early days some lucky ones climbed on to the housing ladder. Ownership brought rich rewards. They converted the houses into multi bedrooms and flats which became money-spinning gold mines. Every bed in the house was let on a shift basis. The one who slept there during the night, would get up, eat his breakfast, organise his lunch in the Tiffin and would be on his way to work for his morning shift. The one who was on the night shift would be on his way back to cook his meals, eat and would be in the same bed which had another occupier only a couple of hours earlier. He would then have his sleep, wake up around 4-5pm, yawn and ease himself from his chores of toilet and bath, move to the common TV room if available in the house, have his food and be ready to go his shift. The third occupier would be already there, ready to occupy the bed and use the cooking and resting facilities. In this way one sleeping bed had three occupiers. So each bed in the house was rotated three times a day, seven days a week.

The landlord would buy rations like chapatti flour, sugar, salt, potatoes, onions, lentils in bulk and charge their costs to tenants.

Who are the better entrepreneurs, the British or the Asians? The British blew the opportunity to earn money from the influx of new dark-skinned strangers. This British attitude made the Asians richer sooner than expected. Rather spending that income on women and wine, they started investing into various small businesses. They were buying more houses, shops, post offices, cash & carries, and petrol stations. There were so many entrepreneurs who would fill up suitcases with shirts, underwear, bed linens, towels and other saleable garments, travel by trains and buses to go to small towns and villages, and knock on doors to sell their wares, with good margins, to full-time housewives. The strange part was that they did not know English and all these entrepreneurs were so-called 'uneducated' villagers from Punjab. Once they saved up the income they moved into setting up stalls, buying and opening new wholesaler shops in the White Chapel areas of the East End. This area then became the centre of garment manufacturing and exporting to the Middle East and Africa. I know many in that area who started their early lives in UK by working in bread factories as shift workers and now they are multi-millionaires.

If one is looking for an opportunity to find gold, then only the gold diggers know where to dig for it. If money is the aim in life then going to universities is a total waste of time. If one is a seeker of God then attending the temples and the churches is to listen to this beautiful song, written by an Urdu poet. It says, 'If you think that you would find God by going early morning to the woods, you would only find cows and buffaloes; if you think you will find God by dipping into holy waters, you will find nothing but fish and frogs; if you think you will find God in churches and temples you will find only lizards. But God can only be found in those hearts which are full with compassion and conscience.' How true this poet is!

Racial discrimination was the biggest problem and still is. It was not only rampant in jobs but it was also openly displayed on the roads and social circles. It was so fearful to walk on your own. You could never tell when you would face the skinheads, as these thugs were called in those days, while walking home.

One day in July 1958 as we were walking home in the Acton area, we saw a young handsome black boy sitting on a garden wall of a house, holding his head and in tears. He had a knife wound in his head and it was bleeding. We enquired what happened. He said he was walking home when all of a sudden he was pounced upon by a few 'teddy boys'. They had knives on them. They hit him, kicked him, and one of them used a knife to stab his head. We took him to the local hospital for the medical help.

If you were travelling in the underground, first no one would come and sit next to you. They would only sit next to you if there was no other choice of seat or the person could not stand and had to have a seat. If someone was already sitting and you went to sit next to him, there was a big chance that he would get up and find another seat. This had created an inferiority complex in me. I started feeling small. I started losing confidence in my ability to cope with my life. My ego was hurt and my ability to deal with fellow beings was being shattered. Without an ego I started losing my self-confidence. I started to move within my own shell. Psychologically it made me so stupid that I would not be able to talk to anyone with eye contact. My conversation with others was dithering. The people on the giving end never realised how much damage they were inflicting on the migrants who had come to serve this country and to make it a home. I remember on another occasion as I was travelling from my work to home. A young lad was embracing and kissing a young lady, a common scene which we were now used to. It was not a novelty anymore. I had not picked up the British habit of reading while travelling. So my eyes were wandering around the compartment. By chance my eyes made eye contact with this kissing maniac who was showing off to others so openly that he had a woman in his arms and was enjoying her spit by wiggling his tongue in her mouth. He gave me a very dirty look. I turned my face. A few moments later I looked back again. He was still looking at me fiercely and threatened me with his body language. I was sitting and he was a few feet away from me near the exit door. Since then I always felt very uncomfortable to travel in the underground. A sort of fear was left in my being. Next morning I started buying the Daily Telegraph so that I would not watch what anyone was doing. I had now acquired the great British habit of reading and realised that it was no wonder that this nation has this habit of reading.

The Company of Bajaj, Tully & Co.

All this crowd of friends, Bajaj, Tully, and Malik, rented a house in the Acton area and were living together. They had good jobs with secure incomes, a nice house to live in and share in its amenities. They were also young, and like any young men from India were starved of the company of females. Being enterprising in that game, soon every one of them found girlfriends. They were not bored and homesick as I was but were enjoying the real life of London. They would go to cinemas with their girlfriends and go wining and dining at restaurants at weekends. For them the life could not be better. In India they had a control of parents, friends, relations, and even jealous passers-by, but here there was no one to watch their activities. They were completely free and independent, and why not. It is a human dream to be free. It is our birthright. They had left their oppressive society behind.

Somehow they had developed their love and respect for me. So they would invite me to their weekend bonanzas. I too welcomed it as I was alone and it gave me the opportunity to mingle and make friends with theirs. They also had some others with whom they were friendly and they would invite them too for going out together or just to stay at their flat where they would cook an Indian meal and we all would share it. One of the invitees whom I met a couple of times at their residence was Dr 'Shanti'. She was a medical practitioner at a hospital. She came from Indian Bengal and had qualified from one of the medical colleges there.

The Lady Proposed Marriage and why not?

All courting couples experience romance before marriage. The romance then turns into love (really, I think love is on first sight; courting love is based on scheming and calculating), a natural and mysterious phenomenon only found amongst humans. The smoke always precedes the fire. Similarly the love has to precede the marriage. Without love the marriage is nothing but to satisfy the human urges as is found in the animal world. We all know that sex is animal, love is human, and meditation is divine. But this natural phenomenon is missing in arranged marriages. There is no romance, no love, but the two totally strange beings are tied together with marriage vows and then both struggle to adjust, give and take, and try to make the head and tail of the relationship and by that time the whole life has slipped away in struggle. The following episode breaks down all the traditional taboos of the Indian system. I leave you to find those taboos in the story yourself.

That is how it happened.

One Sunday, I, with all the crowd at Acton, went to an Indian restaurant for lunch. I happened to sit on the table where Shanti was sitting. As usual, we had to talk some rubbish to keep the conversation going rather than look at the walls and the surroundings. If there was nothing else to talk about, we would always talk about Indian politics or Bollywood movies. The Indian crowd is quite comfortable indulging in these topics. Many a time these discussions led us to very heated arguments but it never ended in dog fights. They were meant only for an exchange of views and never meant to humble or win points. They may also end up in agreeing to disagree. It was an intellectual way of sharing opinions. During these talks, we started talking about boy and girl relationships and how do they marry. I innocently gave a comment that, 'Why it is always the boys who have to take the initiative in asking the girls for an outing, courting them, having a romance, and finally proposing marriage. Girls are now liberated. They have the same rights as

A JOURNEY THROUGH PARTITION AND BEYOND

the boys. Why don't they take the initiative to ask the boys out if they fancy them, or even propose to marry them?' Shanti contested my statement. She felt that if the girl did that she would be considered cheap and the boys would not like them. I maintained my reasoning and convictions. Then she threw a straight question at me, 'If I did that with you, phone you, ask you for an outing, how would you feel? Won't you think that I am not of good character?'

'No, I wouldn't.'

The lunch finished, and satisfied and happy with our meals and the company, we all went back home to follow our routine life for the week. I never gave any importance to my statements and forgot all about them.

A week later, I had a call from Shanti. This was a total surprise as we had never exchanged our phone numbers and I never had the intentions to be closer to her or to any of the girls who used to be in that crowd.

'Hi, I am Shanti. We had lunch together last Sunday with Bajaj.'

'Oh yes, I remember. How are you?'

'You might be wondering how I managed to call you. I got your number from Bajaj. So I thought why not call you to have a chat. We had talked about a lot of subjects on that day.'

'In a crowd you have to talk about something. I hope I did not say something offensive to anyone as you normally can get carried away during those discussions.'

'Oh, no no! I like discussing with others as it improves your own knowledge. So it is always a welcome occasion.'

So the conversation went on for a little while on generalities until she unburdened herself from the bottled up ambition to release her emotional clouds of loneliness from which all we young people were suffering but without admitting it to others. We always put on a brave face with the opposite sex to maintain our egos and to show that we just don't care about the opposites; but inside our hearts we crave to be near them, sit and admire them, love to dream about them, and yet in their presence we just pretend and hide our feelings. We behave like hypocrites. I think Shanti was very brave when she phoned me and said, 'You know when we were at the dinner table, you were very blunt to ask why girls are not brave enough to propose to a boy if they fancy him. Well, I thought a lot about it and asked myself, why not? So here I am asking you, let us meet at my house or somewhere else where we can talk about our marriage. I like you. You are quite a mature person compared to the others. So I collected all my courage to phone you to give a proposal to you provided you are happy with it.'

I was dumbstruck. I admired her courage, being an Indian girl, to come out of the repressive background of nearly all Indian families and propose to marry me. I had no guts being a boy to propose marriage. The fear was 'do not wish to be rejected, too much ego', plus I had no clue how to propose. I was not a man of today's world. I lived life as I thought fit without any influence of the outer world. But I had to say something.

'I never thought of marriage, as you know I am studying for my degree and my exams are very near. However, if you are proposing that we should talk about it, then why not?'

'Then let us meet at lunch this Sunday – just you and me. We do not wish to involve the crowd in our affairs.'

'Ok, done.'

So we decided the venue and met up to talk about the nitty gritty of moving forward. We first talked about our relations in India and then how to handle the entire proposal leading finally to marriage.

Our conversation went something like this.

I explained, 'I have parents, 4 brothers, and a sister. We are refugees from West Pakistan…' and so on. 'But before we marry, we must seek out the blessings of our parents.'

'Well, I have no parents to ask. I have a brother who is not that great. He smokes and drinks heavily and we are not on very good terms. He is not bothered whom I marry and what I do in my life.'

'Whatever the relationship, I believe we should have their blessings. I have to have the permission from my parents. They sent me here for education. It would be very insulting to them if I do not have their permission to marry you.'

'But as you know I am from Bengal, would your parents permit you to marry me?'

'My family is very enlightened and broad-minded. They would certainly accept my decision and allow me to marry a girl whom I decided to marry. Besides, you are a Hindu girl; you are from India; you are well educated and so I do not believe that they would have an objection to which part of India you come from. It is only a matter of time and it is only a formality.'

'Ok, if you feel that way I will write a letter to my brother. But I doubt that he will reply to my letter. Even if he does not write or does not permit me to marry a Punjabi boy, I would still defy him and marry you.'

'That is very courageous. I will write a letter to my father and I know his views. But suppose the permission arrives then when do we get married?'

'I would like to marry as soon as possible. I am a doctor and I don't wish to delay the marriage - as being a girl, my best-before date is decreasing by the day.'

'Oh, I don't know what that means.'

'Because girls can only have healthy children up to a certain age; after that the chances start decreasing. Also it is time that I settle down.'

A JOURNEY THROUGH PARTITION AND BEYOND

'But I have a big problem. I am studying and I cannot marry before I finish the education. I have not enough funds to study, marry, and support a family.'

'Don't be silly. I have a full-time job and get good money on which we can both live comfortably. I am also studying to improve myself for my profession. In life, marriage should not be a hindrance, but it should rather complement each other's efforts to maintain a family cohesion.'

'I do not feel very comfortable that you should be supporting my education. I am a self-made proud man and I do not wish to be supported by my would-be wife.'

She immediately scolded me for my 'arrogant' views. She was of the view that once you were married, there should be no divisions between the two resources. They should become a common pool. She also assured that it would be her greatest pleasure to give me her moral and financial support and share the life which we were going to live together. She also gave me a bit of a brief on the cultural and family attitude of Bengali girls. I agreed with her. The Bengali people are culturally and educationally a lot superior to the other Indians. They have produced some of the best artists, poets, singers, writers, scientists, revolutionaries and politicians in India.

After a lengthy discussion to know more about one another's background, we parted. In the first instance, we both agreed to write to our respective relations to have their permissions and their views. Once we knew their views, we would then meet to decide the next course of action.

I wrote a letter to my father, giving him all the details about the girl and asking his permission to marry her in UK provided we cannot make it to India.

In the meantime we were in touch with one another by phone. I would ask her if she got a reply and she was also eager to know about the response from my parents about the proposal. When I got the reply, I immediately phoned her to let her know that my father had unreservedly permitted me to marry her. She was very happy. But her brother's reply had not yet arrived. However we moved on and planned to marry just after my 1st-year examination.

We were arranging everything against all the conventional rules of an Indian marriage.

1.   This marriage was not arranged by parents or a man but was proposed by a daring lady. She was also ready to defy her elder brother if the permission was not granted.

2.   The same father, who had once refused the permission to his second eldest son to see the girl he was marrying, sent me his permission within 3 weeks, allowing me to marry a Bengali lady and in UK.

3. The permission was totally unconditional, no strings attached.

It is well said that man proposes and God disposes. We both were in agreement to marry and were moving confidently in that direction, but the nature had some different agenda. And I mean it when I say that. We both were proposing to marry but God was working in disposing it off with his unmatched powers.

The Disposer

It was quite a routine to talk to Bajaj on all my important matters. It was nearly a weekly feature. When he called me during the week, we shared about all the pleasantries of the week gone by and by chance, I don't know how, we started talking about Shanti. Shanti and I had agreed to keep our affairs confidential between us until the day we were ready to announce our marriage plans to others. However the conversation between us moved to a point where I mentioned that I had met Shanti again at a dinner and we had discussed the possibility of marrying. The cat was out of the bag. I could not hold the water within me and told him the entire story, how it started with her telephone call to me from her, with a proposal for the marriage, and at what stage we were now. In a way, with hindsight, I had broken my agreement with Shanti. Effectively I had cheated her. I had exposed her broadmindedness and frankness to those who happened to be narrow-minded and did not appreciate the openness coming from a lady. Bajaj said, 'How can a girl propose, she must be out of her mind.' He did not seem very happy. I had broken her trust and she must have cursed me for that. I had exposed her to the viciousness of those traditional thinkers who believed in maintaining a status quo. The world was changing and what was wrong for a girl to propose to a man she fancied and that man happened to be a chicken who had no guts to move forward to propose to her. The traditionalists always feel bad when a girl proposes because they feel that she has made herself cheap and corrupt. Why do girls have no right to go for a boy whom they fancy and with whom they would like to share the rest of their lives? I was broadminded on such issues but I was very naïve on human relationships. I did not appreciate the difficulties I was putting her into. Under pressure she could withdraw from the proposal and change her mind to marry. She might even dump me thinking that if I did not keep my word to her in the initial stages, then how on earth would I be trustworthy later on. It never dawned on me that to be an open book with a friend would land me into a situation where my decision to marry would be ridiculed simply because the proposal had come from a girl.

So the conversation with Bajaj continued: 'How dare she phone you with such a proposal? It is too cheap for her being a girl to propose to you. She could have asked any of us to act on her behalf.'

A JOURNEY THROUGH PARTITION AND BEYOND

'I know but it is not her fault. I innocently encouraged her at the dining table that the girls should feel free to propose if they so wished. I did not know at the time that she had her eyes on me,' I said in her defence. But Bajaj was not to be convinced.

'That may be so, Khurana Sahib.' That is how he always addressed me with great affection and respect. I don't know how I deserved that. 'But my objection is that she is not of your type. She will not make a good partner to you. I know a lot more about her than you do as I have been meeting her more often than you have. She is too modern. She smokes, she drinks and has been tipsy so often in the party. She is totally opposite to what you are.'

'That may be so. I did not know that she smokes and drinks. I smoke too. Who knows she might change after the marriage.'

'People don't change, Khurana Sahib. You are too good not to recognise that.'

'She did say to me that she would try to change and accommodate to suit to my habits, without expanding on it.'

'No, they don't. Anyway, I am against this proposal. I will not support this marriage. I will meet her this weekend and tell her that she is not suitable for you and she should stop taking this matter any further.' Wow, very strong views. Was it interference in my personal life or was it a genuine concern? I don't know.

'Bajaj Sahib, you will hurt her. We will see what happens next. Who knows, I may not get the permission from my parents as well. Besides, we had agreed between us that we would not discuss our affairs with any of you. I am breaching her trust if you go and talk to her directly to dissuade her from marrying me.'

'Leave it to me to tackle it. I am very upset how she dares to propose to you.'

So the chatter finished and I felt guilty that I had betrayed Shanti's trust by discussing the personal issues with Bajaj. Despite my repeated interventions to dissuade him not to talk to her, Bajaj was determined. However, surprise, surprise, I got the letter from my father, not only permitting me but also encouraging me to marry her. I telephoned Shanti to give her the good news. I also enquired about whether she got a reply from her brother or not. She had not. So now I was building up hopes of getting married soon after my 1st year's examination. Shanti was not bothered about her brother's consent or denial anyway. I could see sprouting of seeds of love, the admiration, and the dreams about Shanti in my heart. Was it a torch of love beginning to shine? It was. I was beginning to think more about her. I would not get tired of talking to her on the phone. As the love affair was sprouting, it was also creating worries in case I mucked up my examinations. I was declining Shanti's requests to meet her at the weekends. I told her that if I met her more, I was worried that I would spoil my exams, which were important to me.

Time was moving fast. The exams were coming nearer and I was spending more and more time to meet my exams' requirements by working late nights. Bajaj did not phone too. I did not know whether he had gone ahead with his determination to rebuke Shanti and if he did how did she react?

It was the end of February; the winter was still at its peak. I was well wrapped up to cope with the winter days with woollies and blankets, as there was no central heating in those days. It was the afternoon and as usual I was on my study desk with a dim ceiling light in a windowless dark room where even the sun would shiver to show itself and I was trying to finish my assignments.

The mind is a globe trotter. It never rests and would always wander around, leaving the job at hand. The thoughts were hovering, 'Why had I chosen to be in UK as my home. While the sun never sets on its empire but tragically it never shines on its own soil.' It reminded me of a lecture which a Buddhist monk from Sri Lanka had given a couple of years earlier in which he said, 'This country is hell and the people have made heaven out of it, our countries are heaven and we made hell out of them.' How true it is. With every day passing, I was now digging my roots deeper and deeper into this land. My dreams of getting the education here and then getting back to my country were diminishing by the day. Now I was trying to marry here and it would all depend on Shanti's consent too whether we should go back to our country or stay here. As those thoughts were puzzling me, the phone rang. Shanti was on the line.

After talking some usual familiar stuff, she decided to throw a bombshell at me.

'I have not got good news for you. So please listen to me very carefully.'

'Tell me, what happened?'

'I have decided not to marry you.'

'What? Tell me why? Has your brother opposed the marriage?'

'No, I don't care about his opinions and I have not heard from him either yet.'

'Then why are you changing your mind? I have been planning all these days in my mind how we are going to get married and now this bombshell.'

'No, I just cannot marry you. I am not suitable for you. It was childish on my part to propose to you.'

'Has Bajaj talked to you?'

'No.'

'Are you sure? He did not dissuade you. Has he?'

'Yes, he did talk to me but that has not influenced me.'

'Then what made you change your mind? Only two days ago we were talking on the phone about the arrangements for the marriage and now you say you are not marrying me. You have to tell me the reason.'

I was now persisting to find the reason. I was also getting emotional to see my dreams being shattered. I reminded her that I had the permission from my parents and we had now advanced so far and we would be marrying in a couple of months.

'Sorry, I cannot marry you. I am not suitable for you.'

'But you were suitable for me only two days ago but today you are not. How can I buy that? You have to tell me the truth.'

'Certain things cannot be said. They should be accepted. When I say I am not suitable for you, you accept that.'

'No, I like to know what made you to come to that conclusion.'

I burst into tears. I was crying uncontrollably. She tried to calm me down but I was in real emotional pains. Then she said, 'Ok, I will tell you as you are insisting to know.'

'Please tell me.'

'I am a lesbian.'

'What is that?'

'Don't try to be so ignorant and smart that you don't know what a lesbian is?'

'No, I have never heard this word before in my life and I do not know the meaning of it. You are a doctor, you may know more than I do but I do not know it.'

'Ok, you know the meaning of gay for the boys.'

'Yes, I do.'

'Well when the girls are gay, they are called lesbians.'

'It is personal. It does not bother me. But I don't understand what the girls would do between themselves when they are gay.'

'I am not going to tell you what they do.'

'You may be able to get rid of that once you marry me. I may be able to help you.'

'No it would not be fair on you because when the girls are gay, they hate the men folk. They just cannot stand them. Sometimes they are all right but another time an urge comes to hate. In those moments, I would not bear to hate you. It is not good for your future wellbeing.'

'I don't care. You may hate me when you like but I would still like to marry you.'

'I think, let us meet at my room and talk about it. I may be able to explain to you better. When a gay woman hates, it is really uncomfortable. They are really anti-men and can be aggressive towards them. But we can still meet and continue to be good friends.'

'No, if you have decided not to marry me, I would not like to meet you after our next meeting. My exams are so close and I do not wish to jeopardise my results. But now I will go to India after exams to get married. It is the right time for me to settle down in life.'

Next Sunday we met up at her room. I sat on a chair while she sat on her bed about 10' away. I was crying. She continued to pacify me by explaining the reasons why was she not the right person for me to marry. Maybe she was right. She knew herself better than I did. But it had created a big turmoil in my life. Sincerity and faithfulness are two painful attributes, I realised. They exact and inflict a heavy toll on the practitioner. I did not acquire them or copy them. I was born with them and now I was to pay a heavy price for that.

I was there in her room for about ½ hour. She offered me a cup of coffee. We parted and never met again. I am still not aware what part Bajaj played in all this saga. He never shared with me anything about any conversation with her. I did ask but his reply was summed up in two sentences. He told her that

1. She should have asked him to approach me directly and

2. She was not suitable for me

Did he know that she was lesbian? He never confided to me and I did not wish to tell him either that she gave me that reason for not marrying me. After that episode we never talked about her, ever.

I have heard she lives in Delhi, never married, and is teaching. I am really sad about what had happened and I hope she told me the truth and did not quit on Bajaj's insistence.

The whole episode started very suddenly, full of promises for the future, but ended up abruptly leaving a trail of frustrations and sadness. Relationships are not that easy to start, then to maintain, and finally have a happy ending. They have to be nurtured with love and understanding. They are painful. But we have no choice but to relate with others to maintain sanity. We are social animals and loneliness is the biggest enemy. If we live without a companion for three months, without chatting and sharing our lives, it is true that we can end up in a mental hospital. It is also a known fact that when one spouse dies the other follows sooner than expected. Even the animals live in their own crowds. Look at the clear sky in summer; you would see a huge number of birds touching the sky with beautiful formations, creating such wonderful scenes that give us a great joy. We would wonder in awe how so many thousands of birds are flocking together with everyone knowing exactly its role and its position in that formation. Who is the leader, leading them to such spectacular scenes?

A JOURNEY THROUGH PARTITION AND BEYOND

Again look at the elephants, the rhinos, the cows, the deer, the wild dogs, and the ants - they all flock together.

But in my experience I always found that God never exposes you to such experiences which are not going to be useful to you in your later life. You may feel the pain and the agony at the time of happening but it always gives a lesson to prepare you for the unpredictable future life. I felt the heartache at the time of breaking the relationship. The memories of that fateful meeting at the restaurant, then building up hopes to live with a caring person, and then final separation, all those happenings within weeks were torturing me. Luck can play strange games at times. If I was not going to have a lesbian wife, then nature had already planned to bless me with a daughter who happened to be gay. Years later when my daughter declared to us that she was a lesbian, I gave a very silly comment to her, one that I regret till this day. I said to her at the time, 'Only people with a perverted mind are gay.' She was shocked and I could see the pain on her face. But I was ignorant and stupid. I could have been born with one eye, a hand missing, or any other deformity, would that be my fault? The chemistry of developing a human body in the darkness of the womb is very complex. Anything can happen during that development and one can never put that blame on the receiving person. It can happen and does happen to a lot of people. No one likes to become gay by choice.

So that episode had a message for me for the future, which I did not know at the time.

Shortly after my conversation with Shanti I had a call from Bajaj. I told him that the marriage proposals had been dropped for good. He was very happy. He assured me again that she was not a right partner for me. He also said that he had talked to Shanti and had expressed his disapproval of her marrying me. She also thought that what Bajaj was telling her was true, like she would not make a good match for me. But it is still a mystery to me whether she changed her mind because she was gay or because Bajaj scolded her. I would never know the truth of what transpired between the two. But knowing Bajaj for so many years, whatever he did was all in good faith to protect me. Bajaj is a very loyal and sincere friend and I always admired his great qualities. He is now finally resting in the bosom of God, the resting place for all of us once the body, made with some elements of this mother earth, deteriorates to extinction. I do miss him as I do all those who have departed this planet before my time to be there arrives.

When I decided to go to India to get married, Bajaj wrote letters to some of his good friends to look for a girl who could be recommended to me. They did, but nothing materialised because of the Divine intervention.

The exams were only weeks away. I was really worried in case this unhappy episode affected my results. It was difficult to control the emotional upset. The memory of Shanti continued to haunt me. I had asked her not to phone me in future so that I could concentrate on my studies as well as plan my future without any further agonies. She kept that promise and we never talked after that or met. I am a very emotional man and I had already gone through a love turmoil in Gwalior and I had no nerves to go through that experience once more.

The Two Visitors from India

The Bicycle Manufacturer from Panipat – An Inspiring Story

This person had set up a plant to manufacture bicycles at Panipat. His story in brief was very inspiring and showed his entrepreneurship. He was in his early fifties, slim, bony, sunken cheeks, and melancholy eyes. He looked much older than his age. The miseries and years of toil had tired him. He was not that literate, not even matriculate. He was a refugee from Pakistan as we were. He had lost all his possessions in Pakistan. He was penniless, sleeping rough under the thick tall green trees on the wayside of the road. They gave him shadows and kept him cool during the summer hot days. They also sheltered him from the torrential rains of the monsoon. The bed was nicely laid down every evening under a tree. He shared his single jute bed with his nephew. In the moonlit night, when the birds had retired to their nests, the cool breeze of the night made him go into his deep sleep. He woke up in the morning with *cock-to-coo* of the cocks and the melodies of the birds. He would tuck away his bed against a tree trunk and walk into the open fields to ease himself and then walk down to bathe in a little pond, filled with fresh water out of a well by an ox going round and round endlessly in a circle with his eyes blindfolded. He was making friends with the loyal dogs, with cats, with cows, and the goats. They never hated him. They never looked at his rags or his appearance. They loved him as he was. His life was a misery but he never complained about it. He lived like a penniless maharaja. He was contented with his lot. He never talked about miseries when I met him. I noticed serenity and calmness on his innocent face. He was abundantly contented and when you are contented, you have won the glories and the admiration of the divine which then goes into action to shower its endless blessings. How he behaved with his employees and staffs, I don't know but that is how I found him and I admired his down-to-earth qualities.

He would also while away his time in daydreaming, gossiping, and playing cards with his mates. But he never abandoned his dreams to do something extra-ordinary. All the refugees were penniless and had no money. They were stripped to their bones. They were living on the handouts from the government. The fate had played a joke on their existence. They literally lived from hand to mouth. I have seen it and lived it. It is not hearsay but experience talking. Millions were slaughtered, raped, and converted against their will.

A JOURNEY THROUGH PARTITION AND BEYOND

People talk about the sacrifices of Gandhi and Nehru and the others like them who had gone to jail as guests of the colonial government where they were served foods lavishly; the servants looked after them and massaged their inactive limbs; they walked in the well-maintained gardens with roses and jasmine; and they read books and wrote autobiographies. If that is suffering then millions of poor Indians would be happy to be there. Nay, they had never experienced the deprivation in life. They lived as aristocrats in their homes and honourable guests in jails. Going to jail had become the qualification and the passport to line up for the loot from the country's resources. They had lost nothing but only their freedom of speech and the separation from their families. But got a rich reward by becoming Prime Ministers and the ministers. But we, millions of us, ended up as destitute for life and yet the people like us have never been given any recognition for the never-ending suffering we have gone through and the sacrifices we made for the freedom of our country. Page after page of history is written to drum up the sacrifices of these ex 'prisoners', but nobody sang a song about us. Instead we were labelled as 'refugees' and were made to live on the handouts and crumbs of the communities who were lucky not to be caught by the turmoil of the partition. All the doors to opportunities to better ourselves were closed and denied to us unless we knew someone in the hierarchy. The seeds of corruption and bribery were being laid openly for everyone to witness. We commoners' lives were only hanging by a thread. Only some dreams were keeping us sane. We believed in ourselves and in our efforts and in our hard work. There was never any help from the government, never except a few crumbs thrown in our way to keep alive this rejected body. We managed to survive by self-help, by self-reliance, by begging and borrowing from relations, and a do-or-die motto written on the walls. The banks had never existed for the hand-to-mouth people. There were few, they were only for the rich to hide their stolen wealth. They were there only to serve them.

It was those dreams and entrepreneurship of this penniless 'refugee' which were guiding him and leading him to his way to success.

After the partition the bicycle age had arrived in India. Before that most people travelled on foot and if lucky on horseback or camel. Another mode of travelling was a donkey ride. We could also travel on bullock carts, while in the towns we had the horse carriages. Of course we also had the trains connecting a few major cities and towns of this vast subcontinent. They were built to ferry the colonial soldiers and the armaments to keep the vast subcontinent under their foot. They were also installed to receive the exported tracks and engines from Britain at exorbitant prices thus creating jobs for the British boys while the Indians paid for that equipment with their toil and sweat. Not feeling ashamed with all that plunder, the British cunning PR was hoodwinking world opinion by telling them that they were building those rail networks to develop the economy of the backward Indians, a total lie. It had misled a lot of people of the world. Some people in this world have that knack and a cheek to tell lies.

Nobody was allowed to make any industrial goods in India under British rule; the British would never let them. They would not even allow the engineering education. The college where I studied was not given permission for years to admit students. Bicycles were introduced in Europe right at the beginning of the industrial revolution. But India had to import even that humble two-wheeler transport and such things as needles in 1947. India was forbidden to make any industrial goods.

Once one reaches to the abyss, there is no other way but to rise. It is a law of nature. Look at the ocean waves. Once they have touched the bottom of the ocean, there is no more depth to go to but to rise and rise with hurricane force. This 'refugee' had reached to the deep valleys. Now the time was ripe for the existence to move him to the skies.

One day some cycle repairer asked him to find him a bicycle seat as the bicycle he was repairing needed a new one. He looked at it and thought, 'Well, why don't I try to make it.' It was very simple to make or even assemble by procuring the parts from the various suppliers. So he said to the repairer to give him a couple of days and he would get him a seat. The history of ascent had begun.

On that evening he only had Rs 10 in his pocket. He was 'living' away from his family with his nephew. In the evening, the uncle asked the nephew to go and eat something with the money they had and the nephew insisted that the uncle should go and eat as he was the older and he should have some nourishment. During this insistence to send the other to eat, they both went to sleep without eating anything. This saving became the investment to buy the materials for the new seat next morning.

They went to the market, bought the bits they needed to make the seat. With whatever money was left they both went to eat some food for the day. They had now no funds to see them through the next day. Next morning, after finishing the seat, they went to deliver it to the repairer. He inspected it, tried it on the bike, it fitted well, and he bought it. The pair made some good profit. Encouraged with their success they made one more sample seat and took it to a cycle factory in the neighbouring town. This factory was assembling bikes with foreign parts, mixed with some made at the factory. The seats they were using in their bikes were imported. The cycle factory tried the seat and liked it. The price they offered was good and they got the contract to supply it. They came back and got busy in sourcing the money for the investment. They begged and borrowed from their friends and relations. They also collected some money by selling their jewellery. With this money they set up a small workshop, bought the materials and started selling the seats to the cycle company. So that was the beginning of his venture.

A JOURNEY THROUGH PARTITION AND BEYOND

He expanded the factory and eventually started making bikes of his own design with his own brand name. The market was growing. Millions of bikes were needed all over the country for the newly appointed bureaucrats to travel to their offices. When he came to London, he was given a foreign exchange of £7000 to buy a broaching machine to make chain wheels. This was an aid grant (loan in fact to India) given by the British Government to be spent in Britain to buy capital goods to boost the British economy.

He was a very good entrepreneur but lacked education. He did not speak much English. He was not an engineer but had the vision of a good businessman. He was a simple man; he dressed like a villager, walked like a commoner, and behaved like a commoner. In the streets no one would ever guess that he was a rich businessman and employed a hundred people. He was now making most of the cycle parts in his factory and importing only the chain sprocket wheels. To make that part he got the 'grant' to buy the machine in UK. When he left India he was given the names of two British companies, which made those machines. One of them was in Acton.

He came to stay with Malik and we became friends. He needed me as I was an engineer, I lived in UK, and I knew a bit more English than he did. He asked me to accompany him to those factories to see the machines. Being a student, I could take time off from my college whenever I wanted.

We used to sit and talk about our experiences. He shared some of his personal views with me too. He once commented, 'The white girls lack charm and beauty.' What experience he gained with the British women and when I did not know. I did not ask further to dig out how he reached to that conclusion. I did not wish to enter into his personal affairs but I was very much surprised at his comments. I had no experience to contradict his statement or support it. I did not go with him everywhere except those two factories.

He made an appointment to meet the sales director at the factory in Acton. I accompanied him. We reached the factory at late morning, reported at the reception desk, and asked to see the sales director. The person came down to the reception desk and introduced himself. The sales director already knew that a licence had been issued to my friend's company to buy the equipment, and the director also knew the amount my friend had been allocated by the government of India. Once we knew this, a number of issues were raised in our heads.

1. If this guy knew the name of this Indian buyer and his company in advance, and the money he was allocated, how could we negotiate the price with a British company?

2. There were only two British companies making those machines; both companies had fixed the same price.

3.   Both companies knew that the money had to be spent in Britain and both were not soliciting the buyer to buy their machine. They had made a cartel to get the maximum money they could. They were not competing between themselves to bid for the business. The director talked to the buyer in the foyer without even showing a courtesy of taking him to his office to show some respect. They never had the decency of offering a cup of coffee. When my friend asked the director to show him the machine he was buying or the factory where they were being made, the director bluntly refused. The whole behaviour was so rude and insulting. We were just shunted out from the reception area as if we were just some kind of trespassers. The colonial mentality of superiority of dealing with a 'native' was still shamefully visible to witness.

The tragedy was that the allotted money had to be spent in Britain only. Nevertheless the buyer decided to go to Germany to see what kinds of machines were available there. He contacted a company there, gave them the date, the flight details, and his personal data so he could be recognised at the airport. The company made the booking for a hotel for him to stay. They collected him from the airport in a company car, left him at the hotel to make sure he was comfortable for the night. Next morning they took him to the factory, showed him the manufacturing area of the factory, offered coffee and biscuits in the office, negotiated the price, took him back to his hotel for lunch, provided a guide to show him around the city, and finally left him at the airport to fly back to Britain. He stayed there for three nights at their cost. The price of the machine was cheaper; he saw the actual prototype of the machine that would be supplied. While in Britain he was given a brochure to show what the machine would look like. I did not go with him to Germany but he told me how he was treated there, a tremendous difference in the attitude and the behaviour of the two companies. One was behaving with a colonial mentality and the other with commercial interests. In those days Britain and its elite who were controlling the infrastructure of Britain were still living in colonial times. Their mentality had not changed towards the Indians. Racism was at its peak and every Briton had a chip on their shoulder as if they still ruled the world. They never felt guilt that they had subjugated and colonised millions of innocent people of other countries who had a different race, religion, and colour, and whose only crime was that they were too good and too rich, while the British were poverty-stricken and were fighting between themselves for a few crumbs. They were cunning, crafty, sly, and shrewd and had never felt guilty about plundering the wealth of the other nations. I am proud to be Indian born, the country which prides itself that in its whole history it has never invaded any other country, never ruled any other country, never stolen or plundered even a dime from any other nation but has only spread a message of peace, love and harmony. I, and many more like

A JOURNEY THROUGH PARTITION AND BEYOND

me, detest and criticise the attitude of our forefathers who accepted foreign rule for more than a millennium and never fought back to recover their lost lands and their honour. Equally, I wonder how many future British generations would bury their heads in the sand for the crimes committed by their forefathers by subjugating and enslaving the other innocent people of the world. The people of this world are now getting more enlightened and liberal. The past history might have called it a glorious colonial past but the future history will never forgive such acts of barbarism and plunder of other nations. That is why it is most important for the living generations to be more vigilant and be wary of their actions and their effects over the coming generations.

The Indian buyer had no choice but to buy in UK even though the equipment from Germany was much superior and cheaper with iron-clad guarantees of spare parts and maintenance. This also indicates that the so-called 'aid' was in fact a loan to the buyer's country with so many strings attached to it. It was a clever way to promote their own inferior goods and boost their trade. In fact, the word 'aid' was nothing but to deceive their countrymen and the world.

He left shortly after placing the order. He insisted that when I visit India, I must see him. He would take me for a dinner to a good restaurant. He promised that he would show me his factory. He also offered me a job in his factory when I finished my studies in UK.

When I went in 1961 to get married, I contacted him. He took us (with my cousin) to Moti Mahal Restaurant at Darya Ganj in Delhi. It so happened that the dining tables were laid out in the open because of the hot summer. With electric lights all over, the insects were hovering around us. The next table was occupied by a Bollywood known actor with some friends. They were there for barely a few minutes; suddenly we noticed some trouble there. It happened quickly, just like a wildfire. The moment we looked at them, we saw the actor and his brother shouting and bashing the waiter who was taking their orders. How on earth they picked a fight with that serving humble waiter surprised us. We did not know who those occupiers were. Our host said he was a Bollywood actor with his brother and some other friends. It could only happen in India where the so-called elite get away with murder. Soon the manager arrived at the scene to calm down the situation. I asked my host if we could move away from that table or even go to another restaurant for a peaceful dinner. He advised us to wait. The atmosphere soon became normal except the actor continued to brawl for a little while. What an uncivilised man he was. He normally looks that ferocious and arrogant on the cinema screen.

However we spent the rest of the evening enjoying our dinner. We chatted about the politics of India, and the purpose of my visit. We were back at home for the moonlight sleep by 1am.

Malik's Brother Visits

Malik had come from a good, well-connected family in India. Therefore quite a few people used to come from India and stay with him. In those days the visitors from India could stay as long as they wanted as there was no visa system between India and Britain to control the stay here.

Once, his elder brother came from India to visit him. He was quite well placed and I was just like a bee still trying to make some honey for my future, so we could not become that close on his stay in London. When I went to India, Malik sent some presents to be given to his brother in Delhi. I duly obeyed. During my stay in Delhi, Malik's sister was getting married. His brother was very kind to invite me. I did go with a present and joined the marriage procession. It was a well-organised show, fitting for the family and the display of some wealth. I was surprised that during such a happy occasion, Malik's brother found time to moan to me about Malik for not attending the marriage and also not contributing anything financially for the marriage of their sister, thus leaving this brother to pick up the entire marriage bill. I did not stay very long as I don't like pomp and show and extravaganza to display one's status and wealth to humble those who are not that fortunate. The brother did persuade me to stay on until the marriage ceremony and dinner but I made an excuse and left. May be it was unethical, uncivilised on my part but that was how I felt at the time.

Meeting an Indian Police Inspector

Another person who had come from India was a police inspector in the Punjab Indian Police Service (IPS). He came on holiday by air. He was a very nice fellow. He did not act like an Inspector to us but he did say that 'don't think I am that simple. You have to come and see when I am in command at my police station in Punjab.' I knew exactly what he meant. He was young and had joined the police by passing the IPS examination and that is why he became an inspector so quickly rather than getting promotions from the ranks. I had the experience during my training as a policeman at Delhi of how such officers are abusive and use nothing but a filthy language. They treat their rank and file as if they are just dust and they have their god damn right to crush them under their feet with brutality. He used to go for sightseeing to London on his own.

When I told him that I was planning to go by sea to India for marriage, he became quite interested to sail with me. So we both booked our seats in a French ship from Marseille. We both travelled by a train to Marseille to board the French ship some time at the end of June. I was a student and I booked my seat in the 'cattle shed' area of the ship and he had his berth reserved at the next higher class, but we met every day and talked about the politics of India. He was married, had children. He never talked too much about his background. Why, I have no idea.

A JOURNEY THROUGH PARTITION AND BEYOND

My Brother Arrives in UK

I had just about finished my examination when my brother, elder to me, telephoned me from Heathrow airport. I went to receive him. That was a big surprise as I had no information that he was planning to come to UK. I had been pressing my younger brother Ved to come but I never knew any intentions of Jag. He was well settled in his railway job as a stationmaster not very far from the town where my parents lived. He has three children – 2 daughters and a son. However with a bit of luck there was a room available at Malik's flat. So he settled down there. I had only a couple of weeks to settle him down before my departure for India.

I introduced him to Bajaj and co who helped him to find a job and talked about his other plans in London when I had gone for a few weeks. He told me about his experiences while on his way to UK by air. He was allowed by the Government of India, like so many other Indians who were leaving India as immigrants to foreign lands, only three pounds to travel with. It was such an insult to the Indian citizens who were becoming economic migrants not because of their own fault but because of the lack of opportunity and nepotism in India. Anyone would feel angry the way they were treated and shunted out of the country with £3 in the pocket. It was scandalous to put three pounds in their pockets and kick them on their arse to land in UK and live happily ever after. So Jag's story was amusing but horrific. When he landed at a Turkish airport, he felt an urge to ease himself. So he spotted a toilet. As he was going in, a woman attendant at the entrance demanded a tip. He did not understand her Turkish language and she did not know his. But from her body language he could make out that she was asking for a tip. He had no Turkish currency so he gave her a pound and asked her to give him change back. She asked him to go in and she would give the change when he came out. On his return he asked for the change. She refused. So not knowing the exchange rate between the currencies and how much he should get back he just went away in disgust. All their conversation was with body language. So that was the beginning of a lovely welcome to the gateway to Europe. Now he was left £2.

He spent some more money for coffee and biscuits at Heathrow airport before I arrived. He was now left with only a pound + some shillings in change, not enough to reach me where I lived. If I had gone to India he would have been stranded. He did not know my plans that I was going to India and I did not know his plans that he was coming to UK. So that was the beginning of his venture to Europe.

However I made sure that he was well settled before I sailed from Marseilles in France for India to find a partner.

CHAPTER 3: JOURNEY TO INDIA FOR MARRIAGE

Soon after my exams were over, the Inspector and I both travelled by train to Marseille, France. I booked my seat through Thomas Cook of London. While booking a seat I also bought a fridge/freezer to take to India. In those days people in India were crazy to acquire foreign-made goods. Someone suggested that I take a fridge and sell it at a profit. This would give me enough money to pay for my one-way ticket by sea to India. Greed to recover some of the cost of travelling to India was a good incentive to take a chance. Many people travelling to India were doing that, so why should I not join the bandwagon? I did.

In addition to the fridge, I bought a battery-operated radio, a novelty in those days in India. Wherever I travelled I found the crowds gathering around to listen to Radio Ceylon or any other station. The crowd was hypnotised to see a radio operating without connection to the mains. A, B's friend, had made the best use of it. He was showing off to the crowds on railway stations when he accompanied me to Mumbai to take delivery of the fridge. To me it was an embarrassment but he enjoyed every moment of becoming the centre of the crowd's attention. He would get down at every station, tune the radio, set it to its full volume and then sing and walk along the station to show that he was the greatest music lover that had recently landed on the Indian soil. When the curious crowd would gather around him he would fiddle with its knobs to prove his expertise, and would answer any questions coming from them. I would stand away from him in the crowd to see the smile and joy on his youthful handsome face. It was fun to see how the innocent faces amongst the crowd were enjoying the show. The technological revolution had not yet arrived in India.

I also bought some socks and some shirts to give as presents to relations. I bought a wristwatch in Aden. IP also bought a watch that was more expensive than mine. However B's friends had loaded me with a variety of consumable goods. There were at least three big suitcases full with their goods. I foolishly agreed to oblige them without realising the hassles I would face with Customs officers and their delivery to their relations. They knew I was sailing by ship and so carrying the luggage would not be an issue. They were all working, had income, and therefore were mindless in buying and loading me up with so many taxable goods. They included goods such as toasters, kettles, shirts, tablecloths, and bed linen. It created a lot of problems for me to clear through the customs at Mumbai, carrying them by trains, and finally taking them to a place where I was to stay. In fact I had no place to stay in Delhi. I was spending a night here and a night there. They just used me as some kind of an international coolie. I bet they would not take even a small parcel for me. That is how a lot of people on this planet are – selfish, self-centred, egocentric exploiters.

Customs Clearance at Mumbai

It took nearly 11-12 days voyage to reach Mumbai harbour. All the baggage was taken into a big hall for customs clearance. It was about 11am. The thrill of coming back to my homeland soon wore very thin. I had three or four big suitcases full of goods given to me by people to be handed over to their relations in Delhi. B had sent the goods with me to be handed over to his brother in Panipat. M asked that his goods be given to his brother in Delhi. B's friend C sent the maximum number of goods. He sent a list to his parents to make sure that they collected all of them. When his brother came to collect in Delhi, he counted every item. When he could not find a couple of items as they were packed in a different trunk by the customs officials, he took out the list to show that so and so items were missing. I felt insulted and angry. I had taken their goods free with all the hassles to go through and now I also had to prove that I was not deceiving them. B's goods I took personally to deliver at Panipat. I also took M's presents to deliver to his brother. It was a service I provided from door to door like an international carrier, free with no thanks. Greed was on the face of every receiver. They never showed gratitude and contentment but rather 'is that all, we thought…' was the depressing attitude. Maybe I had changed after three years of living in UK and I had forgotten the Indian ways of inquisitiveness and greed. But it was all depressing and I felt low whenever I faced them. My folks felt small too. They compared their handouts to what I had transported for the others. They were right but I had limitations. I was now a student and wanted to conserve my resources for my education. But I also must admit that I did not know what I should take. I am very poor in public relations. From society's point of view, it was a poor performance but that is the way I am and I cannot change and could never learn those social etiquettes.

At the customs, when my turn came to declare, the officer said, 'You have a lot of baggage. Have you brought them to sell?'

'Sell officer, what are we talking about? Are you kidding?'

'No, but it appears that way, doesn't it? So many trunks must be full of a variety of goods carried by a bachelor. You will have to pay a lot of duty and I hope you have enough cash to settle the tax. Have you got any watches, radios, cameras, or jewellery?'

'No problem Officer, open the trunks and check. I have quite a few things to declare. They are not all mine but I have been loaded by friends to give them to their relations in Delhi.'

'Ok, let us have a look.'

So I opened one trunk. He had a good look. Then he opened the second one, and the third one. He was amazed at the number of items I was carrying. His face dropped with envy. He looked greedy to grab the lot. All the consumable goodies of the western world were passing under his nose, and yet he was not allowed to grab any of them as they were under my control. Who could blame him for his lustful eyes? He too wished to see his children wearing those clothes and playing music on those radios. People were hungry and starved with that deprivation of 'luxury' goods. I could understand his greed and yet was ready to battle for the goodies I was carrying for others. They were not mine and were given to me as a trustee to deliver them to the rightful owners.

'But why are you bringing so many goods for others?'

'Sorry, I just could not say no. In fact they just bundled them up together without telling me what they were sending.'

'You know you could be fined as well, in addition to paying customs duty.'

'No, please don't do that.'

'Where did you buy this watch?' looking at my wrist.

'In Aden officer! I needed one so I bought it. They are quite cheap up there.'

'You will have to pay duty on that too.'

'Suppose if I take it back to Britain? I am going back in 7-8 weeks' time. I have only come to get married.'

'Yes, you still have to.'

'Oh, that does not seem right. Why should you charge duty on goods which are my personal belongings and I am using them. They are not meant as presents. In the same breath you can also ask me to pay duty on the clothes I am wearing, including my vest and panties.' I replied sarcastically. That obviously stung his ego.

So he exploded, 'Be careful, you foreign dweller. Let us stay within the norms of the protocol. I am here to impose the law of the land. Accept it gracefully or else ....'

A JOURNEY THROUGH PARTITION AND BEYOND

I got his message loud and clear. I was becoming a bit frustrated by his questioning, loaded with taunts and sarcastic remarks. Suddenly he changed his tone, and said, 'Can you see that man standing over there?' pointing his fingers towards a man looking like a peon, poorly dressed, standing to attention with his watchful eyes surveying the whole scene like a dickey bird. He was being used by customs men as their butcher to slaughter innocent goats and for collecting their bait.

'No, where?' I looked intensely towards the direction his finger was pointing.

'See that man with a Gandhian cap, with a small moustache.'

'Oh, yes that one. What about him?'

'He is my man, go and see him and give him some money and I will let you go without charging you any custom duty. I might take a couple of pretty socks you have for myself.'

'How much do I have to pay him?' I asked innocently.

The conversation had now moved towards bribing, an interesting subject. I just cannot bear giving bribes to people. It is not in my nature. I just loathe the whole idea of giving money to someone who has not earned it. I cannot even give a dime to a beggar. I feel embarrassed and low. I have done it a couple of times and I still feel guilty about it. Who am I to give a handout to someone with a begging bowl in his hand? It is an impossible task to follow. It is so insulting to the pride of the receiver and I am contributing to it. I hate to turn good citizens into beggars. If he starves, then he would soon get out and be seeking some job to fill his belly. I prefer him to steal rather than beg. There is nothing wrong in stealing to survive. If stealing was non-existent on this planet, there would be no saints either. If there was no demon Raven, there would be no Ram. If there was no British Empire, there would be no Gandhi. If there were no beggars and deprived people, there would be no missionaries, no do-gooders, and no philanthropists. They would all bang their heads on the wall and beg God to create some maimed people to keep their profession occupied. God never creates rich and poor, Hindus and Muslims; it is the society which divides them and exploits them. It is well known that in Mumbai there are some evil people who mutilate and disfigure healthy children at birth so that they create empathy and pity within the public to coax more crumbs into their beggar bowls. We see every day on the TV advertising by the charity collectors showing the crying and malnutrition of African children. These scenes are heart racking but these charities have turned it into a money-spinning business. Similarly, no mother gives birth to a prostitute but the pimps steal them and turn them into that profession. In my opinion, it is a logical step to steal to live. It is the protest, it is a cry of the thief, and it is a waking call to the cruel society. But society is deaf and dumb. Rather than helping them, they lock them up. Or some, so-called 'civilised' societies and governments, are now bribing them with hand-outs and 'dole money' to loiter around the streets aimlessly, visit the pubs and clubs, provided they stay away from thieving and burglarising the homes of the well-to-do of the society. What a marvellous solution. It has become a legalised bribery but with the drumming noise of a 'caring society'. Why should someone have billions while the other is reduced to begging? The law against stealing is made by the rich and the powerful of society, like any other law, to protect their wealth. It is not a divine law. The divine law is to survive and live, even by hook and by crook, but live and procreate. No, this is not my cup of tea to bribe to humble someone, and I can never do it. It is like giving away a drug and a tranquiliser to make him an addict. If I bribe a man, his success with my bribery would lead him to demand the same from others. This appetite would continue to grow. He would become a legalised, booted suited 'beggar' and even a crook. He would breed and rear his offspring like himself. He will spread his disease to all those who come in contact with him. His greed would go beyond the limits and destroy his self-respect and ego. He would look like a respectable man dressed with outfits bought with bribed money but his soul would sink to the deepest levels of the dark valleys. I will not play any part in his destruction. Hence, no, I can never play that game of bribery, never ever. It is not in my blood and I cannot convince myself to be a briber.

Whenever I have given such handouts in my lifetime, it always ended up with a bitter experience. Maybe the coins I had given did not have enough honey on them to make them sticky enough to glue into the recipients' pockets. Maybe I was a lousy, miserly giver. I don't know but I always had the bitter experience of giving, except once when I was walking on a footpath of New York with my eight-year-old daughter Ritu in 1971. We saw a blind beggar with a cloth spread in front of him with some coins on it. Ritu asked who this man was and what was he doing there on the footpath. She had never seen beggars in London. I explained, and then I gave her a coin to drop on the white cloth spread in front of him and we walked away. This man did not protest or show anger. Maybe he could not see what he got. But the other experiences were not so happy. I had once tipped a one-shilling coin to a taxi driver in Oxford Street, London and he threw it in rage. Again one day when I was walking in Darya Ganj, Delhi I gave a coin to a beggar with crippled legs who was sitting on the footpath. He did not like the amount of the coin and threw it with such ferocity that it rolled down on the footpath ending up some twenty feet from us. I told him off that it was not his right to demand the amount of money he wanted to. It was my pleasure to give him what I wanted to give. He became abusive. I walked down, reclaimed my coin and walked away in disgust. What a cheek he had. Apart from these three instances, I have never indulged into such evil practices.

A JOURNEY THROUGH PARTITION AND BEYOND

However going back to the customs clearance, 'I am sorry I cannot pay to that man. It will end up in your pocket. I prefer to pay the tax. At least the Government would get the money and it can spend that for the benefit of the citizens.'

'Are you mad? You would be paying me a lot less and saving money for yourself.'

'How much does the tax come to?' I enquired.

'It should be around Rs 300. I am asking only Rs 50 to let you go.'

'I will pay tax. Please give me the tax paper to deposit the money.'

'Look Mr Khurana, just don't be stupid. That man is waiting for you to collect Rs 50. You go and give it to him. The moment he nods to me, that he has the money, I will re-pack your trunks the way they were already packed and you are off to the railway station to catch your train for Delhi.'

'Sorry I am not giving any bribe to you. I will pay the tax. So please tell me how much?'

Now he was put on the spot. His choices in persuasion, cajoling, threatening had all dried up. My eyes were also trying to find the PI to help me in his land of bribery collectors. But there was no sign of him. We had disembarked from the ship together but all of a sudden he disappeared from the scene. Finally the customs man agreed to give me the completed tax form. It was around Rs 250+ all told. He asked me to join the long queues and pay my tax at the kiosk. Lo, who was making noises at the top of his voice there, in the third queue? It was a young Singh, shouting and abusing the customs officers who were charging him the customs duty on the goods he brought from USA. He was such a loud mouth that I could not miss his bigoted comments. He went on, 'I am a Sikh and all these officers are Hindus. I am made to pay this tax for being a Sikh. Look at how so many are going away without paying the tax. I am victimised.' He went on and on. I thought, well it is all right for him to protest his victimisation because he belonged to a minority community of India, but who should I blame that I too was paying the tax as he was. I thought with all my wits to find some scapegoat to blame but I could not because I belonged to the so-called majority 'Hindus'. The minority in every country bash the majority. The minority never thinks that it is also beneficial to them to stay on good terms with the majority. This is how the minority community fans their grievances and finally ends up in strife and disharmony. This young fellow was spreading his venom for everyone to hear. If there were a few more people of his community, he would have created riots within those four walls of the customs house. Soon I saw the appearance of PI.

'Where have you been? I have been looking for you. I needed some help to influence the idiotic customs man who wanted me to pay him the bribe.'

'Oh don't ask. I got into my own problems.'

'What happened?'

'I thought rather than waiting here in a queue with petty officers, let me be smarter. So I went to see the bosses upstairs to clear my goodies free of charge from the customs. You know I bought some goods from Britain and a wristwatch at Aden. Now they wanted me to pay the tax on the watch. I did not want to pay. I said I was abroad for more than three months, so I was entitled to buy a watch and bring it in the country free of taxes. They refused. So I have been arguing with them for the last one hour.'

'Are you off the hook?'

'No, I have to pay the duty. They are so adamant. I even told them that I am a police inspector in Punjab. They didn't want to know.'

So he paid more than Rs 100 for his watch alone. The rest of the goods were not charged as he was away from the country for more than three months. I wondered how that deranged Mr Singh would react to this news that here was a police inspector with some strings to pull and had the position to influence the customs to get out by not paying, but had to pay. Singh's brawl was just childishness which all minorities suffer from in every country all over the world.

Soon my turn came to pay my tax. I paid and came back to show the receipt to the customs man who still had my possessions displayed in the open in front of him as if he was sitting in a market stall to sell all my goodies. He was still restless. His greedy eyes were stuck on my socks. They were just ordinary socks, which we were wearing daily in Britain. I don't know why they were so attractive to him. What was the hidden magic in them that mesmerised him? Guess what would happen to the scantily-dressed girls on the streets of Britain if he ever set his foot on those shores I thought. Would he ask them to take off their socks and give them to him simply because he fancied them? Or in the worst scenario, would he go and hug them, kiss them, ask them for favours? Only God can forbid the world from his lustful eyes.

Our dialogue continued, 'Can you give 4 pairs of your socks now and it is all over?'

'Aren't you cheeky? I have just paid the full tax you asked for and you are still demanding my goods. Sorry I cannot. I brought them to give a little present to my brothers. They would be disappointed if they don't get anything from me.'

'You buy them something else here as a present.'

'But they are presents from UK. They can buy here whatever they want.'

'But you can send them again from UK. Nobody would send me anything from UK.'

'I cannot afford to. I am still a student. I have to study for another two years.'

'No please give me. Don't be too hard.'

A JOURNEY THROUGH PARTITION AND BEYOND

He continued to persist in his demand. Finally, having no choice, I agreed to give him three pairs of socks. I put all the pairs of socks in front of him and asked him to choose the ones he liked. He was very happy with his loot. I packed my trunks in a hurry, found PI, hired a taxi and hurried to the railway station on my way to Delhi. That was Mumbai in 1961.

On the Way to Delhi

The PI was going to Punjab. He did not tell me about his whereabouts in Punjab. He did not disclose the town he was posted to or where he lived in Punjab. He wanted to keep his affairs to himself. So we parted as the train approached New Delhi station, never to meet again. Was he hiding something? Only he knew.

At the railway station my mother, father, sister and Harbans brother were present. As usual in Indian style, I touched my parents' feet, hugged my sister. Harbans brother hugged me and cried bitterly. I was very much touched with the love and affection he showered on me.

My stay in Delhi was like living the life of a vagabond. My parents and Harbans' family had just shifted back to Delhi. They were having a tough time in Ratlam and had decided to move to Delhi. So Harbans' family was living at his brother-in-law's house and my parents were living here and there in relations' homes. For them, they had become refugees once more with no home and no future. Fate was still cruel to their existence in their old age on this planet.

Finding a partner

I had written a letter to my father that I was on my way to Delhi to get married. He gave his responsibility of finding me a suitable match to his younger brother Dr GR who was now retired and living in East Patel Nagar. Whatever the reasons, the relations between our two families had never been that amicable and close. We knew all the relatives of our mother but not of our father. As it happens, a woman of the family always brings her children closer to her own family and ignores the male's family. I believe the problem and distance which was created between us must have been due to my mother and my aunt. However we all know that blood is thicker than water; my uncle had agreed to take on that burden of finding me a girl and he did so nicely. Since the days I knew him when he invited us to attend the marriage of his son, I found him very warm, very caring, and he showed his love towards our family. He had great qualities as a human. I admired him for those qualities. I had a great respect and regard for him and he and his sons looked after me very well when I stayed with them. He used to write to me off and on after my arrival in UK. Quite often he wrote to me about the deteriorating health of Pritam brother. I was lucky and am very grateful to my uncle who spent a lot of time in guiding me in selecting the right partner. He allowed me to stay in his

129

house for a few days when I was in Delhi. He also made all the arrangements for the marriage procession and for the reception at his house.

Mohini, my cousin, and I became good friends. I enjoyed his company. On some late nights, whenever we went together, I would go to their house and sleep on the roof under the moonlight with a cool breeze blowing. I must admit I always felt a bit uncomfortable and not at home. Maybe the plight of my homeless parents was bothering me. Somehow the mind, full of old rubbish memories implanted in childhood by the families was obstructive. But by staying there those memories were being washed away slowly and I was beginning to feel that there was warmth in their love towards me and my family.

They respected me more this time as I had achieved something now and was living in England. I too was a bit more matured and a more socially acceptable creature. I was not feeling that inferiority complex and was more confident in my ability to deal with such social situations.

Uncle had one more son older to Mohini and a daughter who was married to some rich businessman's son.

The Gate Crashers in Delhi

One Sunday a friend came to pick me up in his chauffeur-driven car. It was dusk; the evening was cooling after a day of hot burning sun. The night life for the young rich glamorous Indians was just about to begin in full swing. While we two friends and the boss's wife sat on the back seat, the fourth sat next to the driver to show him the route to follow. The car sped through the new residential areas of Delhi towards New Delhi's posh residential areas where the newly rich Indians were occupying those bungalows which were vacated by the colonial rulers. The tall grown-up trees, with thick green branches shadowing the roads, were providing a cool breeze on that hot day. The cool breeze, loaded with a mixture of the fragrance of thousands of various garden flowers, was changing our moods to prepare us for going to the evening party. As we drove on roads passing through the posh bungalows of New Delhi, we could see some good parties going on in the front gardens of some bungalows with rich ladies in their summer colourful dresses chatting and laughing. 'Let us stop here,' the fourth, the organiser and the boss of the evening entertainment, suggested. 'No, No, that is not the right place,' his wife said. So we moved on. Another place came. The boss asked the driver to stop. The driver overshot. 'No, go back a bit.' The driver obediently reversed a few steps, just opposite to the point of reception. We all disembarked. The boss instructed the driver to park the car a couple of hundred yards ahead and wait on the road. I was told by my friend to follow them and if asked anything unusual, not to reply. I was not to say who I was, where I came from, what are my reasons of coming to the party. So I followed the 'distinguished invited couple'. I just nodded as I passed in front of a receptionist with foreign features of South East Asia. She gave me a smile and we walked down to the party. I guessed that it was some kind of an embassy reception. I did not share my thoughts with friends. I just wanted to learn how the so-called high-class society manoeuvres their lives in the capital cities of the world. Within five minutes, without touching any food or drink, the boss said, 'Let us go out. This is not the place where we should be.' I followed obediently. We boarded the car and went hunting for another party. In a few minutes we disembarked in front of the reception of another party. We went in. This time I was a bit more confident. Timidity and embarrassment had blown away with the cool breeze of New Delhi. I knew exactly how to act now. We followed, as expected, behind the 'The Guest Couple'. We all had a glass of orange squash. We might have sipped only half a glass when the couple concluded after surveying the environment that it was time to quit the party once more. Now I realised that we were gate crashers and not the invitees. After the debacle of the first party I could guess that that is what they were doing but I still had doubts. Be smartly dressed, disembark in front of the reception from a shiny chauffeur-driven car, and invade the party where no one would question the identity. So it was a great evening with no drink and no food. The couple drove us back to the place where I was staying, without even bothering to take us to another restaurant for a meal. I had to sleep that night hungry. So this was the Delhi of those who live in their false pomp and show.

It could not be only them who were gate crashing the parties of the embassies. There must be a lot more of Delhi's well-to-do residents who had the cars and were smartly dressed with good personality doing it. The embassies must be avoiding confronting this type of scandal.

The Match Makers

In India, at the time I was marrying, there were many types of match makers. Everyone would influence the selection of a partner except the ones who were marrying. The priest, the astrologer, the fortune teller, the parents, the brothers and sisters, and even the close friends, they all interfere. In many instances even an old woman would make it her job to go around searching for suitable marriageable young people and then approach the families with her recommendations. She always thought that she was doing a social service in bringing the two into matrimony. She would act as a link between the two families. What was her reward – appreciation from the two families, sometimes financial gains, and mostly satisfaction and enhancement to her ego. Go around and brag about her achieving the number of successful marriages. The arrangement is never based on the love between the couples. They were totally strangers to one another. In some cases they had never seen one another. Some were even married just after their births and they are content to announce to future acquaintances that their marriage was arranged in heaven, as if heaven is a huge administrative complex where all decisions affecting every grain of the Universe are taken. What a load of rubbish.

Soon after matrimony, the struggle for dominance, the jealousy, the comparison between the families would follow with vigour. The daily dose of fights would ensue between the couples. The bedroom which is meant to be a temple of love becomes the battleground for exerting and fighting for the supremacy. The offspring which are intended by God to be born out of love and harmony are born out of fights and jealousies between the young couples. No wonder this world is full with people of undesirable characters. It had to be so because the couples were never compatible to live together in the first place. They never talked between themselves of the likes and dislikes of one another. The struggle of a lifetime had to start on day one. The children were born, not out of love but out of sex. In the darkness of the night no other would be available to satisfy the sexual desires. Therefore the one available to satisfy one's needs of the time would do, resulting into the unwanted, incompatible children. Once the children arrive, the slavery of the two deepens to a point of no return. The life of struggle continues until the ugly face of death knocks at the door. Is that what life is all about? – a horrible thought. It becomes a history of revenge and a bare existence of the two souls. It is a continuous process of destroying the whole family structure from one generation to another.

The elderly people like parents, uncles, and other grown-up relations feel honoured to find you a suitable match. They claim that they have seen the world and are well experienced to know the ins and outs of the human behaviour. They assert that they have the best interests of the couple in mind. They also say that they only recommend the one they think would be the best suitable match for you. But with my experience and that of many others I can vouch that it is not true. In fact they are imposing their choice onto you and they won't admit it. The moment you show your disagreement to their suggestions, they would withdraw their support and their attitude would become cold. They feel insulted and ignored. Indirectly they are pressurising you to accept their view. It is strange that life was gifted to us by the providence who had given us the choices to lead our lives the way we want, but unfortunately its ownership is later claimed by the people who gave us birth.

Arranged marriages 'succeeded' in India, not because the system is right but because the couple that married sacrificed their whole lives in adjusting to live with each other; to keep their vows they said at the marriage ceremony; and to make their elders and the society happy. The bravos would run away from this oppression, face the brutal wrath of the society and its rules, and finally go for the divorce. They will find another one to marry or live in 'sin'. But the cowards would accept their fate and live on with a daily grind. How the system ever came and conditioned nearly all the youths of India is beyond my conception. To be made to pay by suffering the whole life is a cruelty of unbelievable imagination. If God ever comes on this planet he would refuse to accept that he created the humans to suffer, not by their own misdeeds but by the rules imposed by the society that believes that it knows better. He has given freedom to every creature he created to live the life they want to.

I had gone to India with many hopes to find, with the help of the elders, the love of my life with whom I could share the rest of my life, but they were all so sure that the one they were recommending was the best choice. They all showed their sincerity in reaching to that conclusion. For me it became a tug of war. Whom I should believe and whom I should not. People like me were crushed to obey, especially when I had limited time and I was roaming around with a begging bowl to those parents with daughters to trust me and give me the hands of their loved one. In some ways I can understand their reservations and concerns. Some bad suitor could take their precious soul to a foreign land, thousands of miles away where he could mistreat her, beat her, or even murder her and they may never be able to reach her in time to help. I do appreciate their concerns of not trusting me. This is my biggest quarrel with my maker where he went wrong when designing his human creation. He should have imprinted on every forehead the characteristics he bestowed them with. This would have eliminated the guesswork of judging his souls. They all thought that I was the biggest liar and was there to take their daughter by hook and by crook.

However I agree that there are advantages of arranged marriages but there are a lot more disadvantages and one has to pay for them for a whole life.

Advantages:

1.   Both parties do the thorough searches for the other's family. Are there any infectious diseases in the family like TB or hereditary problems? Is that family well settled? Does any family member have a criminal record; is he an alcoholic? Visits prostitutes, or has any other social evils? And so on.

2.   What are the qualities of the boy and the girl? Can he support the family? Is he educated enough to make a living? What are their personal characteristics?

3.   What do they physically look like?

One also has to conquer the social taboos, prejudices, and jealousies of the society. There are a lot of other personal habits checked too. In my case, before

I decided to come to UK, some relation approached my mother for her daughter. In her searches, she went to see one of my relations to know what kind of a boy I was. In that society the people continue to keep an eye on the growing boys and girls and the matchmakers pounce on the family with their suggestions. But when the lady came to see my mother, she narrated the following conversation she had with one of our relatives. She asked them, 'In your opinion is Om suitable for my granddaughter?'

'No I don't think he would be a good match for your granddaughter.'

'Why, he looks ok to me. His family is good.'

'Yeah, but he is of a darker colour. He is not a fair skinned boy.' What racism!

'That does not matter. Lord Krishna was also of the same dark skin.'

'Yeah, but you know he is going to England for higher education.'

'That is even better. That is no disadvantage.'

'But he smokes.'

'Well, my son-in-law smokes too. We will have to put up with it.'

This is what you are given sometimes in your searches for a boy and a girl by the family relations. It depends whom you are talking to. The above dialogue reflects the jealousy of the informer. A sympathetic informer would tell the lies to the other extremes. Therefore, some of the searches could be disastrous. The matchmakers carry their own prejudices and may not let two decent young people enter into matrimonial relationship.

Anyway I was not ready to marry, but this kind of bickering also carries to discredit the family being investigated. Furthermore, sometimes they would also tell you lies about them, especially the girls. A lot of time the families have been cheated. They were shown a girl at the time of meeting between the boy and the girl and then bring a different girl for the marriage. In olden days nearly all girls used to have a veil to hide their faces at the time of the marriage. Another time the boys were not even allowed to see the girls, as in the case of my brother. My father refused point blank to allow him to see his would-be wife. He got married on the recommendations of my mother and father. Similarly when my eldest brother Pritam was getting married with his first wife we were never told that her whole family had a history of deaths from TB and was infested with the disease. We were not living in DI Khan. The matchmaker was a niece to my mother and the girl she suggested was from the same family where she was herself married. Pritam's wife contracted TB just a year after her marriage and died within a year after. Luckily that disease never took root into our family. If you are a decent fellow you will become a victim of one thing – trust. My mother always trusted and took girls for her well-behaved boys, recommended by the vested interests of her relations. We brothers paid a heavy price for her trust. We were all pressurised to marry the girls recommended and chosen by our mother. That is the heavy price we paid for our obedience.

Selecting a Spouse

It is not an easy game. It is difficult for both parties. The selection process is not limited to the two who are going to tie the knot but it also involves the parents, the brothers, the sisters, other relations, and the whole lot of friends. It is such a simple task for the two to marry but it turns into such a complex affair. The society imposes so many terms and conditions, it robs away the freedom to make decisions, and whomsoever you do not please or do not accept advice from, they are unhappy, they may not attend your marriage, they may sabotage your marriage ceremony as a revenge. At later dates they would continue to taunt the couple. I am a bit wiser today with my many years of marriage experience. But the problem is that at the age you marry you would never have the wisdom. The wisdom comes with experience.

At the time, when I was in the market looking for a partner, I was not aware of any of these complex issues of finding a partner. I did not know the professions available to women of those days. I had no experience of dealing with the humans and the complex relationships between them. I was also not as smart as today's young people are. They are brought up in a totally different environment. Their knowledge is far superior than mine was. I had the experience of riding on donkeys and camels. There were no radios, no electric power, no TVs, no computers, no webs, and no mobiles, no social Media to feed you with the vast knowledge of the world available today. I was brought up in a very simple environment. I knew nothing but respect for the elders, even though they may be even just minutes older than I was. I always respected their views. I never thought of contradicting or questioning them. If someone said in the night, 'Om it is day time,' I would agree to that opinion. But if the next moment another one said, 'No, it is night,' I'd nod to that too. I never wanted to offend anyone and so always accepted what they said. Stupid! I agree with you. That is me, I am afraid. With all that knowledge and smartness of the present generation, they select their partners by courting them, even going to the lengths of sleeping and producing children together for some years and only then marrying them. That kind of social behaviour was not for me.

You can never expect a perfect partner. It will never be there. Two people of the same calibre must differ in the real world. They are both unique and were cut by the Divine differently. But it is how you manage the differences, how you sort them out amicably, and finally forget and forgive, that is going to make the life a bit smoother and more comfortable. Confrontation does not help. Jealousies, competitiveness, distrustfulness do not help. However, while selecting a partner it is most important to minimise the differences and choose the one with the same tastes.

Continuing my experiences.

In my case, my parents had no fixed address in Delhi, so my uncle took that burden in finding me a partner. When I got there, I was asked to go and see my uncle and he enlightened me about the replies he had received from the advertisement he placed for me. He took his folder out and showed me the copies of all the replies he had received. He also marked them with 1, 2, 3 etc in order of going to see them. I went through the list with him and agreed to go along the way he had planned. After all, he was well experienced, he had seen the world, he had married his son and daughter. I could not have a better person to guide me and help me.

Selecting to see the right person is a very subjective process and soul searching. One could short list only on the basis of the information given in the letter by the spouse's parents. We looked at the family background, the height, the age (girls have best-before dates), the education, working or not working, interests and personal characteristics, adjustment within the new family, adjustment with the new partner, sociable, homely, strong likes & dislikes, liking of children, and the type of friends she had.

We then looked at her future plans, what are her ambitions? Would she like to study further? For me it was important to know. I was studying myself and after my bachelor degree I wanted to study further. If she was not interested in the further education then she might discourage me from further study. Also the gap between the knowledge of the two will widen and may create conflict. Would she be willing to work or be a housewife only? This was also important to me. I was a full-time student and I could not support her sitting at home until I had finished my education and got a job. In this part of the world, to maintain the higher standard of living both husband and wife have to work. Some parents and the girls wanted to know the importance of this requirement. They thought I was marrying simply to have a wife who would earn and I would enjoy my life as a full-time student. Suspicion is the worst enemy of the human relationship.

Then we scrutinised the family details. Are there any major diseases in the family? Are there any major issues such as marriage breakdowns, and their standing in the community? Any demands in dowry, conditions, vegetarians/non-vegetarians, religion/the way of living/part of the country they live in, all had to be looked at.

Meeting Girls and their Families

Mostly people would select by looking at her figure, her appearance - eyes, ears, facial proportions, height, weight etc. The mind is quite clever in that.

A JOURNEY THROUGH PARTITION AND BEYOND

Within moments it would compare her personality with the approval of his inner woman and report whether it has passed the object or rejected it. One never enters into the being of the subject to know exactly what is hiding behind that beautiful body. Even a few questions cannot reveal the truth of the object's thinking. There are many instances when people were hoodwinked and deceived. You need trained eyes and ears of a good psychologist to distinguish between the truth and lies. If one cannot find what he is looking for then he would run away fast and knock on another door, provided he has the guts to face the cultural and society's pressures. Who knows, one day you might strike the gold you are looking for. That is only the theory but in practice we are all timid and fearful of the society's outrage. You cannot ignore the pressures of the elders and their anger. I was very poor in scrutinising the bio data of the person. I had no eagle eyes to read the facial details and then come to a conclusion. In fact I did not even know what qualities I was looking for in a partner. In one word - I was number one naïve.

Soon a day came when my uncle and I set out to see a young lady after selecting the best would-be match from the list of girls' parents who had responded to his advertisement in the matrimonial columns of Delhi's newspapers.

The First One

On paper the details given were quite attractive. Uncle said let us start from this girl. She was a graduate and was working in Delhi. She also belonged to a good family and lived in some new development of the Capital. We hired a taxi and landed in front of the house, located in the areas where middle-class families lived. We were ushered into a small reception room with all the Indian welcome formalities. The respect and formalities accorded to guests and visitors by the Indians are unbeatable by any other nations. They would shower their love and affection as if you were the only VIP left on this planet. As we entered there were a few chairs with a coffee table in front which had some piles of magazines and a freshly delivered daily newspaper. In one corner of the room there laid a bed with neatly covered bed sheets giving the impression that the room was being used as lounge plus bedroom. The parents introduced us to the young lady, who was the sole occupier of the bed. She was well dressed with makeup to present herself to the new would-be-suitor. It must have been an awful day for the lady with mixed feelings of a lottery of success and failure. Rejection brings a dreadful feeling and hurts the ego of the person. There is an equal chance of being accepted or rejected and the experience stays in the memory lane till death. All young people have to go through this ordeal, including the boys, except that it is the girls who face the pain of rejection most. They are always fearful for such meetings. The ego is badly hurt. It revolts; it becomes revengeful, and is ready to fight back. Our eyes crossed. She examined me from top to bottom. I could not know her feelings. My eyes also surveyed her appearance and her body and her looks. The mind is a good devil. It exactly knows its choices. It had seen many beauties all over the streets of the many cities, in parties, on the screens, and many more such opportunities. It had already selected and decided the type of partner it is going to live with. Within moments it compared the object with its stored images and pronounced its judgement with no compromises in sight. It declared that the girl was plump with a tummy out of proportion to her bust. Her facial features had no attractions. The eyes looked smaller on her cheeks and the nose was dominating her face. Her hair was well groomed and managed but they were not adding to her beauty and appearances. There were no curves in her body. The mind was ruthless to announce its judgement, cruel though it might seem but no, she was not good enough for me to bed with. The make-up and clothes which are meant to enhance her image did not improve it any further either. I had to listen to my head otherwise it would hate the person for life and create misery for the two souls who, instead of tying a knot with love, would end up in courts with heartaches. I did not ask any questions. I could not. It was no good to be a hypocrite and give false hopes. My uncle did ask out of courtesy. We were there only for five minutes. Uncle gave me negative signs with his body language. We got up and were on our way home.

The 2nd One
Don't remember

The 3rd One
Don't remember

The 4th One
A parent kept on writing for his widowed daughter with three children. His letters were touching, heart-rending. He was appealing to the conscience of young suitors and was trying to touch their raw nerves. He was pleading that she had 'three beautiful children, married once, husband had died, and the children need the care and attention of a new father.' I felt bad – rather, I should say awful - to not consider her. Caught under that internal conflict, I asked Uncle's opinion. 'Would you like me to see this girl?' 'No, you should not be a sacrificial lamb. Let someone else do that caring.' So my ordeal was over and we did not go to see her even though the father wrote letters a few times to Uncle pleading to consider her for the sake of her children. I was not aware of those letters but Uncle told me about them after I was engaged.

There was another reason too. I was still a student and I had no means to support a family of four. It would have also put my whole career in jeopardy.

A JOURNEY THROUGH PARTITION AND BEYOND

The 5th One

Uncle knew someone (O) in West Patel Nagar. In fact he arranged the party for a reception at Uncle's house after my marriage. O told uncle that he knew a girl who was studying at Aligarh University. She had no parents or any other family member. She was the only child of her parents who were no more. She had just finished her Masters in history. I was not having much luck with the advertised list. Even the 2nd advertisement had the responses from the same people. Uncle then strongly urged me to go and see this girl.

One day I boarded a train and I went to meet this young lady at the Aligarh University, famous for educating the rebellious, radical Muslim students who played a significant role in creating Pakistan. Nearly all the Muslim League's leaders who started direct actions and massacres of the minorities in the majority Muslim areas of British India were educated at that University. They were nothing but agitators and their only goal was to snatch power by inciting Muslims to slaughter the Hindus and Sikhs. Therefore I was fearful about what kind of a University campus it would be; but knowing that Aligarh was now a part of India and had Hindu students studying there as well, that fear was short-lived.

The time passed in the train in dreaming about this young lady. What kind of a girl she would be, what questions she would ask, what she would look like, and so on. I was very naïve in those days. All these questions were nothing more than mental fantasies. Here was the opportunity, arranged by Uncle, to meet a young lady and I was supposed to make the best of it. I had no courage and initiative to find a lady leading me to the matrimonial stage. I always believed that minus the arranged marriage system in India, I would still be a single soul.

My train reached Aligarh station around 9am. I hired a bike rickshaw from the station and directed him to take me to the University Central Library. I was given the directions by uncle to head for the Campus central library after I disembarked from the train. The library was built on a higher plateau. After getting down from the rickshaw, the driver directed me to 'walk through the vast spacious lawn in front of us and then climb those many steps to reach to the library hall' which I could see. The sunrays were peeping through the windows and the doors of that vast building, thus lighting the inner huge auditorium. It was a very big room with rows of wooden benches with backrests, laid neatly on the steps. There were no books inside the room. I peeped through the door, confused and bewildered with thoughts of was that the right place? It did not look like a library, as I knew them in UK. I had not gone to Indian Universities for studies so I was not in a position to compare.

There were hardly any people there, maybe around ten dotted around on the benches of that vast room, all men except a lone woman huddled somewhere in the middle. She was sitting silently, gazing at the auditorium in front as if she was in meditation or in deep prayers. It was frightening to me. I stood there momentarily breathless and in contemplation to collect my courage to face the situation I was not prepared for. Was that scene happening in the real world? Why did she look as pensive as she did? What was making her to be in that mood? It had gone beyond my wits to understand. I am no psychologist. It made me think that she might be asking her Divine to allow her to succeed in her mission to meet her dream boy. She looked bewildered, fearful, threatened, and deep in deliberation. Who would blame her? She had been a lonely girl for nearly twenty-six years and now the chance of a lifetime was coming from heaven. An unknown young man who lived in UK was on his way to see her to fulfil her dreams if it all goes well. Of course it also depended whether she would like the boy and if he would meet her expectations and imaginations. Who would blame her in having dreams of that kind? Do not forget that she had passed a lot of years of her life without even calling someone her own. Nature had been too cruel to her and yet to reach University level, she must have been of an extraordinary character, of great determination.

Having surveyed the inside scene, cautiously I entered through that wide opened door and walked towards the direction she was gazing. I wanted to walk along that way to show my face. I did not wish to go to her from behind her back and say hello. She may not be the girl I was to see even though she was the only girl there. If she was not, who knows she might have taken out her sandals to sort me out for my advances. After all, I had left India only three years ago and the girl's culture would not have changed that much during those short years.

As soon as she saw my face, she jumped up from her seat and quickly walked towards me, blushing and smiling. Her broad smile reflected the warmth, the welcome, and the happiness in welcoming. It appeared that on the first sight she liked my physical appearance. The imaginations I had built on my first glance had all disappeared from the mental screen. I too walked briskly to greet her. I was happy that I had been approved and she must be the girl whom I was supposed to see.

We greeted one another with folded hands. As we walked out of the room, we introduced ourselves. We came down the million steps and settled down on the lawn under the sun that was shining with its full range of anger. It was getting warmer by the minute.

My first question to her was how she knew that I was Om. The way she had approached towards me showed a familiarity as if she had seen me before. She said that there no one was coming to see her except me and she had never seen me around the campus before. The sudden appearance of a stranger meant it had to be you. She was happy that her guess was right. After a few formalities, I could guess that she was a very smart girl, very intelligent, educated, extrovert, happy, very loving, and affectionate. She had all the qualities of a good partner.

We talked about her living at Aligarh, her treatment there, and her education. Soon we started talking about the issues for which we were meeting. I told her what I was doing in UK, how I managed to get to Britain, my education in India, my family background, and other relevant information of interest she should know. She told me about her birth place, her achievements, about her family, and her future plans. She showed her willingness to marry me, not saying in words but I could see that if I was willing to accept her, she would also be ready to adopt me as her man. I can never forget the dialogue we exchanged within those four hours. They still bother me that why on earth I was not strong enough to oppose the pressures of my mother and consider her seriously to be my life partner. The dialogue went on as below.

'As you know I live in UK and studying, you think you would have any difficulty of communicating in English there?'

'No, I would be fine. I may face a cultural shock in the beginning but eventually I would settle down.'

'Would you be able to work and earn some money to support yourself when I am a student?' I explained to her that I had enough savings there to see me through my education but I may find it hard to support her financially until I got a job after education.

'Why not? If I were marrying you it would be my duty to look after you and my future family. I am a very caring person and take that very seriously. I love to have children, see them growing. I am going to be a very loving and caring mother.' I was surprised at her openness. She hardly knew me and she was already talking about the children and their welfare. She assured me that she was not only going to love the children but she would also be a very loving, caring, and thoughtful partner.

She repeated many times about her loving nature, her duties, and her caring nature during our informal talks. That is what bothers me - how I could not take her seriously to marry her. Maybe it was fate, maybe as they say in India that the matrimonial relationships are made in heaven or in the Garden of Eden. In my case they were certainly written in His Court. Somehow things were never made to move forward between us. We both liked one another, were willing to tie the knot, and yet it never happened. It was certainly a Divine intervention. Out of all the girls I had seen so far, she was the only one who looked promising and willing to marry me. If by chance I had stayed one more night in Aligarh, I believe my matrimonial story could have been different. But it was not to happen, why? This incident puzzled me for so many years until I overheard the following:

In August 2012, I heard Mira talking to a friend about how her engagement materialised with me. Before I came to India, her parents were approached by two other suitors' parents. Her father rejected both of them. Then another offer came through a known matchmaker. Without meeting the boy, her parents agreed with the boy's parents to marry her to their son. All the ceremonies of the engagements were performed at a later date. The pressure of marriage was mounting from the boy's mother. Some disagreements ensued between the boy's parents and her father, who, after six months of her engagement, refused to marry her into that family. It was touch and go and the sadness was felt by everyone in the two families. The boy's family was so much aggrieved that they even threatened to kidnap Mira and marry her forcibly to their son. While this scenario was taking place, one of Mira's students, an amateur palmist, read her palm and declared that her engagement would break with that boy. Mira asked, why? She said that a line on her palm said that she would be going to a foreign country to live. She also said that she would have a lot of turmoil in her married life.

So to achieve His goal of sending Mira abroad, God was playing Ram Lila here and He is quite good at it. I was getting married in UK. He engineered a plot and used B as His tool to break up my marriage plans, then made me plan to go to India to get married, even though I had no such plans to travel. He also created a situation to break up Mira's engagement. He also made sure that no one else would be forthcoming to be my partner. If this is how He manipulates His schemes, then why on earth does He pretend that He has given freedom to us humans. I ask my Maker - if He had decided to bring Mira to UK, then why did He choose me to be His puppet, a robot in this drama. Why did He use B to break up my verbal promise to a lady and finally throw her on the scrap heap with no fault of hers (I know she never married)? I do not know the fate of this Aligarh girl.

But I dare ask God - is that Your justice? It was Your plan to bring Mira to UK. May I ask humbly why did You use me to fulfil Your dreams? Who would love You, Oh God, when the other mortals would read my experiences and the way You manipulated my life? I bet that a lot would question Your integrity when they read this story and would lose their trust in Your so-called compassion and benevolence that You say You have for Your creation on this planet. You cannot be a benevolent God. You are a good schemer, a manipulator, a conspirator. That is why there are so many atheists on this planet, and that includes Bertrand Russell, Buddha and Mahavira. You will stand in the dock of the people's court. I would not like You to forget that justice would be done and it would certainly be in my favour.

However, continuing my story further...

A JOURNEY THROUGH PARTITION AND BEYOND

We were there for a couple of hours chatting and discussing various things, not all were connected with the marriage but in general to know each other. The time came to part as I had planned to return to Delhi the same day. I had already found out at the station the train times for Delhi. So I said, 'Ok it is time for me to go to the station to catch a train for Delhi.'

'I thought you would be staying for the night. I have already booked a room at a hotel for you to stay.'

'Sorry I did not know that I would be staying for the night. So I did not bring my clothes for the night. I have to go, sorry!'

'Why don't you stay? We will go to a movie tonight. In this way you will know me better and I will know you. Regarding your pyjamas, don't worry - we will find some solution for that.'

'Sorry I think I should go. I have told my parents that I would be returning to Delhi. If I don't return they would get worried.'

'OK. Come back in a couple of weeks' time to stay here for a week.'

'I will try but no promise.'

I know she was disappointed. She was very keen for me to stay but being a girl she did not wish to show her eagerness to persuade me. A girl's insistence can be easily misunderstood. We walked down from the lawn to the road, flagged down a rickshaw and I was on my way to Delhi.

I believe if I had stayed for the night and met up next morning I would be writing a totally different story here. The acquaintance could have turned into a friendship and who knows it could have ended up into a marriage. But fate had other plans. Why did fate, destiny, continue to manipulate me without even me being aware of it? I keep on harping on those two words because I cannot find any other reason for why we did not marry. Why it did not turn into a life relationship. My mind was possessed with some outer power which would not let me make my decisions freely. My destiny was sealed and I was powerless. My mental faculties had gone on holiday, my emotions seemed suppressed, and my being was under the control of a Control Freak. I had no idea what was happening and why everything was just moving like a dream. I feel that I let her down and rained on her plans and her dreams, which she must have been building up. Do I regret it? Yes of course I do, and very much. I think I must have hurt her badly. I do not forgive myself for that behaviour. I do not know what happened to her. I was just powerless before the big Almighty Schemer.

After reaching Delhi, I reported to my uncle. He was very keen to know what had happened. He was also surprised that I did not stay longer. We kept on trying to find another match but were not successful. I was a bit disappointed that I had come all the way from Britain to marry an Indian girl but now I was hitting brick walls, built one after the other by the attitude of the people. Most of the time, it was the lack of trust. People thought that what I was telling them about myself was all lies, nothing but lies. They thought that I might just be an attendant in a restaurant or a cleaner at some airport. The following episode will throw more light on this attitude. However during this period my uncle suggested a couple of times to go back to Aligarh to meet the girl again to find out more about her. He said he would play the role of her father, to give her away to me. I reported to my parents but somehow they were not that keen. They had not seen the girl. They had not known anything about her either. I believe it was the prejudice of my mother because the girl was suggested by my uncle. I had no problem in marrying her. I liked her, admired her, but the tussle between the elders to influence their child became an issue of ego and I had to pay the price for it. My parents never supported me. I was a chicken, timid, and fearful of offending them. I could not move decisively to look after my interests and my likings. Also I had no guts to defy the Almighty who was playing games with my life, hiding somewhere in the nooks and corners of this vast multi-verse. I was forced to submit to His wills.

The 6th, an Army Officer's Sister

Someone suggested that there was an army officer who had a sister and he was looking for a suitable match for her. It must be the talk of the town. It was just like the olden days when the kings used to spread the news all over their kingdom that they were going to marry their daughters to the winner of an open contest. I was intrigued and volunteered for the challenge. I had nothing to lose. I joined the bandwagon, not knowing who the other contestants were in the queue to garland the lady. This person gave me his telephone number to contact him. I phoned him and made an appointment to see him in his office. His talk on the phone with me was not warm but casual. It was a tone that, 'Yes I have a sister but if and when I get some suitable candidate I would marry her otherwise not bothered.' So even the beginning of the attempt was on a wrong footing. Had I lost my dignity and self-respect? Had I gone so low? I think I had. I had gone bonkers. I was a boy in India where I should have had an upper hand. Instead I was crawling on my knees with a begging bowl in my hand to plead to those who had some suitable young lady to give away to me because I had a pretty face; I was settled in England; was going to be an engineer in a couple of years; and a self-made, hardworking person. All these were great assets as bargaining tools but were not enough to convince the doubters and were not working in my favour. They had their own agendas. Half the time they don't listen and contemplate. In normal times they would be chasing the boys to get their daughters married but how come, within three years of my leaving India, all that culture had gone upside down.

A JOURNEY THROUGH PARTITION AND BEYOND

Think of fate man, just think about it. I had a battle with the will of the Almighty, the omnipresent and the most powerful.

Anyway, on the day of my meeting, I presented myself at his office. He was sitting in his big office in civilian dress. He thankfully greeted me with respect and offered me a chair to sit down. The pomp-ness of his office reminded me of the one where I had stood in front of a Delhi police chief and begged him to free me from the clutches of those brutal arms of that autocratic bureaucracy. That day I was trembling with fear and was nobody, but today I was talking to the same kind of authoritarian brute on equal terms.

I gave him a glimpse of my background, what I was doing in England, who was who in my family, and what were my future plans. I was now expert in this kind of introduction. I remembered every word of it like a parrot. He listened to my small talk attentively. The dice was already loaded against me. For him to see me was another ego trip for him. I was no match to his expectations. Here was an army officer who lived with his sister in his make-believe comforts and there I was on my knees to be considered as a match for her. He did not tell me anything about the lady. What does she do, what was her education, what are her ambitions? Nothing, but he never hesitated to reach conclusions about me. He pronounced his verdict authoritatively, as the army officers do, and they always think that they are right,

'I don't know if what you are telling me is right or wrong. There have been instances when the boys from Britain have come and have given a lot of tall stories about themselves that they are engineers, doctors etc, and got married here. Later on it was discovered that they were just factory workers or bus conductors, or doing some other odd low level jobs.' He was frank, straightforward, brutal, and was economising on courtesies. The army people like to impress you with their superiority. He had already executed me before getting the evidence. He had already announced that I was a liar without a trial.

'I understand your problem sir. There are all kinds of people on this planet.'

'Therefore I will write to the Indian High Commission in London to do searches on you. You give me all your details of the college where you are studying, your address where you live. Once I get those reports we may move forward.'

'But that would take some time and I have only three weeks left to be here. I have to go back to resume my studies.'

'Yes, it would take about three months. But you may call me in a couple of weeks' time. If I have the replies during that time I will let you know.'

This was the greatest disadvantage, to be seen to be on my knees. I had made him bigger than his boots because I was asking for the hands of his sister in marriage. It was not considered to be mutually beneficial. So we shook hands and parted. I must admit he was one of the typically arrogant army officers who are known for their outbursts. I admired his genuine concerns, like any brother, to protect his sister but it is his manners I am complaining about. I phoned him after a couple of weeks but he said he had heard nothing from UK. He never gave me any info about the girl. That showed that his attitude was that he was everything and I was nobody. So this episode rested to its natural death, leaving a scar on my memory lane.

Another Suitor: On A's Recommendations

When I left UK, B wrote a letter to his chummy friend A, who lived in Rajinder Nagar, New Delhi. I met him a few times as and when I was in Rajinder Nagar. He was working as an Engineer in CPWD (Central Public Works Department) at Delhi. He was young, handsome, and had married recently a young, smart, beautiful lady. His mother lived with him. One day I was at their house and I saw the sudden outburst of a shouting match between the couple. I was horrified. It made me think, 'Is that what I am heading for?' Was it worth going into that kind of a life? How two young people can ever fight on trivial matters - and it was a trivial matter. It just did not make sense to fight for. I do not criticise that now as I am an experienced person but it did raise my eyebrows at the time.

A also accompanied me to Mumbai when I went to get the delivery of the fridge, which had come from Britain. We became quite close as the time went by. I admired B's choice of friends.

He knew a family of two sisters who lived with their brother around Connaught Place. A made my appointment to go and see the younger sister who was an officer in the IAS (Indian Administrative Service) and was working somewhere in the central secretariat. A had already briefed me that out of the two girls it was the younger one who was smarter and good looking. He also said that they were keener to get her elder sister married first. She was working as a nurse in a local hospital. A also warned me that I should be careful in case I am pressurised to see the older one first. He had already given them my bio-data and told them that I would preferably like to marry the younger one because her age suits me better. But they resisted and said to him that they would not be interested to talk to me if I was not ready to see the older one first with a view to marrying her. A had resisted that. A found out when the younger one would be at home on her own and asked me to go and see her. I went to their flat in the evening at the time given to me by A. The young one was at the flat alone. She knew that I would be going to their flat as A had told her. Her brother was still working and was late in coming home and her elder sister was on her night duty. It had nothing to do with the physical attraction that mattered to me that much but I was not interested in marrying a nurse. Somehow I could not reconcile myself to the idea of marrying a lady who was following that noble and caring profession. Family life would be in the doldrums when the man is working and the wife is at home and the wife is working when the man is at home. Therefore A's opinion of physical attractiveness, though important, did not interest me. The beauty and physical appearances are always individual choices and are in the eyes of the beholder. It does not follow that what attracted A would have attracted me too. Therefore there was no point in seeing her and then later on finding excuses for saying no.

Hence it suited me to see the younger one when she was on her own. We talked for about an hour. She explained to me all about herself and their preference of the elder marrying first, as A had already told me. However I persuaded her to think of getting engaged with me now and marry later once her elder sister was married, provided she liked my credentials. She agreed to talk to her brother but warned me not to be hopeful. We parted with an understanding that she would let me know her family's decision on the following Sunday at a religious procession which was taking place at Daryaganj. I went to A next day and told him the outcome of our meeting.

On Sunday as agreed, I went to Daryaganj. I was looking for her in that huge crowd of people, like finding a needle in a haystack. Minutes turned into hours. I gave up hope. I thought the lady of Delhi had hoodwinked me. I was ready to catch a bus for home. All of a sudden I heard a shout and saw waving hands from the other side of the road. Surprise, surprise it was the young lady waving at me to get my attention. For a moment, rays of hope kindled in my heart. It must be good news, that is why she had come and was waving at me with a broad smile. We greeted each other. Then she exploded a bombshell, 'I am sorry to let you know that my brother does not agree with this marriage. He does not wish me to live abroad where if I get into some problems, he would not be able to reach me. So the answer is no.' I tried to persuade her with my positive reasoning that the world is shrinking fast. Foreign lands are not that foreign anymore. Travelling wise, London was nearer to Delhi than Mumbai. It takes only ten hours to reach Delhi from London by air. She said, 'I also tried to persuade him but was not successful. He does not like the engineering profession which you are following.'

'Then what does he like?'

'He promised to find me an army officer. I also would like to marry an army officer. So don't be disappointed. You will find a lovely partner soon.'

Inside I was now bleeding. How could I tell her that I am in a desperate situation because of my circumstances? The clock was ticking against me and within a couple of weeks I would be sailing back to Britain alone without a partner. This was my last hope. I had no one else lined up to meet. Uncle again reminded me to make a visit to Aligarh. I should have but I did not. Fate sometimes could be cruel. It had chosen someone else already and it was only playing a game of Ram Lila.

I came home and announced unceremoniously to my parents my intention to go back to Britain unmarried.

'Then what are you going to do? Are you coming back again to marry?' my mother asked.

'No idea. The future is yet too long to live. Something will turn up. It is not the end of the world.'

Panic Stricken Mother Goes into Action

They got panicky, without displaying their emotions to me. Mother got into a frenzy and went to see her sister's son-in-law who was working for the Indian Army as a civilian. I did not know about this. She had a meeting with him and his wife and explained the situation. They discussed between them some daughters of relatives who were of marriageable age and could be approached. One day mother took me to see him. He put forward some proposals. He suggested three young ladies. All of them were related to him. One was his daughter whom I knew very well. Another one was his wife's brother's daughter. Again I knew her well too. If these were related to him then they were also distantly related to me. I always considered them as my sisters. They all came from my mother's older sister's family. The third one was his brother's daughter. So he said, 'I have these three girls in my mind to suggest. If we have girls in the family, then why go out and seek other girls to marry.' His wife and my mother nodded in agreement.

He then gave me a brief background of these girls. I just sat there and listened to him. Sometimes people do not realise what exactly they are saying. Their intentions are good but they never think about the implications of their suggestions. This was exactly the case in this proposal. I said, 'I am thankful to you for your proposals. The first two are out of the question. I have grown up with them and whenever I met them I always considered them as my sisters. Now I just cannot change my thinking suddenly from a sisterly relationship to a wife's relationship. The mind would simply not accept it.'

'Well, they are distantly related. They are not sisters as such.' They tried to convince me.

'May be so but the thinking would continue to prolong in the mind. It will not be possible for me to marry them, no. But I am happy to see your brother's daughter.'

'Ok. She is also closely related to me. If the relationship materialises with her, I am happy too.'

I had heard about this girl a few years earlier. My mother had told me the approximate location where she lived. I used to walk to Kingsway Camp from

A JOURNEY THROUGH PARTITION AND BEYOND

Rajinder Nagar and her house was on the way. I must admit that I used to be on the lookout as I passed her house in case I could get a glimpse of her. A couple of times I even stopped for a couple of minutes in case she might wander out. But I was not lucky. As they say, the marriages are arranged in heaven. It appears to be true. At that point of time in life I did not know that one day she would be suggested as my marriage partner.

The meeting was arranged between the two families to meet at H's house. After everyone had assembled in the room, the young lady walked in, sandwiched between her two sisters. They deposited her about ten feet away on a chair opposite to me so that we could have free eye contact of one another. The sisters sat on either side of the lady as bodyguards. Being the elder of the three one could see who was in command. The younger ones appeared timid and innocents especially the youngest A.

The lady was not wearing her usual glasses. The game of cheating as it normally happens in arranged marriages was there to see. Some cards of openness were not put on the table. The truth was being economised. I did not know that she wore glasses until I discovered next day when we were going to Karol Bagh after the meeting to buy a ring and marriage ceremonial sari of her choice. Would I have the same opportunity to deceive them? No, I would not. All her family knew, including the matchmaker and yet they hid that fact from us. It was possible that I might have still married her but the freedom to make a decision was robbed from me. I have never said it but this is my auto-bio and I must be honest to say it.

After some formalities of introduction, soon an Indian traditional game of arranged marriages of digging out the truth and assessing the 'suitability' of one another was in full swing. Was it really a meeting of assessing the suitability under so many gazing eyes, I wondered? The game was nothing but eyewash and had to be played to convince the society we lived in. It was already a foregone conclusion that soon it was going to be a ceremony arranged by the 'minders' and the meeting was only a formality of giving the opportunity to the suitors to 'see' one another and that 'see' was only to assess the physical appearances without disapproval. The seal of acceptance and approval had already been stamped by the elderly marriage makers. That seeing between the couples had to be conducted stealthily. There were so many eyes and ears trained on you two. We were only stealthily gazing at one another by eye contact; we were assessing the looks, the behaviour, the etiquettes, and the general appearance of each other. We were looking at the body structure; the blushing mixed with shyness; and at the same time being deeply absorbed in our own thoughts of living together in future. We pretended that we were there; participating in the gossip of the surrounding relatives but nay, we were never there. There were never any dialogues to know the likes and dislikes of one another, what were our interests and hobbies, how we would like to live our future lives. It was the cruellest way to 'arrange' marriages. It was the marriage sentence of the whole life and they were all happy and enjoying seeing you being given a life sentence. Everyone present had some axe to grind. They were all guilty for this ceremonious cruelty. The couple were being crucified at the marriage altar and no one was feeling any guilt about it. I went through all this without any choices. In all the meetings to marry I had, the only time I could discuss my marriage freely was at Aligarh and that was cruelly torpedoed by the parents. However, soon some experienced one suggested, 'Hey, come on you two, talk to each other to find out about one another.'

Find out more about one another under those gazing eyes, impossible! The replies and questions would be all well-rehearsed and said like scriptures from Gita. They would never contain facts, and truth would never be told. Everyone present there assumed that the engagement and marriage were imminent between the two. It was a foregone conclusion unless something terribly would go wrong. The meeting was just a formality, just to rubber stamp it. But the formality had to be done. All these questions and answers were just eyewash. However the questions had to be asked and answers had to be given to satisfy the inquisitive nature of the grown-ups. It was a formality to prove to the world that arranged marriages do give freedom to question one another to make up their minds to marry. It was farce and cheating that was being presented as fairness and freedom to accept or reject the other. Though we were in our mid-twenties, yet for them we were still immature kids. So a typical immature question was thrown at me first.

'Do you smoke?' she asked as if that was the most important issue to affect her in future life.

'Yes, I do but not many, about 6-7 a day.' I replied.

'Do you drink alcohol?' she asked, again a typical question to control the life of a man.

'Yes I do, sometimes in company.' I did. I was in UK where a social drink was never considered as a taboo but a norm.

Now it was my turn. So I put my usual questions. Would she be happy to go to UK? Would she work? Would she be comfortable to live and share her life with my family? And so on. There were some more questions and answers that I don't remember.

It was just an immature dialogue. The present generation would make fun of me.

My ordeal was not yet over. More grilling was still in the pipeline and I was not aware of it. Soon after that first meeting was over, it was now the turn of some well-connected heavyweights of the family to be consulted. They had to consent to the relationship. They doubted my statement that I was studying in engineering. Suspicion is the biggest enemy of human relationship. Life never runs

A JOURNEY THROUGH PARTITION AND BEYOND

smoothly anyway. Nature always makes sure that it has thrown enough thorns in your way and you need to cross a lot of bridges before arriving at the destination. So I was not surprised not to see any roses on my way. To accept me or reject me, soon the investigations started in earnest by her other well-placed relatives.

The real problem was not me, as a person, but some other deep-rooted suspicions and motives within her family. The following were the major difficulties.

1. The attitude and behaviour of my mother that the opposite side had learnt from others. They had never met my mother. Their opinion was formed on the basis of what they had heard from the hearsay. I did not know about this. Even if I had known, my defence of my mother would not carry very far anyway.

2. Mira's aunt, my cousin, was not very popular in her in-law family. She was considered selfish, self-centred, aggressive, and possessive. As she had suggested this marriage proposal, therefore whatever she might have said about my family was under suspicion and scrutiny. Even her mother-in-law strongly objected to her proposal by saying, 'Hum, how dare she suggest that her cousin marry my lovely granddaughter. I will never agree to this relationship. I would not let her marry in her family. Never.' Such prejudices were very difficult to overcome. Such utterances were poisonous for the future relationships. How much that had created adverse feelings towards my family and me in Mira's mind only she can answer. But in my married life Mira certainly had said many unpleasant things about my family. I can only conclude that such outbursts from a respected grandma of the family must have affected Mira a lot. Otherwise, not knowing or even meeting any of my family members, how could she have such views. In such circumstances, I believe that it was better that they had rejected me rather than inflicting on me and my family strong adverse opinions for life. In life, one can only be answerable for one's own actions and not for anyone else's and that includes all relations and friends.

3. Were there any objections from her maternal uncles? I don't know. They were all businessmen, living together in civil lines (the administrative area) of Old Delhi. They were very supportive to the family. They are also Grover family as is my mother.

4. On her father's side, Mira had two well-placed and well-known uncles and an aunt. One cousin in Delhi was a chief engineer (CE) of CPWD Delhi. He had daughters married to sailors and army officers. The other was a well-known doctor. He never married. Their sister (more about her later) was married to a doctor, a very nice fellow who stayed with us in 1980. This couple had one daughter who studied medicine in UK, lived in America too and finally went back to India.

This whole family was in arms against us. The tragedy was that none of them had met my family or knew us. Maybe my family was not to their level. Maybe we were relatively not that well-connected and were of an unknown brand. But if they had some reservations, they should have coughed them out in the early stages rather than showing their colours after our engagement. Or even better they should have helped the family to find a better boy suited to their dreams. But why place all that negativity on me and my family. It left a permanent scar on me for life.

A couple of days after the engagement I had a call from the matchmaker that I was to accompany him to see CE at his bungalow in New Delhi. It was a lovely morning. We sat in his lovely well-maintained garden to answer some of his genuine questions which were bothering him and his brother and sister. As they were a well-connected family, they used to hear a lot of stories in which the boys coming from abroad would boast about their good jobs, good houses and stylish life, when in fact they were working as labourers. So they were keen to dig out the truth of whether what I was saying to them was truth or total deception. I cannot blame them for such an attitude and enquiry. Only those who do such tricks should be worried. I was clean and always believed in putting all the cards, including the dirty ones, on the table for examination. Why cheat, there is no need to do that. It was their genuine well-placed concern. Which parent would not worry about their daughter? No one can hand over their precious loved one to a stranger who may be a criminal. To me, it was a bit annoying, as I was telling the truth, nothing but the whole truth. All the genuine people would feel hurt with such insulting behaviour and questioning of their honesty and integrity. But then it was not written on my forehead that I was telling them the truth. So the enquiry was welcome and amusing. It was a great learning curve for me. It was not so easy to run away legally with a woman without being challenged by her guardians.

I was not the only one who felt that way. A few years later, another person I knew got married in India. He used to complain bitterly about his experiences of matrimonial investigations. He was asked bluntly how much salary he was drawing as an accountant. He told them the real figure, including the tax deductions, he was getting. Instead of believing his words, the family phoned to his office in London to confirm the amount. He just could not believe that people in India could be that brutal. He still continues to bleed with those unpleasant memories. Anyway, with so many questions and answers with CE, I felt that I had managed to convince him that what I was telling him and others in their family was true. The meeting was over and we came back. But the doubts still lingered in CE's mind. He set up another meeting with me and this time with my father. We came back after answering some more questions. Perhaps this time he was happier.

A JOURNEY THROUGH PARTITION AND BEYOND

CE's sister phoned him in the evening and he convinced her inquisitive mind too that I was following my studies. After this meeting with CE the message was sent to Mira's parents that their family was happy and they could go ahead with the engagement ceremony.

The day was fixed and the engagement ceremony took place at Mira's house at Karol Bagh. The marriage day was fixed for 3rd September 1961, again at the bride's house, an Indian tradition. The preparations were in full swing. We did not have much time for the preparation as I had to be back to UK to resume my studies. The marriage procession was to leave from my uncle's home. The dinner for the marriage night was to be arranged by her maternal uncles. Some tussle started between the two uncles on the menu of the dinner. My uncle insisted that the menu must have non-vegetarian dishes and her uncles insisted that they were bound by the family traditions never to serve non-vegetarian foods on marriages. The uncles had a couple of meetings between themselves to iron out their differences. My uncle told me that if the meat was not served, he would not attend the marriage. So we had a stalemate and this skirmish between the uncles went on till the marriage day and eventually my uncle relented and accepted the vegetarian dinner. It was a battle between two egotistical people. I was happy to know that there would be no non-vegetarian dishes. I would have cried all my life for those slaughtered animals ending up on the dinner tables.

On 3rd September as the evening approached and the darkness set in, I was ceremoniously mounted on a horse, decorated with flowers. We reached the marriage house. I had all the relations present. My friend Vohra, from Jodhpur, also joined. After brief introductions, we had our dinner. Around midnight the marriage ceremony started and went on for more than two hours until dawn. It was quite a tiring business. It gave me the taste of what was coming in future – the harder and more demanding life. I have become a wiser man. I just don't get why people get married. Why the two are bonded for life? Why the meeting between the two cannot be a one-night stand with no commitments except if afterwards you get children? Why not negotiate the terms and conditions for the night only with no financial gains on either side? Why does one have to spend one whole life with one spouse when God has thrown so many beauties and handsome men all over the planet? Of course, this would not fit for couples who are in love and would like to stay together forever. But normally the true love in marriage only lasts up until the honeymoon and then it is nothing more than a struggle to dominate and control the other. This system has been operating for millenniums and it is time that it is looked into a bit more seriously. Millions of couples are suffering although no one likes to admit it. We all know that there are only very rare couples who have not played infidel to their partners.

Honeymoon at Missouri

The next day 4th September was spent on meeting the relations. In the evening a small reception was arranged in a small marquee installed outside uncle's house where all my colleagues from NPL had come. After the reception we boarded a train to go to the hill station Missouri. We had planned to stay in a house owned by Mira's relation. My mother tried to persuade me to stay on in Delhi for whatever days I was in India rather than go to Missouri, but I did not like the idea of being part of the crowd. The honeymoon is a personal matter where two souls meet to know each other. So I insisted on going to Missouri. My mother suggested that if I did not wish to be a part of a crowd, I should hire a room at a Delhi hotel but I just wanted to be away. So we boarded a train from Delhi around 10pm for Dehradoon, where we arrived next morning. From there we took a taxi for Missouri. It was just an hour's drive.

When we arrived at Missouri, the tourist season was already over. The main bazaar through which we drove had very few people shopping. The taxi stopped in front of the house where we were to stay. We took our baggage out, opened the door and deposited ourselves on a couple of dilapidated, unwelcoming chairs. The disappointment dawned sooner than expected. The floors were not damp proof and moisture was seeping from the ground thus creating an unpleasant humidity in the room. It reminded me of my old days of living as a tenant at Gwalior. Also we had an added problem of cooking and shopping. No, that was not the place for a honeymoon where we were to indulge in shopping and cooking. I said to Mira that we should get out of that place and find a hotel. Being a tourist place, there were no shortages of hotels in the town to suit all pockets. The tourist peak time had finished and there were plenty of them to welcome us with open arms. We walked out and saw a big hotel around the corner, with a big banner outside 'We Welcome You, Come and Stay with Us'. We went in to inquire if there was a room available. To our surprise nearly all the hotel rooms were empty. There were only 5-6 people staying there. The rest of the holiday-makers were gone, back to the plains where the September breeze was more pleasant and the temperatures were dropping by the day. We were delighted and surprised to know that we had choices of rooms without breaking a bank. We selected a room on the first floor. The whole floor was empty and we were the only occupiers. The stay also included breakfast and dinner. We hurried down the road to fetch our baggage. The staff helped us to take our baggage to our room. Everyone at the hotel was happy and excited to know that they were sharing the company of a newly-wed couple who had come for their honeymoon at their beautiful hill station where in olden days the white employees of the Raj used to come to get away from the burning heat of the plains. But that day a young unknown, turned Wog being in Britain, had come to enjoy his honeymoon. They were also happy that they would

A JOURNEY THROUGH PARTITION AND BEYOND

have something to do rather than get bored all day without any visitors to take care of.

After depositing our baggage we enquired about any sightseeing places in the town. We were told there were none. With no sightseeing places on a hill station, then what do the tourists who flog there in the summer do, just catch flies and have a hate and love affair with mosquitoes?!

'Are there any parks around where we can go out and sit in the open sunshine?' we asked. They gave us the direction but suggested that we hire a cycle rickshaw as it was a bit far away. We came down, walked down the alley, hired a rickshaw that inched its way through the narrow winding streets and dumped us after ten minutes ride to a so-called 'park'. 'Is that a park?' I asked the driver.

'Yes, sir it is.'

'Are you sure it is not the wrong place?'

'No this is the only park in the town.'

Good God, for heaven sake, was that a tourist attraction or was it some kind of funny joke? Or had the tourist industry gone bonkers there?

There were hardly any flowers, bushes, or trees. It was just a vast lawn with dry grass that was praying to heavens to soak it with much-needed showers. Even if I wished to be romantic on my only – the first and the last honeymoon of life - there was no chance in hell. The heart just sank at the sight of that dry wasteland. How some people had suggested to us going to Missouri for the honeymoon was beyond me. What made those uncles buy that 'beautiful' flat there? And what were they doing there for weeks? Were they bored in their high-class bungalows on the plains, fed up with visiting the pubs and clubs, or were they trying to get away from that high society and looking for some lonely corners of the hills for making love to their spouses? I had no clue. It was a mystery to me and I had no time to discover it. I had no idea what I was supposed to do there for a week except to sit there in the 'park' and look at the distant horizon full with scenery of hills and valleys which were dotted with beautiful tall green fir trees. We could not walk down to those miles-away places and get lost in that wilderness. It was too risky to be lost with a young newly-wed girl. Surprisingly there were no waterfalls, no fast-moving streams to create a soothing music for the ears and where you could go and bathe in the morning. I don't remember seeing monkey gods as there were in Dalhousie, where I had gone twice when in Gurukul. There were no malls where we could stroll in the evening to enjoy the cool soothing breeze touching our hearts; to walk around with arms around the waists in harmony under the close scrutiny of the heavens as I had read the Brits were doing in their colonial times. Compared with Dalhousie it was just a very dull and desolate place. I had no choice but to reconcile myself to it and make the best.

We got down and asked the rickshaw to come back in an hour's time to pick us up. He did.

For dining there were hardly any souls around to share the chattering noises of other guests. There was pin-drop silence in the dining room as if the whole world had gone into slumberland when the evening was still so young. In that big dining hall, we were the only two souls. The attention we were getting became sometimes very embarrassing. There were so many questions we were getting from the staff and the manager. What would you like to have at breakfast? What time should we wake you up? Would you like to have tea in bed and what time? What would you like to eat at lunchtime, dinnertime? Are we comfortable being newly-weds? It was more than we could chew. Some people may like that attention but I felt embarrassed. I wanted to be left alone to mind my own business.

My First 'Moon'-Night

On that first night, the usual dark night was there with all its glory in the sky but the moon was missing.

What is a honeymoon anyway? How do you celebrate it? What exactly you do that night? I had no idea except what I had seen on the cinema screens. Nobody enlightened me, and nobody threw any hints to me, including my friends. I had never read any book on the subject and I had never flirted with anyone. I never had romance with anyone and if had made love to anyone, then that was done in dreams, far, far away from the real world. I was still a virgin and so was she. I knew what normally does happen in that lone night but I had no clue how to start the dialogue between two young strangers, finally leading to the actions.

Should I let you people, the readers, peep into my personal affairs on that first night? Would you hate me, would you make fun of me, would you laugh at me once you know what happened? Well, that is your prerogative. Only I know the truth. If I have to tell you about me then I must tell it all, the whole truth what happened. If you don't like it, tough! I handled it as I saw fit at the time. If you had done it differently then it is your prerogative. Whatever you would be saying now, you would be saying it with hindsight after reading my experiences. But you would not say it with spontaneity. So here we go and you read the facts. I let you enter into my private life. Rather than let this episode die with me for ever, allow me to share it with you.

We both had a quiet dinner. The darkness of the night was setting in. It was all deathlike silence in the halls and the corridors of that big hotel. There were no street lights and the inside dim lights were adding to the melancholy of the general environment. There was no music and there were no dancers either. There was nothing else to do so we found our way to our bedroom on the first floor.

A JOURNEY THROUGH PARTITION AND BEYOND

For the moonlight there have to be some vital ingredients in place. There should be a romantic environment, a soothing music to cool your nerves, the vibrations of the two loving hearts leading into that direction, the touch between the two bodies, the dialogue to create the melody between the two souls, finally resulting into the melting of the two energies to merge together. None of these ingredients were there for the two bodies to melt together. If they had, then it would be nothing more than the meeting of two bodies hypocritically indulging in meeting the requirements of sexual lust, and mechanically discharging the energies of one body into the other. For me that was no honeymoon but a 'lustful' moon. But it was all just silence, silence, and nothing but silence. We were both unknown to one another. We were both introvert. We both were not flowing on the wavelength on which lovers should. We were incapable of merging into one another. In that kind of the environment we moved towards our bedroom.

On that first night at the Missouri hotel for which I had defied my mother's idea of staying in a hotel at Delhi, nothing happened. The lady may be in the same bed in which I was but she was totally new to me. She was just a stranger. I did not know her. I did not know how even to converse with her. I was totally ignorant, naïve and I did not know the ropes of seducing a woman. I had no experience of it and I did not know where to start, what to say to her, and how to throw seeds of passion in her direction to incite her and excite her dormant nerves. I also had no idea how to make advances towards her. She might not have liked them. I was scared in case I was invading her privacy and violating her body. I did not know those flattering and polishing words to hoodwink the partner, talking about love but in fact trying to use her body for my selfish motives. I had no clues about verbalising such egocentric phrases. I was a sincere, honest, and decent bloke who was free from the cunning attitudes of the young. Engulfed in those strange thoughts, I went to sleep. I was tired from all the commotions of the marriage, and sleepless nights of not having a settled residence. The cool fresh air of the mountains also did not help. And with that kind of internal mental battle, we both had gone into dreamlands until repeated knocks on the door woke us up. It was a call for the morning 'tea in bed'. Such important nights of life, once in a lifetime, do nothing else but create worries and fear. What would the partner think? Would she think that I am not a man? A lot of ladies would certainly conclude that but I do not know how my other half thought. However if I had failed to do something about it for the second night, I would certainly be misunderstood. The first night I could explain with excuses, but how would I explain the next night. I woke up with anxieties about how I would face this dilemma for the following night.

We got ready, went down, and had our lovely breakfast. There was no one else except us for the attention of the well-trained staff and the chef. We were being served whatever we wanted. While the breakfast was great and delicious and the attention and the service were showered perfectly, inside me I was anxious to sort out the problem for the coming night. The anxiety makes things even worse. Society had set the goal for the moon nights. You've got to go for the body; with love if possible otherwise you've got to penetrate into it without bothering about love. But love is not a commodity which can be acquired. It is a mysterious phenomenon, and it only happens at first sight. It can never be created with time between the two souls on any night, first or last. Some people may say that they 'love' but to me it is a very loosely-used word. It builds its nests where truth abides, where trust is never shaken, where devotion and harmony live. It cannot be shaken by hardships, rather it welcomes it. It takes the lovers to the brink of madness. True love does not care about society and its contractors who try to impose their own rules. It faces them head on with courage and single-mindedness. It does not care about the consequences. It moves towards its goal with vigour and unparalleled devotion. It is the Divine which guides and shows the path and that path has no map, no previous history. It is the path you have to make, you have to search for it. And it would be a unique path only for you to follow and not for others to jump onto it. It will never become a beaten track for anyone. It is just like searching for God, for enlightenment, and for eternal peace.

Love is a mysterious phenomenon. No one knows when, where, how, and with whom it will happen and click. But it is a wonderful feeling to crave for someone; to breathe for someone; to live for someone; and to die for someone. It never happens to everyone. It only happens rarely and to rare people. It is no one's property. Love is for life, for perpetuity, and is to last for seven generations, as per belief in India. It is not something which happens for a while and then shifts itself onto some other being. It never changes its direction and its loyalty. It has no boundaries to localise it. It is vast and limitless. It is something rare and when true love happens, it is a divine gift. It is a suffering, be warned. It is not a bed of roses and has a lot of thorns. But it makes you steely, flexible, humble, and silent. It tempts you to leave this canny world. You hate this world and you want to renounce it. Love can never be explained, defined, and described in words. Words have no expressive power to infuse it with emotions. It can only be experienced. It just wakes up - why and from where, no one knows. It is an inner feeling which arises from one's deep inner being. It sometimes can be confused with acquaintance, affection, and friendship. With love you enter into the other soul, you melt into it, you merge into it, and the sexual act just happens and you do not intentionally make it happen. It just follows naturally on its own accord. And the meeting of those two energies then becomes the divine act and the meeting place is His temple. It is something pure and has the blessings of God. Without love, sex is an animal act and the one who indulges into it is behaving like a beast. The

A JOURNEY THROUGH PARTITION AND BEYOND

offspring born out of love become the sages and the contributors of the future while the others become the burden on this mother earth. That is why most of humanity today is suffering and the planet is being burdened with billions of unwanted, uncreative, unethical human bodies, only representing the matter without soul. But to be a winner in the first night without love, you have to be a tiger in the bed. That is what they all expect. You must be lustful. You must be brutal to violate the privacy of the other soul whom you had just met only a few hours earlier. You must be a winner, a hunter as they say men should be. Failure is the worst disaster. No one permits it. Society only loves the winners. All the close relations and friends would ask personal questions about how the moon was as if the moon is so easily accessible. It is surrounded by the darkest nights. How did you perform? Relations you may ignore but friends would ask searching questions of how, when, and where? They would like to know your juicy story of the first night, how you conquered the other unknown body; and if you tell them the truth that may create a disaster and may prove injurious to your ego. So you worry about how the truth is to be economised and it is difficult for those who are not habitual liars. If you tell the truth you would not be able to show your face to them. Everyone would look down on you. I just did not know how to invade her body, touch it, stroke it, and kiss it. Would she be happy or would she just push me away? A boy has to face all these issues with a girl on his first attempt. These were all fantasies of my mind. It was my mind which was manipulating, planning, and was weak in executing the manly desires. I was confused and I did not know the right road for me to tread.

Rightly or wrongly I decided to go and seek out help. In the morning after breakfast, as we walked out of the hotel to go to the rickshaw stand, I saw a doctor's surgery. I asked my wife to wait outside, as I needed some medication. There were no other patients there.

'Doc, I just got married. Last night was my first moon night with the young lady. I had no biological urge and no erection. I know that sexually there is nothing wrong with my organs and yet nothing happened. Why? Can you help?' I asked blushingly.

'There cannot be anything wrong as you say. It can happen sometimes if you are too anxious for the action. But don't worry. I will give you an injection, which will help. I am also giving you a prescription. You may get it from the chemist down the road.'

So he administered the injection, a psychological trick played in India by the doctors. It boosts the patient's morale. He feels that the doctor has done a great job in sorting out his health problem and it also adds a lot more money into the doctor's coffers. I paid the money and looked for the chemist. Mira asked if everything was ok. I said yes, he prescribed some medicine, which I would get

159

from the chemist. I went into the chemist, asked Mira to stay outside again. As the assistant saw the prescription, he looked at my face fiercely as if I was some kind of a criminal who had done something awful. Then he looked out with lustful eyes to see who that lady victim was and if he could somehow help himself to the prize. I froze. I felt brutalised and low. He knew what that medicine was for. I took the medicine and rushed out. A few steps down the road, I looked back. He was still gazing at us with his sarcastic grin. I cannot forget that grin and I am sure he would not have forgotten the story either. He must have told the story to his lovely wife to prove that he was a tiger in the bed alright. I never went back on that route to the hotel. I felt awfully embarrassed. There was also the danger that such people can take advantage of the situation in which you were caught. The day was gone, the night arrived. I was dreading it. I had no biological urge to do anything. The medicine and the injection could not create any urge either. But who would know if the injection given to me was genuine. It was India. Anything was possible. It could have been just water to create a psychological effect. The days of Viagra were not on the horizon as yet. So the days we stayed there at the hotel, nothing happened between us. Mira never showed any feelings or anxiety about it. We never talked about it either. She showed a lot of understanding and never questioned. I do not know if she had read any anxious feelings on my face. I would never know. This subject is taboo and everyone likes to bury it under the carpet. The doctor must know of such conditions among his many patients and that is why he only showed it as a casual phenomenon, and I agree with him.

We stayed there for four days. We hired a taxi back to Dehradoon, stayed for the night in a hotel, and went to watch a movie, and then went to bed. She had her monthly period now. I felt relieved that God had helped and saved my skin. In Delhi, life was very busy. Every evening we were invited for dinner. Everywhere the food was very rich and plentiful. I just could not manage to eat more than one meal a day. It was getting hard. We stayed in Delhi for six more days. We were then on our way to Mumbai to catch an Italian ship 'Roma' for Genoa and then to London by train. My parents came to Mumbai to see us off. At that point I was short of money to pay for two tickets for London. The fridge which I took to sell was still not sold and hence the shortage of funds. However my mother had some distant relations in Mumbai with whom we were staying. We asked them if they would buy the fridge. They agreed to buy it. I had now enough money to book our tickets plus some pocket money to reach UK. I had charged them the cost of fridge plus Rs 150 more to recover the costs of getting the fridge released from the customs. The buyer still continues to complain that I overcharged them. They are businessmen and insist that the accounts must be right to a penny. It is history. I will be happy to refund that silly small difference of only £2 when I go back to India. However I am grateful that they bought it otherwise it would have created a

A JOURNEY THROUGH PARTITION AND BEYOND

little hiccup in the finances. There were no card systems, and even if there were I did not have any. In the worst scenario, we would have been stranded in Mumbai until I had received funds from UK where I had my savings in the post office.

Back To Britain

During that voyage we became friends with the Handa family. He was coming to do his PhD in Economics from the London School of Economics. His wife was a teacher. They had a seven-year-old son and insisted on speaking to him, all the time, in English. Later they immigrated to Canada in 1967.

We also became good friends with B who was coming here to work. We used to meet very often.

Nasty experiences at the ship

1.   We did not have a cabin as that was expensive. We had booked our beds in a sharing dormitory. I was sharing with a few more men and Mira had her bed in the women's dormitory. All the dormitories had a common bathroom complex where the toilets were built on one side of the complex and the showers on the other. The ship was full of Italian tourists and Indian/Chinese immigrants of all kinds of hue and colour. A lot of them were from Punjab villagers. Some were also from the island of Mauritius. Many did not have the civic sense of using the toilets and showers. I was an early riser to finish off my daily chores before the crowds. On our first morning in the ship, I went to the toilets about 5am. I thought I was the first clever one there to beat the crush. It was all dark and no lights were on. As I walked in the shower areas, I noticed that I had stepped on to some soft dough-type mass. Hey what is that, I asked. I rushed to the toilet areas to find out. My suspicion was right, it was a human shit. My chappals were buried into it. I hurried to switch on the lights. To my horror I saw the whole area was dotted around with shit. It was very disgusting. I took my shower, washed my chappals, and carefully walked through those patches back to my digs. From then onwards I changed my timings to visit the bathrooms. I do not know how the ship staff coped with that situation. They must have hated the type of Indians who were heading to Europe to make those countries as their future homes.

2.   We had sailed a few hundred miles from Mumbai. All of a sudden the ship stopped in the middle of the Ocean. There was no announcement for the reason for it. An hour had gone by, and then two, still with no announcement. We were getting anxious to know the reason. A waiter, who was serving us meals in the dining hall, happened to pass by. 'Can you please tell me why the ship has stopped?' He did not answer but continued to walk away. 'Hey please, I am asking you to tell me why the ship has stopped?' He turned around

and retorted, 'Do you know French?' 'No, I don't,' I replied. 'Then don't talk to me. If you wish to talk to me talk in French.' His tone was now more aggressive and was loaded with anger. 'But you spoke so many words in English; you could have replied to my question in English as well. There is no need to be aggressive.' He just walked away. A proud Frenchman from Africa loaded with arrogance.

The Mauritius community had a couple of cabins booked for them. They were no more than 100. Something went wrong between one of their countrymen (M) and me. I do not remember what it was. I was on my own on the deck, enjoying the fresh breeze and the sight of the rich salty blue water of the Indian Ocean. Normally I had always been with Mira but on that occasion she went with Bhalla (B) and was not with me. A couple of M's compatriots came to me and said that I had to accompany them to their cabin to see M. They alleged that I had said something wrong to M. He would like to sort it out with me. I denied that I had said anything of that sort to anyone. I even did not remember what he looked like. It is obvious that in a human relationship, if you do upset someone, you too get upset and you keep on brooding on it until time heals it. The mind does not allow you to forget the face of the man with whom you had an altercation. So I went with them to remove any misunderstanding. As I entered through the cabin door, M instructed his companions to shut it. There were some 8-10 people in the room. M was lazing on his bunk bed. He instructed me authoritatively to sit on another bed opposite and started throwing his questions at me very aggressively. You had said to me over there, so and so. He kept on saying I did and I kept on denying that I did not and it was a misinterpretation of what I had said. I knew right in the beginning that I was in deep hot water when M ordered the door to be shut behind me and I was confronting about ten fierce-looking young people dotted around the cabin. But I kept my nerves outwardly but in my heart I was very frightened. M was getting angrier as the conversation progressed. He behaved like a ringleader, a gang leader of the crowd present there. His eyes were raining fire; his body was trembling with rage. It was a complete stalemate between us. He insisted again and again with accusations and I kept on denying them. He finally shouted with a threatening voice: 'You know what you have said and you keep on denying it.'

'But I have not said it. You have to trust me. I had no intentions of saying it. I don't know you and why would I say it.'

'You can deny as much as you like. You can see how many boys are here. If we kill you right now and dispose of your body in the sea, nobody would find a trace of you.'

'I understand that. That is why you brought me to the cabin. I know I am facing so many determined people.'

'You don't have to fight so many of us. Just choose any one of us.'

A JOURNEY THROUGH PARTITION AND BEYOND

'Sorry I don't like fighting. I have never fought with anyone in my life. I cannot fight.'

'You are a coward.'

'Maybe you are right but I cannot fight. It is my nature'

As this aggressive dialogue was going on for nearly half an hour, there was a bang on the door. It was Mira shouting and banging on the door. She was saying, 'Open the door.' First they ignored it but then he told her to go away, we were just having a friendly conversation. She insisted that she was not going away. She would like to come in. Now their centre of attention shifted from me to the door. After a few minutes of fierce conversation between Mira and M, and Mira threatening that she would go and fetch the ship staff for help, M relented. He asked the door minder to open the door. B and Mira walked in. Threats continued for another few minutes and eventually M asked me to apologise for what I had said to him and he would let me go. M's ego had to be satisfied. The door was firmly shut again except that we were now three against ten. I decided to withdraw what I had (not) said to keep the peace and we were let out with a warning, 'Watch it in UK. We are also going there. If we ever see you there on the British streets, we will sort you out.' He had to say that to save his face from his crony supporters who were surrounding us and were waiting for their master's orders to thrash us. What a childish egotistic behaviour. You pick up a brick on this planet, and they are there hiding themselves like scorpions. God saved me with the timely arrival of Mira at the scene. I do not know how she found out that I was kidnapped to be murdered that day by some crazy thugs who were looking for some fun right in the middle of the Ocean. Thank God I have never bumped into them on London streets so far.

Outing in Genoa

After a brief stay at Messina and Naples, we headed towards Genoa. We looked around in Genoa. B also joined us. He was surprised to see the bargaining and the cheating displayed at the market places in the European towns. A watch was offered to him for £10 and then finally was sold to him for £2. He said how was that possible? We always thought that the white skins were a lot superior to us in honesty and decency but they were worse. I reminded him of the colonial times when they acted so deceptively, cunningly bribing their way to cheat the locals and the rulers of the countries wherever they had gone. They also plundered those countries to bone dry and left them to their destiny when there was nothing more left to suck. If there ever is a God, they will never be forgiven for the crimes they have committed against the humanity living in those shores.

We spent a day in Genoa, boarded a train in the evening and we were on our way to Dover where we arrived in mid-morning, after crossing the Channel.

We boarded a train for Victoria and H entered the compartment first. There were a few Caribbean passengers who were already well settled and seated and were heading for London. As soon as they saw us, one of them gave some derogatory remarks about us. I did not hear those comments. When we settled down, I asked H what they were saying. He said, 'Here come the coolies of India.'

'But why did they call us coolies. The coolies we have at the railway stations in India. How come they know this Indian word?'

'When Indians were taken as settlers to the Caribbean Islands by the British to control the locals who were also taken there as slaves to be sent to America, the British introduced us to the locals as coolies. Hence they continue to call Indians this derogatory name, "coolies".'

'That is very silly coming from the other immigrants to this country. They are as much hated in UK as we are. I am disgusted with that attitude, coming from the other colonial people who were also oppressed and ruled by the British.'

H had the knowledge of the past history of India. I did not know all that. He was well read and that is why he was heading to LSE for the higher education. It left a nasty scar on my memory. How humans hate each other based on the name of culture, religion, race, and colour. Will they ever learn to live together in harmony? I believe no, never. Human history is very ancient. If they could not live amicably in the past five thousand years, they will not be able to live in future either, until and unless they are enlightened to the core of their heart where only love would have its abode.

We reached Victoria Station in the evening. B, M, and my brother were there to receive us. Malik had not only come to greet us but also to tell me that we should go and live in his room and he would go and sleep in his friend's house. It was an unforgettable gesture. He had no more vacant room in his flat for me to stay. All the rooms were occupied. We have not forgotten his kindness. That offer was open until we found another place to live.

We had a bit of an argument with the Customs at the station. This time I did not wish to entangle myself with fruitless arguments. I paid our tax whatever they asked for and walked away.

We reached home. My brother was also staying in another room in the same house. He had a job now. He made good friends with B & Co.

Next day I resumed my studies and was back to college. Mira was settling well. She did not know cooking at all. So she would ask me the methods of cooking. The time of coming home without any cooked meals was over. There was also a companion at home to talk to. I never felt lonely after that. I had a partner at home – good or bad, angry or loving, caring or hating. One has to accept all of that from your partner.

A JOURNEY THROUGH PARTITION AND BEYOND

The Final Moon Meeting of the Two Energies

Mira was brave and very accommodating for the marital situation she was facing as a woman. That is what I think. I never shared my views with her on this subject; even if I wanted she would not talk about it anyway. It is more likely that any other woman in her position, married for so many weeks to a man when nothing happened between us as a married couple, would have declared me as an impotent and incompetent man in bed. She would have walked out of my life, dumping me while still in India without taking any chances of accompanying me to that far away land called UK.

I would love to talk to some other women, truth tellers, about what they would have done in the circumstances in which Mira was caught. I bet most, if not all, would have deserted me within 24 hours.

Shobbah, a woman novelist from Mumbai and a well-known writer, declares in her book that a woman loves to marry a man who

1. Has a hefty bank balance and an American Express card with unlimited spending limits
2. Has a chauffeur-driven Rolls and
3. Is a tiger in the bed.

She is a woman and she knows what she is saying about most women.

We had two single beds in Malik's room. We slept in our respective beds. There were no advances on my part. I just did not know how to invade her privacy even though she was sleeping on a bed next to me. I did not even know her after so many weeks of marriage, just how to start a conversation which would lead me to intimacy. While I was facing such dilemmas, I did not know what kind of a torture Mira was going through. Would she be thinking that she was now married to a man who was not a tiger as expected by nearly all women? If he is ok, would that mean that she was not attractive to the man she married? A few more nights had gone by. I did not keep count of them. Then on one night it just happened – naturally and when no other thoughts were perturbing me. I was not even thinking of invading her for sex or for lustful advances. I just slipped, to her surprise, into her bed. The winter month of October was just cosy during the day but chilly at night. I don't know how I ventured into her bed but I did. From where came all that courage I had gathered after so many confused and dark nights, I cannot answer. I was not thinking anymore. I had banished all the crony ideas from my head that were obstructing me from building up man-to-woman relationship. It was the heart that took the charge of the bodily functions that night. With no objections from the willing partner, I dared to remove the obstructive sari, and the underwear covering her bottom. She co-operated. She was ready for her long overdue honeymoon. She positioned herself. She knew the position a woman should adopt in bed with her partner but I did not. I jumped up in position and thrust my part in the darkness of the night. Suddenly I noticed the heat on my part. I knew something had happened. She confirmed that it had gone into the right place. In the next few moments we forgot the world. We were the only two. Nothing else existed. It was an unbelievable feeling which cannot be described in words. It only has to be experienced. It appeared that at last we had conquered the world of marriage that night.

So on that night what happened, happened wholly and completely. The whole body went into a feeling of bliss. Every cell of the body was vibrating in harmony and enjoying the gift of Nature. The two energies had finally met. She met her inner man and I met my inner woman and the duality of us both disappeared. We are born out of the two energies and we carry those two energies for life. We disappeared into that memorable experience of life for the first time since the time we both had attained our puberty. It was the meeting of the two bodies in the presence of the divine. It is the divine which created the experience of losing the consciousness and memory momentarily at the peak of the interchange. So how can the divine be absent when it was all happening in the real world?

When the two energies meet, they create a huge spark. They bring about a storm, a tsunami. So we were lost in that first experience of a lifetime to which, as animals, we are all entitled to have. In her rare admissions on this subject, Mira confided to me in her later years with her unguarded words 'I cannot forget the night. I remember everything about what and how it happened in that night.'

That night she too lost her virginity. She gave her body voluntarily yet not the whole one; it was just a bit of it. The permission was granted only to reach as far as the animal instinct of penetration allowed. I had no permission to reach or touch the upper parts of the body where the human love reaches. The two human bodies met but in a very restrictive manner. While the animal instinct was allowed to accomplish its goal, the human element was banned. The hunger and the starvation of the stomach were allowed to be fulfilled but the appetite of the heart remained unfulfilled. I became a tiger in the bed alright but I was still deprived of the human love.

In later life a woman doctor joked in ladies' company that men are only mad to have that 'little hole'. When I heard that, I protested. What we need is not the 'hole' but the love, the meeting of the two souls, and the intermingling of the two energies. The need of a 'hole' is an animal instinct, love is human. It is in the meeting of those two energies that a new energy is created. That is how we are all created. When the negative and positive poles of electricity are joined together, they give birth to a third energy – light. Light illuminates the environment and

A JOURNEY THROUGH PARTITION AND BEYOND

removes the darkness. The feeling of joy is mutual. It has to be. I was thirty-plus at the time. I had attained my puberty and maturity at the age of seventeen. For the next thirteen years, society's rules had denied me legally the opportunity to meet the other energy. Society had robbed me of that freedom that creation had bestowed upon me. Society had deprived me of enjoying the bliss of those thirteen years.

On that fateful night I had lost my virginity. So did she. We look back on our experience of that night. It was natural. It had to happen one day. Nature makes sure that it must happen for everyone. Nature cannot allow its creation to stop and not to flourish and multiply.

From then onwards these two souls, which became as one in that night, continued living together, sleeping together, sharing and fighting together. There were many moments of anguish, hatred, anger, fighting, separation, running away from it all, divorce, and forget and forgive. They are all there. It is a part of life and has to be managed. Life has to be lived in the whole and in the totality. Those who boast that their life has always been smooth, tranquil, and full of love, are liars. I hasten to add that somewhere, some place, they are saving on truth. It just cannot happen and does not add up. Life is full of duality. It does not move in a straight line. It moves through the hills, the mountains, and the valleys. It is like a river, like sun rays. It has to have a turmoil and tranquillity. The universe does not move in a straight line. The stars do collide, the clouds in the sky do crash, mingle together as if they are making love, and then separate and go on their own path. Then why should this life which is part of the universe move in a straight line? It just cannot, it should not, and it will not.

The divine was in action too. The divine has to be in action otherwise the whole creation would be dead. The whole world lives on sex. The whole universe is full of it. Without this energy there would be no animal kingdom, no vegetation in the world; there would no storms; there would be no lightning in the sky; and there would be no flowers, trees, and fruits. There will also be no meeting of the galaxies in the cosmos, nothing. And yet it is considered to be the most hated act by the religions, the priests, and the society. There are more jokes on the sex subject than on anything else. Society has gone bonkers. It is time it changed its tack. It is time to think to allow more freedom to the humans. It is time to look at the marriage institutions which are painful and which bind us all for the next 60-70 years. It is time to look at one-night stands where they will negotiate the terms of their meeting for the night with no commitments but with their mutual agreements at the place of their choice. But they should never be expected to stay together for life as happens now to all of us.

CHAPTER 4: MARRIED AND GRADUATED

Moved to Leytonstone

Within six weeks of arrival, we rented a two-roomed flat with kitchen and bathroom at Harold Road, E11. This house was owned by an Indian who lived downstairs with his young family. It was a big relief that M, who was so generous to give me his room, could finally move back to his flat. We were occupying his two rooms and he was sleeping rough with friends. It was so kind of him and he never moaned about it.

The location of the flat was very convenient. The college was very near here, just a mile bus ride at Stratford. The Leytonstone underground and the shops were only a couple of minutes' walk. The only drawback was that it was called the East End, the hated East all over the world. Whichever part of the world you go to it is always the East which is considered poor, backward, un-intelligent, un-inspiring, and uncivilised.

Allow me to say a few words about the West. I know I will be going off on a different track but still I beg to be permitted.

Of course, the West is rich and has all the comforts of life. But how did the West get richer in the first place? We all know that they had used devious and most unscrupulous means to accumulate that wealth and there is no need to repeat the history here. We all know about the hated East India Company which got rich by plundering; by being cunning, devious, and shrewd; and being ruthless warmongers. Those dirty tricks are still being played even today with impunity. This is all propagated by the West to demean the contribution of the East. But history tells us differently provided it is not written by a western bigot. Talking about the East, the whole history starts dancing in front of me. Numerous books on the contribution of the East have been written by well-known scholars and I am no expert to disagree on those opinions. It is true that the West has excelled in science and technology and has provided the means to improve the standard of living of their citizens. They have made a tremendous advancement in transport and communications. But they have also stockpiled the destructive atomic bombs to wipe out this mother earth, and its whole civilisation as we know it, many times over. And those atomic bombs will also kill those decision makers and the executors of the orders and their families. There are only a handful of them. But these power maniacs would annihilate the entire innocent creation of God to extinction. They would melt every grain of this planet which had nourished those power-hungry decision makers from birth to the day. They are so insignificant a minority. You only need a determined fanatic with a simple weapon and the accessibility to them. They are the most cowardly bunch who sit in their ivory towers, protected by thousands of armed men paid for by the citizens of the land. They in turn would destroy the same citizens who voted for them; the same scientists and technocrats who gave them those destructive weapons; the same doctors and nurses who contributed towards their well-being; the same academicians who nurtured their growth, wiped their tears, taught them manners, and made them bigger than their boots; the same army and police personnel who saluted them and protected them; the same bureaucrats and the millions of helpers who served them so obediently. They are the most ungrateful bunch ever planted on this planet. It is not happening only in the present-day environment, but this practice has been going on throughout the history of mankind. Only the armouries of the weapons have changed with the times and the actors. As the weaponry became more sophisticated so have the actors. This is the biggest tragedy of mankind. The desperate and enlightened minds just find themselves helpless and restless to find a solution to this ever-going historical problem. Please God save, not only those few, but the whole of humanity. That is my prayer.

When you look at the planet as a detached spectator from space without humans on it, you would find nothing but peace and tranquillity. All the creatures, the vegetations, and the matter would be seen to be living in harmony with minor skirmishes. But the moment you introduce humans on to the scene, the whole environment changes for the worse. This species kills its own kind in millions and slaughters others in numbers impossible to count.

With all those achievements the people of the West have yet to attain inner peace and tranquillity of the mind. They are still restless and unhappy with their lot. The East had seen all that glitter of the modern way of living millenniums ago. All that glitter was blinding them. Then they started looking within. They wanted to have the eternal peace and not the peace provided by the out-worldly comforts. They propounded new philosophies; they debated on new theories about how to achieve that goal. That is when they gave birth to most of the great religions of the world. Other religions have drawn inspiration from them. It had the world-class institutions for the intellectual education. It excelled in sculpture, the arts and crafts, road building and sanitation. It built the monuments, the great temples, the palaces, and the forts with archaeological beauty. They even carved the mountains to depict their thoughts and philosophies. They wrote Vedas, including the science of physiology and medicines; the world-class epics of Ramayana and Mahabharata; the treatise on sex, the Kamasutra which cannot be improved upon; and the first book on psychology, the Gita. It has given yoga and meditation to humanity to keep them physically and mentally fit. It has produced the enlightened Buddha, the Mahavira, and the Guru Nanak and many more. Even Jesus had his inspiration from the East. The sun would always continue to shine from the East and sets in the West; it is an unchangeable law of nature. But it lost all that glory because of the one simple law of nature – what goes up, must come down. Therefore, one can never blame their downfall with the passage of time. That downfall was inevitable, and it lasted more than a millennium. The sun is again beginning to shine from the East. The inspiration and the divine light have always been shining to the world from the East. There have been only two minds that have guided the outer and the inner world of humanity. One is the Greek mind that led to the progress in the field of science and mathematics, and the other is the Indian mind that laid the foundations to the road to mysticism, eternal peace, and the exploration of the inner peace and tranquillity.

However, going back to my history.

I resumed my college nearly five weeks late for my 2nd year. I had not missed much. The tempo of teaching was still sluggish. Mira started looking for a job. She tried Woolworths as a shop assistant, but it was not to her taste. Then she tried a job at a clothing factory where a lot of Asian immigrant women were working. There was good overtime but a lot of hard work. It mostly suited women from the continent who were un-educated but it was not for the educated. So, Mira quit the job within a couple of weeks. In the meantime, she had applied for a teaching job with the London Education Authority. She was interviewed, and after the LEA had checked her credentials in India she got the job. She had been a teacher in India since her graduation, so this job suited her most. She was interested in the education of children. She felt fulfilled once this job came through. She opened her bank account where her salary was directly transferred.

One day a topic came up when she asked if I had some savings. I said yes. Mira protested about why I had not told her that I had some savings in the Post Office.

'How much have you got?' she asked

'I don't know. It could be around three hundred pounds in my savings account, tucked away in the Post Office for my education.'

'Why didn't you tell me before that you have some money tucked away?'

A JOURNEY THROUGH PARTITION AND BEYOND

'It never occurred to me that I am supposed to tell you that I have some savings. Besides we were married only 12 weeks ago, then we were travelling, then trying to settle down. Where was the time to tell you such small things?'

'No, you were hiding it from me.'

'Why would I be hiding a few hundred pounds?'

'You did.'

The dialogue turned into a heated one. I brought my post office savings book and threw it in front of her.

'Here you are, look after this money too.'

Since then I have no cheque book, no money, no regular income except £200+ cash in my pocket for any contingencies. I not only live for small mercies from her but also for a hand-out when I need to buy some books to satisfy my intellectual needs. She buys me clothes if and when she is in a good frame of mind; or when she likes that her husband should have a presentable outfit for her friends; or sometime woollies may be thrown in my way as a birthday gesture. I am not complaining. In a way it is good. Money makes people arrogant and corrupt. At least I have been saved from that ordeal. Quite frankly I do not need money anyway. What I am going to do with it? I am not going to take it with me. There are no shops in heaven or hell where I need to spend it. However, some say that on the day of judgement, God would bless all the dead in their boxes and bring them back on the planet. Indians call it reincarnation. I might like to take a blank cheque in my box that would be handy for me to cash in for the rainy days when I come back. Who would cash it I am not bothered yet. Maybe God would open some banks especially meant for those who have been sent back from their judgement day. Cashing a cheque may not be that big a deal but to accommodate so many mortals on this blue planet would be the biggest challenge for the Almighty God. However it is good to keep on wishfully thinking for the distant future, extending it to eternity if I can.

I had already lost my virginity. Now I had lost my wallet too. The God-given financial freedom for the last three years had gone once more to a woman. I managed my finances when I got my first job as a policeman. I continued to enjoy that freedom when I was a student and during the period when I had my second job in Gwalior. In Delhi, where I had my third job, I used to hand over my pay packet to my mother, without opening it. In UK once again, I became free to manage my finances and I was nearly saving one-third of my salary until I married and became a prisoner for life in 1961. Since then I had been in difficulty a few times when I had no money on me. Some incidents in life can not be forgotten, never mind how much effort you make to shake them off. They reside deep in your unconscious mind forever and bother you whenever those memories surface.

171

Once it happened that in 1973 I was driving on the A12 in the morning to my school where I was teaching. Suddenly, my car stopped. There was no petrol in the car. I had no money, not even a penny in my pocket. What to do? A few hundred yards away I saw a petrol station. I left the car on the busy dual carriageway with hazard lights flashing. Timidly I went to the cashier and asked, 'My car has no petrol and it stopped on the main road. I have no money on me. Would you let me have a gallon of petrol? I will pay you the money on my way back from school where I teach.' (Petrol cost around 50p/gallon in those days.)

His reply was abrupt and cold.

'We are not a charitable organisation. If you have not got the money to buy petrol, then go away.'

The brutal message was loud and clear. He was right. His pump was not a charity. It was true that I had run out of petrol. But unfortunately, I was not a certified honest man; it was not stamped on my forehead. Honesty must be earned.

I came back depressed and stood on the pavement near the car. Moments later I heard a horn and the driver pulled in front of my car. The driver was none other but a teacher colleague from the same school.

'Hey, Om do you want a lift to school?'

'No, my car has run out of petrol. I would be grateful if I could borrow a couple of pounds to buy some.'

'Yes of course.' He took out £2 from his wallet and gave them to me.

'Thank you. I will repay you tomorrow.'

I could only dare ask for two pounds because I hardly knew him. I had joined the school only recently. I was even surprised that he offered me a lift. I was worried that he too might refuse to lend me a couple of pounds. I was disgusted with the insult heaped upon me by the cashier at the garage. But he was only doing his duty. But I take him as the messenger of the Divine. He had decided to teach me a lesson not to be so sloppy in managing my affairs. But with that lesson, He also managed to send this angel teacher to help me. Without his offer and stopping to enquire, I dread to think what would have happened. I would have been stranded, with no help from anywhere. There were no mobiles to contact my wife and I had no credit card. I thought of walking back four miles to home to get some money.

I went back to the cashier at the petrol pump and said, 'I have the money to buy some petrol. Would you let me borrow the petrol can? I will return soon after emptying the petrol in my car.'

'No, you have to put one pound deposit for it and it will be refunded when you bring back the can.'

'Ok.'

A JOURNEY THROUGH PARTITION AND BEYOND

I got the petrol, paid for it and the deposit, went back to my car, emptied the can, went back to the garage, got the refund, went back to my car, and drove off to school.

On the way I thanked my stars. Suppose I had borrowed only a pound, just enough to buy a gallon of petrol but not enough to pay for the deposit, I would be back to square one. What a fate! What an experience. Life never shies away from playing games with you, does it?

After reaching school late, I straight away went to the Head Mistress to apologise. Next day I returned £2 to the angel, with thanks.

There have been some more instances like this. They are buried comfortably down in the memory lane and will stay there until the day when this life meets its final destiny, the ashes to ashes.

Buying a house

Owning a house was a dream from the day I arrived here. I was messed around by the landlords who were prepared to let me a room, not on economic grounds but based on my colour, on my gender, on my age, on my status, on the structure of my family, and on my looks. There were so many prejudices and conditions I had to face before I was given a key. That dream remained buried for all those years because the circumstances were always against me. The problem was not unique in Britain; I found the same prejudices in Gwalior as well as in Delhi. In Delhi to get a room was not only very difficult but I was also loaded with so many restrictions as a tenant. I shared a room of 10'x8' with three more adults. We slept in that room; we cooked in that room, and we studied in the same room. The set-up and the room furniture were to be adjusted so many times in a single day. It was just a nightmare. It was not living, but a bare existence. The renting of a room in London was insulting and below the dignity of any self-respecting individual. My family had never lived as tenants before the partition. We had plenty of land with houses on them. Having so much property, that was left behind in Pakistan, the dream of owning and living within my own four walls was always lurking at the back of my mind. So, the forces of owning a property within me were so powerful that I could not ignore them. Also, a house is not only for you to live in, but it is a future security for you and for your future generation.

The dreams always remain dreams until one tries to act to fulfil them. So, I started investigating how to find a property, its funding, and its legal implications to completion. I had the inspiration, had the need as I was now married, and the determination to achieve my goals. As I dug more into the subject, I found out the whole thing was loaded with many intricacies and problems. The biggest issue was to find the funding for the house. And that was not so easy for a man like me who had no income, no chance of having a job for another two years, and no cash for a deposit. It was the most daunting issue for a prospective homeowner.

The present landlord had been in the country only for a few years. He worked in the bakery, earning around £10 per week with overtime. He assembled the 30% deposit with his savings and by borrowing some from friends. The other 70% he funded with a mortgage from a building society. He owned the three-bedroom house. He improved his weekly income by renting some rooms to tenants. That rental income was more than enough to pay for his mortgage. He then got the rest of his family from Punjab and was living in comfort, free as a landlord. Did I need more incentive to go for home ownership? No, the example was all there, right under me, on the ground floor of the house, occupied by the landlord.

If I had continued to work in my old job, I was getting double the amount of wage per week than my landlord, but I had some different goals in life that made me leave that job. Therefore, to buy a property became a lot more difficult for me.

Another Asian in Stratford had three houses. He was renting them to students from the West Ham College. The three-bedroom house prices in the West Ham area in those days were a mere £800. But no building society would give mortgages on those houses as they thought the whole area would be demolished in a few years' time to be rebuilt. The same houses are now changing hands for £1/2m.

The dream of buying a house was not new after marriage. It was there when I came to this country. It was there when I was in Delhi. The subject was alive when I was working and living at Muswell Hill. I came across an estate agent. I asked him to help me buy a house. He showed me a four-bed house near Mill Hill Tube station. I asked him to help me get the mortgage. He dragged his feet. I also did not pursue it vigorously as I had not saved enough deposit. I went to another estate agent in the Highgate area where the houses were big, with four storeys. The agent asked me what my price range was. I boasted that I was happy to go for a house of up to £3,500. The agent looked at my face and said, 'The minimum house prices around here are £9,500+. The day I sell a house in this area for £3,500, I will quit my job and sit at home.' He was very right. Today those houses are worth multi-millions of pounds. The world of property investment today has gone crazy. I could dare think to buy a property in those days as a student with zero resources. But today with all my resources and knowledge I cannot even dream of buying a flat.

The Search for a House

The search for buying a house became more urgent because I was married. Rather than living as a single in one room, we needed more space now.

A JOURNEY THROUGH PARTITION AND BEYOND

Economics dictated that for the rent of £7/week that we were paying for the two rooms flat, we could buy our own house with the same weekly commitment. But there was a big handicap. I had no job. I was a student and had no regular income. Furthermore, we did not have 30% deposit to get the rest of the mortgage. Whatever savings I had, I wanted to keep them for my education as well as our daily grind in case Mira did not get a job or may not like to do the available menial jobs. So, I decided to buy a house in my brother's name as he had a regular full-time job. I asked him, and he agreed.

We found a three-bedroom house, selling for £800 in Stratford. As there were no mortgages available for properties in Stratford, I decided to approach a Stratford landlord for guidance and help in finding a mortgage. I knew him because one of my classmates was renting a room in his house. His house was only ten minutes' walk from the college. Whenever I went to visit my friend, the landlord opened the door. Therefore, I began to know him well. He enquired about the details of the property and its location. Guess what happened. Within two weeks we had a letter from the estate agent saying that the house had been sold. On my further enquiries I came to know that the house was bought by that landlord whom I had asked for help. We thought that with his experience in buying houses he would help me to find the mortgage from some sources he knew. Instead he double-crossed me and cheated me. There were so many more houses in the market he could lay his hands on to buy, so why did he get involved with the one I was trying to acquire? That showed his character and his ethics. That is how the big experienced fish swallow the smaller to get fatter. I never thought that a man of that polite nature and nice talk had the heart of a sly fox. He hoodwinked me and deceived me. It left a bitter taste about whom to trust and whom not to. He already had a few houses in the area and it was his full-time business to rent them. I continued to meet him later and never mentioned to him about his deception.

As the Stratford area had funding problems we decided to go a bit farther away from the area. One Saturday we decided to go to the Ilford area. As we came out of the station we saw an estate agent office on the first floor of a building opposite. We reported at the reception and she directed us to wait in a small adjacent reception room. There were no other house-hunters waiting there at the time. A few minutes later, a middle-aged gentleman, with good personality, walked in. He was a typically well mannered, kind, and very helpful English gentleman. There were no signs of any prejudices in his behaviour. In one word he was a thorough gentleman, ready to help. He belonged to a noble profession to help provide shelters and he was a god-sent angel to assist us, the newly-wed couple. There are professions which exploit, cheat, send fears into your being, and manipulate to earn their living. But he was coming from a different species.

175

He brought out the brochure of the properties for sale in his area. He scanned through the list and took out three of them which he considered would be suitable for us.

'Before we go any further, let me know a little more about your tastes.' He asked, 'What kind of a property are you are looking for?'

'What do you mean by what kind?' I enquired.

'Are you looking for three bedrooms or a four bedrooms house?'

'Prefer four bedrooms if we can afford otherwise three would do,' I said.

'Is that for you? You seem to be a recently married young couple. Which country do you come from?'

'India.'

'Ah, the land of Gandhi, I met him once when he came to this country to attend the Round Table Conference in London. I am an admirer of him. He was a great man. I admire his philosophy of non-violence. Have you met him?'

'No, I was too young and am a commoner so there was no opportunity.'

'How long have you been here?'

'Just three years. I got married last year in September. I am a full-time student at West Ham College. We are buying the house in my brother's name.'

'Why is it in your brother's name and not yours? You are a married couple. You need a house for yourself, don't you?'

'Because I am a student and have no full-time job. Therefore, I may not get the mortgage.'

'We will see about that later.'

With that brief friendly rapport, he got up and said, 'Let us show you the houses. I have two with three bedrooms and one with four bedrooms. They are in different areas. But don't worry if you do not like any of them. Say so and I will show you some more on my books. But the one I am going to show you is more suitable to your taste and in a good neighbourhood. I have a car; let me get the keys and we'll go to view them.'

We both settled down on the back seat of his car and away we went on an adventurous trip of buying a first ever family home. A ray of hope kindled in my heart with a mixture of fear, what if it does not materialise because I had no income and not even a penny deposit? The fear was genuine and real. Mira was nagging me all the time in the back seat since the agent's suggestion of us buying it rather than buying it in my brother's name. She kept on pestering me not to make a commitment to buy it in our name. 'If we must buy then it has to be in your brother's name. He is employed and has a regular income to support the borrowing and we do not.' She kept on insisting. She was right, and I was quite happy to do that as long as we had a shelter, it did not matter whether the house was in my brother's name or in my name. I was not a selfish person and I had already told my brother and the agent that we planned to buy the house in my brother's name. Having the same views as she had, I don't know why she went on and on, repeating the mantras like a parrot.

Having seen all the three properties, we were back in his office an hour later. During the car journey and viewing, we continued our dialogue about his experiences of India and his queuing up in the East London streets to have a glimpse of Gandhi when he visited the country to attend the Round Table Conference on India's independence. He also showed his appreciation of how Gandhi was dressed in his simple attire to display the poverty of India.

As we settled down in the office, he continued, 'Now let us know which property you would like to buy out of those three I have shown you.'

'I would go for the four-bedroom property at Seven Kings. This property was in an open, nice clean area.' I said without any hesitation. 'I love bigger properties.' I do not remember which property Mira liked.

I had some good reasons to like it. This property had four good sized bedrooms and a toilet/bath upstairs; three reception rooms and a small kitchen downstairs; a toilet outside with a front and back garden. It was a semi-detached house in good condition except that it needed redecoration. It also had good potential for renting the four rooms upstairs to enhance the income to pay for the mortgage.

It was owned by a family who bought the house in the thirties for three hundred pounds and they were now selling it for £3,600. The family was buying a house in the Chadwell Heath area.

Going back to the negotiations, I asked, 'Is there any room to manoeuvre on the price?' This is what we had learnt from previous buyers that you never pay the asking price for the house. You always knock it down by a few hundred pounds. I was not a good negotiator anyway. However, I collected some courage to ask the question.

'What offer have you got in mind?'

'I don't know. You know better than I do. You deal in properties every day.'

'I know there is certainly some room. Let me offer the vendor £3,300. Let us see what he says. The house is worth that much money.'

'Ok, I will leave that to your expertise.'

'Ok, I will offer him that price and I am sure he will accept it. Now let me try to arrange a mortgage for you. You said you cannot buy it as you are a student and you want to buy it in your brother's name.'

'Yeah, that is right.'

'How much per year are you getting? The building society rules are that they offer you a loan of two-thirds of the price of a house which is £2,200 and your yearly income should be at least one-third of the mortgage. Therefore, your yearly income should not be less than £750 per year. You said you get £290 from GLC as mature student's scholarship. Therefore, are you getting around £450 per your parents in India?'

'I would say I am getting that much from India. Besides, if the worst comes to the worst, I can pick up a job which would give me at least £1000 per year. That is what I was getting when I left my job for the full-time studies. In addition, Mira is a teacher and she is trying for a teaching job. If she gets one she would earn more than the income required by the building society.'

'No, they only look at your present status. They are not concerned what happens in future.'

'I do get some money from India from my brother when I need it.'

'No, the building society does not want income based on an on-off basis but a regular income. Should we say it is the regular income you can lay your hands on?'

'Ok, you can say that.'

The income was only to be given but was not to be proved in those days. Building societies were not asking for proof. The country's institutions were run on absolute trust. Whatever you say was always considered to be true, a great cultural asset of the country at the time which is now being slowly eroded by the foreign settlers of all kinds of hue and colour. That culture is being modified every day with ever increasing stringent rules. It is now reaching to a stage that 'you are guilty until and unless you prove it otherwise'. In those days we could walk into a building society, the post office, and a bank to open an account without showing our identity. But now every citizen of this country must produce a passport and a utility bill to prove your identity and the address. The whole world has gone upside down here and it is largely done by the foreign settlers who have brought their culture of cheating, deception and lying to this land which was totally free from such human evils.

'With these joint incomes, let me try if I can get a mortgage in both of your names. If the building society is happy to consider you both for the mortgage, subject to a satisfactory survey report, you both go for the house in your names. Let us leave the final decision until I have tried for the mortgage.'

He disappeared to his little office. He came back after a little while, with a broad smile on his face. 'Yes, everything is ok. The building society is ready to advance you a loan £2,200. You now go away and find a deposit of £1,100 plus the solicitor's fee and the survey fee. Do you want me to introduce you to a local solicitor I know in Ilford?'

'Yeah, that would be nice.'

A JOURNEY THROUGH PARTITION AND BEYOND

'Ok, give me your address and other details. I will pass it on to him. He will write you a letter to introduce himself with his charges. I will also write to you and the vendor confirming the buying price of £3,300. I know he will accept this price as I have known the owner for a long time. He is a very nice fellow.'

So, we got up to go away. He congratulated us for our first ever step on the property ladder.

We had accomplished the first step on the housing ladder, but we still had a long way to go on that arduous journey.

We humans are our own worst enemy. First the mind creates desires; the desires lead us to make financial commitments to accomplish those desires. Those commitments would then lead us to become the slave of the financial institutions. Effectively we sell our freedom to become prisoners of our own making. This is the worst scenario of modern day living. Happiness runs miles away from us and the struggle of a lifetime begins. When it becomes hard going, we either end up in madhouses or in temples with a begging bowl in our hands for the mercy of our God. This is not my story alone. All humans play the same game and are suffering. It is a rat race no one wins. I wish we were made to be content to live in huts. But we are not. We were made to be ambitious, egotistic, jealous, and competitive. Then finally when we have achieved our goals and ambitions, the box is ready to mingle us with ashes to ashes. Is that the type of life we should live? Not really! But that is what we all do. We know it is wrong and yet we follow the rat race. We find no other solutions to our present way of living. In fact, this is the effective way of buying all expensive necessities of life like a house or a car. The other solution we had was to continue to pay rent, regularly save money, and then buy with saved cash. This would have taken another twenty-odd years before we would be able to go for a house and during those twenty years the prices would be a lot higher because of inflation.

Raising a deposit

I had no bank account. The savings account in the post office had only £s which we could count on our fingers. I was in the market to find a deposit of £1,100, the most arduous task of my life. I was on my own in my mission to achieve my impossible goal. When I say on my own I mean it. Mira was all the time nagging me to say no to the estate agent because we had no deposit and we did not want to buy a house. That is the truth and I am not bragging to have the credit for this acquisition. I had no expectations of co-operation from my brother either as we were buying the house in our name. I could understand his reservations. He must have been thinking that I double-crossed him. It was far from the truth. It was not selfishness that made me want to buy the house in my name. It was the agent who manoeuvred the situation to put me in the front line to buy the house even though I had said to the agent, right in the beginning, that we were there to buy the house in my brother's name. However, it was also true that we could buy another house in my brother's name any time later as he had a job. It was only a matter of finding another suitable house and then arranging the mortgage. However, the misunderstandings always create problems in maintaining good human relationships. Therefore, I never raised this issue of finding the deposit with him.

Not finding any solution, I just left the whole issue in cold storage to gain time. One Saturday on a shopping spree, we spotted a money lender's shop at Leytonstone High Road saying, 'You can borrow money for any purpose.' We walked in. I did not know what to ask. It was just a stab in the dark. However, I assembled some courage and asked, 'You say in your window that we can borrow money for any purpose.'

'Yes! You need to put some jewellery, some valuable painting, or some asset as collateral to borrow the money.'

'How many years?'

'Up to ten years.'

'We want to buy a house and we need to find a deposit. We have some jewellery which we can put as collateral. Would you lend us some money against it?'

Now it was not right to say that, as the jewellery was Mira's property and I had no right to trade it. However, Mira did not object. The lender was a decent, honest man. So, he said, 'Sorry we do not lend money for home deposits. It is very expensive borrowing. Your first port of call should be your bank. They too would not give you the money for a deposit but if you go to them and tell them that you are buying a house and you need a loan or overdraft to buy furniture, they would certainly be kind to lend to you for three, four years. Have you got an account with a bank?'

'Yes, my wife has.'

'Oh well try there and good luck.'

That conversation gave me a clue about how the financial system works. So next Saturday we went to the Natwest Bank Branch at Leytonstone where Mira had an account. The banks used to open on Saturdays for full service in those days. We saw the teller and said that we would like to see the manager. She went into his office and within ten seconds, the manager came out of his door to receive Mira. The manager must have been in his sixties, looked a tall, elegant, respectable, and soft-spoken banker. Mira asked me to accompany her to the office. I refused; I was a reluctant chicken to face the man. I said, 'No you go as I have not got the account here. It was your account and it is appropriate that you go and see him.' While following him, she continued to signal me to go in with her.

A JOURNEY THROUGH PARTITION AND BEYOND

I kept on saying no. All this dialogue was going on in our body language. The manager was watching it. I must admit I was timid and shy about facing the gentleman. The manager shut the door behind him and I waited at the door like a gatekeeper, not knowing what to expect. Within seconds, Mira opened the door, with the manager just behind her. She said, 'He wants to know how much money we want to borrow and for how many years.'

'I don't know. Ask for two, three hundred pounds.' The manager interjected, 'No you have to be specific.'

'You can ask for three hundred if that is ok,' Mira asked me.

'Ok, three hundred,' I said hesitantly. I knew if he refused three hundred we would be back to zero. So, they went in. The manager asked Mira if I had a bank account in another bank. Mira said, no. He asked her to call me in so that he could open a joint account for us and then he would put three hundred pounds into our joint account to spend whenever we would be ready to buy the furniture. We had economised on the truth here by saying that the loan was for buying furniture. I say 'economise' because eventually we did buy new furniture to furnish the house, but it was bought on hire purchase and the overdraft we got was used as a deposit.

So that day with the manager's kindness and with a bit of a lie we had three hundred pounds in our pocket as an advance for the house. We still had a long way to go. We had now climbed on to the 2nd step of a winning ticket. We had first managed the mortgage and now three hundred pounds. We had to move forward to find another eight hundred pounds. That money had to come from some other sources but not from a bank.

We looked around the list of friends who would give us a short-term loan, provided they had the spare cash tucked away somewhere. The greatest advantage was that there were very few people here from our country. The community feelings and helping each other in times of need was deeply rooted. Of course, there were jealousies too. Everyone was trying to get onto the property ladder. It was but natural because all of us were facing racism in renting as well as in buying a property. The neighbours hated those whites who sold their property to us. Some vendors even would slam the door on our faces when we would go to view their 'little' houses. It was like a death sentence to the neighbours wherever we had bought the house. However, the solution for the community was to help someone now and once he was settled down then he would return your cash and top up with some more so that you could also buy a property. Some were very generous and were more than willing to help with no strings attached, but on the other hand some clever educated people bargained by insisting to be partners in your property or charging high interest on their mean contribution. The so-called un-educated who came from the Indian villages were generous, trusting, ready to help, and very broad-minded.

A Story of Genuine Help with no Strings

Here is a true story that was narrated to me by a person S I knew. This clearly indicates the generosity and the community feeling of a man who had come from an Indian Punjab village.

S, a young, very polite, decent fellow was walking one evening along the Romford Road, West Ham. Suddenly he saw a middle-aged Singh, waving to get his attention from his front garden on the other side of the road. He did not know English. He could only communicate in Punjabi. It was a winter evening when the days were short, and the dusk was just around the corner. S was also a Singh and hence the older had a natural affinity to wave to him for help. S crossed the road and walked over to him. After a brief chat and introduction, Mr Singh asked his help in finding a fault causing his house lights not to work. It so happened that S was an electrician and knew all about the wiring system of a house. That is what he was doing for his living. For him it was such a simple job to restore the lighting. He checked the fuse board and found that a fuse had blown. He repaired the fuse and the darkness from the house disappeared. Following the cultural traditions of India, Mr Singh invited S inside the house and offered him a cup of tea. After that brief socialisation they parted. So that was their first brief encounter and the matter finished.

A couple of months later S wanted to buy a house and he needed a deposit like I did. After pondering around to see who could help, S thought of approaching Mr Singh. He knew the chances were very slim as he did not know the person that well. However, he thought of trying it in case the luck favoured him. So, one day he ventured out to see him. After the usual greetings and settling down with a cuppa, S told him his problem. To S's surprise, Mr Singh took his cheque book out, signed a cheque and said, 'Here is a blank cheque. You can fill up the amount you need but no more than two thousand pounds as that is what I have in my account, and return the money whenever it is convenient.' Two thousand pounds was a lot of money in those days to part with to a stranger whom he had met only once briefly for a few minutes. Mr Singh had no education, was a simple decent person from a village in Punjab. His generosity would never be matched by an educated person who would call him stupid, illiterate. He would have probably loaded S with many conditions before parting with that sum. After that S told me that they became good family friends.

So, we approached B (do not wish to identify him as he did not return the extra money we gave him to buy his house), one of our friends. He was willing to part with £300 with a promise that when he would be buying his house we would

A JOURNEY THROUGH PARTITION AND BEYOND

also advance some extra money as a loan so that he could buy his house. We agreed.

Now we were short of £500 + fees. The agent continued to send me reminders that the vendor was getting uptight for not seeing any further progress. By this time, I gave up hope of getting any more money for the deposit and I was ready to give up. The agent wrote to me again to ask how I was getting on about the deposit, and this time I decided to come clean and inform him about the difficulty I was facing. I telephoned him to say, 'We have about £700 in our bank and are short of the rest of the deposit. We cannot find any more money. It appears that we would have to give up the idea of buying the house.'

The agent said, 'Let me see if the vendor is ready to give you some loan for three years. With my experience it has happened before that a vendor loans some money to the buyer. The vendor had bought the house for £300 before the war and he is selling it for £3300. He is buying a property in Shadwell Heath for £2,500 and so he would have spare cash to lend. Let me try and I will come back to you. I know him well and I am sure he would not say no when I recommend your name.'

'That would be great. We would be very grateful for your help.' I encouraged him to try.

A week later, I had a letter from the agent saying that the vendor was willing to loan us £500 with the same interest rate as the building society was charging. The loan would be payable in three years, by monthly payments by a standing order, and it would be registered against the house. I agreed to the terms. Within days the solicitors did the completion. We had the house and we moved in there in September 1962.

We got the house. We were to pay £17 per month mortgage to the Halifax Building Society for 25 years. We went to Boardman's at Stratford and we bought all the beds, the sofa, and the floor coverings on HP. The vendor had kindly left a couple of light bulbs, an old dining table and four dining chairs for us to enjoy our meals in the approaching winter nights. I say 'kindly' as most of the vendors in those days would not leave anything, including light bulbs. They would just strip the house naked, or, should I say it more brutally, they would vandalise the whole house where they had lived for so many years and had already made a good fortune by selling it. That shows their meanness and poverty of their soul.

We managed the repayments to Halifax, to the vendor, to the Bank, and to the hire purchase company. We had also paid back the borrowed sum to B within 3-4 months. We met those commitments by converting the upstairs four rooms into a flat. One room became a kitchen, there were two bedrooms, and one lounge with a common bath. We rented this to a family with a young daughter and son. They were paying £7-10s-0d (£7.50) rent per week. Downstairs we rented a room to one of my classmates at £3-10s-0d per week, sharing a kitchen with us. We had one room as our bedroom, one as a lounge, and a small kitchen with a toilet outside. In addition to the rental income, Mira now had a teaching job with ILEA. The income was good and as she loved teaching to infants it worked out well for her. But life was hard in the beginning as we were to pay a lot of initial debt.

A year later my brother also bought a house in Leytonstone and called his family to come over from India.

My Marriage Ring

It was November 1962. We had moved to our first new house at Seven Kings. The winter used to be bitterly cold and humid with plenty of smog. Central heating was non-existent. The news arrived that the Chinese had invaded the North East of India. Their invasion was swift, brutal, professional, and intimidating to the Indian pride. They marched through the hills and mountains of the North East for nearly twenty kilometres inside the territory claimed by India and then, adding insult to injury, they withdrew from the occupied territory within three days. Nehru gave a statement that they were marching through the Indian Territory like wave after wave and he did not know how to stop them. The Chinese army is sophisticated, battle-hardy, well equipped, and a well-trained fighting machine because of their internal civil war. On the other hand, Nehru was a Gandhian and was following the stupid policies of idealism of the Panchsheel treaty in this dangerous world we live in. He had no international friends to bail him out in that crisis. His army was starved of modern equipment, and was fighting with the WW2 infantry guns. He issued a statement that, 'We would fight the Chinese with bamboo sticks if they do not stop their incursions into India.' Being educated in UK, he was trying to step into Churchill's shoes - 'We will fight the Germans in the hills…….' We, Indians in UK, were frightened to see India reverting into colonial times, this time under the control of the Chinese. Someone organised a meeting at Toynbee Hall in East London to enlighten us about what was happening in the North East. I went to attend the evening meeting after attending my college. The Indian community was very small but very dynamic. There were fiery speeches, challenging our conscience, and reminding us of our duties to rise towards the need of the hour to protect our motherland. It was an occasion to prick our nationalism to stand up and fight for the cause of freedom – physically, morally, and financially. The speeches certainly aroused our passions. And finally, as it normally happens, the speakers first brainwashed us and then opened the collection box to throw in whatever we had. Some people chucked in their unopened pay packets, others wrote cheques, some put in cash, and I volunteered my marriage gold ring, the only gold possession I'd had in my life for the last fourteen months. And this was the first and the last jewellery I ever had. We

A JOURNEY THROUGH PARTITION AND BEYOND

Indians were not very rich in those days. We had only arrived in the country a couple years earlier. Most of us were either students, as I was, or factory workers who earnt some crumbs from the jobs the locals would not like to do.

Going back into the history now, I do wonder whether that money did reach the purpose for which it was donated – to buy arms for our Indian soldiers – or did it end up in grafts, in personal pockets of the organisers, or in the coffers of the corrupt bureaucrats of New Delhi. There is no way to find out and we would never know. It is filthy muddy mire. You can dig and shift more and more muck and still the truth would not be revealed. God forgive those if they had betrayed the trust we placed as the donors.

Living Conditions in London

The living conditions in London were hard and tough. It was not the repayments that made life harder, as they were met with the rental income, but the way the people of this country lived in those days.

The floors of the house were of wooden planks with an open space underneath for air circulation. This was done purposely to keep the wooden planks free from dry rot. In wintry winds, the cold air would find its way into the rooms, making the whole house unbearably cold. The mice and rats would also find their way in to share the warmer rooms as well as to eat the leftovers of the food.

We travelled to and from work by buses, undergrounds, and trains. Very few lucky ones had cars. The winter used to be very cold, no sun during the day, and the environment was polluted with a mixture of fog and smoke produced by coal burning at home fireplaces. The days were short, and it used to be dark when leaving home and arriving back at home. At times the fog used to be so thick that the visibility would be down to only ten feet. The conductor would walk in front of the bus to guide the driver to stay on the road. After reaching home the first job we did was to light a kerosene stove to warm one of the rooms. These kerosene heaters were also a high safety and health hazard. They would produce a typical burning smell, loaded with traces of carbon monoxide. They also produced a lot of moisture in the room thus creating many health hazards including bronchitis. Furthermore, there were risks of fire and monoxide poisoning when left on during the night. They would also leave a very unpleasant smell when turned off before going to bed. Even this little stove was shivering to warm the place up - a losing battle.

The whole house would hardly reach to around 0-degree temperature. The cold walls, the airy floors, the draught coming from the French windows and the leaky doors were all playing their part in keeping the whole house cold, thus making life very miserable and uncomfortable. We would huddle around the stove. The front part of the body would be warm, but the back of the body would be freezing. We all know that the flesh is not a good conductor of heat. Therefore, the body was sending two signals to the head and both parts were telling their own miserable tales thus adding to the woe. As we moved from the warmer room to the kitchen to cook, we felt as if we were moving from heaven to hell. The windows of the kitchen and the warm room would become foggy with dripping moisture. We dared not go from warm rooms to the cold rooms. When we went to our bedroom to sleep, the bed, the linens, and the blankets would all be bitterly cold. So, we took a warm water bottle to warm the bed but some parts of the body outside the blankets were exposed to hell. Being young we took it all and coped well with the wintry weather.

Weather was literally making life hell in those days. It is also no wonder that the people of this country being poor, destitute, and living in a hellish island, went out to seek warmer countries to live.

A Racist Attack
Examinations always give you a tough time. They test your memory, your stamina, your endurance, and your ability to retrieve the data you have stored somewhere deep in your unconscious mind. A lot of factors affect its retrieval. With all those worries of performing well in the examination hall and many other odds against, I believe I had prepared myself well for the last subject of my final year examination. I used to study late into the night and I had done well in all the papers before. I had only one final paper. With this routine of working every day like a workaholic at the desk, with a tiny table lamp and books and notes spread all over, I was getting a bit fed up with studies and wanted to have a change. I had done whatever I needed to study for the final paper and it was time to have a bit of a relaxation and diversion from studying.

It was May 1963 and it was Sunday of the long weekend with bank holiday. I thought that it was my last paper on Tuesday and I had Monday available for a quick revision of the subject. Also, I did not like studying right up to the last minute before the examination. The memory could get jammed up to create a blockage in reproducing the subject matter. So, yeah why not have some socialising. B invited us to have dinner with his family at their house in Leytonstone and we accepted. So, we went in the evening. We had another young fellow named M who also accompanied us. He was living at Leytonstone too.

We travelled from Seven Kings station to Stratford and then changed to the underground for Leytonstone. Mira was six months pregnant with our first child.

We had a good dinner and a lively chitchat. Around 10.30 B, M and we walked to the underground station. B's house was around half a mile from the underground station. We walked on Ferndale Road and turned right at Leytonstone

A JOURNEY THROUGH PARTITION AND BEYOND

High Road. We were chatting as we walked. Conversation amongst Indians never stops. They are good chatterboxes whether it is day or night. Even walking on footpaths in the residential areas did not deter them from their national habit. They feel insecure if there is nothing to talk about. That habit remained even when in Britain where to talk loudly in the residential areas was frowned upon for fear of waking the children. The usual talk is mostly on politics.

Soon we approached a busy pub on our right on the main road. It was summertime. The locals were busy quenching their weekend thirst and were getting tipsy in that process. We were not aware of the British culture even though we had been living in the country for some time. The locals never mixed with us and we also moved among our Asian circles. It was voluntary segregation. There was nothing in this to worry about. Even the animal world only mixes with its own kind. One would never see cows grazing with buffaloes or pigeons flying with sparrows. And we have evolved from that animal world. So, to know each other's cultural habits was not possible. We now know that the British have a habit that whenever they have alcohol in their tummy, they cannot remain peaceful. We Asians also drink, sometimes heavily but it never results in fights or misbehaviour. If it does happen, then it is a rare occasion and not a norm. So not realising the dangers involved in passing by a busy pub at its closing time (11pm), we continued to walk our way towards the station. Soon after passing the pub we heard some abusive language from behind. B looked back and found three young blokes following us. We decided to turn onto the next road on the left to avoid them. This road passed through a quieter residential area (Harrington Road). We thought they would continue to stay on the main road. But we were wrong. They followed us. We increased our pace to get away from them. Their abuse became louder and more aggressive. We were just about approaching Harold Road on our left, when all three of them jumped in front of us. They blocked our way and kept on abusing us with their filthy language. We did not hear much of it as we were so fearful of the whole thing. A fight was now on our hands, with its dire consequences whether we liked it or not. None of us was a fighter. We were all timid and cowardly, especially me. B was the same. I had never fought with anyone in my life. I had learnt to walk away from such troubles. But this time there were no choices. We never said a word in response to being provoked. Now under these circumstances, the safety of Mira became a paramount objective. I whispered to Bhalla in my language to whisk away quickly with Mira to the station which was only a couple of hundred yards further on. He resisted and asked me to go with Mira and he would face the consequences. We knew in our mind that whatever they might do to us, they would not attack a pregnant woman, with any colour or creed. But when one is drunk, one can never predict the behaviour. As B and I were arguing between us who would accompany Mira, two of them grabbed hold of M. They

187

were beating the hell out of him. B and Mira rushed towards the station. I became more aware of the dangers surrounding M and me. The third was standing right in front of me. He continued his abusive mutterings, 'You bloody bastards, why have you come to this country? You f...... c..., go back to your country.' The next thing I knew was that I fell on the footpath and my nose was swollen and paining. There was no other soul around to help us at that time of the night. I looked back, M was not there either, nor the other two who were beating him. The one who hit me also disappeared. I don't know how long I remained on the footpath. I managed to get up. Those boys had their fun at our cost and walked away.

I walked briskly towards the station. Bhalla and Mira were waiting for me at the ticket office. He looked at me and said, 'Your nose is bleeding. They have hit you on the nose.' I touched my nose and saw blood. He asked, 'What happened? Did they walk away?'

I said, 'I don't know. The only thing I remember is hearing his abusive language and then I lost consciousness. When I came to I found myself on the footpath, with a pain on my nose.'

'What happened to M? Did you see him?'

'No, I don't know. He was not there. I thought he might have come to the station as he knew you were going to the station with Mira.'

'No, he has not come here.'

So now we got worried about the safety of M. We did not know what to do. If we went back to search for him, we might come across more of the drunkards who would still be finding their way home. I was also worried that we might not get a connecting train from Stratford to Seven Kings (SK). So, we decided that Mira and I should be on our way to SK. B said he would find his way back to his house and he would stick to the main road. We had made a tactical error of turning to the side street. But who knows, that could have happened even if we had stayed on the main road as those blokes were looking for a fight. They were just trigger-happy. They must have met up later to brag about their 'killings'. People like them are like wild dogs, looking for fun by inflicting pain on the innocents. They enjoy cruelty to their fellow citizens. They have no conscience. Otherwise they would not be doing such wrongs to others.

Next day we learnt that M had managed to run away from those two thugs. They were beating him with fists and with a belt. As his house was at Harold Road and was not very far from there, he managed to extricate himself from their clutches and ran like a wounded fox to his house. They were young, well built, and drunk but could not keep up with M's running speed. Luck also favoured him that he lived nearby and he escaped with some nasty injuries.

I could not sleep in the night due to the pain. I had planned that I would be able to revise the exam subject during the following day. I could not concentrate

A JOURNEY THROUGH PARTITION AND BEYOND

on it. I went to see my GP who gave me some painkillers to relieve the pain of my swollen nose.

Final Day Examination at the College

Tuesday came, and I was on my way to my college for the final day final examination. That was the routine for the last three years and it was a beaten track. It was a bright sunny morning. As usual I got off the bus, crossed the road, and then walked to the main college building where I was asked to go to the annex where this exam was being conducted. The annex was behind the main building. I walked on Water Lane and entered the courtyard, leading to the annex. I was just about half way through that when I heard a shout behind me.

'Hey, do you know where?? Street is?'

'No, I don't know.'

'It is somewhere around here on the map, but I cannot find it.'

'I don't live around here. Sorry I cannot help.' And I started walking towards the annex. He did not give up. So, he shouted back, 'Where are you going to?'

'I have got to appear for my exam in that annex.'

'Oh, bad luck.' He uttered those wishes completely unknowingly and innocently. As I turned around to walk towards the annex, he realised the stupidity of his outburst. And he shouted back, 'I am very sorry. I did not mean to wish you bad luck. I don't know how it just came on my tongue. My apologies! Good luck for the exam whatever it is.'

He did not realise that those words were not his, but the Divine was speaking through him. He was only a tool used by the Existence. The die had already been cast, the results of my exams were already declared through him even before I appeared for it.

'That is ok.' I responded and hurried towards the annex without paying much attention to his outbursts.

The exam paper was served. I glanced at the paper. There were two questions which were copies from the book and I had done them at home. There was one more question I knew I could do. A fourth question I could also do. A fifth I would attempt, but I was not sure that I would do it correctly. I was very happy that I would certainly be able to do 4 questions right, thus giving me 80%. So, I started with the two I had already attempted at home. I started one and I got stuck. Just could not reproduce. The memory lane was blocked. I decided to go to the second but again I got stuck. My memory was now failing me completely and utterly. I went back to the first to have a go again, but luck was not favouring me. I left both and went for the third and fourth. I had done them and in between I continued to go back to 1 and 2 but no success. The time was running out. I tried the fifth, got stuck again. The time was up, and I was not very happy with my exam. Nothing more I could do. If I could finish those two first questions I would have been heading for a plus degree, but I knew that I would be just a borderline case. Now it was a matter of waiting for the day of destiny.

The Hard Times as Student

The financial situation at home was deteriorating by the day. The rental income from the house was fully committed in repaying the mortgage, the loan for the deposit, and the repayments for the furniture. Mira was not working and was heavily pregnant and was waiting for the delivery due in early September. Her income had totally dried up. We were now heading for big financial trouble. Life is a cycle of ups and downs. It moves into the valleys before climbing up the hills and the mountains but that climbing is painful, full with thorns and sweat, and loaded with agony. But it must be climbed, and life must be faced totally and squarely with steely determination. Quitters never make good in life. They give up too quickly, without tasting the fruits of the Garden of Eden. They are too worried that they would be expelled from their own Garden. I was prepared to face it. In fact I never thought at the time that it was all part of growing up. My mental faculties were still in infancy. The wisdom of growing up had not caught up yet with the age I was passing through.

To cope with it all, I was desperately looking for a job, in fact any job. All graduates suffer but mine was the most difficult case. I was an Indian and I had to fight a systematic and institutionalised racism in the job market when there were no laws against it. My age was also not very helpful. I was 32 at the time. The expected graduate should be around 23. That also did not help. After graduation I was competing for the managerial jobs. Normally in those days, a manager's job was offered to those who were coming from the elite universities. In life you win one battle, and then there is already another one taking shape to be fought. Human prejudices are many and of enormous proportions that to win them all on every step of the way is the most daunting task we all face. If the prejudices in the British society were racism and bigotry, then they were different in the Indian society but equally daunting. Humans are such a lousy species, created by God in such a way that they have never learnt and mastered the technique to live and let live in peace. God must shiver in his holy den by creating the humans as we know them today. And they are never going to be improved. So many Buddhas and Jesuses have come on this planet to improve the lot of this creature. They all failed, and some were even murdered and crucified. It is a sad tale to tell but it is there to witness, to live, and to be part of it. You only need look from a distance with an empty mind, totally detached without any prejudices, thoughts or opinions, and you would think, 'Where on earth are they all going to and for what?' While

A JOURNEY THROUGH PARTITION AND BEYOND

in New York, I once stood on a bridge under which cars were being driven with maddening speeds in both directions of a four-lane highway. I wondered what was going on in this technologically advanced country. So many souls are competing like mad robots. Where were all these people heading to and for what? I just could not comprehend. Is it a harmonious world or a lunatic place? Why were they all in such a hurry, some heading towards one direction and the others in the opposite? I still cannot figure out why and where they were all heading to.

So, I moved on to try my luck in the job market. I had to fight every inch of the way. That is the thing called 'life' which moves all the way like a stream, fighting all kinds of obstacles of rocks and pebbles; through the various terrains of mountain tops and the valleys; negotiating also with all kinds of vegetations and the animal world, and finally merging into its destination. That is also the source of my origination and where I would finally end up.

Go, Go Man and Try your Luck

Interview at CEGB (Central Electricity Generating Board)

Just after the final examination, as usual, a season of horse-trading began in earnest in which the big employers started recruiting their graduate needs for their future expansion. They were sending their personnel officers to select the 'best' from the elite universities that are infested with nepotism and corruption. I call them elites because they earned their names by a self-perpetuating mechanism: graduates of these establishments who attain high positions in commerce or politics then recruit only students of those universities. I say 'best' but in fact they were recruiting from the offshoots of the ruling classes of the country. They had joined those universities, not on merits but with their family connections and by whom they knew. If my statement is wrong, then I'd like to know how the daughter and grandchildren of Nehru had managed to get into those elite universities. Did they join on merits with good grades? No, they joined because they were offshoots of the Nehru family, and later in life they proved utter failures in their academic fields. And yet they went on to become the prime ministers of the country, by hoodwinking the commoner, the simple, and the trusting voters. However, knowing all those disadvantages, I still had to compete in that unfair job market. I had applied to several places but had the honour of getting regrets from all except the CEGB (Central Electricity Generating Board).

CEGB was the nationalised central electricity board. It was a very big employer, spread all over the country.

On the day of my interview, I went to their head office at Euston where the interviews were being conducted. It was an elegant building with posh offices, creating awe and fear in the minds of the job seekers. It was also an eye-opener to a simple soul like me. The inside décor clearly reflected the fitting image of a very big nationalised corporate employer. The walls were panelled with expensive wooden boards. While the elite members of the board of governors controlled and managed the production and supply of electricity to the country, humbles and ordinaries manned the entrance doors to show off the power of the industrial giant.

When my turn came I was ushered into a huge meeting hall. There was a very big long table. On either side of the table there were seated several heads of the departments. At the top of the table sat the Chairman of the CEGB on his elegant chair with a high back reflecting his power, position and his authority. I could sit at the opposite end to this most powerful man who could give the nod to the incompetent who had good connections and a 'nay' to the clever from the wrong background. As I glanced around, I took in the wood panelled-walls, the hugeness of the table and the chairs on which were seated so many personalities with powers to hire and fire and control my future destiny. The whole intimidating scene sent shivers down my 'native' spine. It reminded me of the scene from the epic Mahabharata where the frightened *Dropdy*, the wife of the loser brothers, was presented to the winner brothers. Even the brave would run for cover from that frightening environment. It reflected the powers of a colonial system rather than reflecting the compassions of a benevolent service-provider giant. Was it an interview room to recruit or was it an intimidating chamber of torture to frighten the simple and the innocent, I had soon to discover. Those elites were a mixture of young and old; they were all well-booted-suited with smart neckties as if the whole English gentry had landed in that room to impress me with their imperial past; they frightened me and disarmed me from asking any questions to these well-placed aristocrats. They were all representing the elite universities of the country. A man like me - with humble background of an Indian origin; with a beautiful brownish skin to dazzle the non-existent lady on that top table; with a degree from an unknown college of West Ham; located in a poor district of hated East End London - had to have an enormous intellectual power to convince such egotistical people about my suitability. There was no chance in heavens even to make an eye contact with any of them. They were so many and even a well-trained eye would not have enough time to look at them with the spoken speed of the words of the chairperson. However, the formalities of hallow lofty ideals of an 'Equal Opportunity Employer' had to be seen to be completed for the whole world to see.

So, after I was ceremoniously seated, the Chairman roared at the top of his voice to make everyone hear him without the aid of loudspeakers, 'Mr Khurana, we are an equal opportunity employer here. On my either side are the representatives of the various departments. They know their needs. If they are interested in your candidature, they will be asking you questions. They are fully

A JOURNEY THROUGH PARTITION AND BEYOND

independent to make their decisions. So, you may please answer their questions when asked,' thundered the chairman of the board.

He sped through his introduction of the various heads of which he now had mastery. I heard his roaring introduction loud and clear, even though I was seated quite far away from him. My mental faculties and the listening abilities were at their top gear. I responded, 'Yes, sir.'

'Also, I might point out from the outset that, you being from India, no British would like to work under you. So, we must find you a job in which you will not be supervising the British labour, but you would be working on your own, such as in the design office.'

'Yes, sir I understand your problem,' I replied sheepishly without showing my annoyance or disappointments. Who was I to question his authority and his declared policy of an equal opportunity employer? And yet he was condemning me, a candidate, for my origins? He was sheltering behind the prejudices of his country. The declared policy of equality was a farce and it was only meant to throw dust into my eyes and the others on the street. Before I was to be asked a relevant question about my experience, my education and my background, I had already been discarded. I was insulted, reduced to a meaningless dust. He had robbed my self-respect as if I had dropped in from another planet. My father was quite capable to serve them in India to prolong their colonial rule, but I was not competent enough to serve them in their own land. It was so hurtful. My ego and my confidence were totally shattered. I had never come across such hypocrisy in my life. But there is always a beginning for everything. So here was the beginning from learned, booted, suited, and well-placed elite in the land of gentlemen, blowing hot and cold as if the man sitting opposite had no brains, no heart, no emotions, and no self-respect. Simply because he happened to be of a different skin colour, does not make him inferior. The skin only gives the outwardly appearance of the body. Inner soul has no colours. Colours do not make inferior or superior. Instead they enhance the beauty of the creation. Without those colours the bees would never be attracted to the flowers. But then man is a man. He would always give reasons to hide his prejudices. All those sitting on the table were nodding their heads in obedience to the chair as if the chair was pronouncing a sermon to impress them. It was a brutal reminder of my origin. No wonder Gandhi and Nehru turned nationalists after coming to this land of 'opportunity' and went back with fire in their bellies to retrieve their self-respect by agitating for the independence of India.

From that moment onwards, I knew the whole show was a farce. I was already working as a designer before I went for the degree. What was the point of sacrificing three years of life and financial security if I still had to end up in the same kind of a job? There were hardly any questions coming from those 'enlightened' heads. The heads knew from the summing up and introduction by the chair where they stood. Why on earth they would call me for an interview if that was the policy they were to follow. Perhaps it was to teach me a lesson for the future. The outcome of the interview which would come in a few weeks' time was obvious. Within minutes of my going in, I was escorted out from the same door through which I had walked in with hopes for my 'bright' future in Great Britain. I was dressed down, intimidated, and demeaned by those heads, coming from the elite universities. Their hatred towards my origin and my skin was so obvious that even an ant would understand their body language. The strange part is that no questions were asked by the heads even for the sake of a formality. Why did they ever bother to call me for an interview? Did they wish to prove to the outer world their label of 'Equal Opportunity Employer' at my cost by robbing me of my dignity and my self-respect? I continue to wonder. Even after fifty-four years of that incident the country is still struggling to achieve that 'Equal Opportunity' badge. Will it ever get it? No, never I believe. It is all eye-wash. Humanity will never reach to its perfection. It is the same as it was in Buddha's and Jesus' times.

A few weeks later a regret letter, as expected, arrived at my address. I did not shed tears on it. I just threw it into a waste bin, the fate it deserved. I did not get the job, not because I was not experienced or did not have enough education but because of my origin, my colour, and my appearance. All those assembled heads sat there like robots, rubber-stamping, without moving their tongues to ask one single relevant question to find out more about my background. They had already decided my fate before I even had entered that fateful room, lit with chandeliers, energised with free electricity. Today my company employs 40-50 people of all colours, creed, race, religion, and nationalities. The times have changed. The Chairman had no vision. He could not envisage tomorrow's world coming to Britain. His mentality remained localised to a resident of a small islander. He was wearing the coloured glasses and his vision was blurred, mixed with the colours he wanted to see. He was just a narrow-minded man, full of prejudices.

I had come from a country which was infested with prejudices, not based on colours, but on the religion, the race, the community you came from, the gender, the province, and whom you knew. I thought I had beaten that when I came to UK. But alas sadly I had fallen from a frying pan into a fire.

<u>Trying for a Job Through a Local Job Centre: A Heart-wracking Experience</u>

Beggars never have choices, but they must just keep on knocking the doors in case something drops into their bowls. Opportunity only knocks once but misfortune keeps on knocking until it succeeds in its mission. Desperate as I was

A JOURNEY THROUGH PARTITION AND BEYOND

for any job, I ventured to walk down to the local job centre at Seven Kings to try my luck in case some job was available. It was just 5 minutes' walk from our home at Seven Kings. I was ready to accept any temporary stopgap job if it gave me some income to prop up our finances. Mira was not working because of the expectancy; the financial resources had dried up because of the studies for three years. So, we were just broke, a hand-to-mouth situation. Nature was watching me closely for my patience and perseverance. I was ready for its scrutiny.

It was around 3 o'clock. The queues had finished by the time I got there. The interviewing officer must be in a receptive mood, I thought, to indulge in helping a needy man with problems. There were about four interviewing cubicles manned by different officers. All were busy when I reported. There was no one else in the waiting queue. Soon an officer became free and I walked into his cubicle. As soon as he saw an Asian face, his wits disappeared. He showed signs of stress as if I had stung him. His manners became rough and crude. His language showed the signs of rudeness. So, looking fiercely into my eyes as if I had done something terribly wrong to be there, he opened the dialogue with abruptness.

'Yes.'

'I am looking for a job if you can help me.'

'Where do you live?'

'Oh, just 5 minutes' walk from here.'

'There are no jobs now.'

'Can you suggest anywhere I can try? I am willing to work at any place as long as I get some money.'

'You know there are a lot of people like you who are coming to this country; they do not know any English. As soon as they land at the airport they are taught a couple of English words. One of them is "dole" and the second one is "thank you". You lot are just the lowest of the low of your country and are flooding this country to exploit its benefit system. They get down at the airport and go straight to the dole queue next day to claim money.'

'But...'

'No, buts just leave me alone. Come and see me tomorrow if you want.'

That outburst was very hurtful and insulting. He never offered me a chair to sit on while I saw all the other white locals being treated with dignity and respect. I listened to his outbursts in silence without reacting to his insults. Inside me I was bleeding. Oh God, why did you have to expose me to such a brutal, heartless, and uncompassionate person? He had touched my raw nerves with his stinging words. I was already wounded and was going through very difficult times and now this.

I just walked out. No further dialogue was possible with him. On the way home tears were rolling down my cheeks. How many people saw me in that state on the way I did not care to know. I was not in a mood to accept any etiquette dictated by the society. How to behave in the public arena was not for me when I was wounded in the heart. The emotions have no boundaries and they do not allow you to control them. It was time to let the world see your inner pain. As I walked in that state, the mind was pondering all over the horizon. I just could not find the answer to 'why?'

Wounded people can react badly but for me, a gap of seventeen hours was the God-given opportunity to cool down and respond to his insults with dignity and calmness. Next morning, I walked down to the exchange and sat down on the chair provided for the job seekers. My turn came and someone from another cubicle asked me to see her. I declined.

'Sorry, I am waiting for this gentleman to be free to see him.'

'I can help if you want.'

'No, thank you. I saw him yesterday. So, it is him I must see.'

'Ok, as you wish.'

She walked away.

When he became free, there was one in front of me, waiting to see him. So, I waited. When my turn came, I went in.

'Hello! You remember me sir? I came to see you yesterday for help in finding me a job.'

'Oh, yes in the afternoon.'

'You mind if I sit down?' seeking his permission to occupy the chair opposite to him. This time I was not prepared to be treated as a second-class citizen. In life those who accept insults are as bad as those who inflict them on you. I was not in a mood to be offered a chair, but it was time for me to have it and sit on it.

'Yes, yes please have a seat,' he said.

'I only wanted to see you today because you were rude to me yesterday with no apparent reasons.'

'I am sorry I was very tired by the time you came.'

'That does not give you any right to insult me. You never asked me who I am. What do I want? What is the purpose of my visit? You just started narrating me the incidents which I have nothing to do with. You cannot tarnish everyone who comes here with the same brush. Do you know the agony I have been through since yesterday? That is why I only wanted to talk to you and no one else to clear the opinion you have about all those who look like me. We are not here, trying to stand in the dole queue. We too have dignity and self-respect. You insulted and condemned all the people who are coming here from my subcontinent.'

'I am sorry I didn't mean to hurt you. But tell me now how can I help?'

'You are here to help people get a job. We come to you to help us and listen to our problems and solve them if you can. How can you jump to a conclusion by looking at my face that because I look like some of those who are claiming the dole, I too am going for it?'

'Ok, let me know how I can help?'

I had now cleared all my mental blockages which had been bothering me since yesterday. I had gone over those arguments within me, time and time again. I admired his coolness and his good manners to conduct the meeting. It put my mind at rest. This quality you will only find among the Englishmen who would admire the point of view of their opponents. So, I started the dialogue again.

'I have just appeared for the final examination of engineering degree from West Ham College. As I was studying full-time my financial resources are very strained. We are expecting our first child in a couple of weeks' time and therefore I desperately need a job.'

'Why did you not tell me this yesterday?'

'You did not let me tell you! You just went berserk the moment you saw my face.'

'That means you are a professional. This side of the job centre is not for you. This area is meant for those who are looking for factory jobs. You should not report here.'

'How do I know where to report?'

'You should be going to the other side of the building.'

'Where?'

'I'll take you there. They will register you and put your name in the professional register. They will then circulate your name to the companies interested in your background. They will call you for interview if they are interested.'

'That is a long procedure. How am I going to survive for that long?'

'Once you register yourself, come back here. I will get you registered for the dole here. You don't have to queue for that as those people are,' he said, pointing towards a dole queue waiting to collect their handouts. The whole scenario appeared to be insulting and degrading to human dignity. It was like monks roaming around with a begging bowl. But they must have had some compulsions in their circumstances as I had. Perhaps they had no alternative but to have a begging bowl in their hands. They might have been caught in the doldrums of their economic situations, sacked or laid off by the companies who employed them. No sane self-respecting person would go down to that level and stand in a queue for a free hand-out. We all have ego built into us. I went on, 'No, I will never go in that queue,' I said very bravely even though I knew that the circumstance I was in was not favourable.

'Don't be silly. It is your right to have money from the Government when you are looking for a job. Nobody is obliging you. The law allows you to claim that money.'

'I know but,'

'Let me take you to the other side and get your name registered. After registering there, come back here and I will do the required formalities to get you the money from there. You don't have to queue up. Come and see me and I will get your money here from them.'

He got up and led me to the back of the building. On the entrance door it said, 'Professional Registration Office.' We went in. There were hardly any job seekers there. He left me there to see the interviewing officer with the words, 'When you finish here, come back to me to sort out your dole money.' We parted on a 'goodbye and see you soon' basis. He was transformed and had become very caring, polite, and ready to help a person. His arrogance of yesterday had all gone. I admired his quality of an Englishman and his generosity to understand the problem. Once understood, he went out of his way to help and mend those mistakes he committed in innocence. These qualities are rare among other people of the world. There was no sign of vindictiveness, jealousy, and anger. I became his fan and admired his qualities of accommodation, forget and forgive, and wanting to mend the mistakes he knew he had committed against my being.

The professionals don't find jobs through exchanges. They campaign, sitting in their homes by sending their CVs to various companies of interest or through responding to advertisements in the newspapers. I was doing that, but luck was not helping me, or should I say my colour and my Indian name was filing my job applications in the dustbin.

The officer at the professional centre gave me an application form to fill up at home and then I should return it to be registered. I asked, 'How will you help me find a job?'

'We only register you. When a company needs a man of your calibre and they cannot get them by advertising, they refer the vacancy to us. We then look at our register to find a suitable candidate who would fit their requirements. We write to them if he/she is still available. They then contact the company.'

'So effectively you only introduce the two parties.'

'Yes, you are right.'

'But I need a job now, any job.'

'Sorry, it does not work like that for the professionals. But you may apply for the national assistance and get some money from the Government until you get a job.'

'No. I don't want to do it. I will bring the form filled up tomorrow.'

I left. I did not go back to the previous officer who was going to put me on the dole queue. I just hated those queues and it was not in my blood. I would rather starve to death than have a begging bowl in my hand. To me it is an affront to human dignity.

No Nothing Yet

I filled up the form next day and returned it to the professional job centre. I continued to apply for vacancies. I used to go to the library to see the vacancies in the newspapers but nothing concrete was coming through except polite regrets, wrapped up with nice words of apologies saying, 'Your application has failed on this occasion, but we will keep it on file for future reference if there is a vacancy.' I knew that the 'file' mentioned in the regret letter was nothing more than a dustbin, a garbage rack to be thrown on the scrap heap.

Heating and Ventilation Engineer

I remember applying for a vacancy for a heating and ventilation engineer. I never got any reply from them. I telephoned. The man said, 'Come and see me.' So I went. The office was above a shop in a shopping parade. I went up, knocked on the door, and went in. There was a man sitting behind a desk. The office was poorly lit. There was no secretary. It did not look like an office. It appeared to be a one man show. I became hopeful that perhaps here was a single soul and not a corporate juggernaut that would decide quickly.

'You have a vacancy in heating and ventilation. I telephoned you and you said, "Come and see me". Here I am reporting to find out.'

'There is a vacancy, but I am afraid I cannot consider you for that vacancy. If I give you a job you may go back to your country and set up a company of your own.'

'But I live here, and I have a family here, I have a house here. How can I just leave and go back to India'?

'I know but sorry I cannot consider you as fit for this vacancy.'

There we are. A corporate does not give me a job because no Englishman would like to work under me and another, one-man-band business owner says I might steal his tricks of the trade and run away to my country to set up a business. Even if I were to set up a business in India how on earth would it affect his one-man-band business in UK? His reasoning just did not add up. Both were guilty of damn naked racism and they were just finding excuses not to consider me for the job they had. Here I am today serving the UK PLC for the last 50+ years and still working and paying taxes. I have created many jobs with my sacrifices and I still live in the country and serve it with the best of my ability without claiming even a dime in any form or fashion. I wish God had written on our foreheads what we are and what is hidden behind our heads and hearts.

The Divine's Cruel Verdict

Soon the day came when the results of the examination were to be displayed on the college billboard. The University sent the results to individual candidates by post, but the college got the results earlier. I was not aware of the date of the display but one of my classmates Z who was from Mumbai and was studying civil engineering and lived with us, told me the date. Mira and I went to the college. It was around 11am. There was a big crowd of students gathered around the board. We had to push in the front to see the results. I hated that struggle. So, I stayed away at a distance until the crowd eased up. Z pushed in and came out after seeing the results. I enquired about his results and he said, 'Yeah, I have passed in lower 2nd class. But I could not see your roll number, maybe I missed it.'

Shock waves shook the whole body. Still not losing hope, I pushed through the crowd to see for myself if that was true. Yes, it was. I could not see my roll number either. It confirmed that I had failed in the final examination. The bad news always sinks in with a tremendous jolt. In bad times you always find yourself at the crossroads and you are always on your own. Therefore, there was no one around me to know my inner plight and the pain I was going through. Even my own, the so-called kith and kin, departed and would not hesitate to pass on their evil opinions. Mira was the first one to comment 'I told you so.' She said that I failed because I did not take her advice not to buy the house, a cruel analysis to prove her point of view at the time when I was sinking in life and passing through a most difficult time of my life. I guess that, for her, it was the right time to teach a lesson to the one who had defied her opinion.

I had failed for the second time in my life; the first time was when I appeared in the Physics A-level. It altered the whole course of my future career. If I had got into the elite Imperial college as an internal candidate, I would have got a good degree and then would have got a very good job anywhere on this planet. But now I was ending up struggling to find any job. The greatest opportunity thrown by the Divine in my way was lost forever. This was a real disaster for my future career and my immediate financial well-being. But new in the country and not knowing the difference between studying at an elite college or an ordinary college and its effect on my future, I now think that I should have made some more efforts to pass the A-level Physics. I must blame myself for that and my ignorance. But then a contradictory thought does come, how would I have financed the education for three years. I had no financial backing.

A JOURNEY THROUGH PARTITION AND BEYOND

Why does the world only crown success in life? Is failure not the other side of the same coin? Is it not part of life? As an individual I can handle my failures. I can philosophise on them. I can cope with them but what do you do with society's taunts and cruel comments - impossible to handle them. People will hit you hard in life when you are down. They would never have mercy on you. They only need the opportunity to achieve their goal – to see you in the gutters of life. Society hates you when you are down and feels jealous when you are climbing up the hill. Either way you are a loser.

We came back home. I sat in the lounge on a sofa, in a very pensive and sad mood. Someone took my photograph as I was sitting in the lounge. It tells the whole story. I was utterly devastated. I just did not know how to go from there. No job, pressure of finances, and now failed the finals – the last hope to get a job had all gone. It had created new problems to tackle. Now, when I would fill up an application form for a job, what would I say to the 'would-be employer' – "failed degree holder"? Or how would I account for the gap of three years between my last jobs and the one I am applying for. With racism on the high, this failure added another blow. There was no solution except to move on. I just could not quit life. It was dynamic; it had to move on to something, to somewhere with or without a goal. The only thing which does not move is the dead corpse which I was not. I was a living soul with bubbling energy that could still make me a dynamic achiever. So, I decided to move on to continue to apply for any jobs wherever they were. The only logical position I could apply for was for a designer job in a contract Jigs and Tools design office where I had experience and that would fetch me some quick income. They would not ask me about the past three years of my life. Even if they did, it would not concern them anyway. They needed my experience and my good output which I had, and they did not need a degree to design the special purpose production machinery.

Was it an Intervention of the Divine; if not then Who Mucked up my Degree?

During those days when I was campaigning for the job from home, I noticed a single plastic flower in a pot, placed on the wooden cover of the electric meter in the hallway of our house. I was intrigued. This flower was offered to me by a gypsy woman who was going around in the street from house to house. One day near the examinations, I was staying at home for my studies. She knocked at the door and offered, 'Take this flower. It is a very lucky one. It will give you a big success. Just give me a pound for it.'

Big success, I thought! A plastic flower, no it must be a con. So, I responded, showing my scepticism, 'No, thank you. I don't need it.' And as I was shutting the door, she bargained, 'Ok, give me ten shillings (50p) and have it.'

'No thank you, I don't want it.' And I shut the door on her face.

A few days later, she appeared once again on the door and tried to persuade me to buy the flower. I refused again. I did not buy it. I did not wish to part with ten shillings for dubious reasons. The matter ended there.

Now if I had refused to buy that, how had it appeared there? I asked Z if he had any knowledge of it.

'Oh, yes I bought it. You know she was so insistent that it would bring me luck. So, I reluctantly bought it.' Reluctantly! He was lucky that he bought it.

'How much did you pay for it?'

'Oh, she was asking a pound and I said no way I would pay that sum for a plastic flower. She accepted ten shillings. So, I left it on this cover.'

'I saw her too. She was offering it to me too. I did not buy it. You bought it. I failed, and you got lower 2nd class. Therefore, it was a lucky flower as she said.'

'Yeah, with hindsight it was a good investment even though I always felt that I did not do well in one of the papers. I was expecting a pass degree and not the lower 2nd class.'

In my whole life, I have tried to find an answer to this million-dollar question. And I am still at a loss to understand why. I am not a great believer of God although society had given me not one but many Hindu gods. I was born to a Hindu family and my early education was in Gurukul where I learnt all the Hindu scriptures, reciting and praying twice a day with hymns from Vedas on the holy fire to keep the gods in the sky as happy as possible with my innocent mind. I rebelled and became an agnostic. How do I reconcile the ideas that there is a divine power controlling me? Why on the day of my exam did another 'fortune teller' appear on the scene from nowhere and wish me innocently, 'bad luck'? I failed in the same subject on which he had said 'bad luck.' I had already successfully solved two questions which appeared ditto from a book in the exam and yet my mind went blank and I could not reproduce or redo them. Where is this Divine power and why does it control my life and for what reason? Where had that freedom gone which the Divine claims that He had given me on my birth?

This was not the last time a gypsy lady appeared in my life. In the late 90s, a gypsy woman again appeared at the factory and said, 'You will be selling your business and will be a free man within a year.' With my previous experience, this time I obeyed and gave her £20 as that is what Mira would give me to give her. A year went by and I was still there. I had not sold it. She dropped in once again. Very surprised, she looked at my face, and said, 'Are you still working here? Have you not sold your business yet?'

'No, you said I would sell it within a year and the year has gone by, but nothing has happened.'

'I don't know what went wrong. This time you give me a lot of money and I will pray for you.'

'What is a lot of money? Should I give you £30, are you happy?' As I offered that sum, I looked at Mira who controlled the finances. I have lived on her mercy all my life. Her face was disapproving the figure. She was saying, no that is too much. But still defiantly I enquired and tried to negotiate.

'No, no. A lot more money you have to give.'

'But I cannot afford more. I have not got it. Ok, I will give you £50.' On my offer, Mira's face went red with rage that how on earth I was offering £50. The gypsy lady still insisted on a lot more. However, I persuaded Mira in my language to part with £50. She gave it to me, and I slipped that money in the gypsy lady's hand. Disapprovingly and reluctantly, she said, 'Give me your hand.'

'Which hand?'

'Your right hand.'

I did. She held my hand in her delicate, soft, warm hands and said, 'Now close your eyes. Ask only one thing in your prayers to your God. I will pray for you.'

'I don't know what to ask for, I have nothing there to ask.'

'It does not matter; just ask whatever is in your mind.'

Guess what? I closed my eyes, and, in my prayers, I asked for world peace. 'Please God do not destroy this lovely planet and be merciful to it.' That was my prayer. It was the year 2010 and I still have not managed to sell my business. I continue to work and only Heaven knows when it will retire me, if ever it would.

I still have a lot of questions for which I do not find an answer. Be frank, you reader, and tell me if you have the answer? You may call me an idiot that I prayed for world peace at that time and not being selfish enough to ask for the help of the divine to sell my business. I also don't know what you think of my exam results? Was it a divine intervention? If not, what was it? I am still searching for the answer and I do not find any to 'why did I fail in my exam?' Is it because I failed to buy that plastic flower? How could that simple gypsy girl know that I would only pass my exam if I had bought that plastic flower? Was that plastic flower only a symbol of submission to the authority of the gypsy girl? 50p was not going to make her rich. What is it and why did it happen? After the exam results, I wrote a letter to the University explaining the details of the incident on the night of my visit to B and asking them to show compassion and give me a pass degree after getting my references from my lecturers at the college. The University showed sympathy but nothing more. So, I had to take the exam again next year and I got a humble pass degree without distinction. Was my wasted one year with all the struggles in store worth only 50p? Where is the justification in God's house that he valued my one year with that 50p?

Talking about the Divine control of our lives, I had some other instances in my life for which again I do not find answers. Why had they happened? I will mention them later as I write further my story.

The Birth of Our First Child

I was still unemployed and had no source of income. Nature does not wait for your circumstance to change. It just moves on with its calculated speed. Soon a nature call came on 30th September or 1st October 1963 for the imminent arrival of our first child. I called the ambulance and we took Mira to the Newham Maternity Hospital, Forest Lane. She was admitted. There were no complications. Our daughter was born on 3rd October. I used to go to my class fellow R, who lived only ten minutes' walk from the hospital. We used to sit together and share the miseries of our exam results. He used to make me delicious onion sandwiches and after eating them we would both walk down to the hospital to see Mira.

R too had failed in his 2nd year. He later moved to live with us at Seven Kings. He was quite an intelligent person and came from a good family in India. He used to have a lousy habit of betting on the horses rather than spending time to study. His failure was not a God-sent punishment, but it was his own fault for indulging in bad habits. This habit had inflicted unnecessary miseries on him. He had an account with a bookie near our home. He would bet on the horse by telephone and then see the races on the TV to find whether the horse had won or lost. I had seen the stress on his face when he was watching those races and his horse had failed to win. He used to shake his body to encourage his horse to run faster. He knew the bio-history of all the horses in the race. It took him another two years to get a pass degree.

Within a couple of days of birth, Mira was discharged from the hospital. Poverty was taking its toll and had reached to its peak. We had no money to buy clothes to dress the little girl, our first loving child, to bring her home. A good friend, on her visit to the hospital, had given a gift of a white shawl on her birthday. Mira wrapped her up in that to bring her home. In those days there was a maternity allowance of £12 for every newly born child. We were denied that handout too because they said that, according to rules, we had not contributed to the NI when I was a student and therefore we were not entitled to that. Racism was at its peak, even if there was a way to help, the bureaucrats would not help. At every step in life we found stumbling blocks from those who were able to help the needy. Those times have passed but those cruel memories continue to haunt and inflict pains.

Within days of our daughter's birth I got a job in a contract jig and tool design office at Harrow, a long way to travel from Seven Kings, but I had no choice. I was used to this kind of work and I think I was getting around £30/week plus overtime. During my interview I told the Head that I had appeared for the degree exam which I had failed. They needed my services and my experience and were not concerned about my failure to obtain a degree or where I lived, except that I would be able to travel that distance and be there every day on time. He encouraged me to finish the degree next year and they might be able to offer a job to suit my qualifications with better pay. I was not sure where and how they would. I knew that they were not doing any complex calculations such as designing bridges etc where a degree holder's expertise was required. The head also encouraged me to move to Harrow to be nearer to the office. However, we stayed where we were as we had now a good circle of friends. I remember it used to take me nearly two hours to travel one way to Harrow station and then walk down to the office another 5 minutes. The office was above a shopping parade. I used to leave home early around 6am and reach back around 8pm. But I was grateful to God for this small mercy that at least I was back on financial stability.

A Year Later -Ritu's First Birthday
We celebrated her first birthday with a big bang. I bet she did not know much about what was happening. Mira made lovely and tasty food, fitting for the occasion. A variety of foods were prepared, some for the grown-ups with hot curries and others for the children. The sitting room was decorated with all kinds of balloons. The table was set with a decorative cake to be cut. All our friends with their children were invited and the party began in the evening and finished around 11pm. It was an experience not to be forgotten. Only a few months earlier we were penniless and were trying to find money to clothe her. Things had now changed for the better within these few months. I had a designer job and Mira had also gone back to teaching. My brother's family which had arrived to join my brother were all there. When my sister-in-law arrived in the country she said to me that she had come to take us all back to India. She is still here in the country and well settled with her children. At the birthday party we took quite a few photographs.

The Growing Child
The daily grind of family life was also in full swing. The little girl was growing. She was being deposited with a housewife baby-minder in the morning and collected in the evening. Mira detested that. But when you are an immigrant, settling down in a foreign land and building your future with meagre resources, there were no choices but to accept such headaches and move on. Life had to be compromised on lots of issues whether one liked it or not. Without those sacrifices at the time I believe we would probably be living somewhere in a council house and on a handout from the government, a totally unacceptable situation. I say this

because without those sacrifices I would have had no further education, no marriage, and no home. There was no need to leave my country, stay away from my loved ones for the last fifty-five years, and then turn into an NRI (non-resident or non-returning Indian), a tag given to me by the incompetent leaders of my country of birth. It is a sad and hurtful tale to tell.

Ritu, being a child, was prone to a lot of infectious diseases. She used to be ill quite often. Nearly every third or fourth week she would be down with high fevers reaching to 103-104 degrees. Her whole body used to shiver, an unbearable scene to watch. Sometimes Mira would take a couple of days off and other times I used to stay home to look after. The diagnoses were that she was suffering from the growth in tonsils which, when infected, were making her suffer from high temperatures. A few times when tending her, I cried as I just could not see her suffering. The doctors would not operate to remove her tonsils until she was three. Going through that routine at nearly every three-week intervals was a very painful experience. Sometimes Mira had got into difficulty with her head at school because of her repeated time off from work. A big relief came when Ritu turned three, a magic age for children to undergo an operation. She was operated on at Barking Hospital. She was admitted for the night to be operated on next morning and we were asked to collect her next midday. It was very painful to be separated for those two nights from her at that tender age and leaving her in the care of nurses. For them she was only another patient, a number in the ward, to be operated upon next morning. That night I remember we both could not sleep the whole night. We counted the hours and minutes so eagerly for the time when we were to go and collect her on the day after the operation. She still had pain in her throat and could not speak and eat. The nurses asked us to feed her ice cream. Soon those fevers and infections had passed into history.

A Bad Accident

As you will see later, in 1964 I started work at Borough Polytechnic. One day in 1966 as I arrived home from the Poly, Mira was at home with a family friend S. I was surprised but not alarmed as we used to meet them at least two, three times a week. After I settled down, we decided to go for some local shopping. I picked up Ritu. I was told that we were not taking her in the pram. I obeyed. I walked a few feet in front of them. We must have walked only a few hundred feet on the footpath when I overheard S coaxing Mira to tell me about the accident that had happened during the day. Mira was hesitating and was saying that she would tell me later. I slowed down and joined them. I asked, 'What is Mira going to tell me later?' S volunteered, 'You know, Ritu had an accident today on the road with a motorcycle.'

'What happened? She looks alright to me.'

A JOURNEY THROUGH PARTITION AND BEYOND

At that point Mira coughed up, 'This morning I was late to take her to the baby minder and I was crossing the main road. I looked on both sides and after seeing no vehicle on either side, I started crossing. As I reached to a couple of feet from the kerb on the other side, a motor cycle came at speed and hit the pram. Ritu's body flew out of the pram and dropped on the footpath. The pram, with the impact, was snatched away from my hands. It was all twisted and bent and landed on another place on the road. I stood there in shock. It happened so fast that I did not know how all this had happened.' I heard her story in total amazement and concern.

'But I always asked you many times that you should never cross this busy road anywhere else but at the zebra crossing.'

'I know but I was late, and I took the chance to cross the road there. Someone called the ambulance and I rushed to see Ritu on the footpath; she was crying with shock but thank heavens she was unhurt. The whole impact force was absorbed by the pram and this saved her from getting injured. The motorcyclist apologised and drove off.'

Mira came back home with the broken pram and hid it under the staircase so that I didn't get a shock when I come back home. Then she called S who stayed with her the whole day. When we came back from shopping, I inspected the pram. It was very badly damaged. Ritu escaped bad injury or even death because of divine intervention. I was upset but, to the surprise of Mira and S, I did not say much. They were expecting that I would be shouting at Mira. I knew it was an unfortunate accident and Mira was shocked probably more than I was when it happened right under her supervision. She coped with that shock very well. Under the pressure of life which we were all going through in those days it is amazing that we coped so well.

We used to get up early morning, do our daily chores, get the child ready, then walk to the nursery, walk back to the station, and then be off to work. The process reversed soon after working hours finished. We would then cook an Indian meal, eat, and by seven one of us would take Ritu to bed. We used to read the same book to Ritu, like a parrot, until the little madam would nod off. That depended on how tired or alert she was. I remember that when a couple of times I cheated her by missing a few lines or a page, she would immediately point out that I had missed a page. I would deny it but she would insist that I did. I had to go back to the previous page and read it to avoid a problem. She was always a winner. After that, with a bit of luck, we might get a few minutes to watch the TV and then go into the cold bed with a hot-water bottle. That was every day that was, a routine with no excitements.

Beggar Chased the Bank Again

It was summer 1965. Ritu was approaching two years old. The pressure from Mira's family was mounting that it was time that she should now go to India to see them. Ritu was the first grandchild and they were getting very excited to hold her, to adore her, and play with her. We both were working, and yet we had no savings to pay for her travel to India.

On one Saturday, I made an appointment to see the manager at the Westminster Bank, Seven Kings. At the appointed time I presented myself in his small office. As I entered, he looked at me fiercely, and examined me from top to bottom with his suspicious eyes. He gave me the impression that I was an intruder into his office and was disturbing his peaceful life. The bank managers were second only to God in those days. What they said or did was a firm line drawn on the rock. Nobody questioned their authority. They held your future in their closed fists and if the fist remained closed it was very hard to open. They decided your future prosperity. But when it opened, your stars were woken up from their long sleep in heavens. I had had that experience only a couple of years earlier when a manager granted us an overdraft facility that opened all the locked doors in front of us. We then, with not a penny in savings, managed to buy a house.

He raised his eyebrows and roared from his rotating comfortable chair.

'Yeah, what can I do for you?' he asked with his stiff authoritarian tone, without any welcoming gestures of politeness. I had just stepped into his office and barely had a chance to see his face before he froze me and disarmed me instantly. That treatment was unexpected from an English gentleman of financial clout. I became fearful. However, I collected my courage and asked with tongue in cheek, 'I would like to send my wife and daughter to India for a holiday. I wonder if I can borrow some money for the airline tickets.'

'We do not lend money for holidays.' He refused my ill-conceived, though genuine, requirement bluntly. I froze but did not give up and continued cheekily, 'I am a teacher and so is my wife. You get our regular income directly paid into our account in the bank. It is quite safe to lend to people like me for a couple of months to buy an air ticket. So where is the problem?' I insisted.

'No, we do not lend any money for holidays. So please do not waste my time.'

I just walked out in disgust. I knew that these bank shops were just hollow. They boast that they are the financial seeds for the growth in the economy but sadly they are empty with no oil in them. They never germinate, and they die no matter whether the soil is fertile or sandy. One manager of the same bank was quite happy to lend to a student like me with zero security while another one just four years later was refusing the same person who was a hell of a lot better off than before. I now had a secure government job and was also a homeowner. Maybe he was right that the bank did not lend money for holidays, but they were certainly taught and trained to show dignity and respect to their clients from whose deposits they earn money by lending it. He was totally out of order here.

With hindsight, it was my stupidity to expect a loan for a holiday. But that request was from an innocent man who was not aware how the banks operate. I know that now. It was just a silly idea to ask for loans for pleasures.

However, it was a good experience.

CHAPTER 5: EMPLOYMENT AFTER GRADUATION

With only a pass degree in hand, I was not good enough to head for the teaching career where racism was at a bit more tolerable levels and hence there were better chances of getting a job. Industry did not insist on higher level degrees but was rife with racism as I have mentioned in Chapter 4. However, I was keeping all my options open and continued to apply wherever there was a vacancy. The best reply I could get was 'regret' and that had become a norm of my life. I accepted that with dignity and with a pinch of salt. One can never change the human prejudices. We are all born with them. We can only work within their limitations, accept them, and hope for the best. It is always an uphill task for a commoner, with no connections, no bribery to give, or approaches, to accept second fiddle in life. It happens in every country. The human society will never be free from it. It does not matter what kind of political system the country operates. So, continuing our dialogue,

Designers Job at Ford Motor Co

This job was advertised for their local Research & Development office near Dagenham. I was called to attend the interview. First, I was interviewed by the Personnel Department. They found me a suitable candidate for the job and sent me to see the head of design under whom I was to work.

Everything went well in the interview with the head. He was a young, energetic, and nice fellow to work with. I had the education; had the design experience; was living only four miles from the factory; and was sure that I would be in for the job. We discussed the salary, the office where I was going to work, the type of work I would be assigned, and the working conditions. But then suddenly, we hit a rock. He finally asked, 'Which church do you go to?'

It was a very delicate and political question. It had huge implications. He wanted to know my denomination, my beliefs. No one would ask such questions until and unless he was trying to recruit a like-minded person. In any case, why did it matter so much to him that he wanted to find out my personal beliefs? They were very personal to me and even I was not sure about them. They change with the time. They are never fixed. The route to God is infinite. There is no set route how to get to Him. It is all individual. All the enlightened people before us have left no traces of it. They all got enlightenment by following their hearts. The route to enlightenment is like a bird flying in the sky. They never leave any traces of their flying. Why was this silly question being asked by such an educated person? I was being hired as a designer and not as a priest to preach theology. I was flabbergasted. I was being employed by the Ford Motor Company to do a certain job and I should be employed if I was capable enough to do that job. The Ford Company had no interest in my beliefs if those beliefs had no conflict with their business activities. So, I did not know how to respond within moments and on the spot without given time to think on such a complex issue. However, I said, 'I was born to a Hindu family. They gave me a Hindu name and taught me to follow the vast philosophy of Hinduism which gives freedom to go to temples or stay home. I do not go to any church. I even do not go to temples as such.'

That was true. Hinduism is very vast; it is like an endless ocean. It has no boundaries. The sky is the limit to its vastness and it bestows complete freedom to its followers. They can even choose their own God to worship. They can pick up literally any object of choice from anywhere in the natural world – a piece of stone or wood - install it anywhere, bow down their heads in reverence and lo, he has made a temple for worship. There is no figurehead, as in other religions, to guide you or dictate to you to follow the rules of the religion in certain form or fashion. Its real beauty is that you are completely free to do what you like. For instance, I can bow or not to any deities in the temples. I can pick and choose my unique deity to worship from anywhere on the planet. I can treat the deity the way I want, I can roughly treat it, I can sleep with it, sit with it. In one sentence I can do what I like to do with it and yet it would not be considered as sin or any offence to any Hindu in any form. It is a very, very tolerant religion. I can write my own scriptures, I can say my own prayers in my own words and the way I like. I could even be an atheist and yet I will remain part of the Hindu society. No Hindu would protest, or agitate to have me thrown out of the religion, or murder me. Not only this, but this religion also allows you to enter into your inner world and you can declare yourself Avatar, a great Saint.

Now how could I tell him the whole philosophy of ancient Hinduism in seconds? He was able to hire and fire me, but he still was a human being like I was. He did not have the super powers of the divine. They reside solely with Him. Humans try to occupy that chair, but they forget that soon their time will be up. God made them mortals because He knew that one day they would try to snatch his omnipresent chair. So, he gave them only eighty odd years to show off their arrogance.

However, in those days there were hardly any temples in UK. Even if there were I was not that much of a dogmatic religious buffoon to rub my nose in front of a deity. Of course, as a human we are beaten in life by our circumstances as I was and as all the commoners are. I was scared too with my recent experiences. I too needed some godly figure, in front of whom I could kneel to beg for His mercy and help remove all the pains of life I was going through, but these had nothing to do with beliefs. It was just a psychological brainwash and human weakness to relieve the pains of life. His face said that he did not like my reply. He impatiently intervened, 'But you must be going to some church on Sundays to pray.'

That told me that he was ignorant about the other religions on this planet. His knowledge was limited. He was too narrow-minded, a bigot. I responded with a bit of a confidence, 'No, I do not go to any church. I am not that religiously minded. To me humanity is more important, and I belong to it, I was born into it. That is my religion and I strive to be a good human being.'

I knew I would now be thrown out of the door. This man, although foolish enough to ask such questions, was delving into the muddy waters of personal beliefs. I could not be dishonest and tell him lies about my thoughts on religion simply because I was on my knees and was in the marketplace to find a job. Telling lies to achieve a certain aim of life would have been a naked deception. I would not be able to forgive myself for all these years I have lived although I might have secured a job to satisfy my immediate needs. So, we got up and he said, 'I will be writing to you if we are ready to offer you this job.'

'I look forward to hearing from you and thank you for allowing me to see you to discuss the employment opportunity at Ford's.'

We parted with a hand shake. I went back to the personnel department to tell the guy there how the interview went. He asked if I was given a date of joining his office. I said, no and I don't think he would offer me the job.

'But why not?'

'He asked some awkward questions like which church do I go to. I said I do not go to a church. He did not like it.'

'But he should not have asked these questions. We had already interviewed you and selected you for the job. We only sent you to see him to get you introduced to him as he is head of that department. It was just a formality really.'

'Well I may be wrong, but I don't think he will allow me to work there.'

I left. When I reached home, Mira asked me about the interview and I told her the story.

A JOURNEY THROUGH PARTITION AND BEYOND

Within a week I had a regret reply. Another episode of human prejudices had passed by. If it was not my colour, then it was my religion. Or someone picked up my place of origin, my native country where I come from. If at the time of my birth, my mother happened to be on the British Island, or on a British owned ship, or on a British aeroplane I would be British. What nonsense! What baloney! These boundaries are drawn by humans and not by the planet itself. The planet is one and we all humans should have the right to live where we choose to live. Suppose if all these characteristics were matched up, then the interviewers would have invented some other reasons to reject me. They could have then said the candidate is too fat, too slim, too young or too old. His features were not acceptable to the eyes, his nose is fat or slim, and his eyes are wonky. His lips are ugly and are not kissable. In fact, they could pick up anything to show you the door.

Research Assistant at Borough Polytechnic

I saw two vacancies advertised for research assistants for the Mechanical and Production Department at the Borough Poly, London. The yearly scholarship was £850/year. The candidate was to help in the departmental research and work for the External Master's degree from the University of London. I thought it was a great opportunity to get a master's degree which would wipe out all the bad record of final year failure and the effects of my pass degree in getting future employment opportunities. Next day I went to the Poly and knocked at the door of Dr Douglas who was the head of the department. He was a tall, gentle, polite, handsome, and bespectacled middle-aged gentleman. I was impressed with his personality and his civil manners. He could not afford to be prejudiced as he was working in a college in the heart of London which had students of all kinds of cultures, colours, and nationalities. As he opened the door, I murmured timidly, 'Sir I have come to see you about that research assistant job you have advertised. I have just passed my degree and I am looking for some opportunity for a higher degree.'

'We had two vacancies – one in the mechanical department and the other in the production department. The one in the mechanical department is already filled. He is a graduate and will be joining soon. He will be working under me. The production side is organised by its head, Principal Lecturer Mr G. Go and see him. He will be most interested in your candidature and will explain to you the requirements. If he is happy with you I would have no objection.'

My goodness, how simple and easy it was made by that easy-going head. For the production department they had already tried to recruit someone before but without any success. I went on to find Mr G. It was tea break and some student suggested trying the canteen. He was there and was having a break with some students. I introduced myself. He explained that he had the funding and a project to cut stainless steel sheet with a tool, superimposed with axial vibrations on a routing machine. I would have to help him on the project so that he could get his PhD and I could apply for my Master's. If I was ready to work on the project, he was willing to offer me the job.

I did not have much experience on the subject. I had a mechanical degree, but I had a lot of designing experience of jigs, tools, and various special purpose production machines to produce a variety of components used in the automobile and aeronautical industry.

I accepted the job on that brief. I was to get a yearly stipend of £850 with a possibility of part-time teaching in the evenings. I started the job at the beginning of September 1964, and started evening teaching in January 1965.

I was totally free to work on my own. I could go to the college at the time I wanted and come back when I wanted. But I never took liberties with that freedom. I maintained the discipline as I wanted to have M. Phil to wipe out the blot of failure in my third year and getting a pass degree. I used to be there by 9am and leave by 4.30pm. Sometimes I was absent when my daughter used to be ill. She used to suffer from high fever because of the tonsillitis. The choice was either Mira taking a day off from school or me. We shared that absenteeism as was convenient for us.

G never gave me any guidelines or directions. He himself had no research experience or knowledge of it, although he pretended that he knew it all. He was as much a novice in getting a master's degree as I was. Rather, I was more educated because I had a degree in engineering and he had a higher national certificate. He never provided me any facility. I had no place to sit and work. I used to sit in the college library and search the literature on metal cutting, its various parameters affecting the machining of metals. Slowly but steadily I started to understand the subject and started collecting the data for the research project I was going to work on. It was all wishy-washy, without any systematic approach to the subject, but I had no choice but to move on into the dark valleys of the subject. Sometimes I wonder why it had always been a nightmare for me to get the education I wanted. First, partition came when I was in the 9th class and I lost my systematic learning of science subjects. Then I had to study at home to pass my matriculation. My Diploma in engineering I got from a third-class institution which was begging for students to start the engineering college with hardly any laboratory facilities available. It gave the basics and incentives to go for something better but never gave planned education in engineering. Then I continued to study at private colleges in Delhi while working to pass degrees in English and Mathematics. Even in Britain I lost the opportunity to study for an internal degree at Imperial and ended up going for an external degree at West Ham, a college with meagre facilities. Now I had the opportunity to study for the Master's but without a guru's

A JOURNEY THROUGH PARTITION AND BEYOND

guidance and help. The only time I could have had the chance to gain a PhD in Industrial Engineering, under good supervision and guidance at a known institution, was in USA. But it was bungled up by my other half who did not like to live in USA and used to often repeat, 'How long will you continue to study?' It is said that 'behind every successful man, there is a woman', but I would like to add that behind every unsuccessful man there is also a woman, unless the divine is fiddling with his flute and not allowing him to play a beautiful melody. So, I lost that opportunity too. I cannot figure out why the divine enjoys throwing so many thorns in the way of some people while some ride higher and higher in life without much ado.

<u>Research Experience at Borough Poly</u>

However, one must move on in life without worrying about the thorns and flowers laid on the path. The learning curve and the experience in life must move on like a stream of water, fighting its way, avoiding the pitfalls, and serving and quenching the thirst of anyone and everyone on the way. It was September 1964. I was now a simple, ordinary, and without any distinctions, an engineering graduate. I had achieved a lifetime ambition but without any fanfares. No one could predict whether I would have been more successful in life if I had a better degree than I have now. Success never comes with education alone. There are many hurdles to be crossed. Success and failures are society's labels. The amount of wealth one has accumulated is measured, but society never bothers to know how it is collected. You may collect it by devious and illicit means; by bribing, by corruptions, by selling drugs, or by selling bodies of innocents. But it still showers the honours and higher positions on those who don't deserve. Look at the House of Lords where you become a lord simply by donating to the political parties. It is an unnecessary pressure. Everyone is running faster and faster to get ahead of the other until death catches up. See for yourself when you drive on the motorways. Stay in the slow lane. You will find someone who has overtaken you in the next lane looking at you as if saying, 'Hey, you are an idiot driver.' Then lo, some clever one in the fast lane flagged this driver with a whoosh, showing him his two fingers, not visibly but that is what he is trying to do. What is going on man? What is all this stupid rush to beat the other and for what? You also may notice, which I have many times, that, if you are driving a banger, and a convertible well-polished Rolls with a bird on the passenger seat passes by you, the show-off driver will look at you to see if you have been impressed by his presence or not. If you ignore his presence, you would notice his face would flop. His ego would be hurt. His body would sink in his seat. He was trying to intimidate you with his possession. Achievements depend upon the opportunities thrown in the way of individuals and they only come with one's contacts in the hierarchy. Those contacts are only available to those who are born with a silver spoon or if they have something under their arms to bribe their way up on the ladder. The rest are all used as the serving classes for the rich and the powerful. Success also does not mean that one is happy.

I had no intentions, no desires, and no inclination for the research or to pursue the higher degree but it was the circumstances that pushed me into it. But I do not regret that push by the divine.

A couple of months after I joined the college, G, realising his mistake, provided me a desk and chair in a shared room, somewhere in the hiding places of the college. It was solitary, dingy, dirty and un-inspiring where concentration was impossible. The college was ready to give me the bursary of £850 per year but never considered investing some money to provide me the amenities where I could sit in peace and deliberate for the project.

In my case, the Principal Lecturer told me that the equipment would be coming for the research in a few months' time. He had no plans yet where he was going to install it. In the meantime, he said that I should start finding information on the methods of measuring metal cutting temperatures, the power requirements to cut a given sheet of metal, and their instrumentation. He never asked me to register for the master's, leave aside encouraging me. Therefore, I would go to the college library, read the latest research on metal cutting and their measuring instruments. I also read quite a bit in the books about the electronic equipment which was needed to construct measuring instruments. I had no guidance from PL and he was never available for help. If I wanted to see him, either I could not find him, or he would be lunching in the canteen and chatting with other students he was teaching.

A few months had gone by and one day we met in the canteen. He started moaning that I did not come to the college regularly, mostly I was absent. I denied that because I used to be in the library to research the subject I was to work on. He also wanted to know if I had written a brief on the metal cutting and the type of instruments required for the project. He demanded that I should have done all that by now as he needed all that info for his project to gain his PhD. On his unreasonable demand, I protested that it was not the brief given to me when I was appointed as a research assistant. I was told that I would be working under his guidance to obtain a Master's for myself but now he was twisting that brief. 'You are asking me to find all that info for your benefit. Can you please tell me that you can hire a graduate for £850 a year just to do your donkey work so that you can get the PhD and I get nothing? If you wish to work for the PhD, you find those details yourself,' I replied in disgust.

'No, your brief is that you do what I tell you. If you are not doing that, you will lose your position.'

'Being my supervisor, you are supposed to guide me to work for my Master's, but you are never available. You just have not taken your responsibility seriously. If you wish to take my job away, do it. The world is bigger than this Poly and who knows I might get a better opportunity than this.'

And I left in disgust. I had uttered those bold words but inside me I was frightened. Opportunity had come and now I was blowing it away. I was getting some income and our finances were a bit better in this racist land of opportunity but with a heavy price tag. I left the entire outcome of this debacle to the lord to work out.

Time was moving fast, and I had made no progress except to read some research papers and books to decide the rudiments of the topic to work on. When I was in those doldrums of not knowing how to finalise the topic and how to go about registering it, I got lucky. One day when I was walking in the corridor, I met a young fellow R. He knew who I was, but I did not know him. We introduced ourselves. He had also joined as a research assistant to work under Dr D. He was a lovely young fellow, very articulate, decent, humble, and free from prejudices. With time we became good friends. He registered himself for M. Phil for the London University, chose a topic, got the money from the head, and was busy in digging out the info from the library. He was getting good guidance from D and would routinely discuss all the problems and issues with him. He was well guided. His topic came under Mechanical and hence the guidance from D who was Mechanical himself. It worked well for R and I found myself greatly handicapped without any supervision. I had not even seen or heard the name of the machine that I was to work on.

One day as I was walking through the corridor I bumped into R again. We chatted briefly, and he wanted to know how I was getting on. He suggested that, to know one another better, I should follow him to his room where we could discuss our mutual problems. So, I followed him to his small room where he could work in peace without any disturbance. His first question was, 'How long have you been working as Assistant?'

'About six months.' I then gave him brief details about who I was working with, and the subject I was working on.

'Oh, you are working with G. You know you must be careful with him. He is also trying to get the Master's or PhD. He might exploit you. He is competing with you. He might try to get all the info from you and use it for his own thesis. He may not also even allow you to use the equipment. He is getting the equipment from a company which manufactures those woodworking routing machines and they want to investigate if metal sheets can also be efficiently machined on those machines. You are on his mercy to provide the facility or not.'

'So, what do I do then?'

'Just be a bit selfish. Be good to him so that he does not deny the use of the equipment to you and keep all the data you are collecting to yourself. He cannot force you to give him the data you are collecting.'

'Oh, it is quite complicated. I already had a bit of a tiff with him. He wanted me to hand over all I have written about the subject so far, for his own use,' I said disappointedly.

'No, as I said - do not give him any info you are collecting for your project.'

'Then what do I do when he is demanding it. He is threatening me that he would take my job away.'

'No, he cannot do it. You are employed by the college and not by him. If he bothers you, go and talk to D. He is the head; he will sort out your problem. When I am with him next time, I will mention to him that you are having some problems from G.'

'Ok, thanks for your help.'

'Have you registered yourself for the Master's yet?'

'No, how do you do that?'

'Well, you get a form from the university and write a synopsis.'

'What is that?'

'It is just a paragraph written about your intended research and the areas which you will explore. You may alter it later if you do not follow that line of research. I will help you write that. Let us get the form first.'

Don't you think, an angel appeared on the scene from nowhere.

He wrote for the form for me as he knew where to get it. He had done that for himself. When the form arrived, we went to his room. He filled in the form for me, including the synopsis, and I signed it. In the synopsis, in addition to measuring temperatures and power requirements, I also added measuring the change in the hardness of the metal after routing it. Effectively, with that addition, I became my own enemy. I had increased my workload a lot more than was required. Perhaps the research topic became closer to getting a PhD. Now for the first time in six months I had moved a step forward in achieving a goal towards a master's degree. From then on, we became good friends. Every day at lunch break we would go to the pub opposite to the college to have a pint of beer with some hot meals of the day. Mine was always a vegetarian dish of the day. We would share our progress on our research topics. His topic was on the airflow on aeroplane wings. He was way ahead of me because he got the money in time to buy his equipment and, he was not competing with his supervisor. More months went by, I was still not getting anywhere. All of a sudden I learnt that the routing machine, loaned by the manufacturer, had arrived. G gave me the news with a clear warning that I was not allowed to use the machine when he was using it because

A JOURNEY THROUGH PARTITION AND BEYOND

he had preference over me for its usage. Also, I would have to design and build my own instrumentations for measuring cutting temperatures and power requirements. I accepted his challenge.

R had done his research, collected all the data, written the thesis, got a lecturer's job at the City University and moved away. I was still struggling. I had not even seen the machine yet; leave aside being allowed to use the machine. G was guarding all the secrets of the machine jealously like a snake.

The M. Phil Project

The project was to investigate the changes in the cutting parameters - such as cutting temperature, cutting torque, and the micro hardness of the material when the routing cutter was to be superimposed with axial vibrations. I used a stainless sheet as the cutting material. The machine was supplied by Wadkins, but it did not arrive until the end of 1966. I had by then, in September 1966, left my research assistant job at Borough Poly to start teaching at Barking College (see later). Barking College allowed me to continue my research part-time, and G didn't object either, and I also continued teaching Engineering Drawing one evening a week at the Borough. When the Wadkins machine arrived, G told me in point blank terms that he would use the machine first and I was not allowed to touch it without his permission.

I knew it would happen as it was turning into a rivalry of who would be the first to submit the thesis. R had already warned me that because G also wanted to use the equipment to get a higher degree, he was just using me to provide him all the initial research info required for him to move forward. He was right. G was using me because he asked me a few times about what exactly I was doing in the library and when I was going to give him the research report. First, I said I was working on it but after R's warning I said to him that I was preparing the report for my thesis and I would only let him look at it, but he was not supposed to use any of the info in that for his thesis. He refused to accept that and continued his threats with grave consequences. I just ignored them. And so far, he had not allowed me to see the machine either. Finally, one day, and I don't know why, wisdom dawned on him. Somehow his heart melted, and he agreed that I could use the equipment in the summer holidays of 1968. But if I missed that opportunity, I would not be allowed to touch the equipment. The ultimatum was accepted.

So, the priority was to know exactly how far the research had been done on the subject. There was none on the routing machine but there was a lot of work already done on the subject by using other machines and materials by superimposing the vibrations on the tool. So, I had to first learn about the various cutting parameters involved, their measuring techniques and their design and instrumentations. I chose to measure the cutting temperature, the cutting power requirements, and the resulting hardness in the cut metal.

My chapter for the introduction, which G was demanding to be handed over to him, was ready. Also, having learnt about the subject and the measuring techniques, I now started designing the equipment. Designing special equipment was my expertise anyway. Then I started making the parts in the college workshop. The most precision pieces were the octagonally shaped rings for measuring the variation in the electrical signals generated while cutting. I also needed to learn about the properties of photo detectors and the choices available. Each detector required instrumentation for reading the variations of the cutting temperatures. Furthermore, I also had to learn how to measure the micro-hardness of the materials before and after cutting. I got a big help from the Indian technicians who were working in the various departments of the college. Micro-hardness help came from the metallurgy department, the instrumentations required for measuring the various parameters came from the physics department.

So, I worked hard to learn all those techniques from books and from the technicians by using them in their department labs. It was a tragedy that there was no help available from my supervisor or from the Head. I only scratched the surface of the instrumentations and devices I used. I only learnt what I needed to learn, and that too in small bits without going deeper into the subject. The same way when I was analysing the data on a computer, I did not know anything about how the computers worked and how they analysed the data. I had to take help from a friend to analyse my data. More problems were added when I started writing my thesis. I had no knowledge, no experience, no guidance in how to write and present a research paper to the well-known academicians. It was all a nightmare to achieve without proper supervision. It was like someone throwing me into the sea with no swimming experience. All the time I was heading towards the darkness.

Later, when I went to America, I found that this was the biggest weakness in the British educational system. The American system is far superior on this. Their system prepares the student first under the guidance of a tutor in those subjects which the students need to learn before embarking on researching the topic. In my case it was nothing but a do-or-die situation. Either I had to find out all the relevant information myself, analyse it, solve problems and write them up, or, failing that, just quit. Quitting was not in my blood. I had never allowed that word into my dictionary. The lucky ones would have guidance from their experienced supervisors who would act like mentors to feed them and help them in times of trouble. So, I had to carry on regardless. It took me longer but then I had no choice.

I designed my measuring equipment and got the components made at the college workshop by buttering up the technicians. I tested the components,

A JOURNEY THROUGH PARTITION AND BEYOND

perfected them, installed them and I was ready to use them in the midsummer college break of 1968. I only had the last three weeks of the summer holidays to beat the challenge thrown at me by G. I was going to the Borough in the morning to collect my data with and without superimposing the axial vibrations on the routing tool. If I required any know-how about the measuring instruments, the lab technicians in the other departments were still available and were willing to help. They were angels and helped me a lot in lending me their equipment, assembling them, and teaching me how to use them. I collected my data within those three weeks. I even measured the hardness of the cutting materials in the metallurgy department of the Borough. I had no facility at Barking College where I was teaching. As soon as Borough opened I went to see G and told him that I had got all the results I wanted. I had left all the set-ups I had used, including the measuring devices which I had made and used for my experiments. They were all there for him to use for his experiments. He pretended to show his satisfaction and happiness on my achievements. He also congratulated himself on how nice he had been to help me to get those results. I did not wish to hurt his ego and thanked him for sparing me the machine during the summer vacations so I could get my results.

However, I am happy to agree on one point here. When the paths on which one must tread are strewn with thorns, the human ego is then challenged. The determination to win and conquer always gets a huge boost. In my case the gauntlet of time limitation G imposed on me boosted my inner core to accept that challenge and finish the job in time. That way he really helped me, but apart from that I had no guidance from him as he himself had no knowledge to guide me anyway. He had no degree or educational background to help.

I told him that he could use all the equipment I had assembled, designed, and constructed for getting my data. But he never revealed to me what type of degree he had registered for. He always kept his plans close to his chest. I don't think he ever used the equipment or pursued it further to get any degree. He was a hollow bragger who had all the opportunity and position to achieve his ambitions but lacked the drive. The drive comes only if you have the ambitions to fulfil. The ambitions arise only when you are struggling to succeed in life. In his case he was already earning a fat salary, with high position, with a good pension to retire on in about ten years' time. The attitude then was 'why bother and for what?' My position was totally different. I was an immigrant with all the disadvantages strewn in my way; I had left my country to succeed and was just on the first steps of a ladder to build my career; I had no money and had not yet gathered any achievements to show to my next generation; and therefore I had no choice but to succeed and win the battles with all my shortcomings.

However, I thanked G for the help he had given me and for allowing me to use the equipment during those summer holidays. After that I never went back to Borough and I don't know what happened to the equipment. I was not allowed to take that equipment anyway because that was the condition G had imposed on me that whatever I developed and used for my thesis would be left behind for his use. I could have patented the instruments for measuring the cutting temperatures and the cutting torque; I designed and made them. But I never bothered.

At Barking, I continued to teach and was using their poorly equipped library to write my thesis. In the summer of 1969, I submitted my rudimentary thesis to the University of London. No one had read the script or its presentation. I wrote the way I thought was right by following the presentation of the research topics in the magazines. In January 1970, when I was teaching as a lecturer at Glamorgan Poly, I was invited to attend the viva at the Imperial College of Technology, London, the same college where I had failed to get admission to do my degree because I had flunked my A-level Physics. My examiners were a senior lecturer in mechanical engineering at the Imperial and a very well-known authority on metal cutting, Prof. Koenburg (my spellings may be wrong) of Manchester University.

I had a very good grilling for two hours. They did not wish me to have the master's degree that cheaply. They wanted to make sure that I had earned the degree with a hard sweat and not by gimmickry. They were right, and I was ready for it. My frame of mind was in top gear during the viva. I had no fear and no panic in my veins on that day. It was nothing less than a fight to win the battle of the day. I answered all their questions with confidence and with eloquence. I always thought that their grilling was on the results I had obtained. As I had done all the groundwork myself in obtaining the results, I answered them very forcefully. But later it emerged that the Senior Lecturer was not concentrating on the results but on the presentation of the thesis. He insisted that as it was a historical piece of research which would be in the archives of the university, its presentation and its few grammatical mistakes must be corrected. He emphasised that I should not do it only for the sake of the university but also because of my name printed on the thesis. I must protect my name as well as theirs because they were the examiners. The Prof agreed with SL's analysis. The SL said he would write to me about the minimum corrections which he would like me to do, and then I could resubmit the thesis. Once the presentation was corrected as per their requirements, there would be no need for me to attend the viva again. I would be granted the degree of M.Phil.

I came back a bit disappointed. I knew that everything they said was right and I must admit that their criticism was genuine. I had never submitted before any written reports to anyone in my lifetime. I never used to answer essays in my examinations. My vocabulary and the grammar of the language were poor. On my return I showed my thesis to a PhD Principal Lecturer at the Glamorgan. He read it and agreed that their criticism was genuine. Theses are presented in a set format;

A JOURNEY THROUGH PARTITION AND BEYOND

that format was missing and obviously I was not aware of it. He gave me some examples. That confirmed that the rewrite was justified. With hindsight I should have read theses in the university and should have followed the norm, but it never occurred to me. However, I had a 6/7-page letter from the SL, listing the minimum corrections to be made before the thesis would be accepted for the degree. With the help of the PL at the college I made the corrections in my thesis, got it typed again locally by some housewife and submitted it again in September 1970. I had a message in January 1971 that I had been granted the degree of M. Phil in production engineering. At the time I was in New York and was once again hunting a teaching job. Again, I was an immigrant in a new exciting country and totally in a new environment.

Was I excited after having the news of my M. Phil? No, not really. It was just another day in my life. It took five years of my life to achieve that. Just to add another two words after my name to impress those who liked to be impressed and are more egotistic than I am. But it certainly helped me to get a teaching job in USA. It wiped out that blot which was added by nature to my career over which I had no control. It was the divine which was playing those tricks. It also removed to a certain extent the handicap of getting a pass degree as well as failure in my final year.

Exposure to Teaching

Just a few weeks after joining Borough as a Research Assistant in September 1964, I came to know that a part-time evening job, teaching engineering drawing, was available there. I applied to the head and I was given the job. That boosted our family income. Mira also got her job back with the Inner London Education Authority; to teach infants in Tower Hamlet. We became financially more secure. The bad times which had taken their toll were now over. The world looked more beautiful once more to live in.

Teaching adults was not a joke. I had to stand up in front of intelligent grown-ups and therefore I had to know my subject better than the students I was facing. The anxiety and fear of public speaking had always ruled over my nerves. Some have a natural gift of public speaking and they are born with it. I have seen even some under the age of ten speaking so confidently without any preparations. But I was always conscious about the opinions of the listeners. I always felt that whatever I was going to say, my words would be rejected, or maybe badly interpreted. In any dialogue there is only one speaker and millions of listeners and readers. All those millions would interpret your said words differently, depending upon their moods, their experiences, and the frame of their mind at the time of listening. Even the words uttered in good faith may end up in debating circles. When the mind was clogged up with those ideas and fears, I just could not speak with single-mindedness; the memory would not co-operate and would fail to maintain the fluent flow of thoughts. The words were uttered but in bits. The lesson which I had prepared would disappear in bewilderment. Therefore, my first encounter in the classroom was full of feelings of fear and panic. In teaching you must be a good speaker like a politician, with ample knowledge of the subject, and with confidence. I was an engineer but had no training in public speaking like politicians to impress the listeners. But luck had it that in my first lesson, as I glanced at the class, 95% were Asians and most were Indians. Being an Indian I knew the nature of my countrymen. They are culturally drummed up, right from early childhood, to respect the elders and especially teachers. They revere them and call them gurus. They are taught to bow their heads to them with respect because the gurus impart their knowledge to them and train them to be good citizens of the world and teach them to be successful in their future lives. It used to be a tradition in olden India that a disciple had to spend years and years to prove their mettle and worthiness to their gurus before the gurus would impart their inner knowledge and secrets to the disciples. I was also aware that they would not be racist and would not be hostile to me because of my colour. Armed with that knowledge, my morale and confidence were boosted, and I was ready to face the music of the evening.

I started with my introduction. I told them about my education, my experience in designing production machinery, how long I had been in the country, and finally explaining that engineering drawing was the language of engineers to express their inventiveness of thoughts to others by the lines, circles, and geometrical shapes drawn on the paper. I explained to them that it was based on the imaginations of the mind which it experiences from our early childhood. As we, the people coming from the subcontinent, never had the experience in playing with various toys - constructing something with building blocks, or breaking them and assembling them again - we lacked the vision of imagining the engineering components. We cannot visualise what the various parts of the toys look like. Therefore, we suffer from not understanding the engineering drawings and how the parts are to be drawn.

The students from the subcontinent agreed. They said that they had a lot of difficulty in understanding the subject. I knew that because I had faced all those problems myself. I assured them that my teaching would be based on the practical side of it. I would first show the object we were going to draw. Then we would look at one side of it and draw what we saw. After drawing that, we would turn the object on its side and would draw what we saw by placing the side view relative to the front view. Then we would draw a plan view by looking at the object from the top. I finally discussed how to interpret those three-dimensional views to visualise the object in three dimensions.

A JOURNEY THROUGH PARTITION AND BEYOND

Next, I turned to know their backgrounds, to know them individually, where were they working, what other subjects they were studying. During this introduction I was shocked to learn that nearly everyone had failed in the subject at least once and the majority were repeating it for a third or fourth time. This subject was only a complementary to their main subject in which they were to get their degree or diploma. However, because of the repeated failures in this subject, they were being deprived of finishing their diplomas. Their future was in the doldrums and uncertain. A lot of them were thinking of quitting for good. That increased my curiosity to know further why they had failed. The various replies came in. The lecturer before me was an Englishman who was a permanent member of the staff at the Poly. They said that he used to say the following to them openly with his cheeky tongue, 'I don't care how clever you people are and what you achieve in the examination, I will only let two or three of you pass in a year. I will fail a lot of you because I do not wish you people to become engineers. If you go out after becoming an engineer to work in this country, you will be competing with my people and I don't want that. If you go back to your country after passing the exam your country will compete with us.'

And so on.

Hence, he designed his genius policy of hatred, bigotry, and racism to destroy the future of so many young ambitious people who had come to this country in good faith, believing in the honesty and sincerity of the educational system, but he failed those who revered him as their guru. He simply abdicated his responsibility towards his noble teaching profession to be honest in discharging his duties. He abused his authority to decide and control the destiny of so many young ambitious students.

'Why did you people not report him when he was expressing such views so openly?' I enquired in desperation.

'Sir, we are part-time students, he is a senior lecturer in his department. He teaches us some other subjects as well. So, if we report him he would fail us in other subjects too. So, we were in a no-win situation,' one said disappointedly while others nodded their heads in agreement.

I was disgusted to know all that. So, I assured them that I would do my best to help. I also said that I would not fiddle the results, I would not help them by any devious means as that was not ethical being a teacher, and I would not pass them by cooking the results, but I would help them to pass by explaining the subject in a manner which they could understand and visualise better. In return they would have to work hard, not miss my lessons, and must do the assignments in the classroom. They must help me to help them.

They did. At the end of the year only two people failed from the whole class. I was proud to kick them out of the class to get their degrees that were being denied to them by a bigot senior lecturer. There was nothing wrong with them or their learning capability, but it was the sheer, naked racism of the senior lecturer who was bent on destroying their future.

Assistant Lecturer's job

The God is great. I was at Borough for nearly two years and yet I was not getting anywhere. I saw a vacancy for an Assistant Lecturer in Production being advertised at Barking College of Technology at Longbridge Road. The college was just ten minutes' walk from home. I applied, attended the interview, and was offered the job to teach Production Engineering subjects with a salary £1250/year. I resigned my research assistantship and started the new job in Sept 1966. Barking college allowed me to carry on my research at Borough for my master's degree. I also continued to teach engineering drawing at Borough in the evenings. G did not object to my carrying on research as part-time. He was rather happier and relaxed as he would have no competition with me anymore. Instead he became lazy as he was in no hurry to work for the higher degree. He kept on dragging his feet on the project. The router machine when arrived was housed in a room but was still idle. He would not do anything himself and would not allow me to touch it either.

Teaching Profession

In Sept 1966, before the start of the classes, all new faculty members at Barking were given an induction course by the vice principal of the college. This course was quite helpful. The teaching was a combination of day and evening classes. Most of the students were from the Ford Motor Company at Dagenham. My timetable involved teaching classes from the lower levels of ONC to the higher classes of HNC. It was hard work to prepare the lessons for subjects which I had never read myself. I had never taught production engineering before. So, I had first to learn the subject myself and prepare the lessons from the books for the syllabus I was to teach to the class. There were also practical lessons to be conducted at the workshop. Again, I was a layman in using the machines. However, I managed lecturing well. I took the attitude that all those sitting in my class were totally ignorant and I was the best. They would have to pay attention to me as I knew it better than them and that is why I was teaching them. They also knew that I would be marking their examination papers and their results would depend upon my marking. So, they had to behave well. Once upon a time, someone passed a judgement on me too. It was a psychological trick for the mind. That attitude was wrong I know, but I had to boost my confidence to give lectures without being fearful of those grown-up, mature people. To maintain that confidence in a classroom is the most important trait of successful teaching. Also, I had to be egotistic, totally out-of-character for me, to win the respect of the people sitting in front of me on those chairs. Without that I would not be able to stand in front of them. I was also teaching quality control methods on the workshop floor. This subject involved a lot of mathematics and my degree in maths from India helped me to teach that subject more effectively.

The head of the department was a very nice man, kind and considerate. No signs of racism in him. Once, right in the beginning, I did get into trouble with him. He lent me one of his files and asked me to return it to his filing cupboard when I had finished with it. I did not, I took it easy. A week later he needed it, did not find it there, called me to his office, and told me off. 'I lent you the file and by not returning it to me you made me disorganised.' I apologised but he never forgot that incident.

Soon it became a routine. I would teach my lessons and in my free periods I would go to the library (not that well equipped as Borough's) to collect data. I started writing the first chapter on introductions for my thesis. Once a week in the evening I would go to Borough to teach engineering drawing.

Bought a Car

Financially we were now getting more comfortable. I had two incomes, one from full-time teaching at Barking and the second from part-time teaching at the Borough. The third income was from Mira's teaching. We had paid back our vendor's bridging loan with interest and with a million thanks. Feeling financially secured, we bought our first new car, a white Ford Cortina mark two, a troublesome car. It was very moody. It had so many manufacturing and design defects. One day I mentioned these troubles in my class to my students from the Ford Motor Company. They told me that the car wiring was too thin, and the voltage dropped on the starter motor significantly when the engine was cranked. Therefore, it did not have enough power to crank the engine efficiently. They offered to bring me a do-it-yourself kit which would cure this problem. I refused the offer as I knew they would nick it from their company to oblige me. The starter motor also would jam the starter gear. It was exposed to the dust and rainwater on the roads. I had to go under the chassis to take out the starter motor nearly every two weeks to clean the mechanism and reinstall it. It was just unpredictable whether it would start in the mornings or not. I used to come out of the house 20 minutes early in case the car did not start and at least I would have enough time to walk down to the college. There was not much competition in the car industry in those days. The Japanese cars had not arrived yet in the market and Fords had the lion's share of the market. In those days they would sell you a basic car. We had to spend a lot more money in installing a lot of extra safety features, such as an interior mirror, side mirrors on the doors, bonnet lock, petrol cap lock, radio etc.

The Driving Licence

Just one day after the warranty was over its front suspension broke down. I had to get both suspensions and stabilisers changed by the Ford dealer. That cost us £30, a lot of money in those days. You could only get the job done from the Ford dealers who had the monopoly of spare parts. I vowed at that time that I would never buy another Ford in my lifetime and I never did. I hear that the technology is much improved. Maybe so but I am keeping my vow not to buy them.

The Driving Licence

We got the car first before getting a driving licence. It was like putting a cart before the horse. Anybody would comment on what kind of stupid decision we made. Mira and I debated who should get the licence first. Mira refused. I did not want to be the first either. I was a chicken and too scared to handle the speed. I did not wish to learn even after some coaxing, and Mira would not budge. The car was outside on the road, waiting for someone to sit on the driver's seat and fly away. It was a GT manual with high performance and needed skill to handle it. I finally decided to try my luck. Maybe she too was scared but she would not admit it.

I contacted one driving school who had their office on the Seven Kings Road. They were charging 10 shillings per hour. The instructor was a lovely man, very kind, and helpful. He came around to pick me up at the college, drove me back to the main road, Green Lane at Seven Kings, parked the car and started his introductory lesson as below:

'I am sorry the first lesson is only to chat about you, about the car, and other problems associated with driving. So, I am afraid you will not be driving in this first lesson.' I was surprised but accepted. I was keen to lay my hands on the practical side of it.

So, he continued, 'I can see that you are in the teaching profession. How old are you now?'

'I am thirty-four.'

'Now you have both things against you. You're a teacher, a responsible and caring profession and you are thirty-four, a mature person. Give me a young man of sixteen and I will get him a licence in 10 lessons and he will pass the test on his first attempt, because that age group is more daring, careless, and has a go-go attitude. Therefore, I am afraid in your case it will take at least 15 lessons before I recommend you for the test and I would not like to bet that you will pass at the first attempt. If you do it will be a big surprise.'

That verbal blast was a great 'confidence' booster and a challenge to beat his predictions. He had one error of judgement – to generalise his forecast. He was telling me that he would rather have a reckless teenage learner than a mature responsible person like me.

A JOURNEY THROUGH PARTITION AND BEYOND

Then he started explaining to me about the major functions and the controls of the car such as the gearbox, clutch, the braking system, the steering wheel etc. The first lesson was over, and he drove me back to my college. I took thirteen lessons and he encouraged me to apply for the test. I did.

On the day of the test, my instructor loaned me his car to take it for the test although we had our car. He felt that as I had been learning on his car and knew all its controls better, it would be easier to pass the test in his car than in mine. I took his advice, borrowed his car while he waited at the examiner's office. The examiner hopped on to the front passenger seat with a motionlessly grim face. As we settled down, he said, 'As we go along, I will give you the instructions to turn left or right or straight. I will give you enough warning before the road comes to turn and I want you to follow those instructions.' I nodded as I looked at his glum and serious face with no smiles. We reached a main road with a T-junction where he asked me to turn left. The right side of the road had a bend and the view was concealed. I could not see the traffic coming from that direction. The flow of the traffic was fast and continuous, and I was not too sure whether I should wait or take a chance and turn left. After a few seconds waiting I looked at him in case he would give me some advice, but he turned his face away towards the left. I knew then that these seeds were not available for the cold press oil. I thought, well I am in charge of the car and was in the driving seat. Therefore, from now on I would treat the passenger as a dummy sitting next to me and would just ignore his presence. So, I moved forward on my seat to look right properly and the moment I found it was safe to turn left, I turned. I confronted the same situation on a high street traffic light where he asked me to turn right. There was a car in front me to turn right too. Because of the traffic coming from the opposite side, the driver waited until it was safe to turn but during that waiting the traffic lights went red. The back of my car was still near the lights. I decided not to turn. As my car was nearly blocking the pedestrian crossing at the lights, I looked back and safely reversed my car to the line of the traffic signal. I just did not bother whether he would approve of those decisions or not.

I brought him back to his office intact in one piece. He declared, 'Congratulations, you have passed your test. We will issue you a licence to drive on British roads.' I thanked him. My instructor was waiting there. The examiner told him the result too. He was very happy. On the way back home, he gave me the following million-dollar advice which I have never forgotten.

'From now onwards you will be on your own in your car. You have the licence, but you are not a perfect driver yet. You are liable to make mistakes on the road. So, go home, hop in your car, ask your wife to accompany you and keep an eye on the road to warn you about the approaching traffic lights and zebra crossings etc in case your attention is on the clutch controls. Always remember one thing. "This vehicle can be used as a destructive weapon or for pleasant travel." Use it for pleasure and not as a killing machine. The choice is yours.'

I took his advice in letter and spirit. I came home, asked Mira to accompany me to Ilford. We drove off in style. He was right to say that my attention on observing the road would not be 100%. While disengaging the clutch and shifting the gears, turning on the road to the left or to the right my attention was diverted from the road. At a traffic light on the High Road as we were turning to the left, the traffic light on that road showed red. Mira shouted, 'STOP! the traffic light here is red!' and I banged my foot on the brake pedal to follow the emergency procedure to stop. Soon I realised that those lights had to be red because the road I was turning from was green. So, for a moment it created confusion, not for me alone but also for an inexperienced and more careful passenger. Luckily there was no car behind me and I resumed my driving.

Driving in Darkness

Nervousness and lack of attention in driving remained for a few months. The coordination of the feet and the hands to press the clutch pedal and change gear was still not perfect. The subconscious mind had still not mastered the skill of coordination. The fear of driving at high speeds on the countryside roads and in darkness persisted for quite a long time. I remember once on 25th December when all the people of the country were having their Christmas pudding, we, with Mira's cousin and husband, decided to go to Cambridge. There were no motorways, only single lane roads. All the garages were closed, all the restaurants were closed and there were no other souls on the road. We were the only four mad and crazy occupants of the car in the country deciding to be on the roads. The whole country was busy in boozing and enjoying their poor Christmas turkey on their dining tables. When the norms of the society are not in place, it is bound to bring about some unpleasant events. On the way to Cambridge, I wanted urgently to go for a pee. There were no garages open. In desperation, when the next garage came, I parked the car in the front forecourt, walked to the back of the building and eased myself. Guess what happened. As I was coming back to the car a police officer drove in. The police would always appear as soon as an innocent man errs. They are never there when the criminals break the law. I don't know why. But my experience is that it always is the case. However, he confronted me, 'What were you doing behind the building?' It was a normal question to ask. It is the nature of policemen to be suspicious. They always feel that the people are always on some mischief.

'I am low on petrol officer. I was looking for an attendant in case he was at the back of the building to help.' I had to tell a lie, otherwise he might have nicked me on that celebration Christmas day.

'It is 25ᵗʰ today. All businesses are closed. Didn't you know that?'

'No officer I did not. Otherwise I would have stayed home like anybody else.'

'Where are you going?'

'We are heading to see Cambridge.'

'Everything there will be closed. You will only see empty roads and buildings. There will be no restaurants open, no students; it will be a totally deserted town.'

'Oh, well as we are already around, we might as well go and see the place.'

'Ok, that is your choice. Good luck and behave yourself.'

'Yes sir.'

So, he went away in his panda car. I felt bad in telling lies to him. I still feel guilty of soiling the back of the petrol station. If I had told him the truth who knows, I would have been in a hell of a lot of trouble with the law as we all know that racism was at its peak in those days. All these people were just trigger-happy to book us and to take credit for their crime-busting activities.

At Cambridge, we found that whatever the officer had said was true. All the shops were closed. There was nobody on the streets. Nothing was available to eat; it was just a ghost town. We had left home early after breakfast and we were hungry. However, we managed to get some petrol. By the time we were on the road back to London, darkness set in. The visibility on the roads was poor and some scattered fog patches made the driving conditions even more difficult. The road was narrow and winding and that made me very nervous. Some silly thoughts, such as that I had the safety of three more lives in my hand, made me even more jumpy. Mira's cousin, who had been driving in India, noticed my erratic driving. She offered me help a couple of times to drive, but being an egotist, I declined her offer. Also driving conditions were totally different in India. I preferred to keep the reins of my life in my hands. I have never experienced such an agony in my life. After a couple of hours drive, when we approached nearer London with street lights, it appeared as if I had come back to heaven again. It was a great relief to know that I had finally brought those four souls safely back home.

Soon the car became a part of our lives. For me it was for pleasure and for going from A to B but that does not mean it was without any life-threatening accidents. These accidents continue to live in the memory lane and are unforgettable.

Here are some more driving experiences.

1.   Just a few weeks after I passed the test, I parked my car at a pump behind another car that was parked at the next pump. I filled up with petrol, went to pay, came back, and as I sat in my car, ready to crank the engine, I noticed that the driver of the car in front put his car into reverse gear and bang, he hit our front bonnet. The young driver realising his mistake came rushing to us, apologising that he just did not know why he reversed his car so fast. However, he promised to repair the bonnet and he did. The matter was amicably sorted.

2.   Again, once we were driving on Ilford Lane. We were only driving around 20 mph; suddenly we were jolted with a bang. A car had run into our car from behind. The back bumper was badly damaged. We stopped, the driver of the other came out, and apologised. He said that 'momentarily my wife diverted my attention to show me something in the shop window. As I looked towards the shop just for a few seconds, I found that I hit you. That was no excuse but that is what happened.' He worked for a garage and he installed a new bumper. The matter ended there.

3.   Whenever I was in the driving seat, the last advice of the instructor always echoed in my ears. Therefore, I was a bit more careful than most. In addition to that, I had studied in engineering that the destructive power of a moving vehicle is its mass times the velocity squared. That knowledge made me a lot more careful than most other drivers on the road. Furthermore, racism was at its peak and the locals hated people like us driving better flashy new cars. Our car was considered flashy with high performance in those days. Naturally they were jealous and that would show up in their behaviour towards us by giving us dirty looks or with some abusive f--- off language. On one occasion, as I waited and took a few seconds to safely turn right onto the main road at a T-junction, the middle-aged driver behind me got agitated, opened his car and rushed to my door, shouting and abusing, 'If you do not know how to drive the car, you should not be on the road.' Very aggressively he jolted my steering wheel and said, 'Why don't you turn the wheel this way and get the hell out of my way.' I shouted back angrily, 'Don't you dare touch my car. You have no business to touch my car. I will turn when it is safe to turn. You can overtake me and go where you like but don't dare push me to do what you want me to do.' In frustration he went back to his car still abusive about how on earth such people had been allowed to come to this country.

4.   Another day I was turning to the right on Green Lane, Seven Kings, when two young hotheads started hooting. I had no clue why. Then I heard one of them opening the car door to rush towards us. I got scared. I locked my doors, quickly turned right, and sped off towards my house. There were no central locking systems in the cars in those days.

5.   It was a lovely morning, October 1985, and the clock had just struck 11.30am. We were just beginning to build the business back after the

A JOURNEY THROUGH PARTITION AND BEYOND

cheating of the manager who had taken all our business, all the employees, and everything else. I was taking the delivery to London in the van. Mira was looking after the factory when I was away.

We loaded the van and away I went with all the invoice papers. I had just passed a petrol station on my right on the bend on the old A120. The road was now clear and straight for a good few hundred yards. I saw another white van coming from the opposite direction. When it was about 200 yards from me, I noticed that it started crossing the white middle line. As a precaution I moved to the left a bit. Then I saw it crossed the middle lane markings and was heading straight towards me. I drove more to the left; hit the curb and moved the van on to the green. I had only the right side wheels on the road and the rest of the van was on the green patch of the path. I could not go any further on the green unless I had taken all the four wheels onto the green. The white van was only about thirty yards away from me before hitting me head on. Just then I noticed that the driver woke up and realised his stupid mistake and took a corrective action. Even then the whole side of his van grazed along the side of my van, leaving a deep dent nearly an inch deep in my van. I stopped right there but the other driver went on for more than 100 yards before stopping. I could not read his number plates. It was all intentional as will be shown later.

He came running towards me, profusely apologising again and again and enquiring if I was hurt. I said, 'Heavens no.' 'Ok let me give you my van details, my contact number, and insurance details.' I had no paper and no biros to write with. He also had none with him. So, he scribbled all his personal details – his name, his address, and his telephone number - on my invoice book with his van key. As he wrote, the details were copied below on the carbon copy of the invoice. We parted with good wishes to one another and he assured me that he would sort out everything for the van repair from his insurance.

A couple of days later I telephoned his number just to check the contact details. The number would not connect. I thought maybe the telephone was out of order. I tried again in a couple of days but no joy. Then I tried the number a few more times at intervals but without any success. Eventually I gave up. I knew I had been hoodwinked. But hope is always a good friend in times of desperation.

One day I was working in my factory. It was a lovely day with the sun shining brilliantly in the horizon. A police officer stopped his panda car outside and walked in, how and why I don't know. He enquired, 'Is everything ok here?' I said, 'Yes officer everything is just fine.' His sudden arrival and asking a simple question surprised me. 'Oh, I was on my round and I just dropped in to ask if you were ok.' As soon as he turned to walk away, I remembered my accident. 'Officer, yes I have a problem. I had an accident on the A120 a couple of weeks ago. The driver gave me his telephone and address. I am trying to reach him by phone but without any success. Would you mind trying this number for me?' I showed him the copy of the details, filled by the driver on the invoice book. He noted them down and said he would call this number from his station and let me have his findings. 3-4 days had gone by but no news from the officer. A week later the officer came in, apologising for the delay. He said his findings were that: The address does not exist, there is no village of that description, there is no one of that name, and the telephone number does not exist. He had checked with the DVLA about the van. There existed no registration number of that description. Therefore, all the information given to me by the driver was false right from the very beginning to the end. The officer could only help if I had some more information about the driver. I had none. So, the matter finished and added a page in my history book.

It is amusing to find that such cheats do exist on this planet, thus making this world so colourful. God has created all kinds of people. This world is like a big museum, with multiples of mini theatres where all kinds of dramas are being played by the various groups and individuals. One should only patiently sit silently and attentively to watch them. They are all created so that no one human complains to the Mighty on their final meeting that they got bored on the greatest planet that we know of so far.

How nice, the man who had nearly killed me was so clever that he wrote everything wrong on the paper. He parked the van at such a distance that I could not check his registration number. He must be quite clever with a great presence of mind. When I asked him, 'Can I see the insurance details,' he apologised that the van was parked at a distance and he could not go and get it. He was also in a hurry and had no time to prove his details. He promised that the details he was giving were true and I should trust him. That I did, and you can see the deception. Oh, people tell me why trust is going out of the window in human relationships. Every day we are getting better financially, technologically, but morally and ethically we are sliding downhill. Why?

6.   It was the late 90s. The millennium was just a couple of years ahead. I was driving a Nissan Sunny and was on my way to the factory in the morning. The new A120 was still not built. The old A120 (now designated the B184) was the main road from Braintree to the M11 to London. It was a very busy road. The rush hour to London in the morning and then the traffic back from London in the evening were the most dangerous journey times. I call this road 'the killers' road'. The disgruntled, frustrated, half-sleepy drivers would overtake a lorry in front and crash into vehicles coming from the opposite direction. It used to be a nerve-racking, scary and daunting road to travel, especially in the winter months when the days were shorter.

A JOURNEY THROUGH PARTITION AND BEYOND

That morning, as I approached on the bend to the right near the garage, I noticed a car from the opposite side, driving behind a lorry, giving a signal to move out to overtake. It accelerated and started coming towards us with an impending head-on crash. I moved to the left, then on to the footpath. I screamed, so did Mira. We thought that the end of our lives had finally arrived. It was a spontaneous reaction when the end is so clearly visible. The crash seemed inevitable. Rather than slowing down and go back behind the lorry, the driver was speeding the car with full throttle. The driver was just about 20 feet from us and I could see that he was desperately trying to avoid the head-on crash. I believe the lorry driver noticed the stupidity of the car driver and moved to his left as much as he could, thus giving enough room for the car to pass through between our two vehicles. The driver continued his misadventure journey. However, the head-on crash was avoided because of the gap given by the two vehicles. No injury was inflicted on any one of us, but our car was badly damaged all the way down the side with a few inches deep cut into the body. I turned my car into the garage. The other driver parked on the curb on the other side and came to the garage, and said, 'I am very sorry. I just don't know what I was doing. I am tired because of bad sleep.' I responded angrily, 'Are you mad? You were going to kill both of us with no fault of ours. I am calling the police about your stupid driving.' He had nothing to say. I called the police. I also called my neighbouring factory to inform my staff who were waiting outside for us to open the factory. One of my staff members came and took the key to open the factory. The police officer came, took our statement and then went to talk to the other driver. The officer came back after a few minutes. 'As there is no injury and he is not under the influence of a drink, we cannot prosecute him. He admits his mistake. The only thing we can do is to prosecute him with dangerous driving if you want us to.' 'Well, is it worth all this aggro? We know he is wrong. We are happy to let the matter go,' I replied. The matter finished there as far as the accident was concerned. But what about repairing the damage done to the car? After that incident we were so scared to drive on that road that for a few months until the days got longer we started driving through the winding country lanes, a much longer route but a bit safer.

The car was insured with AXA fully comprehensively. We informed the company; their rep came to inspect the damaged vehicle and said that the vehicle would be removed to a garage for the assessment of the costs. So, they took the car away. A week later, we had a call from the DVLA that our car had been spotted in the London congestion charge area. We explained to them that the car had been in the possession of the AXA insurance company and we were not driving it. In the meantime we had a letter from AXA that our car was a write-off and was not repairable. Therefore, the best offer they could give was £350 as settlement. We protested as the car was in a very good condition and there was nothing wrong

235

except that damage. We had bought that car new about 7 years before. The insurance company would not budge. We asked that they give us that £350 and the car and we would get it repaired. They refused. In frustration we accepted the offer with a vow that we would never put our business with AXA ever again. As we had no more cars to insure, we asked AXA to refund the balance left for the insured car. This was nearly £200. They said, 'We do not give refunds. When you are ready to insure another car, we will give you credit for this sum.' We had no intention of buying another car. So effectively we got £150 for the car. A week later we had another letter from DVLA that our old car had been spotted again in the London area.

The mutual insurances which were started with good intentions by the forefathers for the benefit of those unfortunate members who were caught in some tragedies beyond their control has been now turned into a big business to exploit all those insured. The noble idea of helping the insured has now been turned into an area of exploitation by the insurance companies, the selfish fund managers and rich shareholders who are sitting in their ivory towers of the major cities of the world. This has become a legal business to hoodwink the common citizens of the land. The whole system is corrupt and full of exploitation. If you are ever caught in that web, you would get into a tragedy of double whammy. I am not the only soul who has paid the price. It is millions all over the world who are done, and the newspapers are full of such stories and help lines set up by the charities. It is a necessary evil in life. If you don't insure you may get into big troubles if heavens become angry at you; and if you are insured, the unscrupulous companies will exploit you and may not pay you what you had insured for. Either way you are condemned.

7.   Another time in the morning, we were driving to the factory as usual. As we reached the same spot on the bend near the garage, I saw a car driving behind a lorry. Suddenly he gave a signal to overtake the lorry. Oh Lord not again, same spot, near about the same month except the year, we were nearly being hit. It is said that history never repeats but it did on that day except the vehicles coming from the opposite direction were different. We thought this road was now safer as a new A120 dual carriageway had been built and the crazy speedy driver could vent their maniac habits on that; but nay, I was wrong. The lunatics were still out there, testing driving abilities. Again, I moved to the left as far as I could to touch the curb. The driver realising his stupidity went back to his lane behind the lorry and we escaped again. But my mental psychology is bothering me.

Three near-fatal accidents within 300 yards of the same spot make me wonder if that is my death spot where I will finally meet my maker. To avoid that from happening, whenever I drive through that spot, which I must for going to Braintree, I take extra precautions. I observe carefully if there is a truck coming from the opposite direction and if there is any vehicle behind it trying to overtake it. My fate is not under my control. I can only slow down as I approach that spot and take other precautions but if something does happen in future, so be it. But the thoughts do shake my nerves. Bad experiences always take a much longer time to fade away.

Lecturer at Glamorgan Poly

In early 1969 I applied for a Lecturer job at Glamorgan Poly, Pontypridd in South Wales. I went for the interview. There were two more candidates for the same job. We were shown the facilities at the college in the morning by the principal lecturer who was also in the interviewing panel. After touring the college, we were taken for a free lunch in the dining hall.

Being a vegetarian has always been considered a handicap by meat eaters. Here I got into a sticky situation and I was at my wit's end to tackle it.

We all were being treated as VIPs by the staff who were attending to us. As we approached the dining hall, the dinner lady started taking the orders. She explained what was on the menu for the day. I became a bit apprehensive about what I should order. If I had said that I was a grass eater, it would certainly have bunked my chances of being selected for the job. But if I ate meat just to get a job, it would be impossible to live with my conscience. Also, how would I eat it? When my turn came, I spontaneously responded, 'May I please have only the vegetables because my stomach is playing up, and I am not that well.' But it did not help. The lady felt a bit concerned and said, 'I am sorry to know that. Would you like to have a fish instead? That is very light,' she insisted.

I had now opened a Pandora's box, full of lies. I was not used to telling lies; therefore, it became difficult to cover one lie with so many others.

'No, I would stick to the vegetables of the day please.'

'Are you sure that's enough? I have only potato mash, peas and carrots.'

'That would do me fine,' I insisted, to get out of it but at the same time calming her anxiety about my wellbeing.

'What about soup? I have got tomato soup with meaty bits in it. That is the soup of the day. There is no choice for that.'

'I would like to give it a miss too as it has meaty bits in it.'

'No, it is very good for you. It is light and has some protein in it. I'll serve you with that,' she insisted. I had no choice anymore. Next was the order for the sweet which had no issues and the selection was settled quickly.

When the soup was served, guess what - I had to swallow it. I hated every mouthful of it. Was it a politeness towards the caring serving lady or just a stupidity? Was I a chicken? I don't know why on earth I did not face the facts right in the beginning and say that I was a vegetarian. Maybe they would have appreciated it or maybe they would have rejected me thinking that I could be a misfit in their faculty. I don't know what could have happened, but I should have had the guts to face the truth. I scold myself even today for that mishap. I failed to keep up to my basic guiding principles of life. And without principles we are reduced to the animal world. With hindsight I can now only cry. Those little bits of meat long ago digested and turned into human flesh are still part of me. They continue to bother my conscience about why I was so weak not to face the music of the day bravely. Why did I compromise, why? I just cannot answer.

Later, after the dinner, we were interviewed, and I was offered the job. I accepted. I was to start the job on 1st September 1969.

After I received the appointment letter, I first announced it to my colleagues in my room back at Barking. They encouraged me to leave. They asked me to go and see the Head right away. I went to see him to resign. He was very upset. He said that he was not accepting the resignation and would talk to me later in a couple of days. He called me into his office a week later and announced that he did not want me to leave and he would promote me to a lecturer position in September. I said I would come back to him after consulting my wife. I went back to my office and told my room colleagues that I was being offered a lecturer's position if I didn't go to Wales. They were surprised. They advised me that I must go to Wales because I was committed to that job as I had already accepted their offer. They said if the head was so nice now then why did he not offer me the promotion before. They opposed the withdrawal of my resignation like hell. I talked to Mira and we believed it was better for us to stay in London. Mira was still pursuing her M. Phil at the Institute of Education. We were well settled in London in our own home and we had good friends. Then why uproot for an unknown Poly in Wales? However, a couple of weeks later, I was sitting in my office with other colleagues. They asked about my decision for the job. Had I confirmed to the head that I was leaving? I said, 'No, we have not decided yet.'

They started persuading, pressuring, and coaxing me that I should go right then and tell the head that I had decided to leave. I said ok I would do it later. They insisted that I should do it that minute. One of the colleagues got up, held my hand as you hold a child's hand, and said, 'Let us go now to the head's office.' He walked with me to the head's office and knocked on the door. As the head said 'come in' my colleague opened the door and ushered me in. He insisted again that I must say no to him now. I went in and I did, as I was under the spell of a witch. The head was disappointed. He tried to persuade me that I had all the advantages of staying there rather than moving to Wales. He said that I would not like to live there. He had lived there himself once upon a time. He even offered to talk to Mira, but I said that it would not help. In fact, he did talk to her when we had a departmental get together before the summer break but there was no going back.

He even offered that we could join Glamorgan Poly in September, resign and come back in January and he would keep the job for me. The fate was already sealed. The point of no return had been reached. It was impossible to work with such colleagues who were hell-bent on getting rid of me. None of them were graduates and feared that if I was there, they would never have the opportunity of promotion over me. They were motivated with their self-interest. They were not interested in my well-being or my family's.

The head had a different agenda. The college was trying to move onto a polytechnic status and therefore the qualifications of the teaching staff were the most important factor in achieving that status. In the whole department I was the only graduate except the head. Therefore, he was very keen to keep me on the faculty.

During the summer recess we started moving our baggage in our car to Wales. The poly had arranged a new council three-bedroom house on the hill where we could sit and see the poly buildings. We made quite a few trips. We even took our own beds there on the roof of the car. We rented our house at Seven Kings to students in our absence.

Soon I was settled down in the department. The faculty members were very friendly and co-operative. We did not find any signs of discrimination there. Right on top of another hill nearby to us I would go and play golf with my other colleagues. The social life was much better there than it was in London. But the family life was a bit difficult. Mira has a nature that if you do not do what she asks you to do, she will make your life very uncomfortable. She was against our move to Wales. She was working for her M. Phil; her tutor was in London and a well-equipped library at the Senate House, where she used to collect data for her thesis, was also there. She had to travel to London and stay at the YWCA to see him. She had a lot of disadvantages but rather than adjusting she would blow her head off when she would come back from London. She was very frustrated and often would take it out on me. Even if the decision to move to Wales was wrong, even then one would expect the other partner to co-operate and accept the *fait-accompli* rather than continue to bring strife on the relationship.

Ritu was only six; she too lost her school friends, family friends, and was a bit upset. But children cope better than the grown-ups. However, she was going through a rough patch. We did not know it until one day she said that she was not going to school anymore. After talking to her, we found out that in the school some children were making some racist remarks. She was the only brown colour child. She was very unhappy about it. However, Mira went to her school, spoke to the head, brought to her attention the problems, and it was sorted out. After that little hiccup she was well settled there and made some good friends who came over on her birthday in October.

The poly already had the charter for giving its own degrees. It had big expansion plans to build multi-storey students' residences and for the extension of departmental buildings. We started making good friends. In those days there were a lot of Indian doctors in hospitals, as GP's, consultants, nurses, and so on. The life in Wales was much better than in London. The countryside was beautiful with hills and valleys. The people were friendly and would invite us for dinner and other social occasions. There were a lot of beautiful sandy beaches within an hour's drive. We were well settled and forgot all about London until a physical ailment hit me.

Struck with mysterious illness

We were there for only a few months when I was struck down with some unknown mysterious illness. I went to see my GP who checked me over and pronounced that there was nothing wrong with me. I was losing weight and energy. I had gone a bit pale. I was feeling fear in the body and I would feel nervousness. When the condition did not improve, the GP sent me to a consultant in the hospital for investigation. They checked my heart beat, took my ECG, had X-rays done, and got my blood tested to find out what was wrong. All the results were negative but there was no improvement. They also investigated if I was under stress at home or work. The summer holidays were around the corner. The Baggas came to stay with us to enjoy their holidays. They would go out in the morning for sightseeing and come back in the evening. They showed their concern too. That showed that I was not making things up. I rang my brother in London to take me to London for a couple of days in case it was the Welsh weather and environment that was not suiting me. We stayed with him for 3-4 days. I felt a bit reassured and better. During that time, when the doctors were busy in finding faults with my body, I had a letter from the American Embassy that I had been selected for immigration to USA. I had applied for the Green Card a few months earlier on a general visa quota system which used to take a long time to materialise. It was a big surprise when I got the news and it was the most welcome opportunity. A good riddance from a racist country, I thought. The American Embassy in London gave me the date for the interview and the medical examination.

The Interview at The American Consulate

The Americans are proud to say that theirs is a land of opportunity for everyone on this planet except the communists. I agree with them. This was the time when Enoch Powell was making fiery and provocative speeches of 'rivers of blood' all over UK. It was also the time when people of the Asiatic and African colours were the most hated species in UK. Nobody gave a damn what kind of economic and social contributions we were making to this country. The locals were well fed with loots from the colonial exploitations; had chips on their shoulders of their recent win in the WW2 over the Germans and Italians; and were arrogant and aggressive in their attitude and behaviour towards all BMEs (Black and minority ethnics). They were aggressive towards the foreigners and supported the derogatory racist speeches made by their small-minded leaders. But they had forgotten that they had won the wars by using the Indian and Nepalese soldiers as frontline fodder. They were also lucky that they had manipulated the Americans into their war with their cunningness. Because the Americans had joined the war effort, the British got the financial and war material support. It was sheer luck that fate had favoured them to win the WW2. But when the peace returned on the planet, they had to run away from their colonies because the world had become more open and wide awake. The Communist movement was on the move and the people of the world were in no mood to tolerate that oppressive colonialism. The two major props behind the British – American finance and the withdrawal of Indian manpower which had helped Britain to maintain the evil colonialism - had collapsed. The country had reached its economic downfall because of the mounting war debt and the wide-awakening of the loyalty of the stupid Indians who refused to be used as fodder for their world domination policies. The British had no choice but to withdraw from the occupied lands of the world. So, they ran from all their colonies because they had no more human resources to control the colonies. So, I was eager to get out from the Britain of that day and live somewhere else to breathe freedom. Who would live in a country which hated our guts? It was also a country where they were insulting the integrity of the young girls coming from the subcontinent. They were checking their virginity at the airports on arrival to marry their spouses in Britain. The recorded history will never forgive them for the evil deeds they committed in those days to people like us, who were called British citizens but treated worse than their cats and dogs. This country had none of those virgins. Some girls here were having sex even at the age of eleven. It was a curiosity for the immigration officers at the airport to find out what are the traits and characters of the virgins of the other land. It was not the first time I tried to get out of here. It was suffocating here. I walked on the streets with head down. The inferiority complex was humiliating my ego and my self-respect. The freedom to live independently, the freedom to think, the freedom to lead my life the way I wished are the God-given right, not only for humans but to all creatures on this planet. And that freedom was robbed by the European colonialists. They could suppress that freedom for a few decades, but it could never be sustained for ever. No one with a grain of self-esteem would ever tolerate it. So, it was time to move, and move for the good.

To say goodbye to this country, I had already applied for a Reader's job at the Varanasi University in India. I was in correspondence with them. The Indian bureaucracy moves slowly. Nevertheless, my application was in the queue. I had a reply just before I got the Green Card for America that shortly they would be calling me for interview. I did not respond to that as I knew I was on my way to the land of opportunity and freedom.

I also tried to go to Australia; another racist country colonised by British expatriates, outcasts, the young destitute and illegitimate children who were made to settle there. That country was also racist to their deepest core. They had deprived all rights to the locals who were the original Australians. They had grabbed their lands and shoved them into the forests. They called them barbarians. If India had also been as sparsely populated as were Australia, Canada, and USA, and their culture was also like those locals, India would have met the same fate as the locals of those countries. But India was lucky in that sense. It had a rich culture, was well advanced in religious philosophy, had a well organised educational system, was well governed, and tremendously rich in resources and wealth. It was a heaven on earth for any would-be colonialist to have and possess.

It happened once that when we were living at Leytonstone in 1961, we invited for dinner a young Australian couple who were going back to their country after a short stay in London. The man was working with my brother. They were very much impressed at our hospitality and the respect we showered on them. After dinner, when leaving he said, 'Sorry I cannot invite you folks to visit us in our country. We are not yet civilised enough to have people like you over there.' The message was loud and clear. How would they be civilised when they had the same genes as the British?

I'll let you know another factual story. At the Barking College, I had a Chinese colleague who was married to an English woman. They had five children and another one was due within a couple of months. He was offered a job in Australia, in a college. He applied for a visa to the Australian High Commission to emigrate. He was called for the interview with the whole family. Every one of them, including the children, had photographs taken to be sent to Australia for the features of the cross-breeds to be reviewed. After being thoroughly examined at the time of interview, their features were carefully looked at, and my colleague was told that they could not commit to giving him a visa until they had also seen and photographed the new baby and got him/her approved by the Australian immigration authorities. He waited and wrote back to his employer in Australia about his predicament. They kept his job open and asked him to keep on trying until he got the visa. Finally, when the new one was born her photograph was sent for approval to the racist regime. His application to immigrate to Australia was rejected. I too had applied to Papua New Guinea a year earlier but was rejected. It is a story of, 'My country is mine because I am born there but your country is mine too because I have forcibly trespassed there and occupied it.'

A JOURNEY THROUGH PARTITION AND BEYOND

Oh, I forgot to say that I applied for Canada just after graduation. I was interviewed by a young Canadian who asked me if I didn't get a suitable job to match my education, what I would do. I said, 'I have sacrificed a lot to become a qualified engineer. So, I would always seek out a job to suit my qualifications.' He knew his country better than I did. He knew that there were not many engineering jobs there. It was mostly a mining and agricultural country. So, he asked if I would be willing to work temporarily on other jobs, even a labourer for instance. I refused to consider that kind of status. He refused my application and advised me that I should be a bit more flexible and accommodating to live in Canada. More flexible to sacrifice! What nonsense. I had only this life to live and why on earth should I sacrifice even a day of my life for that idiotic country. But then he politely suggested that I should try again in a couple of years. I never did, although a lot of my friends had gone there, and I was tempted to do so. Even when leaving America in 1972, my friends asked me to go to Canada to settle down there. I simply refused. I even refused to visit the country. I was too egotistic to accept 'no' from that immature young fellow. I was not prepared to take his advice about what I should be doing in my life.

I also believe this world belongs to all of us. We must have a right to live and work where we want to. It should not be the diktat of some who happened to be there before my turn came to live on the planet. This mother is divided into bits by narrow-minded self-centred people. We humans must protest the legitimacy of this division of the planet based on religion, caste, colour, and the way we think. One day, I bet, these man-made barriers will come down like the Berlin Wall. Because the people of the world would be more enlightened, more tolerant, and the planet would become a melting pot for everyone to live where they choose to live. There will be no organised religions to achieve political aims. There will be no priests to force their beliefs down your throats and condemn your thinking. There will be no one to give you the Bible with one hand and take away your land with another. All the religious philosophies will one day find their way into the history books and will be read by the generations to follow for the folly of their forefathers to kill, maim, rape, and slaughter their own kind because of their own convictions. Everyone will follow their hearts, their souls, and their inner voice without being condemned and molested. The planet itself will become a heaven to live in rather than trying to find it somewhere up in the sky. It must come one day, and it must come before humans blow themselves up with the enormous stored energy in the atomic weapons.

My brief American visit appears to be just a mystery. The reality as I see it is nothing more than a dream. Why it happened and how it all happened I do not know. I applied for the immigration Green Card with no reason and then I forgot all about it. When the invitation came to attend the interview, it was a big surprise.

I was ill with some mystery bug and never thought I would ever make it. Who would give a 'permanent stay' visa to a sick man of thirty-nine? But when everything went so smoothly, I began to believe in the miracles of the existence. The divine was dismantling all the stumbling blocks to smooth my way. I still get dreams that I am in America, trying to obtain the education I had not completed when I left the country in a hurry. Once I dreamt that I opened an Indian restaurant there. Another repeated dream is that I am trying to find desperately some toilet facilities without any success. It shows as if some unfulfilled tasks remained to be fulfilled. Why did I leave that country so suddenly with all the promises and opportunities it offered? I had kicked away everything that opening had thrown in my way. I search for the answers, but I cannot find answers to so many 'whys'. Sometimes I conclude that fate led me there to find a cure to my illness. That is why I say that it was a divine intervention. The moment I got well I got the ticket back to UK where my destiny was.

On the interview day we, the whole family, went to the American Embassy in London. There were a lot more candidates of various nationalities, of all sorts of colours, ages, and religions. There was no sign of any discrimination. They were all going to that land of opportunity to fulfil their dreams and they all had their dreams. We assembled in a hall. We were given an introduction by the immigration officer. We were then sent for finger-printing and individual photographs. We went for a high-tech screening for future references for the American archives. It was just a numbers game. Some of us might have been saints, innocent children, or god-fearing humans, but our individual data had to be stored. I must admit that for the first time in my life I felt intimidated and treated as a criminal by an organised state. I had travelled through Europe, but my human dignity was never raided like that. I felt that I had been put in the dock already without any evidence and proof. However, if one had to settle in a superpower country, I had to obey their tough rules without a protest.

Finally, all the people were asked to go for the medical test, except us and two other families. We were asked to go and see an officer in the basement of the embassy. I was intrigued. I checked once more from the directing officer, 'Are you sure we are not to go for the medical?' and he confirmed. Surprise turned into a mystery and I was not very happy to accept 'no medical' for us, and I wanted to know why. However, we went down in the basement. An officer was sitting in his small office. We three of us went in. I do not remember what conversation we had there and what was the real reason to see this person. In fact, he never asked any important questions; otherwise they would have been in my memory forever. As it was puzzling for me not to be sent for the medical but to this officer, I could not resist asking a million-dollar question to him, 'Why are we not being medically screened?'

A JOURNEY THROUGH PARTITION AND BEYOND

'There is no need for you to be medically checked,' he replied.

I was very keen to be examined because I wanted to have another opinion in case they could discover something about my health that the doctors in Wales were not able to. The American doctors are known for their expertise and thoroughness. They must be also better equipped at the Embassy to diagnose my illness. I too wanted to know that if I was suffering from a mysterious illness, it was better I did not go to that country where private medical treatment was very expensive. During that brief interview, I raised the issue at least three or four times. Eventually he got fed up with my repeated questions on medical screening. He turned to Mira and said, 'See he is lecturing me too. He has not left his lecturing in the classroom.'

We all laughed. That was it. That played the trick and I hushed up. I dared not ask again that question, but I must admit I was disappointed and someway felt concerned that if there was something wrong with me then it was better it was found out now. So, the interview finished, we were selected for immigration, and told that a Green Card would follow shortly, and the family could make plans to go to America.

Thrilled, astonished and riding on the mighty waves of hope and opportunity, we made our way back to Wales. On the way we made plans about how to go and where to live in America. I looked towards the sky in thanking my stars and the existence. We were going to America on a discovery trip to explore and experience the true soul of the country. I know millions more had done so in the last few centuries and they wrote about what they found. The discovery of any subject is the individual's own experiences. We were itching to discover the truth and greatness of that country in our own way.

I resigned my job, declared openly in my resignation that we were on our way to America. As it happens in life, some people would support you to fulfil your dreams; others would feel jealous and envious. Some would be indifferent, and some more would disapprove it. One such disapproval came from a good, sincere colleague with whom we had become good family friends. He had lived in America and came back because he did not like the social structure of that country. Knowing a bit about me he predicted at the time that I would not be able to live there and I would be back within a couple of years. Surprisingly how spot on he was in his predictions; I still cannot digest it.

We planned to sail from Southampton. I did not like travelling by air. It is a phobia stuck in my head and I cannot dislodge it. I loved sailing and that is how I planned to go. We wanted to sail by the QE 2, but the timing was not right for us so instead we booked a three-berth cabin in the SS France, the heaviest passenger ship in the world in those days. It was to sail from Southampton on the

245

17th December in the evening and was to reach New York harbour on the morning of 22nd, just a four days sailing.

We went to London to sort out our house affairs. We put our house up for sale with estate agents. I asked my brother to supervise its sale and the collection of its rent until it was sold.

We found out the contacts in America who would help us there to ease our settling down in the country. We knew a K family whom we had known well in London. They got their visa a couple of years earlier and were settled in New York. They had set up a travel business there. I also knew J whom I had met quite a few times in London at one of our good friend's house parties. He was now living in New Jersey. I got J's address and my friend K told me that he had written to J a letter and that J would be happy to accommodate us for a few days and help us find our feet in the country.

At Pontypridd we sold our car for a mere £100. We tried to sell the furniture – the beds, the sofas - but without success. We left them with a young brother and sister from Kenya to use or to sell and keep the proceeds. We also left a lot of our other baggage such as books, some clothes etc to be sent to America when we contacted them from there. That never happened. I miss those college books and the other interesting books I had accumulated.

We got busy in organising our exit from UK and entry in America. We went on a shopping spree. I had three new suits stitched with ties and shirts. We bought all new crockery, utensils, linens, towels. Bought three new big trunks and filled them up with all the goodies we were taking with us. We had the false impression that America was a very expensive country. When we got there, we felt that whatever we took with us was a stupid mistake. It was better to travel light. Anyway, what was done was done.

The poly was on the way to celebrate its Christmas break. It organised a Christmas party in a big hall where all the faculty members were present. A programme of dance and dine was arranged to cheer up the hard-working faculty. It all started with speeches during the dinner, the congratulations to those who had contributed more to the life of the Poly. It was also an exercise in self-praise by the management and of boosting their egos. Soon the stage was set for the dancer to appear on the stage. My colleague who was against my wisdom of going to America whispered in my ears, 'Let us go out. You will not like it as here the management brings in striptease every year. It is very embarrassing to see a woman going totally naked for a few pounds to entertain the men folks.'

'But there are wives too. Don't they protest?' I enquired while leaving the hall.

'No, some of these ladies don't mind these scenes. There have been some protests from the enlightened ones, but their protests have been ignored and they

A JOURNEY THROUGH PARTITION AND BEYOND

continue to exhibit such ugly scenes of humiliating women. It is the old boss of the college who enjoys the naked bodies most. You can see him bend down to look deep in the naked bodies. He is such a horrible old chap,' he continued.

We went out onto the balcony. As there was nothing much to do and we had already had dinner, I found my way home. That was the final 'goodbye' to the academic life in the valleys of Wales.

On 16th we boarded a train for Southampton where we arrived at dusk. We had already sent our baggage to Southampton to be delivered direct at the port so that we would travel light to board the ship. We hired a taxi and asked him to take us to a good hotel to stay for the night. He took us to a Greek restaurant which had some upstairs rooms to rent. Next to the restaurant was a big multi-storey hotel. I protested to the driver that we asked him to take us to a good hotel and so why on earth had he brought us there. He lied that there were no rooms available in the hotels as they were all fully booked, including the one there next to the café, so in the circumstances he had to bring us there. However, there was nothing we could do. As the driver was leaving, we noticed the owner handing him some money as commission for bringing the family to be crucified for the night. The restaurant's owner very kindly gave us a room above the kitchen where we continued to hear shouts of orders and the tinkling noises of the utensils until 2am. The worst was the humming noise of the extractor fan which was blowing the fumes of the kitchen right outside our French windows. The environment of the cooking smell, mixed with Greek shouting noises, were deafening and only those with no-mind, no ears, and no nose could sleep. The whole night became a sleepless nightmare. In the morning breakfast was being served frighteningly with all the meat and fish dishes. The whole air was filled with horrible smells that were lodging into our nostrils. That was a night not to be forgotten forever. That was also a final 'great' send-off of an innocent family whose only crime was that they had trusted the goodness in the human species, the same cruel species which was carving, grilling and roasting the pieces of meat from the same innocent animals which had suffered in the past in perfecting our body tissues and the organs from which we had evolved. Effectively they were eating their forebears.

We left the restaurant in the morning of 17th December 1970, had a bit of an outing in the town, and in the evening reported at the ship. As we passed through the immigration check out, the officer kindly enquired why we were leaving Britain as he could see we had a Green Card to live in America for good. Well, I said, it is an opportunity we did not wish to lose, even though Britain is a good country to live in too.

'Then stay on here. Why are you leaving? Either you don't go or you'll go and then come back after a short stay there.'

His comments amazed me and made me think, 'Am I making a right move?' I was leaving the country because I was tired of fighting racism in my daily life but here was a man who was making me guilty about quitting Britain. His kind words were too late to change my mind at the time. I had already burnt all my British boats and pulled all my roots which I had been nurturing for the last twelve years. This was not the time to look back. But these words did find their way into my unconscious mind and eventually surfaced again when we started thinking of relocation two years later. Every British citizen was not Enoch, shouting the 'rivers of blood'. There were a lot more decent and loving people who made our living enjoyable and smooth in Britain. Those words continued vibrating in my ears and finally made us come back here and not go to India. And we never regretted to be part of the British society again.

A JOURNEY THROUGH PARTITION AND BEYOND

CHAPTER 6: USA, THE LAND OF OPPORTUNITY

The ship was huge, very big. You had to sail in a bigger ship (this was 80,000 tons) as the frightening waves of the Atlantic Ocean are devastating and well known. We had a 2-berth windowless cabin somewhere below the sea level and we were fast asleep. We don't know when the ship set sail in the night. But by the time we woke up we had left the British Isles far behind. We hurriedly had our baths, went for the continental breakfast in the dining hall and we were on the deck to survey the vast, mighty Ocean. We were negotiating and riding over the mighty waves and challenging them arrogantly with impunity. We were showing off man's superiority to conquer them. Even the very stable stomachs would churn up to make you sea-sick. You needed the stomach of a fish to gently ride over the highs and lows and withstand the turmoil of the waves. The ship was just like a toy, shaking and moving in that endless vastness of the blue horizon. The scenes of waves smashing on the ship's side in the daylight were breathtaking experiences and frightening. I had not seen such an angry ocean before in my life, although I had sailed through the Indian Ocean and the Mediterranean Sea. Its waves moved with enormous power. And yet our little powerful monster, the genius of human invention, was piercing and cutting through these powerful, destructive waves. I was very proud to belong to a human race which now, for the first time in its history, was conquering nature in a small way. We moved around on the deck to survey the ocean from all directions. Then we went for our lunch and had a bit of a rest in our cabin. We went back to the deck again as we did not wish to miss the scenes of a lifetime. So far, so good, until by the evening, Mira's stomach gave up its fight to stay healthy and she started suffering from sea-sickness and she went back to the cabin to be confined to bed. It was Ritu's first experience in sailing. She was ok and bore the brunt of the first two days but on the third day, she also gave up and started feeling sickness and stayed in the cabin. I repeatedly told them the secret of staying free from sea-sickness was to stay on the front deck and watch

249

the up-and-down movement of the ship in sympathy with the waves. It was my experience and I never had sea-sickness. I believe the sickness is not created by the weak stomach but by the wavering mind. Once the mind moves with the waves its shakiness disappears. It becomes part of the moving waves. But they ignored my advice. I persuaded Ritu to be with me as I felt that she might be feeling sick because of her mother. Maybe they were right as they knew how they were feeling. However, I was enjoying it because I always loved sailing. Now I was on my own, both my family members were in the cabin, and I learnt to wander around on the deck on my own.

<u>Encounter with a Returning American</u>

On the third day of our sailing venture, I was moving around the deck standing here and there, scanning the ocean, and watching the huge waves battling between themselves for the supremacy to conquer the race to reach Land's End. The battle was so fierce between them that they would sometimes crash between themselves refusing each other the chance to win the race. Those scenes were exhilarating to the inner soul. The amazing part was that their behaviour was an exact carbon copy of humans and the so-called animal kingdom. Where had all this water come from? Who dug such multi-mile deep valleys into the belly of this mother earth to receive that much water for the fascination of the inquisitive human race which came to abode millions of years later? With those thoughts going around in this little head, by chance I stopped to survey the ocean just a few feet away from an American who was returning home after his holidays in Europe. Our encounter was brief and intense. We got into some silly discussion. It was not that I wanted to talk that way, but it just happened. We talked only for a few minutes:

'Hey, you are going to the States I guess.'

'Yeah! We are going to New York. I am an engineer and I have a green card to settle in USA.'

'Yes, the whole world is dying to go to America and there are not enough resources left there to satisfy everyone.'

'Did you find out the reason why?'

'No, I never bothered.'

'You should have cared to "bother". It is a land of immigrants who have displaced the natives who were simple decent people. The Statue of Liberty right at the entrance of New York is a clear proof of it. They have grabbed all the resources of that virgin continent. You don't look to me that you belong to the aborigines or the so-called native Red Indians. I come from a subcontinent called India and I am going to discover why these locals have been dubbed Red Indians. We know that there are Whites, Browns, and Blacks on this planet, but Red I am very eager to see and meet. That is another purpose of my visit to USA. Do you know when your ancestors immigrated to USA?'

He had no answer. His face dropped. He thought it was only the Americans who knew it all. He also forgot that it is the cream of intellectuals of the other nations who went there to make that country and I admit he too was one of them. It was the concentrated talents of so many who contributed to America's greatness. God has also gifted huge natural resources to that part of the world and the exploitation of those resources has added to its richness. Guess how it would be if that land was just like the Sahara, the land with nothing else but sand dunes where only the mental would venture to go. His outburst gave me the impression that he probably disapproved of my going there. His comments that the whole world was dying to go to America made me feel disgusted. I was going there like many before me to live and make some contribution to the wellbeing of that country. He lived there but his mental faculties had not broadened to welcome those who were in the queue behind him. Within a couple of minutes after our meeting I just moved away from him. I thought his comments were quite rude. That 'welcoming' from a recently settled American was disgusting. We humans always forget that we are travellers, the Universe trotters, and after death no one knows in which part of the Universe we will settle. All these galaxies, the twinkling stars are slaves of the Universe. They are going to stay there for billions of years. They are not free. We humans are free within a hundred-odd years from this enslaving body and then we become free birds again to trot the Universe. We have no permanent abode. We are the citizens of this vast Universe and we are so poor when we fight on this planet for a small plot of land.

New York

It was early morning of 22nd December 1970 and we had just finished our breakfast. We went on the deck to see the approaching New York harbour. We had already collected our cabin baggage and were ready soon to be on the American soil. It was the moment for which we had been waiting for months. We were ready for disembarking on that famous land of Manhattan where stood the world-famous Statue of Liberty. We saw the hugeness of that statue as the ship inched towards the harbour to dock. That reminded us that from now onwards we were going to live in liberty and would be free from political oppression, racial inequality, and the menace of poverty. We disembarked, got our trunks and the baggage collected. The immigration officers were there in force to check our papers. When Mira's turn came for checking, the officer was amazed to see a woman with a handbag slung on her shoulder and gold jewellery on her neck and ears. He could not resist issuing a dire warning to her. He said, 'Ma'am, we do not walk on the New York streets with handbags and jewellery. You would be mugged. Please take them off now and put them in your trunks. Is it your first visit to USA?'

'Yes, it is,' we replied.

'No wonder you are naïve to the culture of Americans.'

Then he asked to check our baggage. We took him to a place where Ritu, the seven-year-old child, was in control of all the six suitcases and the other baggage. He got frightened and very alarmed to see an innocent girl sitting on one of the suitcases as a guard to protect the baggage. He strongly suggested that we should not leave a kid alone as in-charge of baggage.

'This is New York Ma'am; we do not do things like that over here. She would get hurt, kidnapped, mugged, or murdered.'

Welcome to America, a great land of opportunity and freedom, we thought! The enthusiasm and ambition of living and making America our dream home evaporated instantly. We had waited for months and had been building castles in the air to see and live in those lofty sky-high buildings, but now the castles were shattered. That was how we were introduced to the American dream as we put our first steps on its soil. That introduction was within minutes of reaching there. We were obviously jolted and very nervous. In fact, I could never shake off that frightening introduction to America by an American. There is only one life to live, why live in fear? Those early experiences played a large part when we made a final decision to quit America. There were a hell of a lot more experiences to follow.

Having cleared from the immigration protocols at the port, we came out to the meeting areas. A man called G, a friend of accountant J was there to take us to Newark where J lived with his wife and a three-year-old daughter. J was away on a tour and could not come to take us. G said that although he had the instructions from J to find us an apartment and drop us there, he did not have time to find an apartment and so was taking us to J's flat which was in a 21-storey building, just outside downtown Newark. As we had a lot of baggage, he arranged for that to be kept at another flat in the same building. This flat was rented by a single Indian professor at a local college. We reached the flat in the evening by a taxi, going through a very long tunnel under the Hudson River.

The lady was not amused to see three of us there. She never expected us to be there. She showed her annoyance at G. However, she had no choice but to accept us as unwelcome guests. Soon G left, wishing us well and bon stay at the flat. With some chatting with the lady, after a dinner we retired to sleep. Next morning, we got up early as usual. The time passed on, the lady dragged her feet. The clock was ticking 9, then 10, and by 11am we managed to have a cup of tea and a toast for our breakfast. Ritu wanted to have an egg, cereal or any other breakfast. There was none. We cursed our silly habits of living at our home in UK

A JOURNEY THROUGH PARTITION AND BEYOND

with relatively more luxurious food habits. We always had a fresh orange with honey, then egg, cereal with milk, toast, and then tea. Ritu was also ignored and felt jealous while the lady fed her own child with different foods. About mid-day the lady put on lentils to boil with a promise that lunch would be served by 2pm. The time came and moved on and yet no lunch. With one excuse or the other finally we got our 'lunch' at 8pm. We then knew that we were not welcomed there. G had dumped us there without J's permission. J came back from his trip on 24th December. We thought we probably would get better treatment after his arrival, but we were terribly wrong. He moaned and was very much annoyed that G had deposited us there and not found us another apartment. I hardly knew J and I felt it was a big mistake to become an unwelcome guest in the house of someone we hardly knew. But K in London had told me that there would be no problems to stay with him. In fact, we had asked J through K to book us a flat before our arrival. We did not wish to be a burden on anyone, but G had bungled all that. Therefore, the J's were not happy to keep us, and we also had a rough time by staying as unwelcome guests. The pinch and hurt were on both families and yet I would blame J for passing the buck of finding a flat onto G. He should have known himself better that his family and he himself were not very good and caring hosts, even temporarily. But it left bitter tastes in us for that bungle.

In desperation I telephoned K in New York to help me find a flat urgently. We knew the Ks when they were in London. We used to meet up quite often in our circles of friends. We decided to meet on the 26th in Manhattan. We walked through the streets, bending the head upwards to 90 degrees to see the heights of the huge apartment and office buildings, a breathtaking experience. The temperature was below zero and as we walked through the streets, the gushing wind chill was even lower than minus seven. I noticed that my face was frozen, and I had no ears on my head. I had never experienced that kind of cold so far.

All the streets were deserted. Like London, people were lying in their beds and were trying to shake off the influence of over-eating and boozing. However, the public services were moving. K had seen an advertisement for flats to rent. We took a subway and went to Queens. We saw a two bedroom flat about five minutes' walk from the subway station. We liked it, paid the deposit, and could move in on the 1st January 1971. When I came back 'home' and gave the news, the host was happy, but we were not only happy but thrilled and relieved that finally we would move out to our own flat. Mira later told me that Ritu had been confiding to her that when we moved to our own flat, would Mira cook an egg for her every morning. Her wish was honoured to the letter. She was just dying to eat an egg and cereals. The child was so badly deprived of even the basic food by the host in the land of plenty where the food was cheap and plentiful. It was not that the host was poor and was struggling for money. He was a qualified accountant and was earning a lot of money. He had been well settled in America for the last three years. But it was the mental poverty which he could not shake off even in the land of plentiful.

New York Times

It was 11am Sunday. The bitter chill of Newark was discouraging me from strolling out of the building. But the old habits of reading newspapers were lingering on. They would never take rest until the demands of the mind are met and are met fully. I hopped onto a local bus making its way to Downtown to buy a newspaper. I spotted a newspaper stall with all the variety of papers stacked on it. I stood there to glance over them to see which one would be interesting to buy. Well if one is in New York, one should read the New York Times. Its headlines looked attractive and convincing. Following my British habit, I picked up the paper, intending to pay the stallholder. It was nearly three times bigger in size than the Sunday Times in UK. It was bulky and heavy. I felt lucky that I was still young enough to handle its weight. As I was taking it to the stallholder to pay for it, he angrily shouted at me, 'Hey, don't you touch that paper. Put that away where you picked it from. Pay me first.'

'I thought I would bring the newspaper to you to show you what I am buying and then pay for it,' I mumbled.

'No, we don't do it that way here. First pay the money, then touch the paper,' he retorted.

'Yes sir!'

I placed the paper back to its position, came back, paid him first, then took the paper, and waved him back to let him know that I was now taking the paper away.

I got the message loud and clear. A new country, new culture, new environment, new people, everything was new; it was us who were to readjust and learn to live their way and with their etiquettes. I was an immigrant once again. It was only the country that had changed. Aren't we all immigrants and travellers on this planet? Why do we start building permanent abodes here and start making our own rules as if we owned the planet for eternity? Stupid! Just stupid!

Tit-Bits of New York

The following are the experiences which shaped our attitude towards that big country and eventually made us come back. Every grain of these experiences was digested by our cells and our bones. We were frightened to live in that so-called free society. We were instructed by our minders and friends that we should divide our cash in two pockets. We should keep most of it in one pocket and 10 to 15 mighty dollars in the other in case we were confronted by a drug addict or any other crazy, who needed money urgently to satisfy his addictions. We must never refuse to give him something from that small change to protect our lives. Refusal might end up in violence, knifing, or even murder. Effectively what they meant was that we should have two pockets, one for the thieves and the drug addicts and the other for our own use. What a country where you had to cater even for the criminals. It reminded me of those American films which they were showing to the Gwalior students about the techniques of pick-pocketing in USA. Were they trying to destroy the culture of the Indian youths? Was it a big American plot to destroy the nation which had gained independence only a few months earlier, I wondered? It had to be. Otherwise why would someone, a lone idiot (must be a paid agent of some country), contact you individually and then take a few of you to the lonely tree-lined places of the town and show the film in the darkness of the evening? Why was this campaign being organised only in a town full of students? When I was taken to be shown the film, we were about ten students. The organiser warned us not to tell anyone that we had been shown such a film. The organiser invited me once more, but I refused. He insisted that the next film was dealing with a different type of crime and was more interesting. Telling us that we should not talk about the film to anyone else and showing it to only a selected few at a time, smells fishy, doesn't it? And now had I come to live in a sick society or a sane one? No wonder it is the Americans who are running after the Gurus of the East for the peace and tranquillity they cannot get in their own country. I was beginning to learn the American way of living.

1. As and when we travelled in the subways, we were literally frightened for our safety. As we entered the compartment, we used to look around to find a seat next to someone who looked decent and peaceful. As we assessed them, their eyes in turn were fiercely gazing at us. The suspicion and terror were mutual. Everyone was distrustful of everyone else and was frightened.

2. One day I was having a cuppa at one of the coach stations where I was to catch a coach for Newark. As I put my hand in my trouser pocket to get the money out, I noticed that so many eyes were watching my actions. When I left the café to board the coach, I was monitoring if anyone was following me.

3. One evening as Mira got down at the subway station to walk towards our flat, she noticed that a black man, heavy, bulky, and fat, who was leaning against the station entrance wall, collapsed and fell on the ground with a thump. Probably he had a heart attack. Many people were coming out of the busy subway but they all just walked past him to let him die. No one had the compassion or care to help him or even to call an ambulance or the police. No one ever knew who he was. His family would wait forever for him to come home.

4. The toilets at the subway had no doors. You even could not ease yourself in privacy. The other toilet facilities, if any, were normally in the basements of the buildings where I felt scared to go in case I confronted some criminal or a drug addict. That fear was not only in me but everyone I talked to was mindful of that too. They all thought the same way as I did. It was the psychology of fear, hatred, mutual mistrust that was the norm of the country.

5. Once, we were walking around the streets of Manhattan, and we saw a poor man with a blanket spread on the footpath in front of him. He was watching the passers-by with apathy and sadness in his eyes. It was a bitterly cold day. Ritu had never seen such scenes in her birthplace London, UK. So, she enquired innocently, 'Who is he and what is he doing there?' 'He is a beggar,' Mum replied, trying to avoid telling her more about it in case Ritu became more distressed. Children are always inquisitive. Their whys never end until their mental hungers are fully satisfied. So Ritu asked further, 'What does a beggar do?' Mira opened up a bit more and said, 'He is poor. He has no money to live or eat. So, he is begging from the passers-by to give some money so that he can buy food.' 'But we never have such people in London, why here?' Ritu said in her shivering tender voice. We could see that she was now feeling a pain for the wellbeing of this soul on the road. 'Yes, we did not have that kind of people there. It is the type of the country we are now going to live in.' I gave her a dime to place it on the blanket. Soon we had gone past from this scene and her attention was diverted to other attractions of the new place we were exploring. But that left a long-lasting impression on us too, even though we had seen it all in India, a relatively poor country. There the poor are in millions and if by the stroke of luck, destiny does throw you into the poverty trap, no one would feel that much humiliated. But here in the richest city of the world, which takes pride in giving billions of dollars in 'aid' to other nations, such scenes were unacceptable to a visitor. It made us aware that if by some misfortune the breadwinner becomes chronically ill, loses a job, or gets into a litigation, on which an individual would have no control, what would happen to his family? That kind of dilemma worried most of the middle-class residents of America.

6. Our flat was a prison, a trap with a lockable door in a corridor. We could approach there through a lockable entrance door at the ground floor, then going to the upper floors by a shared staircase or an elevator. All residents were screened by the management at the time of renting a flat and were given the keys for the entrance door, but when you opened it to enter the building nobody knew who was the resident in that big complex of so many flats. No resident knew that when he entered, the one following him immediately behind was also a resident, or a visitor, a criminal, a burglar, or what. You dare not question the follower or his motives. You could never tell - he might be armed with a knife or

A JOURNEY THROUGH PARTITION AND BEYOND

a gun. If in the middle of the night someone knocked on your door, you would go panicky. Who is it, why did he knock on my door, and what does he want? We had our doors knocked a couple of times. I must admit I was petrified. We learnt later that in the complex of flats where we had stayed in Newark, a young lad followed a middle-aged man at the entrance. The man never questioned the identity of this young fellow. The young man followed him into the same elevator. Later they discovered the dead body of this man. He had only a couple of dollars in his pocket and for that he lost his life. Obviously, the killer ran away. This was not an isolated case in America. It happens all the time. We always felt that it was a sick country, ready to explode. It is only a matter of time.

      7.   We had met a Jewish girl in London through a friend. She was on sabbatical leave from her high school where she taught. She came to stay with us for a week and became quite friendly with us and asked us to meet her whenever we went to New York. We did. We visited and dined with her family. She took us to beaches. Her father, who was quite well-connected and had a practice in Manhattan, was eager to help us find a job in New York. One day the young girl invited us to visit her school to give a talk about India. We went there on the day. It was a huge high school campus with so many facilities compared with British schools. It was just like a university campus. I had not seen even the colleges I worked for as big as that high school. As we walked through the long corridors, we noticed a police mini-station. 'Hey, you have got police stations in high schools?' I enquired from the young lady. 'Yes, we have. Without the police we will not be able to teach in our schools. They maintain the discipline and the security of the pupils and the staff,' she replied. 'But we did not have any in British schools.' However, we gave our talk. It was quite interesting. We were heard very politely and were asked some questions. She thanked us, and we departed. But it was the beginning of our understanding of how the educational system worked there. After this, there were no surprises on the security issues wherever we worked.

      8.   Mira got a job in the City College of New York. She was reluctant to apply but I coaxed her to try her luck. She did, and she got it. We were now short of money. It was taking me a long time to find a job. We had already borrowed some money from relations in Canada. Therefore, it was the most welcome news for our financial survival in that country. After she joined there, she found that there were armed guards in the corridors of the college. The faculty had its own separate elevators and the students had their own. This was done to protect the faculty members from mishandling and abuse by the students. It was totally alien to the British way of life at the campuses.

      9.   We had been in our new flat in Queens for only a couple of days. Ritu was playing and going around and round a chair in the middle of the room.

She felt giddy and hit her forehead on the metal backrest of the chair. She had a deep cut and was bleeding. In panic, I dashed down to a chemist shop, opposite to the flats. I narrated the incident to the chemist and asked what I should do. Should I call the ambulance? He said that they would charge for this service as the ambulances are operated by private companies and therefore it would cost a lot of money to take her to a hospital. The hospitals would also charge you as a private patient as we did not have health insurance cover. His best advice was that we contact a local doctor who would examine her and advise us. If it is only a small cut we should not worry, he further said. It would heal itself. But we were not prepared to accept that. So we rang a local doctor the chemist suggested and made an appointment to see him. We hired a taxi and went to see him. He was a good doctor. He examined Ritu, administered first aid and recommended that we see a surgeon as she needed some stitches because the injury was quite deep and long. He gave us the telephone number of an Italian surgeon who worked in a local hospital. We contacted him. He enquired if we had insurance. We said no. He said he would charge us his fee of $50 for the stitches + another $50 to remove the stitches after three days + $49 for hiring a surgery room in a private local hospital where he would perform the stitches. Did we have a choice? Your only child is hurt; you are in a new world of plenty. No, we accepted all his charges. It took him three days to arrange the room and stitch the wound. After three days we rang, and he asked us to go to his hospital where he worked. We hired a taxi and went. At the entrance to the hospital, there was no receptionist but only an armed guard. Rather than having some kind of a welcoming sign to put our minds at rest, instead a sense of awe and fear was created as if those doors were leading us to hell. In fact, we were being led to hell. The guard informed the surgeon. He took ten minutes to arrive at the door. He took us to his surgery through a long walk in the corridors. There we saw some patients lying down on the floors. Some might be dead, others in agony and groaning for help. It was distressing; we had never witnessed such soul-searching scenes before, even in India. The corridors were dirty. It was a great learning curve about the rich and powerful country. The surgeon removed the stitches, the wound had already healed and dried. He advised us that we should get insurance as soon as possible and it was a shame that we did not have the insurance in that country against any health problems. But I had another nagging question which I wanted him to answer. I asked, 'On the way we saw so many patients, lying on the floors not being attended to, why?' He said, 'In this country as soon as you are admitted to hospital, the first thing we ask is "has he got medical insurance?" If not, then nobody cares here. That is why when you enter American hospitals, as you did, you could be attacked, hurt, or knifed by the disgruntled people outside. They might think that you are a doctor working in the hospital. That is why we have the security guards to receive you and not the

A JOURNEY THROUGH PARTITION AND BEYOND

receptionist. It is not very safe here to work.' I had my answer. The grass looked so green from the outside world, but the big land of opportunity was sick and rotting through and through to its core.

10.　　The doctor, who had treated Ritu, also investigated the health problems from which I had been suffering. I gave him all the details of ECG, blood tests, X-rays, and duodenal tests. His examinations without a blood test showed all the negatives about my health too. However, he gave me some tablets to try, and warned that if these did not help, he would have no further help to give. I took the tablets. There was no improvement. I just gave up and did not go back to him as he said he could do nothing more for me. A few weeks later I rang him again and reminded him who I was. He asked me to go and see him. He said that he had been thinking about my case. 'Let me try this medicine on you. Let me know on the phone how you feel after taking these tablets for three days.' I tried the tablets for three days and rang him about their effect. I said, 'I feel that something is happening in my head. I cannot pinpoint what exactly it is.' 'That is good. That shows the medicine is working. Keep going and let me know when you have finished all the tablets.' I reported back to him that I was feeling much better, the fear which was stuck somewhere in my head was gone, and my weight loss and weakness which I was observing was gone. I was cured. Is that why the divine took so much trouble to take me to that country? I believe so. I may be wrong, but beliefs are beliefs and they cannot be proved right or wrong. Wrong for the non-believers but right for the believers.

11.　　In the neighbourhood, we made friends with a couple from India who had a teenage son attending a local high school. The man worked for Air India. Sometimes we would meet up for chit chat in their flat or in our flat. Their son would tell us his experiences at school. He told us that there was a very big drug problem in his school. He used to wear torn out trousers in the school so that no other kid would demand money from him for their habits or push the drugs on him. He pretended that he belonged to a poor family and he never told that his father was working for the airlines.

12.　　There was another young single doctor who was working at a Bronx hospital. He told us that to go to his hospital he was travelling to the nearest subway that was only 200 yards from the hospital. From there he was ringing the hospital for them to send a transport to pick him up to take him to the hospital. He was not allowed to walk to the hospital in case he was attacked outside. What a stink!

13.　　A teacher's job was advertised in the Bronx. Mira applied for it. We checked with our friends who had been working in the city for some time and knew the areas of New York. They advised us that we should never attempt to go to that area, leave aside working there. There were rapes in the schools, goods were stolen from cars while waiting at traffic lights, and there were more murders in that area than anywhere else in the city. We decided that we would rather go back to UK than risk our lives by working there.

14. I applied for a heating and air conditioning engineer's job at the Newark school system. My weakness was obvious. I had no experience in that branch of engineering except that I had read a bit of theory at my degree course in London. I asked someone's opinion and he said that it was not a difficult job and I would be able to pick up the techniques of maintaining and installing H&V (heating and ventilation) systems within days. So, I applied. No reply came. One day I walked into the council offices at Newark Downtown. The offices were mostly manned by Black Americans (I hate to use this terminology for the people as it is divisive). On the ground floor an officer was in his office. It appeared that he was holding some kind of good job in the council. I went in, introduced myself, and explained to him the purpose of my visit. I told him that I wanted to see the officer (named the man) who was in charge of recruiting and interviewing for the H&V job. He was quite friendly, chatted a bit with me, and said, 'This man is on the fifth floor. Tell him my name and say that I sent you to see him and he will help you.' I went upstairs to the office. The man offered me a seat and asked, 'How did you know that there was a job available for an engineer?' I said that it was advertised in the local paper and I had applied for it, and that the officer on the ground floor had asked me to come and see him. I gave him the name of this guy downstairs. The man said, 'Oh if he has sent you, then I have to look after you.' I realised that he was thinking that I was being recommended by that man. I did not wish to correct that impression as I wanted a job urgently and the pay was very good with extra bonuses. But in my heart, I felt guilty. However, he asked me to come back in a week's time. I went back. He had forgotten me. I reminded him that so and so man had sent me for the job. So, he asked, 'How do you know this man. Is he your friend?' 'No, I only met him when I was trying to find out about your office.' 'Oh, so he does not know you as such.' At that point I knew that the job wouldn't be offered to me. If I had been smart enough to tell the lie that I knew him well, I would have got the job. There you are - next week I got the 'no' for the job.

15. I attended three more interviews. One was at a factory which was manufacturing plastic carrier bags. When I went for the interview, I noticed a strange and tense atmosphere in the office. The interviewing head was sitting in an open office with all the other staff working silently with their heads down. It was like a classroom environment with a teacher ruling the class with his iron fists and the 'kids' sitting on their chairs with desks. The fear of the sack appeared on their faces. It was an awful scene to see in a democratic country. He showed me a carrier bag and explained that the biggest problem they had was how to open the

A JOURNEY THROUGH PARTITION AND BEYOND

bag at a supermarket checkout. They could not find a solution. That problem is still there even today. I did not get the job and I do not regret it. The second one was for a company that was hiring some temporary workers to meet an order. The interviewer told me that the moment their order was finished the job would be gone. Simply it was a hiring and firing operation. Again, I did not get the job. However, I would not have worked there anyway. The third one was at a trousers zip manufacturing company. They claimed to be the world's biggest company for the manufacture and supply of that product. Again, it was regret. I had no experience in any of those kinds of jobs anyway.

Also, my heart was stuck on a teaching job with an opportunity for postgraduate studies. I always prayed to God to help me get a job where I could teach and study.

A Campaign for a Teaching Job

The job market in America is not that easy. It is very demanding, competitive, ruthless, and oppressive. You are considered as a productive unit, a cog in the chain of a production line. If you are a weak cog, you will be discarded and replaced. There is no mercy, no compassion and care in that capitalist system. You must sell your skills to the would-be-employer. The more you brag of your achievements with plenty of cream and some lies added to it to make it tasteful for the employer, the better. It is a skill you must acquire and learn in a very hard way. It is a brutal, tyrannical society. The timid and the shy would lose out in that market. If you knew someone and you had some connection, it would enhance your chances a lot. For instance, I was writing in my first CV that I designed special purpose machines for production. But a well-experienced writer of CVs said that I should add what those machines did and how much the company saved by installing those machines by giving figures into thousands of dollars. That meant I had to exaggerate everything I did to convince the employer that I was the best candidate for the job

So, I learnt the tricks of the trade to sell the skills I had and how I would contribute towards the wellbeing of that company. Having written a good CV, I got 500 copies printed. I sat down in my flat, and then sent the letters to all the engineering colleges and the universities. Soon the replies of regrets started pouring in. Was I disappointed with those regrets? No, never. It was a part of life. Not everyone I wrote to would have a vacant job waiting for me. I also went to a central recruiting place in Washington DC where all the faculty heads were coming to recruit their next year requirements. It was like a cattle-shed, a marketplace, an auction house. It was like a horse-trading centre where an individual was to sell his skills. The heads would paste their requirements on a billboard with their

261

contact details; the seekers would see the ads and contact the heads if interested; make appointments and see each other. The seekers would exaggerate their abilities and heads would attract the candidates with their generous offers. It was like a hell that was painted with big and attractive slogans, with many promises to lure the candidates to apply. One could even draw a similarity with a prostitute's place where one negotiates the deals between the two interested parties. How much she would charge for the services she is offering and what she would offer in return for the money. The horse-trading would be over within a couple of days. I had a couple of interviews which did not result in an offer. I came back empty-handed like a dead dude.

In March 1971, with my CV campaign, I had a letter indicating an interest in my application from the head of IEOR (Industrial Engineering and Operations Research) at Virginia Polytechnic at Blacksburg. I took the news with caution. I'd had so many regrets in the last three months and that taught me to be modest with any ray of hope. It was only an initial acknowledgement. There was no reason to get excited or to rejoice. A few weeks later I had a letter from the head again asking me to phone him. Phone him to say what? I thought. I was nervous. An interview on the telephone between two-faceless people is never a welcome opportunity. I made some enquiries about the Poly. Someone said, 'Going to work in Blacksburg! You know it is the racist south where bigots live.' Bigots! What is the meaning of bigot? I had never heard of that word. I investigated the dictionary and found the meaning. Should I pursue further? I asked myself. Those were the anxious days. Our friend B from London also had a green card and was staying with us. We were both trying for jobs and the whole day it would be nothing but discussion about the problems we were facing in the new country. We would discuss the pros and cons of living in that country, the social problems, the lack of opportunities for getting jobs, and discuss mutual disappointments of regret letters. It was nothing but all day we discussed the negative aspects of life there. The whole environment was full of frustrations for daily life - crime, job hunting, the children's education, the drug problem, and the medical problems – and so on. B was more disappointed than us as he faced more discrimination than us because of the turban he was wearing. He did not say so, but he must have been worried about bringing up his two school-age sons. They were being brought up as Sikhs in UK. So, within weeks of his arrival he had already made up his mind to go back to UK. I must admit that those negative discussions had influenced me so much that finally when we made the decision to quit America, those ideas strengthened the argument to quit that country – the land of opportunity. One cannot live two parallel lives at different places to compare later which one was the right one and why.

A JOURNEY THROUGH PARTITION AND BEYOND

Going back to the story. I collected the courage and phoned the head in response to his letter. He told me about the job. I was to teach production engineering in the IEOR faculty. I would be offered a job of a tutor with a facility to pursue my PhD. I would not be offered a job of an assistant professor as I did not have the PhD, the minimum requirement to be an assistant professor. Also, University rules did not permit me to be appointed as assistant professor as I was pursuing the postgraduate course. I was disappointed at the designation but understood that I had to start at a low level if I was to study for the PhD. I had turned forty and was still struggling to have some feathers on my head. However, he said he would be writing to me about the date of interview at Blacksburg and the arrangements of the visit. I got the letter with details of the arrangement. I was given the date of my visit, the flight times from and to La Guardia airport, New York. The head was to pick me up at the nearest airport Roanoke; drive me to Blacksburg; I would have the interview with him and with some post-graduate students; a lunch; and then he would be leaving me back at Roanoke airport to fly back. All the expenses were to be paid by the University. He had sorted out every minute detail and asked me to ring him to confirm that the dates suggested were convenient for me.

I had a big problem now, the similar kind I had when I went to Wales for an interview. I did not like flying and I had never flown in my life. I was too scared. I had this phobia. I had no choice but to move forward and grab the opportunity being offered for which I had been praying. I phoned. I thanked the head for calling me for the interview. After discussing other relevant issues, I finally came to talk about the mode of travelling to Blacksburg. I said, 'I am sorry I will not be flying to Roanoke, but I will be travelling by Greyhound coach.'

'Why?' he curiously asked.

'Because I am new to USA and I would like to do some sightseeing on the way.' I told a white lie just to hide my weakness for flying.

'But you can have the pleasure of sightseeing some another time. By plane it would take you only a couple of hours but by coach, it would take you at least 16 hours. You might have to spend more time at Washington to change a coach. Also, it is safer by air than in a coach you know. We are paying for your plane ticket anyway so why not travel more conveniently?' he insisted.

'I know it is safer but please let me come this time by coach,' I continued to resist.

He gave up. He said, 'Ok, let me know the coach arrival time so that I can pick you up.' I said ok I would do that.

However, later I had a second thought on my travelling plans and my stupidity of going by a coach. I thought to myself that why was I such a damn chicken. Why am I so scared of going by plane? One day I must travel by this

263

modern way of travelling, so why not now. The life is to be lived only once and why this fear? I made the enquiries to fly to Roanoke. It was only a couple of hours flying from La Guardia airport in New York. I booked my seat and telephoned Dr A that I had changed my travelling plans and would be coming by air as suggested by him. Dr A was delighted and said that he would be at Roanoke airport to receive me and drive me to Blacksburg for meeting the various members of the staff.

The First Flying Experience

On the day of flying, I checked in at La Guardia and went inside a plane for the first time in my forty years of existence on this planet. I had not done badly in life. I had already walked hundreds of miles on foot. I rode many miles dangerously on the back of galloping donkeys and horses. I had bumpy rides for many hours on camels' backs, with humps and intricate backbones, giving a lot of pains and sore to my bum. But that day I was sitting on a comfortable seat and was flying in the sky on a man-made machine which would take me only a couple of hours to travel more than six hundred miles. Shortly I would be talking to the clouds in mid-air. In my early childhood I was fascinated to see those clouds of all hue and colour fly past me. But that day for the first time I would be able to talk to them as equals, to fly over them or along with them with better speed than they used to show off to me. I even could touch them if I wanted to and feel their softness and mellowness. The world had changed within a short span of life. It was a challenge, not to be missed. In my short span of life, I was now moving from 'ride on a donkey' to 'fly in the sky'.

But the fear of flying was still persistent. As I settled down on my seat, I felt suffocated. I felt so helpless. I had a great urge to run out of the plane. No, that was not the mode of travel for me. I loved the ever caring and loving bosom of my mother earth and I did not wish to leave it to go to those heights from where I might fall. The fear was creating a panic - what if, God forbid, just a small part of the aeroplane body breaks off? I looked through the window and saw some people on the tarmac and in the airport building. I felt how lucky they were to be inside the building. They were laughing and smiling and it felt as if they were making fun of me. I was just stuck in and could not run away. There was no way out but to be in the air soon. The pilot occupied the seat and cranked the engine. The huge smoke, from the jet engine next to me, billowed into the air. The engines started humming with reluctance, the body of the plane started shaking; then engines roared with full throttle, the belly of the plane started taxiing on the runway. Then it positioned itself on the tarmac for instructions to speed up with frightening engine noises. Suddenly it started moving, speeding, then running with huge speeds, and hey presto we were climbing with the nose piercing up and we were in the air flying towards the sky. The heart was sinking at the time and I had surrendered all my body to the care of the almighty. The time of turning back or running away from the cabin was all gone. It was too late. The fate of all the fliers was sealed for the good or for the bad for the next two hours. The time of no return was snatched away within moments. We had finally left the warmth and safety of the ever-protecting mother earth. The heart was sinking, the breathing was getting heavier and more erratic, and I was reciting the mantras of the almighty God to keep my fear level low and protect me from this 'evil' invention of engineers. No, I do not wish to talk to the clouds. Let them fly away to their destinations for which they were meant, but leave me alone within the safe havens of my mother earth. Let nature blow them away and I do not care. Soon we were amid the clouds. I looked below and saw the Hudson River, the huge buildings of Manhattan moving away from us with tremendous speed. When we were touching the sky, it looked as if our plane was stationary and the earth below was moving only with a slow pace, although the plane was flying at six hundred miles an hour. I had the huge wing of the plane on my left and I was sailing in the turmoil of the winds. The panoramic views of the landscape were tremendous. I was like a bird, an eagle surveying the landscape of the cities, the forests, and the historical buildings below. Momentarily I forgot my fear of the sky and I was negotiating my way to Roanoke riding over the turbulent winds. It was a huge change in life style. Anyone could go crazy with that kind of a change, but we humans are a very adaptable species. But if there was no change and no excitement in life, we humans would commit suicides out of boredom. These small tickling inventions, the new gadgets, the new toys, coming at intervals with slow pace are God's bribery to us to keep us going. It is a huge technological change in the last two centuries and the pace of change is accelerating with time, faster and faster now so that it is becoming difficult to keep a track of it.

The pilot was politely announcing at intervals the historical spots and the cities over which we flew. It was perhaps useful to the American citizens who knew the history of their land but for me it was just a dot on the ground. Soon the two hours went past, and the pilot announced that we were going to land at Roanoke airport within minutes. What a relief it was! The fear and nervousness had already subsided. I was now calm and in peace.

Roanoke was a small airport at the time. There were only a handful of us who were leaving the plane. A was there to receive me. The moment he saw me he gave a very broad smile. How he recognised me I don't know.

'Hi, I am Dr A. I am the head of the IEOR department. I am very pleased to receive you on behalf of my faculty.' His welcome was most genuine, very friendly, and showed the typical warmth of an American. I was impressed. There was a hell of a difference between the British welcome and the American welcome. The British welcome is cold, cunning, calculated, and not from the heart. They would smile from outside but their inner being is filled with menace. I must hastily correct this impression - this is not true for every British person. The majority of British are very warm and caring too, and that is why we as 'immigrants' could live and settle here in 'droves'. Some are pretentious, and one can see their attitude as if coming from a man with a chip on his shoulders. Some people say that they are very reserved species. I don't agree. They just do not have the warmth. Their outward smile is just made up to deceive, to show that it is a genuine and friendly gesture but in fact they are intensely reading your personality. It is never heart to heart. The American welcome is genuine, and it is from the heart. Their welcome touches your inner being. It gives you happiness. You feel the pleasure in meeting them. But it is not universally true and not applicable to all the residents of those countries. Human relationships and personality are very complex to fathom; even Freud had to spend a lifetime to come up with some answers but failed.

On the way to Blacksburg, he gave me the schedule of the whole day. There were hardly any members of the faculty there currently. The college was closed for the summer break and the faculty members were enjoying their holidays with their families somewhere on this planet. But whosoever was present there I was to meet. Surprisingly one of them I was to meet was an Indian postgraduate student. Later on, I learnt that the American way of hiring and firing the faculty is very democratic. Even the students and postgraduates are consulted. They play their part in advising the head for choosing the would-be candidate. Of course, the final decision is always made by the head. The head is also an elected head of the department from the faculty for a few years. His appointment is confirmed to the headship every year with some added stipend to his faculty salary. So, having met whomever I could, A came to take me back to Roanoke airport. On the way we had a pizza at a small pizza place. Whatever we ate, we ate, and the rest was packed for the head to take it home.

Teaching Job at Blacksburg

A week later, I had an appointment letter confirming the offer of the job, the date of my reporting for work, the subjects I was going to teach and some details about my PhD programme in Industrial Engineering. I was on top of the world. I had achieved a huge breakthrough to earn my living as well as to follow a PhD programme. Was there any other luckier man than I was on that day? No, impossible. I was the only one whose luck was climbing to new heights and I was getting what I wanted in life. It is a rare phenomenon in life that you get what you ask for, and it was happening. This time God was not disposing of what I had dreamt. Rather, he was on my side and was helping me to get what I wanted. I was accepting his mercies with both open hands and thanking Him. I was forty at the time and at the age of 43 I would have my PhD in engineering, not a young age

A JOURNEY THROUGH PARTITION AND BEYOND

but in my case, given all the worst circumstances I had faced, I had done a lot better than could have been expected. Also, I was the only son of my family to reach that stage. I do not wish this statement to be taken as egotistic brag, no never. But it was a fact of life. I am a humble person and would always remain so. Did I ever think even in my dreams, that one day that dream would really come true? No, never. I was offered a salary of $9500/year. Hey, reader, what would you do if you were in my shoes? Yes, I too accepted it as you would have done. I was rejoicing, dancing, and giving thanks in my heart to the Existence. But on a second thought - why I am thanking the Existence? Aren't I part of it? We are inseparable. We are not two but one. I came from it and would go back into it.

B was planning to go back to UK. He tried even Canada but without any success. In his heart I am sure he must have been disappointed. We started packing. Mira's job was already over at the City and she was not getting any renewal. At the end of August 1971, we packed back everything into big trunks, hired a taxi, boarded a coach and whoosh we were on our way to Blacksburg for a new life, away from the crime-ridden city of New York. While emptying the flat, we broke a table lamp by accident. For two days we all were gluing the bits like a jigsaw puzzle so that we did not lose any money from the deposit of $240. We failed in our attempt and gave up. I informed the apartment's supervisor about the incident. But with luck, we got the full deposit back without deductions. We thought the table lamp was an antique and very valuable but obviously it must have been acquired from a second-hand furniture shop.

We informed A of our date of arrival. After reaching Blacksburg we were picked up by the Indian postgraduate who had interviewed me and told me that he had recommended me for the appointment to the head. He deposited us to stay for a couple of days in a local inn as the flat which they had booked for us at a local complex was not ready yet. This complex had around 200 flats, owned by a Greek property owner. When the flat was ready we moved in. It was a two bedroom flat on the first floor on the main road. Behind the flat we had a swimming pool with a party/assembly room which could be hired for small parties with all the cooking facilities. Opposite on the other side of the road there was a gym complex with various exercising machines and sauna. A minute walk from the flat was the manager's office, manned by a lovely, caring and helpful lady. She told us that if we needed more furniture we could have it by choosing from their store room. She suggested that we had everything we needed to settle there, except a car. The campus was about a couple of miles from the complex and, with no transport, the car was a necessity. She said that she knew the owner of a local garage who sold good second-hand cars. She said that she would take us there in her car, help us to select a car and ask the company to arrange hire purchase. So, on the next Saturday, we went with her. We selected a General Motors green car from a pool of cars, but the car had rust damage on the back mudguard. The owner said that if we liked the car, he would get the rusted mudguard repaired and re-sprayed. During the period of repair, he would lend us another car without charge so that we were mobile. We paid $2500 for the car. After the sale was agreed, they then took us to a local bank. It was like a local money-lender shop. After filling up the form and knowing that we had a job at the Poly, 100% loan was arranged with $10 deposit. Now we had the job, the flat, and the car. We were now settled, so quickly. This is America where everything works so fast. It is the buck which moves the American people to their best ability. They know that on the one side there is a deep valley, the suffering of the hell bound poverty and on the side is the steep hill to climb to lead them to the promised land. There is no middle ground to take it easy. Naturally they moved us towards the promised land with brutal speed and with ruthlessness.

The Driving Licence

America has a federal system of government. Each state has its own elected state government. They have their own laws. If you move to live from one state to another, you must get your qualifications recognised. You must register your car there and you must pass their driving tests.

In Virginia, I had to first pass my written test. It was a multiple-choice questionnaire. I had to tick the right boxes and it took about forty-five minutes. I booked my driving test at the same time. I went back for the test a week later. I had secured 88% in my written test. The examiner asked me to hop into his car on the driving side while he occupied the front passenger seat.

'Right, let us drive. Go straight on that road,' he ordered. I followed the instructions. A few hundred yards drive I hit a road. He instructed, 'Turn right here.' I turned right. There was no traffic in Blacksburg as most of the faculty and students were still on a summer vacation. As we reached the end of the block, he shouted again in his American tone, 'Turn right here.' 'Yes, sir, here we go.' At the end of the block he asked me to turn right again. Within a few hundred yards we arrived back where we started from. 'Please park your car there and you have passed your test.' We must have driven no more than a quarter of a mile and no more than 10 minutes. There you are, I had the American licence from the State of Virginia to drive in that State.

Shopping

There were hardly any shops in Blacksburg. We used to go to out-of-town shopping centres. There was no problem of parking spaces. Once we went to buy some furniture from a warehouse. It was a hot day. As soon as we entered, there was a young fellow waiting with a cold can of Coca-Cola. It was very refreshing. The shops made you feel as if you were a king, honouring you to visit

A JOURNEY THROUGH PARTITION AND BEYOND

their warehouse. One day we were at a huge ASDA's warehouse. Suddenly they announced on the intercom that they were auctioning some expensive kitchen appliance. By the time we reached there the auction was in full swing. A huge crowd was around it and they were bidding for it. That appliance was no good to us, so we did not bid. I was told that it was a common practice to start a surprise auction anywhere in the warehouse and at any time of the day.

One day we went to Roanoke for shopping. Roanoke is about forty miles from Blacksburg. On the way back, it got late. It was pitch dark and I was not used to driving in such conditions. It was dual carriageway and I was driving up the hill. All of a sudden, I heard a big thump noise on the front right side of my car and then I heard some screeching animal noise. I must have badly hurt a heavily built animal. I hope I did not kill it. We did not get down investigating and kept on driving, but I continue to feel guilt that I had hurt an innocent soul on that evening. I am a chicken, yes, I am. I admit it, and I would not argue on that point with anyone. I feel that in my past lives I must have been slaughtered many a time. Whenever I see an animal in that slaughtering position, I just shiver in my bones.

Reported for Work

I reported for my work on the day I was asked to. Most of the faculty members were still on vacation. The ones who were there were attending in their shorts and tee shirts. The head apologised that, unlike Britain, the faculty members were coming in their casual dress, simply because they were feeling that they were still on holiday. I assured him that I didn't mind them coming any way it suited them. The IEOR department was moving into its newly constructed wing. I was given a room as my office, with all new furnishings, where I could prepare my lessons and meet the students. I had my privacy, tranquillity, and peace of mind. It was not like in Britain where we lecturers were herded together in a small room to share tables and filing cupboards. As individuals we just had no privacy to prepare our lessons and mark homework if some others had decided to indulge in small talk and smoking to while away their time. Teaching is a serious profession and it must be respected as such, and therefore must have the proper facilities for those who take their jobs seriously. In Blacksburg the working conditions were excellent. The whole building was air-conditioned. If you have good facilities and a good wage in your pocket, then obviously your productivity would be better. Naturally then, the system would also demand excellence from the faculty and they get it. It clearly reflects in the number of books and research papers which are published in America compared to any other developed country.

Soon, more faculty members trickled in the department. A staff meeting was arranged, the new faculty members were introduced and the changes to be introduced in the academic New Year were explained. The office secretaries gave the details of their services and of the new equipment added for the faculty members to use to discharge their duties more effectively and efficiently. The timetables were dished out, and all the other admin details to run the courses were discussed. I was invited by the faculty committee on 15th September 1971 to attend an orientation programme for the entire new faculty members. I attended that. It really made me feel that I was a part of the university, a very different approach than I had experienced in UK. The whole department was now ready to start rolling with enthusiasm for the next year's teaching. It was a great learning curve for me. It was also the time to compare the teaching practices of the British colleges, with their limited resources, and the Americans, with their huge resources. I noted that the gap was the same in the deployment of resources between America and Britain as I found them when I arrived from India to Britain. India was a country struggling to develop its educational base after the disastrous centuries-old colonisation and systematic robbing of its financial resources.

American Way of Learning

The teaching procedures, the speed of learning of the various subjects, and their testing were an eye-opener. There was a hell of a difference between the two education systems of Britain and America. I admire the American system and became a fan of it. I believe it is a much superior method of learning than the British. The British system is based on cramming the subject and reproducing it at the examination. The American system is based on understanding the subject. There is no cramming involved.

The American system is more democratic, free from the faculty interference, better value for money. It achieves more learning within a given time and is humane and friendly. The academic year is divided into three quarters. The 1st quarter runs from September to December, the second January to March, and the third April to June. Every student is first interviewed at the time of enrolment. A tutor is appointed to supervise and monitor his/her progress. Their courses are well planned, considering what their aims and goals of life are. What would they like to become? What are their ambitions? Having decided these factors, the type of subjects a student should take is considered. The student is then guided to decide which of those subjects to take in the next three quarters. Every student then takes the number of subjects according to his pace and ability. The brighter ones would have the opportunity to take more subjects per quarter and finish their course earlier, while the slow learners would have the freedom to follow the courses at their own pace. The system also requires that a student must attend the minimum number of years to gain a degree. If he fails in one subject or he wishes to improve his grades in that subject, then he can repeat that subject again without affecting

A JOURNEY THROUGH PARTITION AND BEYOND

his appearance in other subjects. One never loses a year. He only loses a quarter to re-appear.

The British system is not as flexible as the American one. There is a vast difference between the two educational systems.

British System

1.   The syllabus, the course content, and the number of subjects is decided by a committee and remains fixed. All universities follow the syllabus for the whole academic year of 9 months. There is no room to choose a subject of your interest. It is the academic committee, sitting somewhere in a world of its own manipulation, that decides what is good for the thousands of young people which pass through their teaching factories. The handful of academically 'wiser' men is imposing their will on thousands. It is a brutal, control freak system. It is only they who know best. The learners have no choice but to follow like slaves.

2.   All the subjects are taught on a weekly basis by the qualified lecturers. The subjects are taught with its theory and are fortified with its practical experiments in the labs.

3.   Homework is set and checked but plays no part in the final assessment when the final grades for the degree are considered.

4.   In the affiliated university internal colleges, the examination is set by the lecturer who is teaching the subject. The lecturer would set the exam questions only from the areas he has covered in his lessons. This may result in a very limited and narrow teaching of the subject. The lecturer also knows personally all the students he teaches. During the academic year he may even sometimes sit with them in the canteens to have friendly chats. He builds a rapport with the students he teaches. Because of this personal touch, they would not like to be very strict in judging their examination papers and are likely to award a higher-grade degree than the students deserve. So, the internal students have great advantages over the external students who study in the externally recognised colleges of the universities. In these colleges the students may be taught by more able and dedicated lecturers, cover a lot more subject matter, and work a lot harder than the internal students. But because the exams are set by the internal lecturers for the external students, they get a poor grade even though they have studied the subjects more thoroughly and completely. They not only set the papers, the faceless examiners also check the exam papers. It is a very unfair system of education and I paid a heavy price for this. It may sound that I am complaining because I paid a heavy price for it, but I have seen the unfair working of the system when I was teaching myself at the degree allotting colleges.

271

5.   If you fail in any one of the subjects, you must repeat all the subjects again, thus losing a precious one year of life.

6.   The system only tests the memory and recall of the subject. It does not test your ability, your intelligence, your hard work, your attitude to society. It is a very poor way of testing the contribution a person can make to society and the country in his later life.

7.   The examiners are also humans. Their prejudices, their moods at the time of marking the papers and their mental attitude – is he under the influence of alcohol, is he angry, is he watching football, is he hungry – all these factors affect the marking ability of the examiner. It is a 100% subjective testing on which the degree is granted and is a diabolical, inhuman system. Yet the fact that it has been followed and accepted for centuries by the academicians beggars belief.

American System

1.   The academic year is divided into three quarters or semesters.

2.   You are offered a choice of subjects. You decide in which area of the subject you want to specialise, and you select only those subjects. You take those subjects in some orderly manner. If you are wrong, then a tutor will step in and advise you about how you should be following the course. For instance, if you chose a subject for which the knowledge of computers is necessary, then you would be asked to take the computer subject first.

3.   The selection of the subjects is so vital that you are guided all the way by a tutor, keeping in mind the area of your specialisation. The tutor never imposes his views but just advises you. The tutor is your god-guardian. He is your mentor; he is your all-in-all at the campus.

4.   The college also cares about your wellbeing, your finances, and your progress. If you do get into financial difficulty, they will offer bursaries, help you find a job at local shops and cafes.

5.   Of course, your subject matter is taught by your lecturer, but the exam paper set by him would reflect originality. You would be given a time to answer the set number of questions in your own classroom. You may be given a choice of questions, depending upon the lecturer. You are allowed to take your books, class notes, or any other info you may wish to use to answer the questions. They call it 'open book, open notebook' examination. After handing over the exam papers the tutor would walk out of the classroom and go to his office to do his work. He would return just a couple of minutes before the time was up to collect the completed papers. The only thing you had to do was to sign a declaration at the end of your exam paper that 'I have neither copied nor allowed anyone to copy'

my exam paper. If someone is caught in copying, then the student would be referred to the students' union for a disciplinary action. What a trusting system! Tutors never act as policemen in the examination halls as in the British system.

6. The exam paper is long, and the time given is short and therefore you must know your beans well to complete it. You would have no time to consult the books or the notes anyway. The papers are original, well thought out by the lecturers, and are never copied from books.

7. Each subject is given a grade of A, B, C, D, E. Each of these grades is then given value in numbers such as A is assigned 4 points; B has 3 and so on. For instance, on passing one subject, say with A and another with B, your overall score for the two subjects then becomes 7 and the average grade acquired is 3.5. For the completion of a degree you must achieve an average grade required by the department. It does not matter what you score in any subject; if you maintain your average you would be allowed to have a degree. That is why I called the system as humane.

8. The American system is based on the competitiveness. It rewards those who excel and punishes those who refuse to join the rat race. Your yearly wage increase is not automatic but is based on your achievements.

It is the fittest who survive in that system and the rest are left to heal their wounds inflicted by the system. I was not aware of all that. The well-known warning phrase to every faculty member of the American university is very true: 'publish or perish'. Because the system provides you the amenities, the facilities, and a good environment to work in which is unknown in any other part of the world, one would have to find time to write books, to do research and publish papers in one's area of specialisation, and attend conferences. I learnt this with a tremendous cost to my future prospects when at the end of the year I was told that I would have no increase in my salary next year. At the end of the academic year I was given a 20-page document to fill out with details of my publications and the conferences I had attended. There was no mention of how many students I had taught and what grades they had achieved. We also noticed that well-established wives of the faculty members suddenly became active in promoting and bragging about the achievements of their husbands so that they get more dollars for their department and increases to their pay. It is a very competitive world up there that only the strongest would survive.

Teaching

In my case, I was appointed as an Instructor to teach Manufacturing Processes. I could not be given a better designation to suit my qualifications and experience because I was also going to study for the PhD course in industrial engineering. The university rules forbade giving me better designation. I taught the subject only for the year Sept 1971 to July 1972 because they could not find a man with a PhD level to teach the subject. I worked hard when the faculty was still out on the summer holidays. I got there earlier than I should have so that I had enough time to prepare my lessons and experiments from scratch before the classes began. Therefore, in addition to preparing my theory lessons, I also had to prepare data sheets with information on how to use the machines, assemble the data, and prepare a report. It needed a lot of machine diagrams on those sheets. It was really hard work. There were no such experiments being done by the students before I was appointed. Although English is a common language of America and Britain, its colloquial meaning could vary between the two countries. I got into some difficulty with the workshop supervisor who had a long service in the department. In my experimental sheets I called a threaded bar a 'screw'. He objected to my word and said that I had come from UK and I was using a dirty terminology of 'screw'. I was not aware of the dirtiness of the word. I protested that in Britain it was not a dirty word. I cannot find another word for a threaded shaft, but he would not have any of my reasoning. I asked him to give me an alternative word to complete the sentence, but he had none. So, it left a bitter taste of our altercation. Maybe he did not like my being a part of the department.

From Sept 1972, I was asked to teach Technology of Metals IEOR 211. This course had Welding – gas and electric both - Machining Processes, and Casting Processes. All were heavily laboratory orientated. Again, I had to start all over again with teaching lessons and experimental sheets. Whatever preparations I had done for the manufacturing processes, they had all gone to benefit the assistant professor appointed to teach that subject. The system became unfair but there was nothing I could do to alter the university rules.

So, I taught this subject up until December 72, just one quarter, when we decided to quit America and come back to Britain.

The PhD Programme
While all the teaching was going on I had been pursuing my PhD. For the PhD course in Industrial Engineering and Operational Research, I lacked the fundamental knowledge of some main subjects which had to be taken before proceeding to write my dissertation for the PhD. The subjects that I had to take were

Operations Research Methodology I
Operations Research Methodology II
Human Factors
Probability and Statistics

A JOURNEY THROUGH PARTITION AND BEYOND

Statistics
Research Methodology
Introduction to Operations Engineering
Industrial Computer Science
Linear Programming
Engineering Economy

Within a span of four quarters I had done the above courses in addition to teaching. My supervisor A was quite pleased with my progress. I had achieved an average grade of B and that was acceptable. If I had stayed on I would have got my PhD within the next 2 years. But the fate had different plans. We made a sudden decision to quit America. Why, it is a mystery. I just cannot explain but it did happen.

Social Activities

There were a lot of Indian students at the university, following various courses. We had an Indian Social Club which used to organise a lot of social activities for the Indians. We used to show Indian movies at six to eight weeks intervals and a lot of Indians living at a commuting distance from Blacksburg would attend. The community food would be provided free that was cooked by the wives of the married Indians. We arranged picnics at some beautiful spots around the town. We had a Diwali function in a hall where a Bhangra dance was organised. It was so hilarious and enjoyable that the American whites who attended were so much overwhelmed by the music that they wanted to go on the stage to join the dancers.

In early 1972, there was a meeting of the club at one of the faculty member's house. To my big surprise, I was elected as General Secretary of the Club. I declined, asking the community to keep the present GS, a postgraduate student, because he was doing a great job in managing the events with the help of his energetic wife. But they refused to accept my reasoning and insisted that I should take over the reins of the association. I had to accept. I was surprised that within a few months how I had impressed such a large community to elect me.

The Birth of a Son

However, life moved on and we soon settled down in our routines. Mira was a full-time housewife and she was bored. She did not know what to do all day. There were no jobs at the campus for the wives to work. It was a small student town. There were no industries or schools where her talent could be used. I was going to my college in the morning and sometimes returning late as I was working on computer programming to meet my course requirements for the PhD.

275

Within days of our reaching Blacksburg, Mira was expecting. That was very good news. I always dreaded to have another child when in Wales. I was told that around Cardiff there were higher proportions of births of defective children. Now we were looking forward to an addition to our family. It was time that we had another child to give company to our lonely daughter. It just happened when all the variables met the requirements of nature.

On 25th May 1972, nature's call arrived. It was nearly 9pm. We had just finished meals and were ready for bed in ½ an hour's time when Mira announced that she was ready to go to hospital. We had no insurance for maternity care (we missed it by two days), and without insurance you could only dream of using an ambulance in America. So, we bundled her in the car with her baggage which she had kept ready for the occasion, and we all three dashed to the hospital which was about an hour's drive away. We informed the hospital and they in turn had informed her gynaecologist J who was looking after her. He was going on holiday in a day or two but instead of deputising someone he decided to attend to her himself. The room and her bed were ready to receive Mira when we reached there. I asked if Ritu and I could stay overnight but were politely told to go home as the timing of the arrival of a child was unpredictable. So, we soon left, wishing her well.

It was around 12 in the night. I was still awake but lying in bed next to Ritu to give her company. The telephone rang. I gently got up to attend the phone so that I didn't disturb Ritu. It was from the hospital where Mira was admitted. The message said, 'I am very happy to let you know that your wife has delivered a child. Both mother and child are doing well.'

'What is it, boy or a girl?' I enquired.

'It is a boy. Congratulations.'

'Thank you for letting me know. Should I come to the hospital to see Mira and the baby now?'

'No there is no need as she is very tired. She is not in the labour room. She has been transferred to her room and is now sleeping.'

'We would like to see her.'

'No, please do not come right now. Come and see her in the morning,' she insisted.

I went to sleep. Ritu whispered, 'Was the telephone from the hospital?' I was surprised to find that she was still awake.

'Yes!'

'What is it?'

'It is a boy,' I said.

'Hooray! I have a brother. Let us go and see them now.'

'No, we are not allowed at this time of the night. Also, mum is sleeping.'

A JOURNEY THROUGH PARTITION AND BEYOND

'No please let us go I want to see my little brother.'

'Please go to sleep, we are not allowed to go there to see them. We are going there tomorrow.'

She was disappointed, but nothing could be done.

Next day when we went to see them, Mira was in her room and Vipul was kept in the baby's room where there were other newly born babies too, all lying in their cots near the corridor windows to be seen and with name tags on their arms. We went back to see him. Mira told us how bravely, just after the delivery, she went to her bathroom and had a warm bath to get rid of the stress. She asked the nurse if she could be discharged next day, a big surprise to the nurses. They agreed, as they knew there was nothing wrong with her to cause her to stay longer. At the same hospital there was an Indian assistant professor's wife who also had a boy. She was a bit more orthodox, being from South India, and wanted to stay in the hospital for at least 20 days after the delivery. The hospital was pressurising her to leave early but she was resisting.

Life was normal soon after Mira was back at the flat on the third day. Ritu loved Vipul's company. She was now eight years older to Vipul and would insist on feeding him. When I went to see Mrs J, our complex manager, who knew that Mira had gone to hospital for delivery, she asked me, 'Boy or girl?' and I said a boy. She was thrilled and congratulated me that now, 'You have a complete family.' Before her reminder, it never occurred to me that what she said was true. We now had a girl and a boy.

Soon Mrs H from Canada visited us with her daughter who was only a couple of months old. We had met Mrs H on the ship when sailing from India just after our marriage and we became very good friends. She was very brave. She travelled all the way from Toronto to Blacksburg by a coach on her own with that young kid.

At Christmas break of 1971, J of New Jersey, with whom we had stayed for a week, also came to visit us and stayed with us for a week. It was snowing heavily all over the country, but they battled through the different climates on the way. We gave them a VIP treatment. We gave them lovely, tasty, well cooked, and well organised breakfasts, lunches, and dinners; we took them for sightseeing of the area and gave them good presents to show our appreciation of the initial help they had given us when we arrived in America.

Some Surprises

Once when visiting the gynaecologist, I asked him a million-dollar question. Would he be able to tell us whether it is going to be boy or a girl? He said, 'I would be a millionaire if I would predict that. No, I cannot tell you.' Today we can see how the technology has moved on to predict that with 100% accuracy.

I had one more surprise. Our computer at the Tech was housed in a huge air-conditioned room. We used to feed data with punched cards which were read in a small room adjacent to the computer room. The results were printed on a dot printer after the data was analysed by the computer. Obviously, it was a very cumbersome process and expensive to maintain. One of my students, who was leaving the campus after his graduation, came to say goodbye to me. I enquired where he was going to work. He said that he was going to work for IBM. 'They are developing a small computer which would sit on the desk to be operated and it would be as powerful as the one in the department.' I said, 'Are you pulling my leg?!' He insisted that it was going to happen soon, and he would give me one of those computers as a present. I did not believe him but now it is part of history.

Sudden Decision to Quit America

We were now four in the family and therefore we needed a three-bedroom flat. Flats and houses never appreciate in America. Everyone constructs their dream home with their design and liking on a piece of land they could easily buy. The land was very cheap in those days and there were never any planning issues to give you grief. So, we had a choice to construct our own house or buy a ready-made flat.

In the summer holidays of 1972, we started looking for a new house to buy. Blacksburg University was expanding and therefore to meet the growing demand of increasing numbers of students and faculty, new housing complexes were offering attractive flats and apartments. We looked at a few but did not decide. We had all the intentions to make America our new home as life in Blacksburg was very different from that in New York. But fate had different plans in store. Suddenly just before the college was to be opened after the summer recess, the whole situation changed dramatically with the following chain of events:

1.   There was a post-graduate student in my department from the Mid-West. During the summer recess his wife suddenly died. He rushed back home to look after the children and therefore he had to discontinue his education. There was no one else to support him to bring up the children. It was big news in the department at the time. Everyone was concerned about him, his family, and his education.

2.   There was another young assistant professor who lived with his children and wife in the same complex where we lived. We heard during the summer recess that he had suffered a brain haemorrhage and died within 24 hours. All the families living in that complex were in pains and were talking about the family. His wife and children suddenly became destitute. People were giving the family food and collecting money to support them. That was a community feeling

A JOURNEY THROUGH PARTITION AND BEYOND

and help, and to us it appeared to be a charity. Without this financial support the future of the family was literally grim in that society. They were doing well but all of a sudden they were depending on people's handouts. There were no social organisations to help except the charitable organisations. We felt awful. We started comparing the American social structure with Britain. It was not right as every country has its own political, social, and economic structure. Comparisons are never right. Comparisons bring conflicts. The thoughts are always single dimensional and never multidimensional. We debated the whole situation in our minds, the pros and cons of the social structure and, rightly or wrongly, we arrived at a conclusion that this system was not for us. So, the fate was being sealed to quit.

3.   The insecurity of being thrown onto a jobless heap once more in a couple of years' time after graduation was very worrying. It would be an upheaval task to find a job again in America. We were aware that having to find a job was not unique to America, but it was a problem in every country of the world. However, that is how we felt. While considering the pros and cons of quitting America, we foolishly forgot to consider what would be my future in a racist Britain, from where we had left only two years earlier with those heart breaking, and demeaning speeches of Enoch Powell and other cronies like him.

4.   Mira repeatedly pestered me, discouraged me, and moaned at me, 'You are now forty, how long do you think you will carry on studying?' In life there comes a time when you can stand up to such silly comments and brainwashing but eventually the time comes when you give up and succumb. It is rightly said that behind every successful man there is a woman, but I believe the vice versa is also very true. Behind the disastrous failures of men, there is also a nagging woman's hand. Mira's comments were always in the mind and made me think, 'Am I right to continue to pursue my dreams of getting the education by a hit and miss method.' These negative reminders did play a big part in making decisions in my life. You may think I am talking fibs but there is a parallel example within our circle of friends. On our return to UK we found that one of my friends, who was a teacher in schools and was older than me, had left his teaching job. His wife made him leave his job and forced him to do a PhD because she used to say that, 'I feel ashamed that my husband is not a PhD. He must do it.' He did it and then got a job at Bristol University to teach. The wife was a very proud woman, but she paid a heavy price for that. Her family was divided between London where she had a job and Bristol where her husband had a job. I too suffered for not completing my education. I continue to feel that the resettling back in Britain were the darkest years of my life (see more about my experiences later). Also, incompletion of my PhD still haunts me. I continue to get dreams even today in the night that I am in America and studying at a university. Why? I think it may

be that the dreams of having the higher education were suppressed into my unconscious mind which is a lot more powerful than the conscious mind, and therefore continue to exert themselves in the night dreams. I believe it is also true that the unfilled desires and ambitions end up in dreams too.

5.   We had to change the private health insurance in New York to the University's group insurance when I joined the Virginia Tech. According to their rules, we could only claim the costs of the maternity after the insurance was in force for nine months. Vipul was born just 24 hours before the 9-month completion. The insurance company refused to accept the continuity of the insurance with our previous insurance company. So, they refused to pay the maternity costs of the hospital. We were annoyed by this. It reminds me of a story I read. A fortune teller told an expectant mother that if the child was born on or after his predicted time, the child would be very bright and intelligent and would attain the top job in the country. Otherwise he would end up in a poverty-stricken life. Nature's call came a few hours earlier than the prediction time. It is said that the worried mother hung herself upside down to delay the birth by a few hours. The name of this child was Birbal and he became the prime minister of Great Mogul Akbar. True or not, I am not bothered, but should Mira have done the same to claim a few hundred $s of insurance money. This was the second time we had missed the boat. The first time was in Britain when we were not allowed to have the £12 allowance for the birth of our daughter because I was not paying my national insurance, being a full-time student.

This time too I could not pay the hospital fee because of the heavy expenses involved in moving to Britain. We also had to conserve our financial resources in finding a new job and the other resettling costs in Britain. However, I wrote to the hospital that we were moving to Britain and I would be sending their dues from there. I gave them my British home address. I had a couple of reminders from the hospital. It took me a couple of years before I transferred the money to the hospital, thanking them for the help they had given us for the birth of our second child. They replied with thanks and said that a lot of people would not have bothered to pay them, and we were very honourable to accept our responsibility for paying the outstanding bill.

6.   Mira always had been active in maintaining her career. In Blacksburg there were a lot of faculty wives who were homebound as there were not many jobs to go around. While talking to A about my resignation, he brought about this issue as he felt that it might be one of the reasons that Mira was frustrated by sitting at home and then persuading me to quit America. So, by giving me their names, he took extra pains to clarify that there were a number of the wives who were sitting at home, and he advised me to persuade Mira to join the association of faculty wives to share the problems and keep mentally busy. I said to A that it

was not the case. But it was possible that Mira might have been frustrated but she never told me and only she can answer why she was so keen to quit America without considering the costs of resettling. Why did she insist on leaving America without considering my lifetime ambitions of getting higher education and its effects on my future career? Something was always bothering her and that only she can answer. She was a full-time housewife and had no need to worry about having to earn $s and yet I found her tense at home. I thought she should have been happier as my wages were good, and we were managing very well with my income. She was free all day to mind her children and give them her company, whereas she always complained in UK that she, being the working mother, had missed the opportunity to bring Ritu up. However, I believe that I paid a heavy price for this in my future life and so I call those early resettling years in UK as the darkest years of my life.

      7.   Not being allowed to go to UK after 2 years' stay abroad was a factor of which we were not aware when we made the decision. However, this could have been overcome by visiting Britain and then going back to America, thus extending our stay in America for another two years.

      8.   The UK government had allowed the Ugandan Asians to settle in UK, and this encouraged me to return to UK as I thought that perhaps the racism which was rampant in Britain when we left, mostly must have gone. But the experience in finding a job to suit my experience and education I had on my return proved I was terribly wrong. But the die was cast and there was no way of our returning back to USA. I had resigned from my job; I had packed up the PhD programme. All was gone with just one decision. You, the readers, would call me 'mad', and I would agree with you whole-heartedly. That is what I call fate. You may not believe it, but I do. I have seen its appearance time and again in my life and I cannot find the answer to 'why?' Who is controlling my destiny and why? I don't know but there is some mysterious power taking interest in my life, nay in everyone's life. What is it and who is it? Don't be silly, it is not a ghost.

      9.   We had kept the house in UK and some friends said to me that we had not burnt our boats in Britain. If we had sold the house, we would have no economic link, and we would not have come back. Maybe so. These are all speculations of hindsight. These opinions do not belong to the real world of decision making.

On my insistence A could not do anything but to accept my resignation. He was very kind, very helpful, very persuasive, and he was convinced that I was making a mistake. He allowed me another two weeks' cooling time to reconsider my decision. He also left the door open for a change of mind at a later stage and said, 'After returning to Britain if at any time you change your mind and want to come back, please do not hesitate to call me and I would be very happy to have you back.' But I was too egotistic for that. Even if I felt I was wrong when pointed out by my good friends in New York, I dared not call him to admit my mistake.

The news of resignation was received by some with tears in their eyes. The departmental secretary when I went to give her the news of my leaving USA burst into tears. She pleaded, 'The reasons you have given of quitting America may be right, but we are all together in this country. Don't go, please, and withdraw your resignation. We want you to stay here with us.' Mrs J, the manager of the complex was also in distress and tried to persuade me to withdraw my resignation. For us the die was cast, the human ego became paramount in continuing to reaffirm that the decisions we had reached were the right ones. The fate was sealed and was buried deep into a keyless steel box. Soon the day of leaving arrived. We were on the move again. With a heavy broken heart we left our 'home' of fifteen months just like gypsies, as we were used to it now for the last two years, moving from one place to the other. We had become experts in moving our bags and baggage. All the movable baggage which we had brought from UK was loaded in the coach. The other new furniture like beds, dining table and chairs we gave to V, an assistant professor with whom we became very friendly and who had constructed a new home for himself. We thought they would be more useful to him. The facts that in the last three months we had bought new furniture and were looking to buy a house clearly show that we had no intention of leaving America. Then what made us leave that country will remain a mystery of life to be solved. Who would solve it? I cannot, I don't know, I have no clues. In that case, let the mysterious world stay as a mystery while we get on with our lives.

The mind is not capable of solving mysteries. They are beyond its capabilities. It normally walks away from the mysteries of the world. It can never become the part of the mystery. It can tackle logical problems; it can solve the complex problems of science and mathematics. It is quite brutal and daring in waging wars to kill its own kind. It uses its superior mental faculties in slaughtering the animal kingdom with its technological superiority, and yet it is impotent to tackle the mysteries of the world.

As we were just about to board the coach, the manager Mrs J called me over and whispered in my ears very bad news, 'I have just received a telegram from India that Mira's father has passed away. I do not know how you want to handle it.' She also advised not to tell her now otherwise the whole journey would be painful. I agreed with her. Mira was boarding the coach. I was in a fix. I did not know how to control my emotions so that they would not reflect on my face and in my body language. But it was certainly not a good send off. Mira did ask what the manager wanted and I said, 'She just came to say goodbye.' It was a lie. Nothing I could do about it.

A JOURNEY THROUGH PARTITION AND BEYOND

As soon as we left Blacksburg, I knew that a terrible mistake of quitting America had been made. It was the greatest blunder of my life and I have paid very dearly for that. I had made a cock up of my life. I had trusted the racist institutions of Britain too much. I thought that they had become more humane and compassionate. I had forgotten for a moment its colonial oppressive past. It is they who thought that they were the superior people. Because of the colonies they had a chip on their shoulders. It is also them who spread the gospel of racism in the world and they did it cleverly with cunning smiles on their faces to hoodwink the decent masses of the world.

The cynics, the bigots, and the nationalists would blast that if I am that critical of Britain and its policies then why don't I just get lost somewhere in eternity. That would be good riddance for them. No. The division of the mother earth is man-made. Britain is my postal address where I live and share my life with other locals within this island. I belong to humans and it is my human right to live on any part of the earth. The earlier such divisions are broken down the better. The birds, the fish, the insects, and the other animal world do not have those boundaries around them, then why humans? I am the child of my mother earth. I am inseparable from it. It nourishes me, and it supports my life. I am part of her and she is part of me. All my body parts are made from it. That is why I do not kill and eat the other animal world. They are part and parcel of me. How I can eat my own flesh?

I kept on pondering on such issues until we reached Washington DC. We stayed there for a couple of days for sightseeing. We stayed there in a tourist home. It was late in the evening when we reached there. We waited for a taxi to take us there. The taxi took an hour to arrive. When it arrived it was driven by a Black American. I was very nervous to travel with him with my young family. Would we reach our tourist place safely? However, we boarded. I was on the front seat with the driver. The young fellow was very friendly and very proud of his entrepreneurship. He started talking about himself. He said that during the day he was a student at the University and was also managing a music instrument shop with the help of an employee. He showed me the shop as we drove past it. In the evening he was also running a taxi. One could only get such pioneering and enterprising young people in America. I felt ashamed that I was so stupid to be afraid of him, simply because he was black.

Next morning, we were getting ready to see the American Institutions of government, the Senate House, The House of Representatives, The White House, and The Arlington Cemetery. In the common bathroom there were a couple of guys who were talking between themselves about how to get a green card to settle in America. Here I was, a lucky one, who had it and was chucking it away. I still did not get the message; what on earth was I doing?

Washington did not frighten us this time that much. We felt more at home. We talked about our leaving. Why was this fear of insecurity overpowering us? We debated between us that yes, we were wrong to quit America and yet we never attempted to correct it. We agreed that we were making a mistake but still we continued to keep a brave face. That was destiny, a force which was pulling us towards Britain for good or bad.

After sightseeing in Washington DC, we came to New York and stayed with the Gs'. He was really upset. He insisted that I should call back A and withdraw my resignation. He insisted that we leave our bag and baggage with him and go to UK for Christmas holidays and come back and re-join the University. I agreed with him but without admitting to him our mistake. We continued to insist that we had made a right decision. But inside me I was bleeding. Why was I so deceptive, a liar, and reckless? Why was I defending the indefensible? If the mistake was being made it was better to admit and correct it rather than continuing to maintain the egotistic stand. Next day we all went for dinner at the Jewish family's house. He was also adamant that I should take my resignation back and if I was a chicken and had no guts to talk to A to give me my job back, he asked me to give him the telephone number and the name and he would talk to him on my behalf. We again stood by our decision. The whole evening was spent on this topic. G and the host continued to impress upon us to change our mind, but we remained foolishly adamant.

At times, fate can be very brutal. A lot of people don't believe in it. I just cannot explain why, despite so many people making relentless efforts, we could not be persuaded to change our minds, especially when we knew in our hearts that we were making a mistake in leaving America. Destiny, yes of course it is the destiny. I have experienced many times in my life that it had played a big role in changing the flow of my life. I am a part of this Universe which moves around us so systematically. I believe we are a part of some energy which controls us. Many call it God, but I call it consciousness. Then how would that energy allow me to do what I wanted to do? No, I am just a tiny cog in the whole intricate chain of this Universe and I am controlled by some miraculous forces. Those forces are like a gravitational force that only allows a tiny manoeuvering. The moment we oppose those forces we would be asking for some deeper troubles.

On 16th December, we boarded on two separate planes, Mira and Vipul on one and Ritu and I on the other, at New York airport and we were on our way to UK, not three but four members of the family. It was a brief visit but most fruitful. I feel sad even today that destiny had played a cruel trick with me.

Visit Back to NY at Easter

A JOURNEY THROUGH PARTITION AND BEYOND

In 1973, after my return from America, I was teaching at secondary schools at Havering Borough of London. G from New York was still pestering us to go back to America. He saw a big advertisement in the newspaper that New York City was interviewing all kinds of employees, from managers down to craftsmen, during the Easter vacations. He phoned me and said that I should fly to New York and try for one of the jobs. It was an open walk-in interview. He said that they were recruiting more than a thousand people. My school was closing for the Easter break and I decided to try my luck again, of course against Mira's wishes. So, I booked my seat and flew. I reached G's flat in the evening. We had a good chat and a lovely dinner. Next day I queued up for the interview. There were hundreds of people already lined up before I got there. Every unemployed citizen of that city was crushing in to try their luck. Who could blame them? It is a capitalist society. Hire the people when the government grant is sanctioned and fire them when the money is gone. Therefore, the unemployment is always higher and there are no handouts as in UK. I stood all day; my turn never came. I was very disappointed. G asked me not to lose heart and try next day. The second day, he argued that most un-employed would have been hired on the first and there were likely to be fewer people to compete. So, I went next day again, and I found the queues were equally bad. The history of the previous day was being repeated and I did not get any chance to be interviewed again. As I was battling to get a job to resettle in America again, I had told Mira that when schools opened on Tuesday 24th she should phone my school and apologise that 'Om is sick, and he cannot attend the school.' When questioned, 'When would he be back,' she should say, 'I don't know. It could be a week.' But it was not to be the way I wanted it to be. Mira bungled it all. On Tuesday Mira phoned me.

'I am sorry, you have to come back to London tomorrow morning.'

'Why, what happened?'

'When I phoned your school this morning, I said to your head that you would not be going to school today. "What happened, is he ok?" she asked. I replied that yes you are ok. You have flown to NY for the Easter break and you could not get the seat and you are delayed. You would be back tomorrow or the day after.'

She said all that so innocently that I could not react angrily.

'But Mira I had asked you to say that I was not well. You have blown everything. We have spent so much money in travelling to New York and you have not allowed me enough time to test the job market.'

'I know but that is what I said now. So, you take the next plane and fly back tomorrow so that you are not late in reporting for work.'

G and his wife both were listening to the conversation. They felt disappointed that Mira had bungled the whole thing. But I had no choice, I booked

285

my seat for the next morning, and I was back in London in the evening. Next day I reported to my school. They all pulled my leg that I was very rich to fly to NY for a three-day break. Rich my foot. I was struggling financially after moving to London with no job for a few months.

See, I told you before, fate had intervened again. If it was not fate, then what else it was?

Shooting at Virginia Tech

It was 16th April 2007 when I sat down to watch the news. A lone gunman Cho had gunned down thirty-two innocent students and had injured seventeen more in the same department where I once worked. It was devastating news. Tears rolled down as I heard the details of the massacre. It was so agonising and painful. The old memories were coming back. I followed the details of his shooting from room to room as he went on a shooting spree. When we got there in 1971, we thought that it was a heaven on earth. The whole campus, the town was so peaceful and tranquil. The beauty and the scenery around it were breath-taking. The people were so kind and friendly. But that day one crazy idiot put the Tech on the world map. It was devastating, heart-wrenching news. My inner soul went out to those who were living in that beautiful town where I had spent a tiny part of my young life. God bless those students who lost their lives in that frenzy. That is America, a soulless capitalist country.

CHAPTER 7: BACK TO BRITAIN

Back to UK – The Beginning of the Darkest Days again

We had flown back to Britain on two separate flights. Mira and Vipul flew together on the first flight and Ritu and I by another one with an hour to spare in between. We met up at the Heathrow terminal 3. We still had our Indian passports. As we cleared through the customs, the cheeky customs officer commented after looking at our passports, 'Just in time.'

'No, still two more days to go.' I retorted smilingly. As an Indian passport holder, we were to be back within two years of absence.

That welcome back to Britain had an ominous message. From the officer's comments it was clear what was stored for us in the future. Welcoming other people of different denominations with the dignity and respect they deserved on British soil had not yet dawned on the immigration officer. He felt great in scrutinising the foreigners to his island country. I felt awful and insulted. I thought Britain had become more civilised, enlightened, and cultured after admitting the Asians from Uganda. I was woefully wrong. The officer still had the same British chips on his shoulders. The arrogance and false pride still reflected in his tone. The colonial history which he had read in his school days was still guiding him to be nasty. His tone showed the racist attitude towards people like me. He still thought that the people of my kind were flocking to this little island as economic rejects of their countries. He would never learn. He needed his head examined, not by a doctor but by some enlightened social worker.

However, we got our bag and baggage cleared through customs and found our way out from that suffocating environment. My brother was at the airport to receive us. Driving through the streets of London appeared totally alien, as if I had never been there. There were so many changes in the traffic system within the two years of my absence. The streets looked narrow, ugly, dirty, and poorly lit. They gave the impression that we were back in a third world country. Had we changed so much in the last two years? Everything looked smaller and miniature, the replica of an ancient world. I commented to my brother that everything here now looked funny and strange. He said, 'Don't worry you will get used to it.'

My brother's family had kindly allowed us to stay in one of their bedrooms. We four of us crammed into that room to survive the wintry days of Britain. We knew it had to be very temporary accommodation. His house was just big enough to accommodate his own family and for us to stay there longer would become very uncomfortable for both of our two families. So, on the second day after our arrival, I enquired from my brother about the situation of our house at Seven Kings which he was managing on my behalf. I had given him my arrival dates and had asked him to get the house vacated by the time we arrived in UK. He told me that there were two families living downstairs and one family upstairs. The downstairs families had been given notice to leave. Their tenancy was based on furnished rooms and therefore could be vacated according to the existing laws. But there were no written agreements and they were not moving out because they were finding it difficult to get other accommodation. The law did not allow them to be forced out. So, it was a stalemate and there was no chance of us getting possession until they showed a goodwill gesture to leave.

The upstairs was rented as an unfurnished flat to a friend. The law was that he could live there for life with a nominal rent and could never be evicted. Why had my brother done that? I just could not understand why he had made that decision for me without consulting me or referring it to me. I had never given him that authority.

Now the die was cast for troubles for us to settle back in Britain.

So, we had no home to live in, no hope of getting it vacated soon, no jobs, and no car. We also had no funds in the bank either. It was overdrawn as my brother was not paying the rent into our accounts. With a bit of a luck, the bank had continued to pay our monthly mortgage otherwise the house too would have been re-possessed by the building society. We had to start a life right from scratch once again with a lot of ifs and buts. And when you are in that situation the whole world dumps you as well. You feel that you have relations, friends, and the government agencies to make your landing softer in the bumpy days. But nay it is all crap. At the end of the day you are on your own. No one likes to share your miseries. Only the tarnished memories of the wretched past continue to lick your wounds and you have no choice but to bear them. The philosophy of living would explain that the experiences of hard times make you a tougher and wiser person in later life. But that wisdom is gained at a heavy price and what use is the wisdom at a later life anyway. You would be already on the downhill slope of your life and

A JOURNEY THROUGH PARTITION AND BEYOND

who cares whether you are a wiser person or an idiot. It is only an ego trip for you to feel that you are wiser.

Therefore, the priority was to find an accommodation in the Ilford area so that our daughter could join her old local school where she had friends. I searched for a flat to rent but without any success. Desperately I went to the housing department of the Ilford council in case they could provide a flat. I told them that I had two kids, had just arrived back from abroad after a temporary stay, and I had no place to live. Would they rent me a council flat temporarily? They flatly refused! They said that we owned a house and so they were under no obligation to give us a council flat. Amazing! When we were in USA, we bragged about the superior British social system, but that all seemed hollow now. It became a cruel joke. What surprised me most was the attitude of the employees manning the council's housing department. They never cared to find out where we were living with our two little children. Were they being sent to schools? Were they being fed and how we, as a family, were managing our and our kid's welfare? Our meeting with the council staff had finished with those two cruel sentences and we were back on the road, disheartened, discouraged, and rejected by the welfare system of Britain that brags so much about their institutions as being world class. In my experience of living in UK, no institutions help if unfortunately you ever fall into difficult times. They all dump you and the only people that beat the system are those who know how to make abusive noises and scare the hell out of the bureaucrats who man those institutions. Peace-loving families would always suffer and pay a heavy price for that. This was the second time in the same borough where fate had played its cruel joke on me. Both times I had miserably fallen into the gutter. Once after my degree when I had the house but no income, and no money to care for my newly born child. It was another worst time of my life. The world would always behave strangely when your chips are down. It would just walk away from you. Even the closest ones with whom I had shared some good times at parties had walked away, leaving me cold to sort out my misery myself.

But the existence of which you are an integral part would never let you down. It is only humans who feel that they have been rejected and let down. My friends and other relations were hard on us with no apparent reasons. There were a couple of comments which are unforgettable and unforgivable. One 'friend', to whom I had given lifts many times in my car, once stopped by as I was walking near the Seven Kings Road station. 'Hey, Om sorry I cannot give you a ride as I am in a hurry,' he said after a bit of social conversation. 'Also, I am sorry I have not invited you for dinner at home. You know I cannot afford to buy okra as it is more expensive than meat and you are a vegetarian. But not to worry, one of these days we will meet up.' After these comments, he sped off leaving a trace of hurt on me for life. This 'friend' was a meat eater. Was that comment meant to be

289

sarcastic to point out my vegetarianism or just contempt of my way of living? Only he could answer. But when you are down, such comments are even more humiliating and insulting. That is why they get stuck into the memory lane. Another woman kindly kept us for four days. While in conversation with her friend on the phone, we overheard her saying to the caller, 'Oh no, no I am only keeping them here for another two days.' So, when the chips are down, your stars are also in the fading mode at that time of your life. But the rays of hope do appear, maybe faintly, but they do show up. You can never be down in the valleys for ever. The day must come when you will again start climbing up the hills. You must; otherwise the law of nature would never work.

Two things happened during those miserable times. Some human hearts were mellowing. Compassion at last could be seen on the horizon. The tenant friend occupying upstairs mercifully offered us to stay in the smallest bedroom (7'x7') sharing a cooking facility with them. That was a great gesture of kindness towards us. Small though for the four members of the family but it was most thoughtful and was greatly appreciated by us. Mira and Vipul (only 8 months at the time) slept on the bed while Ritu and I slept on the floor. Realising our plight of no privacy all day, no job, no other emotional outlets, the angel B who stayed with us in New York offered to help. At weekends he would come in the morning and take us to his house. They would feed us with breakfast, lunch, and dinner and then leave us back 'home' around 10pm. It gave our legs an opportunity to spread, and company to Ritu as the couple also had two sons of Ritu's age. This continued until their school holidays were over and they went back to teaching. Soon after the Christmas break, Mira got a job in the school system of Tower Hamlets, London where she had been teaching before. Having established our foot inside our house and realising our plight of suffering with two kids, one of the downstairs tenants moved out within days. We moved down and turned one big reception room into our bedroom. Soon the second one found a flat and moved out as well. So, we had the whole downstairs for our family. We had a huge promotion, from miserably living in a small bedroom to a big bedroom, a lounge, a dining room, a kitchen and with an outside toilet and the garden. We had the entire house to ourselves now.

Ritu was readmitted to her old Good May's junior school. Cruelty has no limits to its boundaries. Insults after insults were heaped upon us as if we had committed a crime in coming back to UK to resettle. Ritu was put into a quarantine room of the school. They said it was normal practice even after finding that all the chest X-ray tests and blood tests were normal. What a rubbishing treatment as if we had come back from mars or a third world country. We think the school was just showing its arrogance of British superiority over the outside world including America. Two weeks had gone by and they continued to detain her in the quarantine room. Ritu was desperate to re-join her friends and resume her studies. We went to her school to protest to the head teacher. Obviously, she defended her decision. However, Ritu did resume the classes within two days after our meeting. This shows the head teacher's decision was racist, hollow, show off, and depressing.

We had now achieved the one family income, a foothold in the house, Ritu's education in her old junior school, and Vipul's admission to a nursery school at Good May's. But the major issue was still unresolved – my job. We still had no car and we were mostly housebound during the weekends. The clock had moved back to 1964. The same struggle of riding public transport and walking Vipul in a pram to and from the nursery was the norm of life. Mercifully B continued to help at the weekends by taking us to his house.

My Future Career

As soon as we had arrived, I started a campaign of applying for jobs around the London area as a lecturer. I was quite used to it and had mastered the tricks of finding jobs in USA. I prepared my CV and sent it to the colleges and polytechnics wherever a vacancy appeared in the national papers. I would go to the local libraries every day to see the advertisements. I also registered with the local professional job centre but without claiming the dole money. Adding my name to the professional register was just a waste of time and I knew it. It was a government's empty gesture to show to the citizens of the land that it cared about the professional people. The registration only monitored the statistics for the government. I applied for a vacancy at the Regent's poly. As expected they were very kind to send me a letter of regret. I applied to a couple more around the London area but without much luck. This time I had no intention of moving far away from London. With my British and American qualifications and British teaching experience, I thought at least the colleges would have the courtesy to invite me for an interview. But nobody did. I went to see my old head of department at East London Poly, there was no vacancy. Racism in employing people of my colour was at its peak. My conclusion in America - that Britain had changed after allowing entry to the Ugandan Asians and therefore racism must have mellowed - was totally wrong. I was now paying a heavy price for that wrong conclusion. They probably had to accept the Asians because technically they were British, living in Uganda. They were not allowed in on compassionate grounds nor had the British changed their racist attitude. With that wrong conclusion, my entire career, my education, and the toil and sweat of my young age were on the rocks. I was on a ruinous path. I had no way to undo my stupid mistake. I had too much pride to call A in America and ask for the job back and get back into my PhD studies which I had foolishly left simply because of my thinking that Britain had become more liberal and less racist.

Applied for Sr. Lecturer at a Poly

With luck, a vacancy appeared for a Sr. Lecturer in Production Engineering at a Poly. I applied for it. Nearly four weeks had gone by but no response. I used my American experience of job hunting that if you are in the market to sell your skill, then do it aggressively and convincingly. Tell the employer what your capabilities are; what your experience is, and how you can contribute better than anyone else for the advertised job. Brag to the employer about your educational achievements and your experience to convince them that you are the best candidate for the job. The worst thing the employer can do is to say, 'No.' Accept that answer gracefully and pitch your tent at another place. So, with that conviction in mind, one day I ventured out to the poly by public transport and a long walk and said to the receptionist that I was there to see the Head of the Production Department. A meeting took place in his sparsely furnished office. I gave him a reference about the vacancy and a brief about my qualifications and experience. He took out the folder and frantically started looking into the file for the replies he had received. After a couple of attempts, he found my letter right at the bottom of the pile. It amused me. He felt a bit embarrassed and never expected that a potential candidate would land in his office to see the position of the application in the file, it was a totally un-British way of doing things. He briefly read through my application and said that the interviews were being arranged within the next 3-4 weeks and if I was selected, I would get a letter to attend the interview. I showed my interest in the vacancy and said that I was very keen to get back into teaching after coming back from America and was very much interested in the vacancy. Again, it was an American way of selling my skills. Had America changed me that much within two years of my stay there? Amazingly it had. On that note we parted.

Four weeks later I received a letter to attend the interview. We were only two candidates. The other one was an internal candidate, always a difficult one to beat. The only time one can beat them is if their education and experience are much inferior to yours or they had offended the management. Otherwise they always have a winning ticket. However, we attended our interviews in turn. I was the first one to be called in. I was quite pleased with my interview and I felt that I had given them satisfactory replies to all the questions they had asked. Who knows, I might get the job. Hope is always a good friend. I went to sit and wait on a bench in the lobby outside the receptionist's office. Half an hour later, the head walked past me with the internal candidate to see him off at the exit door a few feet from me. I could hear, with some difficulty, their whisper. The head was explaining, 'I am sorry we may not be able to offer you the job because the other candidate has degrees while you have HND. It would be difficult to ignore that even though we would like to give you a job. However, I will continue to convince the board and try my best.' The candidate continued to say, 'Yes I understand.' Within this conversation, I must have heard at least 5-6 times the repeating of 'sorry'. I anxiously sat there with mixed feelings. Here was I, an Asian, caught between nepotism and racism. There were no merits being given to my achievements in life. The decision makers would decide, not on merits but whom they knew and favoured. Whose face fits with them better, and not who would make more contribution to the system. These selections are nothing but farce. They are subjective. It was not here in Britain alone. This disease is all over the world. You get to the top not by what you are but by whom you know.

After warmly shaking hands with the internal candidate, the head walked towards me. I got up. He said with cold shoulders and a stiff face as if I had done some awful things to his plans in the making, 'The board has not decided to whom they will offer a job. We will be writing to you shortly. Thank you for attending the interview.'

On that note we shook hands and I was speedily out of the door. What a difference it was, I thought, in the treatments between the two of us.

In those days there was no law against discrimination based on race, religion, colour, gender, or the country of origin. There was a race relations board to hoodwink the world that Britain was an equal opportunity country.

Race Relations Board, an Eyewash

My patience was reaching the end of its tether. I was getting desperate for a job. Sitting home all day was depressing and demoralising. It was challenging for my wits to accept the status quo. I just wondered why I was being ignored simply because of my colour and my origin. The human instinct to know was boiling within. The ego was battling not to accept that kind of treatment. The mind was now getting set to accept the challenge and was in a fighting mood to not take it lying down any more. Someone had to raise a voice against this discrimination. I decided to report my treatment to the Race Relation Board. I sent in the application, listing all the places I had applied for and their replies. I was called for the interview to prove my charge. From the reception, I was taken into a room where six or seven well-to-do citizens were sitting. At the top of the table was a middle-aged pipe-smoking wog, with beard and moustache, as a chairman. The scene was set to intimidate the citizen who had dared to complain against the establishment thus bringing shame to its well-placed ethos. Interrogation started in full swing as if I was the culprit. They placed me in the dock and started questioning me as if I was in a court of law. Maybe some of them belonged to the legal professions and they got these jobs not to find the truth but to hush the matter up and prop up the crumbling lofty rules of the establishment at large. They were trying to show to the world that Britain was free from the racist disease and was a fairer society.

As soon as I sat down a member opposite to me asked me to narrate in my own words, 'What makes you think these rejections were because of your origin?'

'I was not called for the interviews. I believe that I was a suitable candidate and met all their educational and experience requirements they had advertised. In some cases I would say that I had rather more than they asked for. All my engineering education and teaching experience is from Britain. I was not even sent a regret letter saying why I was not called for the interview. I was not given the opportunity to give more info if they needed any.'

Finally, I gave them the gist of the conversation I overheard for my last interview. I said all the above reasons led me to believe that the hiring was not done fairly. Either my application was rejected without going through its contents by simply looking at my name or they did not wish me to oppose a British candidate with inferior education and experience.

Having heard me, the person started analysing and questioning my conclusions. He started speculating the reasons with maybe this and maybe that. At no point did any one of them come up with an idea of investigating any part of my complaints. They were all defending the system and its status quo. They all found faults with my approach. They all started giving me a lecture on how to apply for jobs, what to write, how to conduct an interview. Finally, the wog on the chair authoritatively summed up by pulling a deep smoke from his pipe to invigorate his congested lungs, and throwing his polluted breath in the room. He was now acting to me as a school teacher. He was highlighting his points so egotistically. He was preparing to rub my nose in the ground. It was time for him to show off to his masters who appointed him to the chair to justify the stipend he was paid. He had to defend the system for which he was hired and find the faults with the complainer and not the managements who rejected me. He started demeaning all my education and my teaching experience. I was now to relearn all that I had been teaching myself for so many years simply because he was occupying the seat on the opposite chairs. He was on the winning bench and I was on the losing end. He was clever, and I was stupid. I felt very low, disgusted, and demoralised. His sermon, 'No, we do not find that you were discriminated against. You were not sent replies because you did not know how to write letters. We suggest that you attend a course on how to apply for jobs, how to fill up application forms, and how to attend interviews.'

Oh God, I was reduced to the level of dust. They treated me like a child. They were acting like control freaks. I was 42 years old and they were asking me to go back to school and relearn English. They were declaring me as a total failure in life simply because they had the jobs and I was trying to find one. They were not ready to accept that the system was faulty. Who were they kidding? Of course, they were demeaning the public. They were not there to investigate the complaint but to defend the faulty system, riddled with racism. Were they paid to do that? Of course! They also chose a wog to chair the panel because they knew that the complaints would only come from the minority community and therefore the chair should be occupied by the minority candidate. It is only steel which cuts steel. They were appointed there to defend the system and to show to the world that there was no discrimination in the land which had instituted the system of racism, colonialism, and slavery. That organisation was a farce, intimidating, humiliating, and patronising. It was only meant to blind the public by throwing dust into their eyes and clouding the issue of discrimination.

The whole atmosphere of the building, the set up, and the interview, stunk. I took their advice and ran before my confidence was further shattered to deal with the issues I was facing.

That is why I said that it was the saddest day of my life when I left America, the land of opportunity, and landed back on the shores of this race-ridden country. The British might take pride in their history, but the other foreign historians will never forgive this country for what damage it has done to other lands. Never!

Introduction to School Teaching

Rejected, disappointed, depressed, and demeaned by the fellow honourable academicians and the administrators of the higher education system, I finally gave up the struggle to re-join their ranks. I started to investigate teaching in the school system. There was no help from any other sources. Three months had gone by and yet no luck in getting a job. I was very frustrated. Sitting at home all day was very demoralising and agonising, especially as I had been so active all my life. Every evening on her return from her school, Mira would notice the sadness on my face. One day she put her foot down and insisted that I must seek a job in the school system where the job opportunities were a lot better than in the college system. Reluctantly I agreed. I did not wish to do that job. I had no experience of it. However, I applied for a supply teaching job to teach technology subjects at Becontree Heath School and I got it. I started the job in April 1973. The head of technology was living in Ilford and used to drive past my way. He started giving me a ride to the school and back with sharing petrol costs. That was very kind of him.

On my first day, the head asked me to accompany him to his first lesson to learn the ropes of teaching at school level. His first lesson was to teach metalwork to 16-year-olds. I followed him into the classroom and stopped just a few feet away from where the students had assembled and were chatting amongst themselves without taking any notice of the teacher. As the school technology rooms were new to me, I was taking more interest in looking around the facilities available there. Suddenly I heard two frighteningly loud bangs on the desk, with the teacher screaming, which took my breath away. As I turned around to look, I saw the fearful faces of the students. The head had a big hammer in his hand which he used to bang the workbenches to get the attention of the pupils. The students went quiet and heard the head with fear clearly displayed on their faces. 'Is that how I will have to teach and have their attention?' I asked myself. Was I supposed to frighten them before I get their attention? Am I capable of doing that? It was a totally alien culture to me and was never to fit my nature. From that day onwards, it was nothing but frustration that had lodged itself into my head. The mind was full of questions. Can I change my ways of thinking and doing things? Had I to become a brute, a hard-hearted teacher to create fear amongst those innocent children who would be attending my lessons? Am I to make that classroom into a battleground between the pupils and me? Either they would rule the waves of the classroom by chatting or dancing or I would have to shout and frighten them to get their attention. Should I turn the classroom into anarchy by allowing them to win? And if I do, I would have no satisfaction of teaching them to justify my monthly wage. There were no simple answers for all those intricate and complex questions. I had to forget all the knowledge I had gained in teaching at poly level and forego the latest research in my subject. I had to downgrade my knowledge to the basics of technology. It was going to be a different ball game, a totally different world. I could cry or scream at my fate but that is what I had. And all that frustration and change - for what? I needed the income to bring up my young children. A lot of frustrated people like me who need the income to look after their families also end up joining the kill-or-be-killed war machines of the armed forces. At least I was luckier than those. I was not fighting a war created by the elites and the politicians of the day. I was not killing my conscience by taking someone's life and I was not allowing my body to be used as fodder either. I had a choice to have a go in the profession and if it did not work for me I had the option to get out without harming anyone.

Within a couple of months after I started teaching in the school system, we bought a second-hand automatic Rover saloon. It was a good car but worn out. We paid £600. Now we were mobile too. Financially life became normal but without any intellectual satisfaction. Within a couple of years, the car's clutch

A JOURNEY THROUGH PARTITION AND BEYOND

packed up. The garage told me it was un-repairable. We scrapped the car and bought another one.

The plus side of the story is that we were still very lucky with the type of jobs we had. Being in the teaching profession, we were getting a lot more holidays. Some of our friends were also teachers. So, we would take the kids to the seaside to play on the beaches during the weekends. Our daily grind at work also had fewer working hours than the people working in other professions and on the factory floors.

School Teaching Continued

I taught at Becontree up until summer break 1973. I was still very hopeful that I would get the senior lecturer job at a Poly, but I did not. I had a choice to sit home once again and spend time as a demoralised and frustrated man or swallow my pride and join the school system once more. I decided to bite the bullet again. I applied for a temporary assistant teacher's job at Marshall's Park School at Romford and was appointed to teach technology subjects from September 1973. This school was merged with another school called Pettit's Lane School and I was attached to this school but was teaching the technology subjects at both the schools. In September 1974 I was promoted to grade 2 and was also given responsibility for a class. A couple of incidents which happened during my teaching there are worth mentioning.

1.   For teaching at the two separately located school premises at a commuting distance, we had to inch our ways through the back streets. It was not worth the bother to take the cars. One day as I came out of the Marshall's Park school gate, I saw a man being pelted with some pebble missiles thrown by a couple of youngsters. He was ducking them to escape injury. As soon as the youngsters saw me they ran away. The man walked to me and asked, 'Are you a teacher in this school?'

'Yes, I am.'

'Are you going to Pettit's Lane?'

'Yes, I am.'

'May I walk with you if you don't mind? If I walk with you, they won't attack me again as you are with me.'

'No, I have no problem. But why are they attacking you?'

'Because I am Jewish and they don't like me. I have been attacked before as well and that is why I do not walk on my own.'

'That is disgusting. I could be attacked as well if I walk on my own. Who are they anyway? Are they from our school?'

'Yes, they are.'

297

'You should report them to the Head.'

'I did but he did not take any action.'

'Well report again and I will give a statement about what I saw, and I recognise these boys.'

This time he did. The head called me, and I told him what I had seen. The head questioned me closely and I replied to all the questions he asked. I had the impression that the head was trying to avoid facing the issue. He did say that he would take some action and would let me know. But I never heard of it again and I don't know what action was taken.

2.   One day a regular class teacher was absent, and I was asked to cover him. As I entered the class, I gave the assignment which I was asked to give by the deputy head. There were a couple of boys in the back row that continued to chatter and would not listen. I insisted that they did not chatter but do their assignments. They ignored me again. I persisted and warned that I would report them to the head if they didn't. One of the lads got up and walked out of the lesson. I asked him to sit down; he just walked out of the classroom. I got worried in case he would leave the school and get hurt on the road. I went out of the classroom into the corridor and saw the deputy walking towards my side. I told him the incident and the name of the boy. He just smiled and walked away. His attitude surprised me. After the lesson was over, I mentioned the incident to my colleagues in the staff room. Having known the name of the boy, they advised me not to tackle him in future as he was a criminal. He had been caught burglarising the neighbourhood and was well known to the police. I took the message. I had him in my lesson one other time. We had no confrontation and the lesson went without any hitch.

3.   It was an open day at the school when the parents come and have meetings with the teachers to know the progress of their children. It is normally arranged once a year. All teachers were in their good attire, presentable, well behaved, ready for the answers to the parents, and were on their chairs and assigned desks to receive the interested parents. I had a big problem because I was new. I knew the children better by their faces but not by their names. However, a very distraught and unhappy mother came and plumped herself on to the chair opposite my desk. After a brief introduction of herself she started the conversation. I could not place the boy, but she gave me enough info to place him.

'Now you are not going to tell me the same as the other teachers are telling me about my son.'

'What are they telling you about your son?' I enquired.

'Well, they are all saying that he is very naughty in the classroom. He mucks around too much. He is always in a playful mood and disruptive. But he can understand the subjects well. He always does his homework.'

Her tone was filled with disappointment mixed with annoyance. She was feeling a bit small. All parents like to hear some tall talks about their children to boost their pride and ego.

'So why are you unhappy? It is time to celebrate. It is time to be happy and be elated. Why don't you recognise that only clever children would be mischievous in the classroom? They find the ways and means to be naughty. They use their cleverness and intelligence to do silly things in the class. Dull children would just sit there and would do nothing. So be happy that your child has the brains and he is clever. Don't forget he is a child. Soon he will overcome these problems when he grows a bit older. Maturity will come with time and the negative activity will change to the positive side. Just wait and have patience.'

'You know - you are the only teacher who has reassured me. All were just giving me very discouraging comments about my son. I really feel very happy and what you just said is true and a positive way of looking at my boy.'

I was very happy that I made her day.

I left the job as I was under pressure to join full-time at the shop, something I had never bargained for. I only invested the money in the venture.

Business Venture

I never thought of going into business, certainly not the retail business. I did think of setting up a manufacturing business in India. But to go for the retailing of grocery was a dumb decision but I had made it due to a couple of compelling circumstances. One was that G wanted a partner to set up a business. The idea came from him. I perhaps agreed because I had an uninspiring and demoralising school-teaching job. There was no challenge in the job and it was very frustrating. I could not go down to the level of reluctant teenagers who came from all kinds of home backgrounds. They were disruptive, unmotivated, rude, and aggressive. I did not wish to make a career out of baby minding. I also felt that if my heart was not in the job, it was immoral to go to work just for the money. Hence, I had agreed to invest the money in the venture as a sleeping partner and to continue to work as a teacher until I had found something better to suit my mental needs.

The shop was divided into three rooms. So, we reorganised the shop by removing the walls and converted it into a mini-supermarket. G worked very hard to bring about those changes. He added Indian groceries. Sales had improved a lot and it became a very busy shop on that secondary street location. That was the time when corner shops were doing well as there were no supermarkets to compete with.

Soon, with the growth of the business, I came under pressure to resign from my teaching job and go to the shop full-time. It changed the whole ball game for me. Firstly, there was not enough income to support two professionals. Secondly, the conflict had to come in managing the place. We both were intelligent, educated people. The business was very small with not many activities to divide between us and then devote our skills independently to manage them. Hence it became a big frustration for both of us. To iron out these conflicts the accountant was also not very helpful. In my case Mira was also dead set against my going into the business. All our financial resources were fully utilised, therefore the chances of quickly expanding the business further were remote. The shop hours were also very demanding. We were opening the shop from 7am to 8pm seven days a week. By the time I reached home it would be around 9pm. Mira would be fed up with her full-time teaching job, collecting the kids, and then cooking. There would be a lot of aggravations at home. Life became literally a home from hell. One Saturday I was taking Vipul to a seaside resort and he did not believe me when I said I was going with him that day. He said to me, 'You never come with me to the seaside. You are just telling fibs.' He was three years old at the time. That hurt me. My mother was also staying with us at the time and I had no time to spend with her. For a person who was only teaching thirty hours a week with so many holidays and all the weekends, it was madness to jump into some business to work for 90 hours a week. Even though my teaching job was professionally unrewarding, I was getting good money, plenty of holidays, and a good retirement pension. The whole life became upside down, from the relatively easy hours of the teaching profession to the slavery of the shop hours.

So, I could see the dead end of my career. It was total disaster and that is why I call it the darkest days of my life in UK. I could not get a teaching job in a poly nor could we expand the business. My whole life was just in a mess. It was easy to go into the partnership commitment but very difficult to come out of it. Finding no other solutions, I made up my mind to get out of this bonded business as soon as possible. In life the mistakes must be addressed, must be faced boldly, and corrected rather than leaving them in cold storage to destroy your life slowly. So, I looked at the following options, keeping in mind the future of G who always respected me and had always given me a great regard as being the older.

1.   Sell the shop to a third party. This needed G's consent. Would he be happy and give a consent? I was not too sure he would and therefore I was reluctant to suggest this option.

2.   Ask G to buy me out. This had some problems and implications I would not like to go into. I was willing to leave my financial commitment in the business if it would allow me the freedom to come out of the business so that I could pursue my future career the way I wanted.

A JOURNEY THROUGH PARTITION AND BEYOND

I discussed that with Mira and we agreed that I should go ahead with that plan. One day I managed to collect my courage, and I put that proposal, the second option, to him. Obviously, he was very upset and refused to talk about it. I tried to persuade him with my reasoning, but he would not have any of it. His reply was that once we agreed to go into a partnership, it should be for life. He was not prepared to accept any of my reasoning. He was not bothered whether we had the income to support ourselves or not. He also never cared whether at the end of the day there was any light in the tunnel or not. The meeting took place in the car and ended up acrimoniously. He was very unhappy even to talk about the subject. He was also of the opinion that he had made the same sacrifices as I had. I did not wish to go into arguments of proving who was the holier of the two of us. He agreed that he would talk to his family and come back to me. I made my position very clear that I had no intention of staying and as it was his venture he should take over. I was happy to get out leaving my house with the bank as it was, except that if or when he sold the business, or he moved house, he would have to take over all the bank commitments for the shop. As far as I was concerned, I had no intention of going into another business and so I did not need the equity in the house to use. But I had one big disadvantage of this arrangement - that if I wanted to buy a better property, I would have no equity available to do that. I also could not sell that property and move to another town if I ever got a job somewhere else. But I was ready to accept that to gain my freedom once again. Days had gone by but no reply came from him. It was complete silence. Reluctantly I reminded him again that I must plan my life and I'd like to know his views. Suddenly one day he announced that he was no longer coming to the shop. He insisted that I had to buy his share of the partnership, release the equity on his house, arrange the stock take, pay him his share of the stock, and then it would be all over. It was a bombshell to me. I did not wish to do anything with the shop. I never thought of that option in my deliberations and now suddenly I was stuck. The blanket was all over me now and I could not come out of it. It was all darkness there. My stake of losing was a lot higher. I told him that I didn't want to have the shop. He should take it over, not me, as he wanted to go into the business in the first place and not me. But he flatly refused. It appeared to be an ultimatum that, like it or not, I had to have the shop and I had to clear his money within the period he specified. As our commitment to the bank was more than his, I was left with no other option but buy it and then sell it. I had to accept it. I had no other alternative except to lock it or run it. Sadly, the whole reasoning for my coming out of the business was misunderstood.

I went to the bank and met the manager. I explained to him the developments. He listened to my tale of woe. He went through all the collaterals involved and offered some money to support me but that was not enough. I then knocked on the doors of some friends and my brother. With some bits from one and some from the other, I managed to assemble the whole money and bought the shop. It was not an easy task to go with a begging bowl to so many for so little. But I did it.

First to Sell Shop

I had a friend B who lived only 5 minutes' walk from the shop. I asked him if he would buy the shop. He was not doing much. It was ideal for him to run the shop with the help of his wife. He was very much interested. He decided to buy it with a partnership with one of his friends who lived at Windsor. He negotiated the terms with him, but it failed. He asked me that he would be willing to buy the shop provided I provided equity of £2,500 on my house. I politely refused. It was impractical. He would have the freehold of the shop, the stock, the business ownership. I was to fund it but without any collateral or security. That meant falling from a frying pan into a fire. This was not an acceptable proposition. The proposal was dropped.

The Problems of Running it

While this was going on, the woman who sold us the shop continued to help us manage the shop. She managed the till while her daughter-in-law (DIL) was helping part-time to fill up the shelves. Her son used to come on some days to do the bookkeeping. The family, even after selling the business to us, continued to have a good hold on it.

One day on my return from cash & carry after buying weekly stock, I found a pile of grocery on the shop floor. I suspected that DIL had collated the grocery to take it home without paying for it. I asked the question whose grocery was that and why was it on the floor; both ladies gave me different alibis which were not that convincing. I did not say anything. They knew that they had been doing that for a long time. In the grocery business you collect pennies to pay for your £s of overheads. Therefore, a little stealing can put you into a lot of cash flow problems which we always faced after turning the shop into a self-service store. The cream of the income was stolen away by the dishonest staff and the rest by the customers. It appeared that it had been going on even when G was there as he used to leave the shop in the care of the ladies when he went home for his lunch break. Both the ladies sussed out that I was watching them. They were under scrutiny. Within a couple of weeks, DIL left as I was not leaving the shop when she would be there.

One Saturday, the son was there to do the bookkeeping and B just dropped in. B used to come in to see how the shop was operating. Some discussion started between me and the bookkeeper. It became a heated argument. I said to the son, 'I find myself cornered in this place as I am managing the place on my own.' The son misheard and thought I had said 'conned'. I had never heard that word and I did not even know the meaning of it. So, the son moved aggressively towards me to hit and said how dare I to say that I was being 'conned'. B intervened to stop him and explained to him that I never meant that, and I had never said that word. However, the situation cooled down and the son left in a huff. When he left, I asked what was meant by 'conned'; B then told me the meaning. A little misunderstanding and that would have cost me some serious injury.

However, a couple of weeks later the woman also left to work for another shop on the high road. I had no one to support me to run the shop. I was on my own. I became the prey of circumstances. I had asked for the freedom to fly away but I became a prisoner of the shop. I was entangled in the web and I did not know how to come out of it. I did not know which way to turn. I was trying to sort out my life, ruined after I left America, by climbing up the mountain to see if any opportunity remained for me to grab. Instead I fell deep into the valleys of darkness with unknown species to deal with. I had no support from Mira either because it was all of my making. Her hands were full in managing the family and my mother and working full-time. We hardly had time to talk. I would just about have time to eat and go to bed.

In addition to working 90 hours a week, I had to go there many times in the middle of the night. The shop was in the area where some families and their young kids were known for burglaries. The two boys of this family worked during the day at the shop. They knew all the security system of the shop. They would break into the shop at night. The alarm would go off and the police would call me. I had to then go to the shop and reset the alarm. They did not know who the culprit was until one night the police caught the younger boy inside the shop after the alarm went off. He was taken to court and he admitted all the break-ins. He was already under the care of a social worker. The judge would ask for the reports from the social services, but they were never sent. Eventually he was sentenced in remand after six appearances. But that made my life hell in travelling from Seven Kings to Leyton in the middle of the night to reset the alarm.

Once it happened:

It was Sunday 2.30am on a wintry dark night. I had only slept for four hours after a hard, busy Saturday with long hours. My shop alarm had gone off. I was tired, and I did not wish to drive. I hired a taxi to go there to cancel the alarm. As we reached near the shop, I asked the driver to wait on a bend for five minutes and I would be back to have a ride back home. I had chosen the bend so that he did not see me going to my shop to cancel the alarm in case, who knows, he may spread the rumours about the shop with no alarm to his cronies, if any, to break-in later. It sounds crazy but that is how I felt - insecure. As I got out of the cab, the driver insisted I paid him before leaving. I assured him not to worry; I would pay him when I got back home, including my return fare. My assurances had no meaning for him. Here was a human problem – insecurity and lack of trust on both sides. We were both acting stupidly with the experiences we both had in the past. He was insistent to have the money first before I disappeared in the darkness of the night because in his profession and experience a lot of customers did not pay him. He told me later when we were on our way back to Seven Kings that he had the experience of some people saying, 'Wait, I'll just go to my flat to fetch the money to pay.' He waited but the man never came back. Whatever he was saying was right as it was the experience which was talking. In my case, I felt insecure that if he had left after being paid, I would be stranded at 3 o'clock in the morning in that unsafe area where anyone could attack me and rob me. So, it was a battle of two anxious minds to resolve the issue on the spot and quick. He must have been thinking that I was a crook and I, in turn, admit that I also felt scared of him in case he attacked me, robbed me and then dumped me and ran away. He had the taxi to beat me and run away but I had nothing. In fact, I was at his mercy. In the circumstances, I gave up and opened up to tell him the truth. I asked him to move forward to a T junction and watch me crossing the road, re-setting the alarm of the shop, and then coming back to have a ride with him to go back home. This way I was more secured too that someone was keeping an eye on me when I was re-setting the alarm. But what can one do with the suspicious mind? Who could predict that in the darkness of that night even the burglar himself might be waiting near the shop to attack me? So, these were the dangers which became part of my daily life while managing that un-wanted business.

Back to Teaching

The shop was not earning much. I was losing sales because the area was demographically changing fast. I had already upset a preacher of a community by not keeping a charity collecting box. So, I was not getting much trade from that community. My mind was also not on the business. I wanted to be out as soon as possible. I was tired and fed up with long hours. Once that woman who manned the till left, I had nobody to help me manage the place. If I stayed in the shop, I could not go to cash-and-carry to buy groceries and if I went to cash-and-carry I had to ask someone to handle the till. Money is such a commodity that even the saints can easily become thieves. I tried to take on some help but later I found out they were also helping themselves from the till. Because of this stealing the shop was not generating enough income to meet my bank commitments. The manager reminded me a few times whenever I went to deposit the money.

Therefore, I decided to go back to school teaching. I applied to a school in Tower Hamlets and I got the job as grade 2 to teach metal technology. Things started working better. The financial pressure eased up. My wages were helping me to pay my bank as well as the money I had borrowed from friends to pay off G.

More Troubles in the Making

I took on board an Asian girl from Forest Gate to manage the place and to look after the till. I would pick her up on my way to school and leave her at the shop. I would also take her back in the evening after closing the shop. I hired a part-time local girl to merchandise the shelves. The PT girl was coming to the shop at 11am and leaving around 3.30pm and I would reach the shop by 4pm. I thought it was working well but my cash flow did not ease up. I was finding it difficult to pay the bank loan again. Then I had the following incidents which resulted into more nightmares.

1.   B who was buying the shop was upset with me that I did not provide him collateral on my house to assist him to buy the shop. So, he stopped coming to the shop, with the result that the moral support he provided had gone. I did not wish to keep my home as collateral for someone who was not prepared to guarantee the loan of £2,500 to me. I bet *he* would have never given that kind of undertaking to anyone. He was never a straightforward man and would not trust even his good friends. This was one of the reasons that his negotiations with his good friend for partnership to buy my shop failed to materialise. He had recorded the conversations with him and asked me to listen to them. Firstly, it was unethical and perhaps even illegal to record a conversation without telling the guy with whom he was negotiating a future business deal. For me it would have been a non-starter if I knew that he was recording our conversation without telling me. Obviously, he did not trust him. Also, he wanted to keep the conversation for future references in case of a breakdown in the partnership and the matter was contested in the courts. He told me they were his motives. A very mean act towards a friend! After knowing this, how was he expecting me to give my house as collateral for £2500 and why? Simply because I was cornered in my life and I wanted an exit route. That did not mean he should have been exploiting the circumstances I was caught in. I was selling the freehold shop at the cost price we bought it six years earlier simply because I was desperate to get out.

2.   Opposite to the shop there was a school. The local Muslim imam negotiated with the council to have the premises to teach Urdu and Koran to Muslim children in the evening. The teaching had been going on for a few months. One evening, a busy time for the shop, I was on the till. A man walked in with a long beard and white robes and whispered, 'Could I see you for a minute outside?' He had a charity collecting tin in his hands with the name of the charity written on

it. I did not read what charity it was as it did not concern me. I went out on the footpath with him. He explained that they were teaching Muslim children their religion and Urdu. He would like to keep this charity tin on top of my till for public donations and collections. I did not know how to react. I asked him to give me a couple of weeks to think it over as I also had other customers who had other faiths and I did not wish to offend their beliefs. From face reading I gathered he did not like it. However, we parted with my promise to give him my response within a couple of weeks. In two weeks' time he was there again with the tin. Most of my customers were British and I did not wish them to be offended and so I had decided to say 'no' to his request. So, I announced my decision to him by explaining, 'I have many local customers who I believe would be offended if I put your collection tin in the shop. Also, what guarantee do I have that some more charity collectors would not come and ask for the same facility. It would become a problem whom to say yes to and whom to say no. It is a private shop, serving the needs of the local population and I would not like to be the charity collecting shop for certain communities. So, my answer is no. I am sorry I cannot keep your tin.' He was furious. 'Do you know what you are saying?' he threatened. 'Yes, I do. My apologies, I cannot keep the charity tin.' He walked away in a huff. 'Watch it now, I will ask my community to boycott your shop,' he warned. He was right. My sales slumped. An already loss-making shop was more in trouble. Jihadis had moved into the Leyton area. Its foundations were laid down a long time ago back in 1976 but if I had said to someone about my experience at that time the Indian subcontinent politics would come into play. And I kept the incident to myself till now.

      3.   One evening about 7pm someone, A, bought some grocery and a bag of flour. He asked me if I could go and take it to his house. I asked him to stay at the shop and keep watch while I was gone so that nobody came and mugged the girl on the till. He agreed. I went to leave the grocery. When I came back he took me to the back of the shop and said, 'I don't know how much you trust this till girl, but I watched her and when she was serving a customer she took out a ten-pound note and slipped it in her bra.'

    'Oh my God, are you sure? I am shocked. I treated her as my family member and if she has been doing that I must have lost a lot of money. No wonder I am having cash flow problems.'

    'I am positive otherwise I would not say this to you.'

    With that warning he left. I stayed there at the back of the shop, shocked and wondering what the hell this world was all about. Had God ever created some decent people on this planet or just cheats and nothing but deceits? A few minutes later a local Bobby, who knew me well, being a local businessman, appeared to say hello. Look at the incidents, how the events change scene one after another.

A JOURNEY THROUGH PARTITION AND BEYOND

When he saw me in that pensive tense mood, he enquired what was the reason for me being so upset. First, I tried to ignore it, but later, on his insistence, I reluctantly told him the incident. He suggested that he should take the girl upstairs and question her. I said that if what I had been told was not true and you question her, she would be very upset and frightened. Also, you being a male police officer you cannot search her physically anyway. Also, she would leave me immediately. However, the bobby insisted that I should allow him to question her. I did. They came down after 15 minutes. The young lady was crying profusely. The bobby said that she denied the charge, but he thought she was telling a lie. Obviously, he could not search her physically, but he offered to call a policewoman to search her if I wanted. I refused. He then left. It was time to shut the shop. As normal I took her to her home in Forest Gate. On the way she told me that she would not be coming to work anymore. I explained to her the whole story. I asked her that she should forget it. If she was taking money from the till she should stop, and I was happy to trust her. She insisted on leaving and she left. She did not report for work next day. Later, I asked another man in his sixties from Mumbai who lived locally to come and look after the shop during the day when I was in school. I had known him for some time. He used to come to buy groceries at the shop. He became quite friendly. He had some property in Mumbai which he went to sell a couple of times but without any success. I told him to be generous and give it away free to some relations rather than spend money on travels. He offered to work on the till. One day again when I came back after buying from cash and carry, someone reported to me that he too was stealing cash from the till. Oh God, can we trust anyone on this planet? Money and women both cannot be given to anyone to be looked after.

Because of the cash flow difficulties in paying my bills, I had already applied for a teacher's job. In 1978 I was offered the grade 2 position as head of metalwork at Robert Montefiore School at Valance Road. I accepted it.

Because of the stealing from the till and with plummeting sales because of the Jihadis protest, I found no other alternative but to start opening the shop at 4pm after coming back from school. I also continued to open it at weekends and bank holidays. It was hard but at least profitable. I controlled the till all the time.

4.   As soon as this girl left, the shop was being managed on reduced hours on weekdays and full-time on weekends. The PT girl, who was employed to fill the shelves, could not work after 4pm and she did not like working during the weekends. She also did not like to work with the man who was managing the place during the weekdays.

One Saturday, it was around 10.30am and the weather was good and the sun was showing off its kindness on the British soil. I was hoping to do good trade that day. A middle-aged woman, with poor presentation as if she had just got out of her bed and with rude manners, just walked in. In her stern voice, she demanded to know if I was the owner of the shop. I said, yes.

'Have you got an office where I can talk to you in private?' she enquired.

'Yes, it is upstairs. But I must arrange for someone to look after the till. It will take me a few minutes to arrange that.'

'Then find someone. It is important that we talk urgently now,' she emphasised by displaying her bossing nature.

I telephoned a local friend to come and man the till. He came within minutes. We went upstairs. She settled down on the chair and started throwing her babbles at me.

'You were employing a PT girl to merchandise your goods on the shelf. She lost her job as you are now opening the shop in the evenings. She is the member of my Union. I am the local organiser for the Union. She lost her job because of you and therefore I am demanding that she should be compensated and be reinstated in her job.'

'I had no choice. The girl who was opening the shop and managing it left. I had no one to look after it once she left. I have a full-time job. I started opening when I come back from work. So how can I re-instate her when the shop is closed during the time she worked.'

'Why did you not ask her to open the shop for you and look after it? She should have been given the first option. She worked here for nearly a year. She had the experience in stacking the shelves.'

'No, I could not have asked her to open the shop for a number of reasons. One – she was hired to merchandise the shelves and not to manage the shop. I have not sacked her. She lost the job because of the circumstances in which I found myself. Two – if she was stacking the shelves, it does not follow that she could also manage the shop. Managing a shop is a lot more complex matter than just stacking the shelves. Three – I do not know the integrity and the honesty of the girl. I had to shut the shop because of the dishonesty of the previous employee. How could I just give my keys of the shop which has thousands of pounds worth of stock to anyone? Is your union ready to give me guarantees that if the funds and stocks are misappropriated by your member, you would compensate me in full?'

'No, we cannot do that.'

'Why? She is your union member, and then why don't you vouch for her integrity and honesty?'

'I am not going into such discussions, but I am asking you to reinstate her and compensate her because she has lost her job.'

'I am sorry I have no job to reinstate her to. I am not going to open the shop just to keep her employed. I cannot afford it and that is why I picked up a full-time job because of the stealing and not getting enough income. I am also not

A JOURNEY THROUGH PARTITION AND BEYOND

paying her because she is no longer working here. I had offered her to work after 4pm and/or on weekends. She said it does not suit her. Now she can choose not to work at the times not suitable to her, but I must keep the shop open when not convenient to me. It just does not add up. We all have equal rights. How come her rights have become more paramount over mine?'

'In that case I am warning you that I will report your behaviour to my union. Shortly you would be hearing from us. I advise you to have a good lawyer.'

'That is your right. I look forward to hearing from you.' I have never come across such a rude person in my life, who had no manners to introduce herself and say even good morning.

I never heard anything from that threatening union boss.

5.　　　　I applied for an off-licence to sell spirits to boost my income and cash flow. My application was opposed by a multi-national company which had an outlet in the area. I was up against a well-trained and clever barrister who bombarded questions at me faster than I could answer. His technique was to put words into my mouth. I could not cope, and this was the first time I had ever gone into those four walls. No good citizen would like to be questioned there. The inevitable had to happen. My application was rejected.

Hope of Selling

The shop was with agents since G had left but there were no takers. I used to pray to get me out of this miserable dead-end business. I remember I would sit in the shop and watch the passers-by walk past the shop. The waiting for a customer to come in became so boring and disheartening. I cannot blame the customers. They had found another shop to buy their groceries as I was a part-time shop. This struggle went on for months and became very demoralising. Life was just slipping away in that endless mire. Surprisingly no one even made enquiries from the sales agent. The economy was bad too. The prices were shooting up. Mrs Thatcher was just about ready to walk into Downing Street.

Suddenly a ray of hope appeared on the horizon. A couple who were working as labourers at the airport and who had two children, came to view the place. For them the shop business was ideal. The husband worked night shifts and his wife worked day shifts. They could never enjoy being together as a family. We agreed a price and they were eager to complete the deal as soon as possible to move in. I too was looking for the divine's mercy and finally I got it. He had already extracted enough revenge out of my veins. He had used me as a donkey for so many years and had robbed me of my valuable years of life but who can tell Him. He was getting away with murder on his planet, simply because he was Omnipotent.

309

The deal was completed and they took over in February 1979. I had had cash flow problems but within days their sales went up simply because he belonged to the community which was now dominating the area. Within months he took over the next-door card shop and opened a cash & carry to sell confectionery, cigarettes, and spirits. Within 5 years they sold the thriving business and moved on to a bigger cash & carry. Today the family are millionaires, rolling with money. The man with no education and no experience made a great success of the opportunity, while we with all the education, knowledge, and expertise proved a failure.

Why? Because I had a different religion for which I was badly punished. That is the world we live in. All the atom bombs, stored in silos in their thousands and ready to unleash their destructive and devastating powers to melt the soil of the mother earth, are proving useless. We are witnessing a totally different kind of world, uncontrollable, vicious, and un-manageable. Is the end of the world so nigh? Only that sleeping Giant knows. I have a feeling when He gets fed up with the behaviour of this humanity, He will unleash one of those huge boulders encircling the earth to finish it off and then start the creation once more. Those boulders are his weapons waiting for his orders. He has used them before and He will do it again. It is only a matter of time. He cannot handover this power of destruction to the impotent humanity which is becoming out of order and out of control.

The Aftermath

The life on a grinding wheel took its own toll. More than five years of my life had gone into the gutters, just to correct a small mistake of going into a business which was not suitable for my tastes, my education, and my likings. It took 4 years to sell the place with so many agonising experiences. Now I had my life back. I paid the loan to the bank with the proceeds of the sale and had some cash left in the bank. I could not sell the shop for what it was worth. The stock taker also cheated me by undervaluing the stock as I did not wish to be there when the stock takers were there. They favoured the buyer, simply because they knew that I was a dying star and they would get nothing more from me in the future. But the new owners were the rising stars and there was a hope for some from them. I accepted all that as a part of the game. I have been a good loser all my life and I acknowledge that gracefully.

Nonetheless, I had still plenty of dough left for the future life to be re-planned. I had accepted the fate of teaching in schools, though not wholeheartedly. The most important thing now was that I was a free man again. Life had to be faced once more with vigour and determination. I was 48 years old. The cream of life was already gone. I was middle-aged and it was time to settle down. The downs of life were over. It had taken its heavy toll of so many years but now it was time to move up the hill once again. One cannot go for the rose bush to enjoy the fragrance and its beauty and ignore the thorns attached to it. Life must be taken and the whole always exists with better and worse, day and night, and light and darkness. So, I did not sit idly to brood on the lost years but started looking immediately for another house and another opportunity to lock onto. It was time to change the house after staying there for eighteen years.

Hunt for a House

We looked at houses in Chigwell, Woodford Green, and even in Epping Forest. While enquiring about the houses in Epping, the local estate agent suggested a property at Stebbing village. It was a newly constructed bungalow in an acre of land with 3 bedrooms. The white local population was leaving London with its ever-increasing pollution and crime rate, and were moving to the countryside. Then why not us, I concluded? I was born at a farm and I loved living in the open countryside. We went to see the house. We all liked it except Mira. London houses of that size were more expensive than what we were paying in Stebbing. The price of the house was set at £49,500 and was reduced to £46,500. Because of the family stalemate, we sat on the decision for nearly two months. Mira continued to drag her feet. One day a man called George (God bless his soul) who rewired our house at Seven Kings, and was quite influential with Mira, raised the issue of changing the house. He knew about the sale of the shop too. I told him the problem that Mira was not consenting to buy a house we had seen in Stebbing. He asked us to go with him to see the house once more. We did. He strongly recommended going for it. Mira reluctantly agreed but raised some other issues.

'How will we travel to the schools?' We did not have the car. We had a van.

'We will buy a new car,' I promised.

'It will not be practical as the travelling distance is too far, and it would take a long time to commute,' she moaned.

'It takes us now an hour and a quarter through London traffic jams and it would take another 15 minutes more to travel from Stebbing. Of course, the mileage is more but the roads have no traffic jams. It would be a smooth run on the newly constructed M11. The quality of life is going to be much better. We work as teachers only 198 (55%) days a year, the rest are weekends and holidays. Why should we muck up over 45% of our life in the unhealthy environment of London?' I gave her my reasoning to convince her.

As usual she was not convinced. She would not like to move to Stebbing because she had friends in London. I countered that how often did we meet our friends during the week and even weekends. This was only a psychological weakness. You need doctors in an emergency and not friends. We three of us wanted to move but Mira was still adamant. However I took the decision to move with or without her consent.

Next day I informed the agent that we would buy the house subject to satisfactory searches. I posted a Westminster Bank's cheque for the deposit. I was short of about £300 in the account to honour the cheque. I went to inform the manager at the Seven Kings branch and he agreed that he would honour the cheque. Surprisingly the same bank, which had earlier supported us to buy the Seven Kings house, bounced my cheque. Why had the manager agreed to honour it and then bounced it, I had no idea. I was very angry when the estate agent informed me. I telephoned the manager from my school to find the reasons. He told me that the cheque was returned unpaid because I had not enough funds in my account.

'I know I was short of funds. I came to see you and explained that I was buying another house and I would be issuing a cheque for a deposit. You had agreed that you would pay it. You have two teacher's salaries coming to you every month. I am amazed that you dishonoured our cheque. I cannot accept that,' I pointed out.

He had no answer. I said to him, 'I am coming now to the bank to close my account. Please keep ready all the money we have in our account.' He agreed.

'But you have to bring your wife with you as it is a joint account,' he insisted.

'There is no need as we Asians normally support the decisions of our spouses,' I retorted.

He insisted again that I had to go with my wife to close the account. I said ok, I would bring my wife with me. I telephoned Mira, explained the situation to her, and asked her to be ready to be picked up in half an hour's time. The head agreed that I could take the time off. I picked Mira up from her school and we went to the bank to close our account. Then we went to Barclays at Leyton, my business bank, and deposited the money in our account. I went to see the manager there, explained to him the situation, and informed him that we were issuing a cheque for the deposit for a house we were buying. He agreed that the cheque would be met in full. I apologised to the estate agent on the phone for the trouble and told him that I was sending another cheque. The cheque was honoured when presented and we were on the way to buy a new bungalow in the countryside.

The Mortgage

Mortgages were being rationed in those days because of the downturn in the economy. We had a savings account with the Woolwich Building Society to get a preference in getting a mortgage when we were ready to buy another house.

A JOURNEY THROUGH PARTITION AND BEYOND

This is what they used to brag about on the TV advertisements - that those who had savings accounts with them would have a preference in getting the mortgage over others. But when we approached them they refused, and the reason they gave us was that they did not have enough cash available. So, they let us down, effectively cheated us with their false advertisements. So, we arranged our mortgage through a broker who managed to get us £22,500. The rest was to be met with our savings and proceeds from selling our Seven Kings house. I was reluctant to sell the SK house as the mortgage for it was only £17.50/month and the years left were only nine. But again, Mira insisted on selling the house. It was just beyond me how her mind operated. Why oppose all the time? I am convinced it is her huge ego that drives her to show her authority. The prices of houses were shooting up at that time. So, I decided to increase my sale price to the person who was buying it. Again, Mira opposed. However, I went to the buyer and told him that he was to pay me £1500 more on a take it or leave it basis. He agreed to pay. He was in the clothing business. He just went to his bank, increased his O/D facility and bought the house, cash, for his son. You may think I was mean and unethical but to me it was a business deal. He had a choice to walk away from the deal, thus leaving me cold in buying my house. I took the gamble to increase the price and he had the right to say no. He knew that he was getting value for his money. In those days the estate agents always undervalued the houses so that they could sell the houses quickly and get their commission.

The New Car

Just ten minutes' walk from our house there was a Toyota garage on the Seven Kings Road. We went to see the cars there. The delivery dates were three days after the deposit. We saw two cars which interested us - a Sporty non-automatic Toyota Celica and an automatic saloon. The saloon was £1500 more expensive because of automatic transmission. Mira could only drive the automatics because of her driving licence. So, we had a stalemate in deciding. I offered to buy the automatic saloon, but Mira was not ready to buy it because it was pricy. Mira wanted to look for some other makes. We did look for another one at Ley Street garage, but its delivery was two weeks later. So, we had a stalemate again. But we three wanted to ride to our new home in our new car.

Everyone liked the Celica, its colour, its style, its interior, and its sporty appearance. So, we ordered it. Mira was now unhappy. The location of the bungalow where she did not wish to live and now the new car she could not drive. It was double trouble in the making.

On the 17th of April we had our baggage moved to our new house. We were now living in the SK house like gypsies. On the 19th of April we had the Easter Break from our schools. We went to collect our car as arranged at 11am but it was not ready. We waited there, and we got possession around 3pm. We came back home, handed over the house keys to the new owner who lived in a house opposite and drove off in arrogance to Stebbing. We, a family of four - middle-aged parents with two bright and well-behaved children - were cruising on the M11 in style in a new car, well-polished, and glittering in the dazzling sunshine. It appeared as if the newly-built, empty motorway had been constructed just for us to inaugurate it by moving onto our newly constructed bungalow. And why not! We had earned it after so many debacles, hassles, and frustrations of many years on a grinding wheel. We had the rights to have some happiness in life.

Ritu was sitting in the front and Vipul and Mira were in the back. Our maiden drive in the new flashy car and our happiness was marred by Mira's sadness. 'You knew I could not drive this car and yet you bought it,' and my reply, 'I offered to buy the automatic but you did not want me to because it was expensive,' created an atmosphere not very conducive to the children. We were all robbed of our joy for a new life in an unknown village, in our new car, and to our new bungalow. When joy and happiness come in life, the long tale of woe is just around the corner to chase you, to snatch away your wow factor. The joys of life are always momentary, it is the woe which drags on and lingers on to leave the memory lanes unmanageably painful.

Our baggage had already been delivered there by the home movers a day earlier. Soon we were settling into the new environment with new neighbours with some fears in the mind that 'would we be accepted by the village community?' That was to be experienced and to be seen later.

Although it was Easter break from school and we were at home, Ritu wanted to go to her school to play tennis and I was taking her. The fresh air of the countryside was overwhelming and was making me more relaxed and sleepy. I found it very difficult to drive down the M11 in those days. One day, as soon as I reached her school, Ritu left with her tennis racket and I just could not keep awake. I parked the car on the main road and had a good nap for half an hour. Later, I discovered the technique to beat the sleep. Whenever I found myself sleepy at the wheel, I would nibble some chilli hot snacks such as Bombay Mix or strong mint chewing gum. The hotter the snacks to burn your tongue, the better is the effect.

Some friends liked our moving to a good neighbourhood while others, as normal, were sceptical. One of the friends said that we had made a terrible mistake by moving to a small village away from friends and the Asian community. He predicted that we would be back in London within six months. He remains disappointed till today as it has never happened so far to meet his prediction. He was wrong to judge the intentions of his friend who was moving out of London with some convictions and not for any financial gains. He also said that the gain in property values would always be more in London than outside. I grant him that,

A JOURNEY THROUGH PARTITION AND BEYOND

but I believe the money is made for me to enjoy my life and I am not there to sacrifice the quality of my life to gain a few pounds extra in my old age.

We had good neighbours. They all came to introduce themselves, sat with us in our lounge, had a cup of coffee. One neighbour took two weeks to visit us but when they did, they became our best neighbours. The husband was a sales person with a building merchant. Nearly every weekend either they would invite us for coffee or they would come over to us for snacks and a drink. The husband would also sometimes come over to help me with the garden chores. We used to have lovely weekends together until they decided to move to Devon after the husband retired.

<u>More about Our Settling Down</u>

1.   Within a couple of days of our moving to the house, I had a call from the local church priest. 'I would like to come and see you to introduce myself as your local parish priest. Is it ok with you if I come to meet you this Saturday at 11am?' I said, 'Yes sir, that is ok. You are very welcome. We would be delighted to see you.' I had never met a priest before in my life. Are they really men of God or are they just like us as ordinary mortal beings? How much was he a man of God and to what extent was I the sinner? I wanted to discover. I was very curious and eager to know. I was looking forward to that experience. As the Saturday approached, the curiosity of finding the truth increased. He knocked at the door exactly at 11am like an English Gent, an admirable British habit. Indians lack that quality of punctuality. They are never on time. They rather take pride in being late.

We moved into the lounge after the usual formalities of introduction at the entrance door. I admit that I was watching his every movement and analysing his every word to discover the difference between him and me. That was my agenda. We went on chatting as we sipped our hot cup of coffee. He said it was his 'job' to inform the parishioners of the services that the church provides. He narrated them to me. Then we moved on to more human and social problems of the day such as caring of the garden and how does he do it; the race problems if any in the village and our acceptance by the community. He assured me that there were no race issues in the village. Before we had arrived there was another mixed married couple living amicably in the village. However, it is normal for the community to watch with suspicion every newcomer coming to live in the village. They would accept the new ones readily if they contributed to the village life. He asked my religion and would I be attending Sunday mass. I said I was born into a Hindu family and I had no reservations about attending a church. He left after an hour. I did not find anything in him to indicate that he was a man of God. He was no nearer to the Divine than I was. He was not an enlightened soul, not even a fraction. He was just an ordinary human being as I was. As a priest he was just

315

doing his job as imposed by his employer - the church. He was trying to earn his living the same way as I was. We belonged to the same ordinary human race.

2.　　　We were in the village for nearly a couple of months. We were well settled with our routine. We would leave Ritu at her Woodford County school first and then I would leave Mira and Vipul who was attending Mum's infants' school, and finally I would go to my school at Valance Road. The return journey was in the reverse order except we had to wait sometimes at Ritu's school until she finished her tennis games, very annoying to her mother, but no choice. The M11 was not that busy in those days and we used to have a smooth, tension-free drive home.

3.　　　One Saturday, as we finished our breakfast, we heard a knock at the door. It was a village policeman. Hum! What had we done that we had the honour to see Her Majesty's representative on our doorstep? Was he also introducing himself? Maybe this too was a village tradition to visit the most un-welcome resident creature. Thoughts are always painful and speculative. They just come unannounced, without any notice. With those silly brain waves, I opened the door. 'I am your local bobby. I live in the village, just a couple of minutes' walk from you on the main road. May I come in?'

'Oh yes sorry, please do come in,' I said with some reservations in my speech.

'I have just come to introduce myself to you as you are new to the village.' He went on explaining his duties, the help he could give in case of some troubles, and the duties he performed at his village office, the integral part of his house. I later learnt that he had a dog at his house. Did he have the dog as a pet or a bodyguard to protect him? I could never find out. If it was to protect him, then I wondered how he was going to protect us. Anyway, the conversation then moved on to our personal movements and activities in the last couple of days. What we do for our living, where did we live before moving to the village. When do we leave home, when do we come back home, how we spend our weekends and so on. They were very searching and investigative questions. But we never felt embarrassed or alarmed. We thought that was his way of welcoming us to the village. We thought the officer was just trying to be sociable and having an inquisitive conversation until he hit the nail on the head and opened his heart. 'Are you aware that recently there was a burglary in the neighbourhood?'

'No, when?'

'It happened just two weeks after you moved to the village,' he replied.

'So that was your reason to visit us,' I enquired, showing some concern that why didn't he say so right in the beginning. Why ask all those questions in some roundabout way? Why not come out clean and be frank? In that social chatter we could have said something innocently which might have incriminated us. 'So why were you not open right in the beginning officer? If that is the case if you wish to know more about us and our background we would be very happy to co-operate,' I said, annoyed.

'I am sorry it is my duty to investigate the burglary as discreetly as possible. I must admit that there was a burglary in the village before as well a few months ago. But you, being a new arrival to the village, we had to adopt a procedure of elimination. I am very happy to say that having talked to you now I am convinced that you are a nice family with a good profession and you would have nothing to do with that burglary. I am sorry if I had not announced my intentions clear to make enquiries about the burglary right in the beginning.' He felt embarrassed and went on explaining his 'good' intentions at length to remove his guilt. In 1979 racism might have been on the decline, but it did not mean that institutions were free from racism in dealing with people like us. The following episode confirms the existence of racism in the police force in this local area. As I had worked in the police in my early days, it is my advice to all to avoid any acquaintances or friendships with policemen. They are always suspicious of your motives and intentions and would like to know everything that you do in life. I prefer a friendship with a snake than with a policeman. It is a horrible statement to give and a slur on that profession, but it is true. That is how they are trained, never to trust and always be suspicious, including their near and dear ones.

4.   It is human nature that when you move into a new place, you would like to explore the area for its beauty, its parks, its schools, its shopping centres, and the other useful amenities available for an easy settling down. As we were teachers and the children loved to read books we decided to go to the nearest town, Braintree, to find out what kind of facilities were available there. We parked our car in the car park and I saw a young police officer walking past us. I rushed to him to ask, 'Hi officer I am looking for a main library in the town.' He first looked at me fiercely; glanced at me with a thorough inspection to check my dress and my personality; and then gave me the directions how to get to the local unemployment benefit office. 'No officer, I am asking for the library and not the local benefit office,' I emphasised again.

'This is the office your kind of people normally ask for, so I gave you the directions,' he retorted by showing his contempt for my 'kind'.

'But officer, I am employed as a teacher in London and have recently moved into the area. I am looking for a library where you can borrow books to read.'

'Ah ok.' He then gave me the directions for the library.

What kind of a town was it where a policeman can treat you with contempt? How this well-dressed body in police garments, representing the bureaucracy to serve its citizens, had such an ugly soul that he had no respect for the citizens to whom he was paid to serve. What could I do? I just had to learn to walk away from such idiots. That was what we did but it was painfully hurtful. Why do I write this even today? Because the hurt is still there alive and as fresh as when it was inflicted. He might be telling these tales to his racist colleagues to make them laugh but these are small men sent on the planet to inflict pain on the innocents. People hate the gun terrorists, but they forget that there are other forms of terrorism too. There are tongue terrorists and there are pen terrorists. Both types of terrorists inflict pain for life and one suffers from its torture if one lives. The gun terrorism may be better as it silences you once and for all and its pain is momentary.

5. It was Sunday when the sun was shining mercifully with all its glory on the village. It was the day when the village folks were celebrating an Elizabethan Fayre. I had not forgotten the advice of the priest that those who participate in the activities of the village are accepted sooner than the others. So, we decided to show our faces to the settled villagers as well as to learn a bit about the culture of the locals. We went all over the village to see the various activities, the different costumes worn by the men, women, and children of the Elizabethan era. They were reviving the memories of their past forefathers and displaying them in their colourful costumes. We had spent about a couple of hours and were still looking around to make the best use of the occasion when an unforgettable scene caught my attention. A pig, slaughtered, dead and with an iron bar pierced through his heart, was rotating and being roasted over an open log fire in the backyard of the pub. He looked as beautiful as Christ looked on his cross except here there were no disciples to cry and wail over his anguished body. Instead the knives were there to carve into his white flesh. My heart sank and started bleeding with woes of pain and agony. I just sweated at the scene. I could not take it anymore, the look of that innocent pig. The scenes of that early morning roasting of piglets and their innocent cries at the temple in India were jamming my memory lanes once more. No, I had no intention of showing my eagerness to participate in the village activities, whether I was accepted or rejected. I just didn't give a hoot for that advice of the priest. The villagers can keep their acceptance to themselves. By their acceptance or rejection, I was not going to disappear into oblivion. I was not prepared to sell out my way of living and thinking. This type of life was not for me. One's celebration should not result in the slaughter of the other. This beggared belief and I did not wish to be part of it. We hurried back home, never to visit such cultural activities of the village again. I must live with my own standards, on whichever part of this planet I live, and not by the standards demanded by the society I am part of. Since then I have never attended such activities and I have no plans to either.

A JOURNEY THROUGH PARTITION AND BEYOND

6. Have I been to the village pub ever? Only twice so far although the pub is only two minutes' walk from my home. In any village, the pub is the central meeting place for the community, though it is a dying tradition. I do not wish the eyes of the people to be glued on me. I never watch sports. I never read sports. I do not support any teams. To me it is idiotic to watch twelve fools play, kick and fight to snatch a ball from each other. I am happy to fail Norman Tebbit's test.

Dinner at Lords

It was one of our good friend's 25th anniversary, being celebrated at the Lords Cricket Ground. They were very good hosts and entertainers. They always arranged their parties in style and for their own 25th wedding anniversary, my goodness they spared no effort to do the best. At the appointed time we were queuing up for the entrance into the car park; we then settled down on the allotted seats; the Indian dinner was to be served by a well-known caterer; and live Indian songs were to be sung by no less than the well-known music director of Bollywood who had sung many songs in the Indian movies. The wine was served, a variety of snacks and food was served, followed as usual with a lot of speeches in appreciation of the hosts of the evening. After all that, some guests went on to the dance floor to reduce their fat intake and some moved to the bar to quench their unsatisfied thirst and gossip about the party and other bits of small talk. We did not fit anywhere. Mira never had the inclination to dance. She also does not indulge in drinking either. It was now nearly 2.30am and it was time for the carriages to move on, and for us it was to travel a long way back home to Essex. So, it was nearly 3am that we took leave of the hosts, collected our car, and we were on our way to the M11 and then to catch the A120, a single lane in those days going to Braintree. We had just reached a few hundred yards away from junction 8, I noticed a couple of flashes from behind. I looked in my mirror; it was a police car giving me the signal to stop. I did. The officer walked towards us, I opened the window, and enquired, 'Hello, Officer have I done something wrong?'

'I stopped you because I'd like to breathalyse you.'

'No problem, officer.'

'I have the breathalyser, but it is out of action. I have asked the station to send me another one. It is on the way. Please wait here for 20 minutes.'

'Ok, officer I will wait.' I had no choice, did I?

So, we waited. The car clock was showing 4am. It took about 30 minutes for the other analyser to arrive. In between the officer came to apologise that it was on the way, but it was taking a bit longer than he anticipated. Finally, it arrived. The officer was now armed with a device to nick me if he could. He was certain that he caught a big fish for his night duty and it would add another success story

319

in his diary of crime busting and in due course promotions. He was quite stiff and every word he uttered demonstrated the arrogance of his authority. As he arrived at my car door, I opened the window. He blurted, 'Have you been breathalysed before, sir?'

'No, officer this is my first time.'

'So, you do not know how to use the analyser. Ok. I will switch on here; you blow your breath in here, and if the light goes red it means the results are positive. In that case I will arrest you and take you to the station. If you doubt the result of the analyser, you may ask for a blood test to be taken to prove your guilt or innocence. If it is a green light that means you are within the limits. So here we go. You will be tested three times to just make sure.' So, he placed the analyser in my hand and watched. It was green on all the three attempts. I was within the limits. I said to the officer that we were coming from a party in London. I had a glass of wine around 10pm and I had no drink since then. Immediately I could see some smile on his face to indicate that he was only doing his duty and was not guilty in stopping me. In his heart he must have been disappointed as he waited quite patiently behind my car for nearly an hour. Otherwise why should he stop me, especially when his analyser was not working also? However, I could not resist my curiosity. So, I asked, 'Officer, just as a matter of interest, why did you stop me? Did I do anything wrong? I think I was driving with quite some alertness.'

'While driving behind you, I noticed that your car crossed the white lines a couple of times.'

'Well you appreciate officer, I am a bit tired with the long drive from London, it is 4am, we had been at a party for nearly six hours. I might have crossed but I thought it was not that important at that time of the night when there is no traffic on the road.'

'But if you are tired, have a bit of break on a lay-by. It is best not to drive. Anyway, have a safe journey home. I am sorry you had to wait so long for the analyser to arrive.' So, we parted with a smiling but disappointed officer. That was the night that was with fun first and then with some hassles. The happiness and the hassles of life are two good mates and they always chase one another and play their own games.

First Time in the Court

Going to a courtroom is a heart-rending exercise for me. It is a demeaning, frightening, and terrifying exercise. I become panicky and disorientated. It is not a place where a decent, law-abiding citizen should ever go or like to go with their own free will. But it is a place where a citizen can be dragged to by the system. Mahatma Gandhi, Martin Luther King, President Mandela are the most recent examples who were thrown into jails, simply because

A JOURNEY THROUGH PARTITION AND BEYOND

they were fighting for a just cause. I believe going to a court is like going into a slaughterhouse where billions of simple, innocents are slaughtered every year. In UK alone seven billion, belonging to the so-called animal kingdom, are 'murdered' every year. The human hypocrisy reaches its peak when some people slit the poor animals' throats on the name of God by reciting the scriptures on tape recorders; while others slaughter them on a killing line by stunning their heads or just beheading them with a sword. One learned person said to me once that 'they were made to be eaten'. What a horrible thought!

For me going to the court was the same situation. I too had to swear on the name of God, 'That I would tell the truth nothing but the whole truth.' But I was not allowed to tell the truth by the 'liars'. It was a place where points are scored, and truth is suppressed. I would also not know how the 'honourable' judge would announce his verdict, what mood he would be in, and would he be guided by his heart or by his head? It is all manipulative, misguided, and subjective decisions, although we are told that there are some guidelines laid down for them to follow. So they say, but in fact it is all deceptive and false. The innocent citizen suffers the same fate as those simple animals – an imminent, unpredictable fall of a sharp knife.

I had gone into a snack manufacturing business in April 1981. I will say more about this story later in another book. I was running the business as a part-time entrepreneur and teaching full-time. A great friend of mine recommended to me his relation, H, who was now free from running his own insurance business in Southall and who would be happy to help me manage my business. He was a single soul, did not care about the wages, and would stay with us at home during weekdays. We welcomed that help. For delivering goods, we bought a second-hand estate car from a car dealer in London. The dealer, in contravention of our agreement, did not provide me the six months tax disc when we went to collect the car on Saturday. I noticed it when I brought the car home. When I phoned the dealer, he denied that there was an agreement to provide the tax disc with it. Obviously, he was telling lies. Everyone knows that to drive the car without a tax disc is not legal. Why did he not warn me that it had no tax disc when I went to collect, and I must not drive it until I had bought the disc? As I was travelling weekdays a long distance to London, working full-time, and running the business, time was a precious commodity.

I used to phone the factory every day for briefings about any problems where they needed my advice. One Friday, when I phoned, the H said that he was to go to Southall urgently in the evening before I came back from London. He would stay there for the weekend and come back on Sunday. He said he was going in the estate car which was parked at home in my garden. For commuting to the factory, he used to be picked up in the morning and dropped off at home in the evening by one of my employees. We used to come back home around 7pm. I pointed out to him that the car had no tax disc and was not legal to drive. He said, 'Don't worry I will be careful not to be caught.' 'But it can happen and if you are caught the police will question me as the car is in my name,' I replied. He insisted on taking the car and said that if he was caught he would take the blame. He also said that he would try, if he could, to cancel the visit to Southall. I told him that it would be good if he could, and I would buy the disc on Saturday and he could then drive to London any day he wished. During that discussion I never agreed that he could take the car without a disc but if he did then it was his responsibility. I could not do more than that. I was dealing with a responsible, grown-up adult and I appreciated his help in managing my business. When we arrived home that evening, the car was not at home. Obviously, he had driven it to London. About 8pm I had a call from him that he had been stopped by the police; they had taken the car details and were going to follow up the offence of driving the car without tax. He advised me to go to the post office in the morning and get the disc. The damage was already done. I bought the disc next morning.

In my summer holidays, I was working at the factory. A stranger, with short build, appeared and introduced himself, saying that he was from the vehicle tax office and had come to investigate the reason why my car was on the road without a disc. I narrated him the whole story, from buying the car to the point when it was taken by H. As it was a long story to tell, during our meeting I was interrupted by an employee who wanted my advice. One time more I had to leave him for a couple of minutes to sort out a problem for another employee. He did not like it. His ego of being a bossy important government employee was hurt. When I came back I noticed that he was tense. In those days I had no office to conduct private meetings. So, after the meeting, while leaving he warned, 'It is a serious offence. I will have to take you to court for the offence. If he drove with your permission, then you are guilty of an offence but if he took the car without your permission, then he will be prosecuted for driving an un-licenced car without permission. And for this offence he could even go to prison.' I said, 'After knowing what you just said, I am in a dilemma and I don't know what to say. If I say he took it without my permission, then he would end up in a lot more trouble than me. He is also a heart patient and I have to be careful what I say.'

'Well when you get the court letter, you have to decide to plead guilty or not guilty.'

With that strenuous warning with dire consequences, he left. A couple of months later I received the notice from a court in Walthamstow to appear on the charges. I had never been to court. I was frightened to go there. I telephoned the court clerk and explained to him the position and asked his advice whether I should plead guilty or not guilty. I preferred to pay the fine by admitting guilt by letter rather than go to the court. But he advised that I should attend the court and tell the magistrate what I had told him about the mitigating circumstances. The court would be lenient and might just let me off with a warning. It was not such a big crime. The court was getting such cases all the time. So why pay the fine? I took his advice.

On the appointed day, I went there with my daughter to boost my fading morale. As the time drew nearer to appear, I was getting more anxious and tense. My daughter read my face and noticed my predicament.

'Dad, the worst that can happen is that you will be fined. It is not such a big deal. It is not a serious offence to worry about. Just narrate the incident in your own words and you will be ok and let the magistrate decide.'

I nodded and showed a brave face but inside I felt just like running millions of miles away from that scene. Soon my name was called, and I was ushered into the courtroom. I bowed my head in front of the three 'enlightened' magistrates; I had to as they were the wise men occupying those seats of judging others in the dock and they knew it all. They were the clever people on this planet. Their role was not to hand over the justice but to win points on sentencing. They may be even half sleeping; their minds may be busy in fighting out some other battles of life facing them. But they knew the standard fines for the standard offences. They just had to follow them blindly. They were part of the establishment to create fear in the hearts of the mortals and to teach the lesson to the generations to follow. They had to make me an example to others to take note not to drive their cars without paying into the coffers of the government treasury. They had the mighty power of the state behind them, the power given by the citizens, by the scientists, and by the technologists. A little protest by a citizen in the dock to plead for his innocence would end up with dire consequences of court contempt. You, as a weak citizen, must accept your sentence without any comments, like a sheep on the slaughter line. All over the world these kangaroo courts, headed by 'intelligent' monkeys, are deciding citizens' fates. It is a one-way traffic. They would pronounce a death sentence on you or lock you up in prison and yet if they have wrongly convicted you they cannot give you your life back or those lost days in the prison. They act like little gods and yet they cannot perform like a god.

However, I was directed to the dock to stand, a humiliating place to be as if you were already dubbed as a criminal. These are the manipulations of the system to humble your ego to make you surrender before even you begin. I was not yet even proven guilty. But this is how they create the environment in the courtrooms, a heart-rending fear amongst the innocent citizens. And that fear travels like lightning into your spine. You are already half dead; your mental faculties would refuse to work. Your brain does not function, does not listen to questions, and finds no answers to the questions thrown at you by the clever, well-trained prosecutors. The investigator who came to see me was sitting next to the prosecutor whose job it was to get the conviction and not justice. For him it was a numbers game, how many cases at the end of the year he had won and lost. That would decide his name, his fame, his pay packet and bonuses, and his position in the profession. The system has turned them into wicked, heartless people. The Clerk of the Court read the charge from a prepared sheet with which he was so much accustomed, and he had a good practice of it. That was his job and he was doing it every day. Failure to impress with his convincing words would not impress the 'honourable' learned magistrates on those tables. The whole environment was created to send the shivers through my being and it was working. They were all, at the end of the day, busy earning their dough from the handouts of the taxpayer's money. He was like a mindless butcher in the abattoir whose only concern was the number of innocent, defenceless, poor animals being slaughtered on that day. He was not concerned for the mental state and the wellbeing of those animals nor was he bothered about where they had come from. At the end of the day he was only rewarded on the numbers. It was only a number game. The Clerk and the investigator were not interested in finding the truth from me, or my mitigating circumstances. They were only keen to get me fined successfully to justify their wages of the day. It was again a numbers game.

After summing up the charges, the Clerk asked, 'Are you pleading guilty or not guilty to these charges?'

'Before I say whether I am guilty or not, I would like to say few words to the judges.' I replied in a broken trembling voice. The Clerk immediately interrupted and said, 'First you must tell the magistrates that are you pleading guilty or not guilty,' he insisted.

That created a big problem for me. I went into my thinking mode. What do I do now? If I pleaded guilty, the case would be over, and I would be sentenced for the crime I had not committed. If I had said, no I was not guilty, and then gave the mitigating circumstances, as the court clerk had suggested, then it would be H who would be prosecuted with the consequences of ending up in jail with a heart ailment. He was helping me in running my business and that too without pay. Now when he was in trouble, I was letting him down and was not protecting him. All the eyes in the court were focussed on me as my thinking prolonged to respond to the predicament the Clerk had put me into. The Clerk was impatient to know the answer and could wait no more and insisted on my reply.

'Mr Khurana, the magistrates would like to know whether you are pleading guilty or not guilty.'

'I plead guilty but...' before I got any further the sophisticated, clever Clerk butted in.

A JOURNEY THROUGH PARTITION AND BEYOND

'You have pleaded guilty and therefore there is no need to add on anything.'

So, he addressed the magistrates and said, 'The case is over from our side sir. We would like you to announce the judgement.'

I looked towards the three wise men, deliberating between them. The court clerk, butting his head in between the three, was whispering his advice to them with a thick book of legal jargon in his hand. Within five seconds they pronounced their judgement with clarity.

'The court fines Mr Khurana for the charge £50, to be deposited with the court before leaving the court premises. The case is now concluded.' They are used to such announcements and they have rehearsed it many times before. I could see no remorse on their faces but a sense of achievement. They had sentenced an innocent man that day with not a single ray of guilt on their faces. Imagine if I was to be convicted for some serious crime which would lead me to prison or even by hanging to death as used to be in the olden days. God knows how many innocents had been beheaded in the Tower of London. But no one protests for that; or lays flowers on those spots; or cries for their souls. They just ended up as numbers and the tourists walk away without condemning the history behind it.

In disgust I walked out of the courtroom. Ritu was surprised to see me out within minutes. I explained to her how the court proceedings were conducted, and the judgement was announced. We went to the court office, deposited £50 and walked out with relief that it was all over even though not in the way it should have been. The state was richer by £50, stained with innocent blood. At least they should have allowed me to have my say, deliberated on it before passing a judgement. But no, that is how this whole brutal system operates. It will never change until the whole system is reviewed. The method of rewarding the prosecutor on successes and not going deep into finding the truth is all wrong. It is the same system as was operated centuries ago when the courts represented the almighty Royalty to punish the citizens of the land. The court language and the bureaucratic texts continue to be the same. It 'orders' the citizens to submit; it creates fear with the dire consequences in their hearts if they fail to do what they are directed to do. There is no politeness, no explanation, only threats to the individuals. The tragedy is that the system is being operated the same way by the elected representatives of the people as in the olden days of kings and monarchs and there is no guilt. The bureaucrats behave and act in the same arrogant way as they did before rather than serving as the servants of the citizens who pay their wages. Who would call this system democracy, government for the people, by the people, and of the people?

Some wise men would sit on the top table. They are the selected citizens of 'repute' from the crowd who have been recommended and nominated by the elites of the system. They are manipulated by the court clerk, told what the law says, and are then guided to pass the sentence within the constraints imposed by the law. Effectively it is the clerk who is handing over the judgement of the individuals, but the judgements are being rubber-stamped by the 'judges', hired from the common citizens. They have no training or knowledge of the law, they are not better equipped or more intelligent than an individual in the dock or on the streets. The citizen is a simple, down-to-earth person, who would just like to get on with his daily grind. He does not have the cleverness, the manipulation, and the lying techniques of the prosecutors who are the masters of that trade. All this bunch of people are abusing the huge power of the state which has been diverted into their hands by the same citizen who is put into the dock to fight for his self-respect and freedom. The same citizen was now being hounded, persecuted, threatened, and manipulated. He only asked this bunch of people to govern the country on his behalf. The whole dramatized show was so disgusting to the core, and I ran as fast as I could. Even to breathe in that environment was like polluting my being.

The prosecutor and the investigator must have gone to the pub to celebrate their score of the day, just like a butcher does. I will continue to lick my wounds till I finally end up in my box.

Joined the Elite Club

It was one summer evening in the mid-1980s. A meeting was called in a big hall somewhere in the Woodford area to nominate new members for the launch of the Lions Club. The rumour reached me through some friends and I decided to attend and seek out membership if possible. It was being organised by C, our good friend. He was running a famous restaurant in the West End area. It was also co-organised by another friend of his friend M, with whom I had close acquaintance. The whole show was being conducted under the supervision of a local senior organiser A of the Lions Club. It was being launched as a new club, with new members, nearly all Asians because of the changing demographic structure of London. The whites were running out to the countryside, the blacks and browns were 'swamping' the streets of London. The flashy cars driven by them were raising eyebrows of the local whites. The shoe was now fitting on the other foot. Jealousies were on the rise, hatred was having its toll, and when the whites could not beat the immigrants' hard work, the unity of their families and their superior work ethics, they were on their flight out. Shops were changing hands and were being converted into the needs of the new residents. Because of this growing prosperity of the Asians, they were now occupying the most sought-after areas in the east of London and beyond. These expensive houses were previously owned by the rich Jewish community who arrived as immigrants from the German holocaust but now these were becoming the pride of the young Asians. The aim of

A JOURNEY THROUGH PARTITION AND BEYOND

the club was to tap the resources of the newly arrived well-to-do community. The same people only a few years earlier were denied the opportunity to join those clubs frequented by the whites. They were banned and were looked down on by the host community. Why must one be rich in life before a due respect is accorded? The poor of the world do not have such low morals.

The hall was fully packed with proud, young, rich businessmen, professionals – the doctors, the dentists, the eye specialists, the accountants, the egotists, the show-offs, the arrogant, the opportunists, the social climbers, and the chatterers. You name it, all kinds of human society were present there, except that they had a brown colour. Within two decades of their arrival on British shores, the fortunes of east London and beyond had changed completely. The men were dressed in their best suits, bows and ties and the ladies, not to be left behind, were wearing their best saris for the occasion. In that well-lit hall they were showing off their newly acquired aristocracy with their glittering and eye-dazzling jewellery and golden ornaments on the exposed parts of their bodies. They had golden necklaces, golden earrings of the latest designs, and bangles on their arms to hide the exposed colour of their skins. They also had rings on their fingers encrusted with diamonds and rubies. Some had their saris and jewellery matching the outfits of their spouses. It was a scene to be witnessed. I saw from a distance, as a stranger, the way of greetings and mannerisms displayed between friends and rivals, especially the womenfolk. They would inspect your outfits at a glance from top to bottom and download your image in their memory lane, an exercise to draw comparisons. It was a futile exercise to determine their position in the hierarchy of the circle, to impress, to demean, and to humble those who belonged to the 'menial' professions of teaching. I was a teacher and had no rings on my fingers either. I was there to take it all. And yet I had the ambition to associate myself with the rich in case I might gain some of their traits to help me elevate myself to their levels. It was a society I hankered to join, a stupid ambition. They were all there to compete with their friends and other families to be the part of that prestigious elite club, just to show a little badge stuck on their shoulder to humble the others. It was a game of jealousy for those better off than you, and pity for those who did not belong to that class.

After entering that impressive mêlée, we went around to greet our friends. I felt low and embarrassed with some and a bit better than others, depending on their status. I too had some chips on my shoulder. I was part of that damned show-off culture. When I bumped into C, I enquired about my chances of being a member of the club.

'Don't worry, I have recommended your name. We need only ten members and all who are here wished to join.'

'Oh, that is quite tough going. Please try, I am very keen to join.'

'I am supporting you. I will make sure you are in.'

'Ok thanks, I will see you around.' And we moved on in the crowd.

After watching and meeting all those friends, soon the bell tolled for the meeting to start. We took our seats. C welcomed the guests, gave the brief of the meeting, and the procedure in selecting members for the new club from the crowd. Then he called upon A to give a brief description and the aims of the Lions Club. So, he went on explaining the lofty aims of the Club to collect for charities with a begging bowl from the public by organising events in public places, and by arranging sponsorships to walk, to run, and suchlike sports activities. Then he threw a piece of bone to the contending 'dogs' saying that whoever ran fastest (that is, collected the maximum funds) would get a free air return ticket and board to America to visit the headquarters of the Club. Here comes the American culture of competitiveness with a reward of a few crumbs. So, it was not a club to enjoy, to be part of and contribute towards its admirable aims, but to compete and be jealous with the same members with whom you would be joining for a noble cause. Was that Club for me, I thought? I kept my options open for the time being rather than sit in judgement. I was still eager to get in to show off the badge to humble those who did not get a chance to get a winning ticket.

A was a very sophisticated speaker and as a senior member he had mastered the art of oratory. In those who had the doubts and were still undecided, he fired the ambition to join. The competition then became even fiercer and more aggressive. Everyone was trying to pitch their flags openly for everyone to see. Then he finally decided to elevate the mood of the audience by telling them a 'joke'. He went on, 'Now I would like to tell you what once happened at Heathrow airport.' He then gave a broad smile. Everyone cheered up to know what happened after listening to his previous eloquent sermon.

'I was flying to Europe. An Asian, appearing to be from Pakistan, asked, "Sir, can you give me £10." I asked "Why, why do you need £10? What are you going to do with £10?". He said, with open hands, "I am flying to Pakistan. I have the rest of the money to buy a ticket but am short of £10. If you help I would be able to return to my country." "No problem," I said. "Here is £20. Get cracking and leave this country. If you know someone else who needs help to leave the country, let me know and I would be delighted to help."'

With his bigoted remarks, he loudly laughed. Some obliged him with a muted nervous laughter. He realised his mistake that he was addressing a largely Asian audience and not the white folks. He immediately added, 'That was only a joke. Please don't take it seriously.' That was the 'joke' of the day. He was lucky that the law against racism was not in place; otherwise he would have found his way into Her Majesty's 'guest house'. He was a charity collector to hand down to the needy but that appeared all farce. Those lofty ideals were only for public

A JOURNEY THROUGH PARTITION AND BEYOND

consumption. I was not amused but I could clearly see the writing on the wall. Yet I was keen to join in and have a taste of the Club's 'lofty' ideals. It was the practical experience I wanted to have - to know how these elite clubs operate. I was mingling with the same kind of people and the ambition to beat them was alive and kicking. My father always attended such clubs in India but then I was just a kid and did not know the ethics on which such clubs functioned. I was an egotist in those days, had a chip on my shoulder, and wanted to show off that I was different than the other-worldly crowds too. I wanted to show that I was there to elevate my ego by helping those have-nots, taking them out of the misery and poverty in which they were caught. It was a trip to ego-boosting leading to arrogance.

After a couple more self-indulgent speeches, M, a 'friend' of C but an arch rival was invited to say a few words. He gave a blistering short speech and demeaned the list prepared by C and said, 'I smell a rat and conspiracy in the preparation of that list and I oppose it.' It was a bombshell for me. My hopes to become a member were dashed. I knew M was pointing towards me and a couple more candidates he did not support. He had his own list and asked the audience to support it. After that speech the meeting was over. The horse-trading session between the sponsors started in earnest. I hurriedly dashed down to C to emphasise once more that I would like to become a member. Once again, he assured me that it would happen. It did happen when the list was announced later; I was declared to be a member of that elite club. So were C and M. I was delighted and looked forward to work within the system to make my small contributions.

How it all operated

The meetings used to take place during the weekdays from 7 to 9pm in a club where food was also served. We paid for the food and the hiring of the meeting room. I used to leave my family after school at the house of one of our friends, where they would eat and wait for my arrival and then we all would return home arriving sometimes at 11pm. It used to be a long, arduous day for all of us.

Meetings were arranged as usual like a business meeting. The chair would ask for the progress for the last assignments, collections during the campaigns, and distribution of the funds to charities. After attending a few meetings, I felt the way they were being conducted was oppressive. The whole environment created was depressive and agonising. It was like you were a cog in the system and the chair would question you as if you were a slave. The chair would act dictatorially, question you and your report as if you were an employee of the organisation. It was never a conducive and friendly environment. You were made small, criticised, and treated like an underdog. All of them present wanted to score a point and try to prove themselves as superior. Their behaviour was as if they belonged to a political establishment where ruthlessness, manoeuvering, and downgrading of others is a norm. Their eyes were fixed on that dangling carrot of a free visit to the promised land of America where the club had its headquarters. I used to be mostly a silent observer. I continued to take all that was given to me and tolerated all that arrogance. I found no outlets for my contributions because everyone else was competing for the time to say something to impress.

They were also arranging some fund-raising parties in some good venues. Again, the atmosphere used to be 'show off' - what you were wearing, how you were talking, at whose table you were sitting, and how noisy and extrovert you were. All these traits were alien to me. I was a quiet, mind-my-own-business type of individual. I was a person who would like to sit silently somewhere in a lonely corner of the hall and just watch the various scenes being played by different groups in a theatrical get-together, without being bothered about who were the actors and what was the content of that story being told. The other people would move around from table to table, engage in a small talk for a couple of minutes, and then would disappear to another table with someone more interesting and articulate where they would get more joy. All this high-class competitive society depressed me. I soon figured out that I did not belong there. I was just wasting my time in trying to butter-up people to have their attention. It was all cheap and demoralising high-class society where jealousy ruled. Rather than becoming happy, dancing and singing, I used to feel miserable and disorientated. It used to take me a few days to shed that lousy experience of the meeting.

I also had some problems with the food being served at the meetings. I like to have a social drink to last me for the whole evening, but I do not want to engage in a drinking spree. I am also a vegetarian and can never eat meat because I do not believe in killing animals to end up on my plate. This obviously offends a lot of people. They feel guilty when they must share the same table with people like me and I don't blame them. Such people even would refuse to share the heavens if they came to know that it is a boring place because people like Gandhi, Guru Nanak, Jesus, and Buddha live there. They would rather go to hell where they can have fun with the virgin prostitutes and with the vagabonds. They would love to loiter around where there are shopping malls, coffee houses, bars, and casinos where they could fool around with the bunny girls. Obviously, my company to them was boring. I hasten to add that I am not trying to compare myself with noble people like Gandhi. I am only saying that mingling at social parties is always more enjoyable by sharing the table with like-minded people.

Because of my food habits, I was always an odd-man-out in the social circle. They all would have their meals to their hearts' content.

I used to be hungry after the whole day's work at school, and then being confronted with a dinner plate in the meeting with unpalatable food was the last straw. To be on the safe side, I used to order salad. One day, salad was served ceremoniously with a piece of ham sitting on the top. The friends looked at my plate with concern, called the waitress, and protested how on earth she dared serve me vegetarian salad with a piece of ham on top. She walked away apologetically with that plate and came back within seconds with a plate. I took my knife and fork and folded the green leaves of the lettuce with a piece of cucumber and as I was about to put the piece into my mouth, I noticed with horror the blood stains on the other greens. The waitress had probably taken away the piece of ham, turned the blood-soaked leaves upside down and brought me back the same plate. I put the knife and fork down and sat there motionlessly. Soon the other diners noticed that I was not eating. So, they enquired, 'Om, why are you not eating?'

'Well, my salad is laced with blood. I just cannot face this plate any more. I am disappointed with the way the caterers are treating me.'

'Well, before we selected this venue for our meetings we told them that there are some people who need vegetarian catering and they promised that they would cater for all tastes.'

The chair called the waitress and protested and asked her to serve me a vegetarian meal. She had none available. I also refused to eat any food. I was feeling pains inside my being and I was no longer in a mood to swallow food from there. I felt grateful that the waitress did not wash the same salad and then bring it back. That would have been awful cheating. However, the matter ended there.

On my way home, I began to feel restless and uncomfortable. I felt depressed about why on earth I was wasting my time with that type of egotistic people and putting up with food I could not eat. With those ideas hovering in my mind, I knew a day had to come when I would say to myself 'enough is enough, I will now have to quit.' That lingering murky situation was not good for mental health and I had to resolve it, the earlier the better. I told my family about the incident and told them that I had decided to quit the Club. From that day I stopped attending the club's meetings.

A couple of months went by and I had a stinging letter from one of the members who claimed to be in charge of the membership. He demanded that I should return all the badges, the membership card, any money I owed, and any other relevant papers I had been given. He also warned me not to use or proclaim myself as part of the Lions Club. The contents of the letter were insulting, demoralising, and disrespectful. I never expected that the organisation of which I was a member, only a couple of months ago, would treat me so arrogantly. But this is how this bunch of people behaved. They felt that they, having joined the LC, were now in the ranks of the elites of the world and the others on this planet were just scum. I wrote back protesting my innocence and giving my reasons for leaving. I said, 'I don't feel proud to be part of such an organisation.' I sent all the relevant papers. I was the most relieved person on the planet on that day. I had my sanity back and the bout of depressions for belonging to such an organisation disappeared like smoke.

A few months later I met this member at a party. He had no membership badge on him. As a curiosity I enquired, 'How are you? I do not see you wearing your upper-class membership badge. What happened?' 'I have resigned my membership. I did not like it. A lot of new blood has joined and some old hats have gone. You left in good time.' I did not wish to pursue the contents of the letter he wrote to me. It was history and there was no need to dig out the old graves to win a point. He is a dentist by profession.

Good-Bye Teaching
Teaching has its charms and those charms are only there if the recipients, the children, are as enthusiastic to learn as the teacher is willing to teach. They are there to share his experiences and he is eager to pass on his knowledge to the future mums and dads of the country. It is his duty to train them to become responsible citizens of the country as well as of the world. The teaching job then becomes most satisfying, rewarding, and encouraging. If these ingredients are missing and the children are not motivated by the expectations of society and the parents, then it just becomes a baby-minding job for the teacher. In that scenario it is better for him to quit the profession honourably and enjoy and indulge in other activities of his life, thus relieving himself from the burdens of minding other people's children.

Most of the schools in Britain, with my experience, are just operated as baby minding places. It is so disheartening to discover that most of the teacher's time is going into maintaining discipline in the classroom. If a teacher can achieve that goal, the heads are happy, the educational hierarchy is happy, and the parents are happy. But the teacher is most frustrated because although he could maintain the discipline, he did not get enough time to teach. All his energy and time had gone in keeping the children quiet. That is why the teachers are under continuous stress. He is sandwiched between the educational bureaucrats, the children, and their parents. It is a three-way tug-of-war. The children are unruly in the classroom because they come from all kinds of backgrounds. The teachers are given the responsibilities but no authority. It is a thankless job. Once a man commented when I told him that I was a teacher in school, 'Oh, only you teachers get so many paid holidays.' I retorted, 'Society has a choice. Either it gives the teachers extra holidays to recover from the classroom stress or open more mental hospitals for them to be admitted.' That is very true. All the teachers suffer from a stressful life in the classrooms. Of course, this would vary from one school to the other. I only speak from my experience and the type of schools I taught in.

A JOURNEY THROUGH PARTITION AND BEYOND

You are exposed to so much noise and behavioural problems that by the end of the school day you are totally exhausted – mentally, physically, and emotionally. In my case I was given a known notorious class in the school where I had joined in September. In my first lesson as I entered the classroom, I found the children were running around everywhere and jumping on the chairs and the benches. They were noisy and screaming. The whole environment was utterly chaotic. I stood there dumbstruck. I was totally lost and had no clue where to start and what to say and what to do. I had no clue how to deal with that kind of situation. I had never come across such unruly children so far in my career. Nearly all the children, save four or five, were Bangladeshis. This was even more surprising. I had the opinion that children coming from parents of third world countries were better behaved, but I was shocked. It was amazing how the new generation of the settled immigrants had changed within the society they were now living. To make matters worse, to my horror I noticed that a couple of teachers and the head of the department were watching me in the corridor and smiling. They knew what kind of kids were in that class. It was obvious that I was given this class to monitor my ability in controlling that unruly bunch. It was like throwing me into a cage filled with monkeys. I could do nothing. I did not know how to shout. So, I let them create the pandemonium in the classroom as much as they wished. They were in-charge and I was only a witness to that chaos. It was their way of welcoming a new teacher, to show him their power. There was no leader to lead them, it had all the signs of mob rule. I looked at the colleagues outside with enquiring eyes for help, but they just shrugged their shoulders and grinned. I only could cry at their treatment. I grant that they were right not to interfere as that would have resulted in my losing control of the other classes too. The rumour soon spreads by word of mouth about the abilities of new teachers. But I was disappointed that the head had given me such a rough class right in the beginning without letting me settle down in the school.

'Am I a failure?' I enquired in the staffroom. They assured me that I was not to be blamed. All of them had the same experience with them. I, being a new teacher in that school – the kids were testing my mettle. The kids always do that. However, that left a long-lasting experience and I started questioning my involvement in that profession even more. When I was transferred to this school, I had a mind to continue to go on teaching but now I was beginning to question it and started thinking about getting out of it for good.

The other events, which affected me most to reconsider my future once more, are worth mentioning below:

1.   I was sitting on my own in the staff room as it was my free period. The bell tolled to announce the lunch break. I heard a deafening noise of

dashing children, running to the playground as if they had been let loose from their prison rooms, manned by the disappointed and disgruntled teachers. The door of the staffroom slammed open and it was D, the science teacher. He slumped himself into an armchair opposite to me. I could see his pensive pale face as if he had been to a mortuary. I could not resist finding out why he was in that depressive state. He was normally always cheerful, happy, and would say 'hello' or 'morning'. He had a master's in chemistry from Cambridge and then had been a research scientist at ICI. I always wondered why on earth he was wasting his life in teaching in such a school where the learners were totally un-motivated and had no clue of the basics of the English language. Fate is always cruel to all of us but in his case perhaps it was worse. So, I started, 'D, what happened, you don't look very happy. Has something gone wrong in the classroom today?'

'No, that is ok. I'd just rather not talk.'

'Why not, it is better to share the mental burdens. It would ease the pain,' I persisted. He still would not come out of his mental shell. I tried once more before I thought of giving up. I knew that Englishmen like to be left alone to sort out their problems. But I knew him well and that is why I tried once more. This time he cracked open, 'You know, today I did a survey with my class children to learn where this country was heading. I asked every child in turn how many children there were in their families. One said five sir, another one seven sir, again four sir, and so on. On average every family had five to seven children. I have only one child and I am fifty-eight and I live in Harrow. I have seen house after house being taken over by people of your colour. Street after street has been lost to foreigners. I walk on the roads and I am the lonely Englishman there. I am a foreigner in my own land. I have calculated that demographically this country will be ruled by foreigners in fifty years. I have lost my country.'

He wailed. His voice was choked, not with anger but with painful emotions. He was on the verge of crying. I could see the helplessness of an Englishman, well educated, decent, cultured, and respectful, in agony to see the reins of his country just slipping away and yet he could not do anything to control that change. He was helpless, powerless. The politicians of the day and the ones before had let him and millions of their countrymen down by allowing a 'free for all' attitude. I could now see why he was reluctant to share his views with me. He thought I was one of 'them'. The school had 95% Bangladeshi children.

'I understand your agony D. The whole world is in a melting pot now. I have seen the same thing in America. I am at a loss to understand why the politicians have opened the floodgates of this country. One can only slow down this change, but no one can stop that change. That is a fact of life. If it helps this country, I am happy to pack up and "go back to my country."'

A JOURNEY THROUGH PARTITION AND BEYOND

'No, that is not going to help. It is the type of people the British government is allowing to enter.'

I knew his concern was genuine and I also agree with him to a large extent. I have seen a huge demographic change since the day I arrived in this country in 1958. His agony was also deep and understandable. All changes are painful when they happen from a settled life. He could not visualise the world in the making. He had no idea about the morrow's world coming. He was not looking at the changing world we live in today. The whole world is in a melting pot right now. It is a change no one can alter and stop. The nationalists of the lands are fighting to maintain their individuality, their culture, their religions, and their way of life. Jihadis are in arms to maintain their hegemony and the tenets of their religion written 1500 years ago. They continue to live in yesterday's world and follow its outdated philosophies. The Sikhs in India had agitated because their offspring were refusing to keep their turbans and beards required by their Guru a few hundred years ago. The Hindus wish us to continue to read the Vedas and recite those scriptures. They also wish to put the clock back to five thousand years ago. The Christians insist on us to keep on believing in the non-written philosophies of Jesus which were added on to their scriptures by later priests. They all want us to live in yesterday's world. The men of the world like to maintain their superiority over the womenfolk by dominating them and keeping them within the four walls as isolated and uneducated. But they will never succeed. The inventions of the Web, mobile phones, computers, TVs, air travel and holidays would never allow that. I have seen a hell of a change within the last 80-odd years, from a donkey ride to a rocket ride. I must move on with the times. While I could see the pain in D's eyes, I could also notice that he was not changing with the times. His suffering would continue to multiply. No one can stop the flow of the rivers to meet their destination – the ocean. The streams will continue to strike themselves on the rocks, the boulders and the trees to gather momentum to achieve their goal. The whole world, including the cosmos, will continue to remain in flux from moment to moment. It is their nature, and no one can stop it. Nature loves change, and it does not stop, ever.

2. 95% of the children were of the recent arrivals of the Bangladeshi community. The children would tell us that they were not allowed to watch TV or listen to music at home. But how are they going to learn the English language and speak like an East Ender cockney if they were not watching and listening to the media? It was a future time-bomb for race relations. Furthermore 99% of the kids were having a free meal. We knew that their fathers were working in restaurants at Brick Lane and were earning good money, but we could not report them because of some left-wing leaning staff who were always fighting the system so that the free meals should continue. The children were also getting allowances

335

for buying clothes and books. Some of the fathers were claiming dole money even while working - a scandal, but we dare not raise our voice. They also had free council flats. They were going on holidays to Bangladesh nearly every two years. The womenfolk were laden with golden jewellery when they left UK and came back empty-handed leaving all their jewellery in that country. Some of the people working there at businesses had never ventured out from the Brick Lane areas. They only know Bengali. They live there as Bangladeshis, they work with Bangladeshis; they think as Bangladeshis, they buy and sell to Bangladeshis, and they hate the non-Bangladeshis. This is New Britain in the making where hatred between the communities will become the norm in the future.

3. A number of times I got into an argument with a leftist teacher who would condemn me for exploiting my staff working at my factory. I was fed up with the job and was not motivated to carry on thankless teaching. It was immoral to keep on teaching simply because it gave me enough of my daily bread. Meanwhile, it was clear that the school was going to be closed down. Somehow, he came to know that I was planning to set up a business once the school was closed. I was 50 at the time. I could not see anything wrong in setting up a business to create a few jobs with my part-time entrepreneurship and risks of losing all my family income. What was wrong if I just did not wish to join the dole queue and claim handouts from the government after being booted out of the school when closed? He could not see the daylight. One day we got into an argument when he taunted me about the ethics of running a business and not giving away the extra cash to the needy. I knew he had a council flat in the area. I asked, 'How many bedrooms have you in the flat?' 'Three,' he replied. 'So, you have two bedrooms extra available at your flat. Why don't you give those bedrooms to someone who has no shelter and share the rest of the flat with him/her?' 'No, I cannot let anyone else share the flat with me.' 'Ok, why don't you ask the council to rent you a single bedroom flat so that someone with a family can live in your flat?' 'No, I like to have a bigger flat. I need to use the second bedroom to play music and the third for my visiting relations from Scotland.' 'So why are you lecturing me about the ethics and exploitations when you yourself are not prepared to share your flat with someone who has got no place to live? People always have double standards. One for themselves and the other for lecturing to the outsiders.' On another occasion we went to attend a meeting at County Hall to discuss the closing down of the school. I took three more teachers in my car. On our return, one colleague suggested that they should pay me 50p per person to compensate me for the fuel costs. I declined their gesture and did not take any but this leftist burst out again with his filthy language, 'No, why should we pay him? He has enough money saved up by exploiting the poor workers at his factory. It is my right to travel free in his car. I would not pay even a penny.' What can you say to this loudmouth, and

he carried on till I left him at his doorstep. He was the last to be dropped and insisted that I should not drop him at school but take him to his flat. I did. On that last leg of the journey, there were only the two of us. He went on with his leftist vendetta without any hitch and I continued to listen to his music with amusement.

CHAPTER 8: HELLO TO A NEW BUSINESS VENTURE

People like me can never sit and wait for things to happen. You make events. You make the future move. You control your destiny against all odds. It is your nature. You never quit when the storms are on the horizon and its wind is changing its direction. You just bend down when the hurricanes hit your boat and you stand up again once the calmness returns. When I put my foot on this soil, my fists were clenched tight with my destiny safely inside them. All the ingredients of life's successes and failures were enclosed there. I must fulfil that destiny. I cannot leave this side of the shores without accomplishing the tasks assigned to me by my maker. And when I finally go, all the fuels stored up in the hands would be used up and I will leave this planet with my empty hands widely open. The share of the energy which was allotted to me by the Existence will be joined back to the maker and this body will return into the mother earth whence it came. For as long as that dust is alive and kicking with that energy I must carry on.

I had such a hard time in my previous venture at the Leyton shop that no one in his right mind would ever think of going into business again. I did. Destiny keeps on knocking at my door and is leading me through my noose. I keep on talking about destiny time and again but that is what I believe, and it has always been a signpost to me.

I saw an advertisement in the local newspaper that there were small industrial units available for start-up businesses. I looked at the advertisement and decided to do something but did not know what. I was fed up with my job. There was no satisfaction in it except that it gave me enough of my daily bread and a pension whenever I retired. Also, I heard rumours that the school I was teaching in would be closed within months because it was dominated by 95% Bangladeshi children and that was not acceptable to the local authorities. They were waking up to the facts of life. The teachers would be seconded to other schools or given an early retirement with an enhancement of 10 years' service to their pensions. I was fifty. I was young enough to take on the world but also old enough for society to

A JOURNEY THROUGH PARTITION AND BEYOND

throw me onto a waste heap. Who on earth would give me a job now when they had never considered my CVs ten years earlier? I was not made for that waste heap and I was also not available to stand in the dole queue. So, the ventures written by the existence in my closed fists were forcing me to go for the destiny, written on the wall. The wise people say, 'Think twice before you jump,' but I jumped without thinking. I was ready to face the music come what may. The music is created with the up and down notes of the rhythm. Life is like music: it moves through the valleys and the mountains. It never moves in a straight, boring line. It is only in death that there is no music. It is a drag. It is a lifeless corpse which never responds to the challenges of life, has no emotions and struggles because the dynamism of life is missing. The rose must die to be recreated. It is the plastic rose which lives forever.

But I knew it was going to be difficult to convince my wife. I knew she would never agree. However, it was time to confront her and I did when I got the moment.

'I am going to lease a factory in Braintree. I know you will be against it, but I have no choice because my school is closing down within a couple of years and I want to set up something as a part-timer so that when it is closed down I have something to do.'

'But what are you going to do with the premises after leasing it?' She asked a genuine question.

'I don't know. I have no ideas. Something will evolve itself but what? I do not know at this moment. However, I am going to lease the premises for three years. I know you are not going to support me, but I would ask you that this time you do not oppose me and criticise me either. Let me have a free hand to do what I want to do without your interference.'

'That is foolish when you do not know even what you are going to do there. Ok, I will not criticise you.'

The die was cast to move forward. I went ahead to lease a council factory at Springwood Industrial Estate from 19th April 1981. It was a newly built factory of 850 sq. ft. I decided on making samosas and onion bhajis and selling them to the fish & chip shops.

We named our company 'Virome Enterprises' from a combination of the letters of our names. Then in the late 1990s we were supplying snacks to a 'John', whose company was 'Natures Finest'. He stopped buying after a couple of years but owed us £25k. He said he wouldn't pay us but by proxy, if we liked, we could use the name 'Natures Finest'. As if he owned it. You cannot trade mark this name as it a is generic common word. So, it cost us £25k.

We went out to buy the catering equipment in Forest Gate, London. We bought an electric chip fryer, mixing bowls, stainless steel tables and other relevant equipment. Then we went to the job centre to hire a chef, a sales/manager and a helper to the chef. Now once more I had changed from an employee to an employer. The job centre provided me excellent help and guidance. They reserved an interviewing room at the centre and short-listed the suitable candidates to be interviewed. I explained to the candidates the whole plan for the venture. I told them that they would have to manage the place themselves in my absence. I would not be there. They would have to maintain their attendance, lunch and tea breaks, their productivity, and open and close the factory. The whole show would be run on their honesty and integrity. I trained the chef how to make the bhajis. I gave instructions to the salesperson to take some of the onion bhajis made by the chef, along with bought-in samosas, to all the local fish & chip shops around us to test the market. He was a very good salesperson, conscientious, honest, and hard working. He used our van which I still had from my shop days. He catalogued all the names of the shops he visited, their telephone numbers, the owners' names, and their replies. For samosas the reply was, 'We have never heard of them,' and for the bhajis, 'No we do not wish to sell them.' The results were surprising but expected. I thought the British tastes were changing and the public was ready to accept the new Indian snacks because of the recent popularity of the Indian restaurants. But I was wrong. The results showed that the public was not yet ready. The salesperson expressed his opinion that these products would have no market and I should find something else to sell. As I was trying to assess what I should try next, the salesperson, knowing that I would have no future and might even close, laid down his tools and left within three weeks. That was a setback as I could not try the market without a salesman. As expected, soon the chef also left.

In the meantime I was also hunting a sweet-maker who could make Indian sweets and samosas. I found one in London who was from Pakistan and he joined me in May 1981. I later learnt, after he left me in October, that he used to work in UK for six months at sweet shops in London, get paid in cash, and never paid national insurance and tax. He would then go back to his country for the rest of the year. On his return he would claim back all the tax paid by the employer. He was uneducated but very 'clever' in his financial affairs, better than the educated. While he cheated the world wherever he could, he was also smart enough to say his prayers five times a day to hoodwink the Almighty too. Why spare Him? It was my beginning in meeting the scum of this planet. He lived in our house. I had to go back to London again every Friday evening, after paying him his wages in cash (he never accepted cheques), so that he could enjoy his weekend with his cronies or might even be working for cash in some other shops. He had been doing all that for years. He built a farm in his country with this loot. He had no fear of the law of the land. That was all settled in bribing the Lord. On Sunday I would go back in the evening to London to fetch him back. I was paying £150 cash in hand

A JOURNEY THROUGH PARTITION AND BEYOND

+ NI + tax + free food + free transport + living. The service he provided – 'great'. One day, I came back early from school and went to the factory. I found the god-fearing man was deep in sleep on the floor.

As the demand for the samosas was not there yet, the staff hired to make and sell them left as they knew that they would have no future with me. I got some orders for sweets from a restaurant at Brick Lane. The sweets business was quite profitable. I would go and see the managers of restaurants in the area at lunch time and get the orders. Later we also added to our product line Bombay Mixes and other related snacks. Again, the margins were good. I hired more staff, mostly of Pakistani origin, and one Iranian. I would call them from school to know progress. I was still losing some money that I would make up from our teaching income, but the progress was good. I was employing nearly six full-timers.

My school closed in July 1984 and I was transferred to Stepney Green School. I taught there until July 1985 and left to work full-time at my business. My daughter had already gone to college in London to study fine arts and my son was going to a local high school. Mira did not like to travel on her own to London, so she also decided to resign her teaching job and joined me in the factory.

At the time the business was being managed by the Iranian. He controlled all the buying, the selling, managing the money and the men. He knew the margins, the customers, and the know-how of the products we were making. I mentioned to one of our customers in London that I was planning to go into business full-time. Greed has no limits. This customer not only told the Iranian manager about my future but hatched a plan with him to open other premises in Braintree with his partnership. The manager, who was already stealing goods from our factory and selling them, speeded up the stealing process to accumulate enough funds to open another factory just a few hundred yards down the road from us. Within two weeks of my joining, he took all our business, all our customers, and all our employees to his new premises. In a nutshell - I had zero sales, zero customers, and zero employees. I had nothing but an empty shell with some equipment. All new staff had to be hired, trained, and then new customers found. Basically, we had to start the whole business again from scratch. So, the choice was to close for good or meet the challenge. I was 54 years old at the time, a critical time of life to accept a challenge. I picked up the gauntlet. Basically, I am not a quitter.

So, we hired new staff, trained them, and started producing once more. We discontinued the manufacture of Indian sweets as they had to be made fresh and delivered fresh the same day to London. It was too laborious and time-consuming. Also, the shops we were supplying to were all taken over by the ex-manager. As we were under continuous threat, we decided to maintain the confidentiality of our business. We decided that Mira would sit at home and campaign for new customers. We continued to make Bombay Mixes, roasting nuts etc. and business started rolling in and within six months we rented a 1500 sq. ft. factory next door.

Every day at lunch time F, my Iranian ex-manager, would send his crony employees, who had worked for me before, to park their car outside our factory. They would sit there for a couple of hours, gaze at our staff to intimidate them, laugh, and make faces at them. He even approached my key staff member, offered him a job, and asked him to quit from my place. My Pakistani driver who continued to work for me was also mixed up with him. This driver cut off our telephone wires and we had no telephone for at least 10 days. The telephone engineer when repairing the system found out that the wires were cut off under the table. The double crossing of the driver was reported to me by the new key employee on one Monday morning who asked, 'How much do you trust the driver?'

'I have full confidence in him and his loyalty.'

'You know he invited me to a house to see another person who owns a factory like yours around the corner. That person offered me a job in his factory and asked me to stop working for you. But I declined. I was horrified that the driver you are trusting was working against you. How can he do that?'

That confirmed that the telephone wires were cut off by the driver. I did not tell him what I knew about his stabbing me in the back. The driver worked for another couple of months and buggered off to help F.

Another previous employee who had gone on holiday did not report for work on the due date. He came back after 4 days absenteeism. Maybe he had joined F's company but came back to me to give some trouble. All these activities were well planned by F. I said to the employee that his vacancy had been filled as he had not come back to report to work on the due date. Also, he had not informed me that he would be late in resuming his job. He went away and sent me a threatening letter from a solicitor about taking me to a tribunal. He had not worked long enough to take me to tribunal. But I was scared to go to court and I paid the damages he claimed. Later I came to know that he was indeed already working for F.

Then F also took me to a tribunal with the help of the woman in charge of a local citizens' advice bureau. His case was for unfair dismissal, even though he had left voluntarily to open his new business. My case was bungled by my barrister who negotiated the settlement out of court to pay F £1700 within two weeks. We were there in the court to argue our case, but the barrister never consulted us before reaching the agreement. In addition to £1700, F also owed us more than £4000 he had borrowed to get his father here from Iran and for the deposit we paid when he was buying a house. All had gone. The house we helped him to buy became his asset and he used it as equity to borrow more money from the building society towards buying the equipment and renting a three times bigger factory than ours. He was kicked out by his wife whom he married as a convenience to stay in the country. She was nearly twice his age. We kept him in our house for nearly three months until the completion of his three-bedroom house. That help and the house he very cleverly used against us. I was shattered at the tribunal's outcome. On the way back from the court I could not stop the tears welling down my cheeks. If that was the reward for helping someone in settling in the country, then it is a stinking world we live in. Was it a crime to go back to my own business which I had set up with hard work and with a lot of investment and losses simply to secure my future when I was made redundant? I was disillusioned, sad, and very hurt. I had treated F like my son and helped him all the way and that is what he gave me – heartache.

F did not survive for very long. He was gifted with one evil. He was a gambler on the horses. With his good income from his business, set up with stolen money from my business, he used to stake all his income on the horses. I was told this by one of his Iranian employees who wanted me to give him a job in my factory when F went bust. F had accumulated a debt of more than £100,000 to his suppliers, bank, and building society. F called me to meet him in the town for a chat to help and take him back into my business again. I refused to meet him. He went bankrupt. His house was repossessed, and he left the town to run a taxi in London I came to know later.

A few months later, I had the opportunity to talk on the phone to the woman who helped F at the Citizens Advice. I mentioned to her that once upon a time she had vigorously defended my previous employee who opened the factory against me but had gone under with £100k of other people's money. He had not paid the wages to his employees. What had she got to say to me about her action of supporting a wrong person that had resulted into 100k losses to banks, to employees, and to suppliers? 'Well Mr Khurana, it is a history now. What is the point of talking about it now?' For her it was 'history now' but for me it was heart-breaking, painful, and sleepless nights which I can never forget until I die. She was aggressive in negotiating the settlement with my barrister at the court and tried to prove that I was a villain. She wanted to forget all that now because it did not suit her to talk about it. It was far easier for her now to pass the whole episode into history that did not suit her. I did not pursue further with her. I did not want to rub in the 'history' she had made and embarrass her. How many other cases had she bungled to punish innocents like me, only she would know.

Another Destiny's Miracle – The Shine of a Glittering Diamond

People say that there are no miracles. I say that there are, and it happened to me so often and so many times. It may be for the good or for the bad, but they have come to change the fortunes of my life. As I said before that it once happened when I was appearing for my finals and a man came to say, 'Bad luck.' Where did this man come from and how did he come to predict my future without even knowing me? He had not seen the life lines on my palm or seen the rays on my forehead that the fortune tellers of India use. Obviously, this man had some intuitive feelings or some other natural energy force in predicting my fate. So, this time another miracle was being enacted in the summer of 1984.

I was working at the factory during my summer holidays and F had gone for the delivery to London. Around lunch time, an unannounced angel walked in.

'Hello, I am Smith and I work for the council. What do you do here?'

'Oh, we make some Asian snacks and sweets.'

'How long have you been doing it?'

'We started in April 1981 from scratch.'

'How is the business now?'

'It is growing. I am very happy with the way it is moving forward. We have some good customers.'

'Are you the owner of this business?'

'Yeah, it is a family business. I am a teacher in London and running the show part-time as my school is closing. We have set the business up so that when I am kicked out of the school system I will have something to do in life.'

'That is a very good idea! It appears soon you will run out of space here. Would you like to have a bigger place?'

'I would love to if I can get hold of it.'

'The council has a piece of land in the east of Braintree. I am authorised to allocate the land to you. It is 0.6 of an acre. In fact, it was allocated to another local industry, but they cannot develop it as they have not got the resources. Therefore, they have returned the land back to us. They have kept some as per their needs. The catch is that you must develop it within five years of the date on which it is allocated to you. Keep what you need for your own use and rent the rest of it to anyone you like. The council would have no objections. The land would be given to you on an option to buy the freehold within five years or lease it for 99 years. I don't know the freehold price yet which I must work out and let you know. Would you be interested in this proposal?'

'I would be delighted to have a factory of our own!'

'Ok, let me go back to my office to find out the situation of the land. If it is available, I will send you a written offer and the price. Here is my card. If you need to talk to me, please come and see me.'

With that note 'the angel' disappeared into the dreamland whence he came. I did not show my emotions in front of him, but I was absolutely exhilarated. If he was not an angel or a messenger of God, then who was he? Who made him come to me and throw that lifetime opportunity in my way? I did not know him. I never met him. I was an Asian; he could have just as soon walked away after saying hello to me. He just dropped in out of the blue, a real blue. To me it was obviously the divine's intervention which directed him towards me, the totally unknown Asian. You may laugh at it but that would not alter my opinion. It must be a miracle, nothing else. I could only look towards the heavens and send my heartfelt thanks. The cosmos was shining at me like a dazzling diamond and was throwing this chance of a lifetime in my way. Why not, I am part of them and the whole universe is mine. I am not going to take it away anywhere. It is going to stay right there where it is now for posterity.

When the offer did not come after a few weeks I felt concerned and went to see him. He said it was being sorted out. The council was waiting for the written reply from the people to whom the land was offered that they were no longer interested in taking up the offer. It took nearly three months before a letter of offer arrived and I held my breath during that time. You never know in case fate was playing a cruel game of hope and hopelessness. We were offered 0.6 acres of land for £52,500 to buy freehold within five years otherwise pay the ground rent of £500 per year for 99 years. The land had to be developed within five years. If it was not developed it would be returned to the council. So, the offer was to take it, develop it, and then keep it for life, or, if development was not successful, return it back to the council with no penalties. The council could not be more generous than that. I accepted that great offer with gratitude but with protests from my wife that I should reject it.

All opportunities create difficulties too in turn. In an unguarded moment, I gave the good news to F that soon 'We would be constructing our own factory designed to suit our own growing businesses.' I disclosed this to him in order to share with him the news of the future of the business. But in hindsight it happened to be a terrible mistake. I had blindly trusted him and had always shared the developments regarding the business with him. That news made him jealous and I think from that point onwards he started planning to destroy whatever we had achieved so far.

New Opportunities with New Challenges

In life it is easy to go down the hill, but it becomes a bigger challenge to climb up again. I had committed to have the horse but how I would ride on it became a nightmare. I was now a lonely man. How would I assemble the resources to develop the land? I had no liquid cash as a personal contribution towards the development of the site. I could offer my house to the bank as collateral, but would they accept it? That was for the future. F was now manoeuvering to destroy my ambitions and grab those opportunities for himself if I failed.

If experience was a guide, I knew that my wife would also oppose me all the way. She had always proved negative to any venture I put my heart into. However, I had accepted the offer and my job now was to get on with developing the land. However, the mantra of 'Sell it, get rid of it, we do not want it' continued even three years after we had developed the whole site, were using two units for ourselves and were renting the other four units.

The business was expanding; we had rented another 1500 sq. ft next door to meet the demand for our products. One big customer, who was deceiving me and was joining F's venture, eventually decided not to join F and came back to us to buy not all his requirements but most. Maybe F's quality was poor. Mira made several more customers by sitting at home. Later she started coming to the factory. To protect one big order near Christmas, we were taking the goods home and getting them packed there in our kitchen so that the information about this customer did not leak out to F by some unscrupulous employee.

It was mid-1986. Within a year of our taking over, we were soon going to outgrow those extended rented premises. We needed to invest in automatic machinery to pack our goods and we had no space for that. So, the land we acquired from the council was timely and needed developing. We had made up all the business we had lost to F and we started thinking of constructing the new units we needed to move to. We were now looking towards the future. The painful past had gone into history. The nuisance of F was always hanging there because of his intimidation techniques, but to me he was a spent force. I took the attitude of an elephant that walks majestically in a street with his trunk saluting to the onlookers but waggles his tail to the barking dogs behind him.

The Construction of Factories

Now the time was ripe to employ an architect to design a building, just enough for our present needs, arrange the finance, and get the construction started. The architect, who was recommended by a friend, made a cock up of the first unit. I, being a novice in the design of industrial buildings, signed the copy of the design. It remains a sore to this day. Trusting people has always been my 'weakness' and for this habit I have paid heavily throughout my life. But still, I would not go against my nature. If the others are not prepared to leave their habits of stinging me, why would I leave my nature of trusting others? It may sound stupidity in the world we live in but that is what I believe and would continue to believe. It was built into my nature when I was only a five-year-old kid. My mother used to tell me some stories while going to bed. She told me the following story many times and that had dug itself deeply into my veins. It is buried into every grain and every cell of my body:

A JOURNEY THROUGH PARTITION AND BEYOND

A spectator was standing on a bridge and was witnessing a scene on a river below. He saw a saintly looking swimmer trying to save a scorpion that was flowing in the fast-moving river currents. He rushed to retrieve it to save it. The scorpion stung him and fell in the stream again. The man grabbed it again and the scorpion stung him again and fell back into the stream. The man attempted again, and the scorpion stung him and fell back into the river again. The spectator could not resist anymore and shouted, 'Hey genius, aren't you mad? You have been stung thrice and you keep on saving the scorpion. Why don't you just leave it and let it be drowned?' The wise swimmer retorted, 'The nature of the scorpion is to sting, and my nature is to be kind and save its life. If the scorpion does not change its nature, why should I change my nature?'

This story has a great hidden teaching in it. I have followed the same rules of that wise man. I have been stung many times in my life and I would not trade my teachings for anything. Without any guiding principles in life we are nothing but animals. Nay, I said it wrong. Even animals have their principles and they would not do what is against nature.

However, the design done, I went to my bank manager with a business plan and he agreed to finance it. The architects, who were also supervising the construction, tendered the project and hired a building contractor. The construction started. We got the first invoice from the architect to pay to the contractor. By law we were to pay the contractor within 15 days of the date when the invoice was raised. I went to see the bank manager to let him know that we were going to issue a cheque for £20,000 to pay to the contractor for the construction. The bank manager refused. He said that he had agreed to give us a loan for the project subject to us injecting some personal cash to show our commitment. They were insisting that we had to sell our freehold property in London rather than giving it as collateral. I did not like it. Now I was desperate to rescue the project. The construction stopped, the contract became null and void, and the builder was demanding compensation and damages for the default. I had troubles, troubles, and plenty of troubles. I looked towards the cosmos and I could not see any ray of hope from the shining diamonds. They had all gone to sleep for a while.

I had met one of my old poly colleagues at an exhibition in Chelmsford; he had set up a business for arranging business finances. I rang him. He said he could arrange it from a commercial bank in the west-end. We submitted the proposals, met the manager but the deal on the table was quite expensive. Also, the manager of the bank was dragging his feet and taking too much time to make a commitment. In the meantime I was also negotiating the finance from Barclays at Chelmsford. They were also taking their time. Finding myself in a fix I decided to sell the property in London and went to see my local manager again. On that basis they agreed to finance the project for completing one building. The construction resumed with the same builder but with new prices, increased by another £20k. I had no choice but to accept.

We moved there in September 1988, within two years of my leaving the job. I was now becoming quite good in climbing the mountains. The learning curve of running a business from scratch for the second time was steep and encouraging. We now had 2000 sq. ft for the processing and packing facility with 750 sq. ft of offices and a staff room on the first floor. We were delighted. We moved all our cooking facility into the new premises. Our premises were on the other side of town from where F was and therefore there was less chance of being intimidated by him. Now was the time to automate the production and packing facilities. We went around buying a second-hand big automatic fryer, a dough mixer, and a dough extruder. They were installed, and the production went up from 1.5 tons a week to 5 tons a week. Soon we also got a contract to pack airline packs – a million units a year. We bought a reconditioned form fill machine with a linear weigher. Within a few months we bought another form fill machine. All this equipment was bought with our own profits. Within a year of moving into the new premises, we had grown out of it. We rented a 20' container to store our raw materials. But the stars were beginning to hibernate. The glittering of the diamonds in the cosmos was starting to fade. The time for sliding down the hill had arrived once again. The era of pain, uncertainty, and heartache was seen on the horizon. I was proposing a lot more to move forward but God was dismantling it all.

Divine's Anger

Who says the Divine is not revengeful? He is just as bad in inflicting pains as He is good in caring. We experienced His full force of anger. He took his toll ruthlessly and with full vengeance. But no religion is broad-minded enough to admit God's anger except the Jewish God who openly declares that, 'Those who do not follow me I would bring havoc into their lives.' In the following episode it was nothing but the uncalled havoc of the Heavens which had befallen on us mortals. Punishment for which crime, I have never been able to discover so far.

The Fire at the Factory

The business was expanding rapidly; packing and production methods were being automated with profits; and all other things were moving on smoothly without any problems - when disaster struck. At the Easter break of 1989, we worked as usual on Saturday 25th March up to 2pm. We fried goods in the kitchen and packed them as a normal routine. We came home to enjoy our long Easter weekend break. The routine remained normal until 2am when the telephone rang. Who could that be in the middle of the night needing our attention? It was a call

A JOURNEY THROUGH PARTITION AND BEYOND

from the burglar alarm receptionist saying, 'Your alarm has gone off at the factory. The police have been informed. They will be there shortly. We want you to go there as they will be waiting for you to check the premises.' This was a normal message from the alarm people. It happened many times – a false alarm. I called a few bad names, got up, got ready to go to investigate the cause of the false alarm. As we were getting ready, a second call came.

'We believe there is a fire at the factory. The police have reached there, and the fire brigade has been called to deal with the situation.'

A fire! From where, who started it, how had it started, the cooking area was all turned off, the gas and electric was turned off, everything was checked before locking the premises, then where had the fire god come from to punish us? And punish for what sins? The mind was trying to find the answers to all those questions. The whole brain was jammed up with fear. How were we going to cope with it? It is a new factory where we have only been for a couple of years and were already planning to construct more units to increase our existing storage. All that had now gone into smoke and into ashes.

We jumped into our car and were on our way to discover what had happened. I was very nervous, fearful and found it very hard to drive the car. However, after we reached there, I was getting out of my car to go inside the factory when a policeman restrained me. I burst into tears.

'You should not go there sir. The firemen are working on it to control it. There is no fire, it is smoke all over.'

'Whereabouts has it happened? Is it in the cooking areas or packing areas?' I asked.

'It is this side of the factory; I don't know, what area is that?'

'Are you sure officer? That area is the packing area. How can a fire start there?'

'It is the job of the firemen to investigate the cause of the fire.'

We were in our car for nearly an hour when the officer came back and said, 'You can go now and see what happened. It is all under control.' We went in. The seat of the fire seemed to be where we were packing that afternoon. Next to that on the wall was the burglar alarm box. Along that wall there were two packaging form fill machines. Both were smoke and heat damaged. There was no naked fire. Wherever the fire had started it smouldered, producing a lot of smoke. The lights and the electric wiring were heat damaged. The inside walls of the packing area were all black. There was no damage in the cooking area. The firemen could not definitely assess where it all started and its cause. One of the firemen, who worked part-time for the local fire brigade, was also working for a local neighbourhood company. He told me that they could not find the cause of the fire. They reckoned it all started with the alarm box which was the only one on. We

349

had always had the habit of switching off all the electric mains and they were all off. One of the electrical contractors suggested that it could be due to a lightning strike from the sky but there were no clouds and the night was clear. He suggested that it has happened in the past that a bolt from the clear sky had struck to start a fire in buildings. It did not make sense to me but there are all kinds of opinions.

On Tuesday we came to work as usual. The staff were there, and they were all surprised. However, we sent them home and we told them that we would continue to pay them even though they were not working, and we did. We hired an insurance loss-adjusting company in London to help us to put the claim. They asked to see the insurance documents. After going through the document, they discovered that our insurance, which was to be renewed on 19th of the month, was not renewed so our insurance had lapsed. I got panicky. However, he continued, the good news was that we were still insured under the ten days renewal grace period allowed by the insurance company. So, they submitted the claim. The insurance company hired a company to clean up the factory, its walls, and the machines to put us back into operation. They also asked a local electrical company to restore the damaged wiring. Within two weeks we went into production again.

The story of the claim is rather more complicated. The insurance company was dragging its feet to meet the claim. They were not even paying the electrical contractor who was chasing us for payment. Briefly, the matter was sorted out as below:

They agreed to pay for sixty percent of the fire damaged stock. The reason - we were under-insured.

They refused to get the packing machines replaced, repaired, or get them sorted by engineers or by the company which supplied us. Eventually we had to get them repaired ourselves. We had used these reconditioned machines only for six months for contract packing. According to the insurance documents, these machines were to be replaced 'new for old'.

They refused to change the roof of the building or its sun windows. They were smoke damaged and were pitch black. They only got the building wiped clean and painted. The whole new building looked disgusting.

They never paid any amount towards the loss in earnings and business interruptions.

The loss adjusters of the insurance company asked me to attend an interview in their Cambridge office with our loss adjuster. As we walked to their office after parking the car, our loss adjuster said to me, 'It is these people who are dragging their feet and not the insurance company. They were not settling the claim as they believe that you started the fire.' 'But why would I set my newly built factory on fire? Our business was doing well. We had bought two machines, and all paid for from our own profits. Am I mad enough to do that? Besides, you have seen that we did not even have valid insurance. We are lucky that we had a grace period of ten days.'

'That is what I have been telling them but they don't listen. They are not going to recommend the full payment of your claim. You will be lucky if you get 50% of your claim.'

'Then it is your responsibility to push to get our claim paid in full. That is why you were hired.'

'I know but they are not listening to my arguments. I have been asking them to prove that you had started the fire and the motive behind it. The insurance company will pay what the loss adjusters tell them to pay you.'

Our claim was settled in January 1990, nearly nine months after the fire. As the loss adjuster said, they had taken away about 50% of the claim. We lost a lot of money in that disaster. When our loss adjuster came to collect his commission of the claim, he told me a sad story. While discussing the issues of underpayment and the insurance company's loss adjusters – the two young handsome fellows – he said, 'Well you cannot now talk to the person in charge of your claim because he is six feet under the ground.'

'What do you mean six feet under the ground?' I enquired, not knowing what he meant by those 'six feet'.

He said, 'Don't you know he died?'

'No, whatever happened?'

'One night he went fishing. He caught a fish and pulled at it. As he applied the sudden force to pull a small fish, his steel fishing rod landed on the naked electric cables behind him and he got electrocuted.'

'Oh. What a sad death.'

He was the one in charge of our claim, had a beard, was handsome, and was married with a couple of kids. What a loss and tragedy.

You would think that the disastrous episode should have been forgotten after more than 22 years. But no, whenever I go back into the memory lane, the warm tears from the eyes still run down on the cheeks to remind me of those painful days. That incident will never be forgotten. There was no reason for the fire to start. It still remains a mystery today. Even the insurance company's loss adjusters must have done their best to find a clue, but failed.

After the incident, whenever we would get a call in the middle of the night we would jump out of bed. It had destroyed our sleep and had made us jumpy. Whenever I used to witness a wailing fire engine on the road, I would start saying my prayers to God to have mercy on the victims of the incident. I had become emotionally very disturbed and weak.

One comment from my previous neighbour, selling engineering goods, I can never forget. I had gone there to buy some screws.

'I had read that you had a fire at your place,' he said sarcastically with a big grin thus dusting salt on my healing wounds.

'Yes'

'You must be a rich man with that claim. Most people put a torch to their businesses when not doing well.'

'Sorry, my business was doing very well at the time. The fire had rather a setback on my growth.'

This man was at least honest to cough up his mental venom on my face. How many more like him might be thinking that way and saying a lot nastier things about that disaster? I would never know, and I would never like to know. They have never been into that type of hell that we had experienced. A lot more people in our society are rotten to their core and stink. They are small-minded, and their thinking is very low.

This matter never ended there. After we went back into production, just a couple of weeks later, there was another big bang on the door to wake us up. A police officer was there, knocking frantically as if some heavens were going to fall on the mother planet.

'You have another fire in your factory. I have come to take you there in case you may not be in a position to drive.'

'Oh, thank you officer for coming. You are right. I would not be able to drive. But do you know where the seat of the fire is this time?'

'No, we did ask the alarm company. They did not know. The only way to find out is to go there and investigate.'

Panic-stricken I went in, told Mira, we got ready and away we went with the officer. The officer warned me that he would be driving fast, and we should not worry. We would be safe. He was used to driving in emergencies. However, I was worried in case the unexpected showed its ugly head. Accidents do happen, and we were going to attend the same kind of accident. We opened the factory. This time the potato chips which we had fried that evening were beginning to smoulder in the kitchen. After the fire, we used to make sure before leaving that we left everything cold enough, but we were wrong.

Then in the next couple of months we had three more incidents like this. One time, before leaving, we noticed that the sesame sticks which we had produced that evening were just beginning to smoulder on the top surface. We separated them, stirred them to dissipate the heat, and stayed there for another hour to make sure they were cold enough.

Because of the big smouldering fire and after so many mini-fires, we were now becoming paranoid and fearful. If there was any call in the middle of the night, we would jump out of the bed, 'Oh God not again.' Some were just false alarms and some from friends, but the psychology was torturing us, and it went on for years. Sometimes in the middle of the night I would have nightmares that would wake me up. I would ask Mira to accompany me to the factory to check if everything was ok there. We not only lost a lot of money, but we also lost our sleep for many years to come until we decided to stop frying Bombay Mixes.

After the fire problems were sorted out, the business was on the move again. To meet the demand, we rented a steel container to store some goods as we had no space inside the factory available. I approached the bank once more to support us to construct one more unit to meet our expansion. The bank refused once again. I had hit a rock again.

The Sharks in the Building Trade

I sat on it, not knowing where to turn. One day an architect from a Brentwood estate agency barged into our office. He said he was looking around for some sites where he could design and build factories. He'd seen this waste land with only one factory built and thought of enquiring if his firm could have the opportunity to help build more units here. We talked about the details of how the estate agency could help in such ventures. I was not aware of this route to build factories. I thought it was only architects who did design-and-build. I enquired about their terms and conditions and asked him to send me his free design proposal. Once we approved the design, we would give them a contract to tender and then supervise the construction.

The Brentwood architects designed to add 5 more factories to the one already constructed. This design was different from what the previous architects had suggested. When they were still in designing stage, the bank manager visited us to look around and after a brief discussion about our growing business and shortage of space, he agreed to provide us the funds to construct one more unit. We were happy that we would get rid of the storage container and would have ample room to store goods and for the packing machines. Surprisingly, after four weeks, I received a letter from the manager who invited me to see him in the bank. In that meeting he announced ceremoniously that the bank had agreed to fund the construction of all the remaining five units. He said it was more sensible to construct all the units in one go and finish the whole development on the 0.6-acre land. The bank had also agreed that they would fund the £52,500 to purchase the freehold land from the council. That was the opportunity we were waiting for and we got it. Now all those directions of that ball game changed. Should I call this the shine of the diamonds over us once more? Was the divine feeling guilty about starting a fire in our premises without any reason and was now in a better frame of mind to help? Or was it a law of nature at work that after reaching into the abyss there was no other choice but to climb up the hills available? I let you decide.

As the funding for all the units had been approved, I tried to contact the surveyor on the phone to move on with the project and issue the tenders. He kept on dragging his feet. I called him on the phone several times but without any success. One day I went to visit his office, but I could not see him. I left a message with his receptionist for him to call me but without any reply. However, while this was taking a long time, another architect's agency at Colchester approached us. I asked them to prepare a design without showing them the one I already had from the previous agency. They came up with nearly the same design. I asked them to go ahead with the construction. Tenders were invited, the contractor was approved, and the date of construction was agreed.

Shortly after the builders had moved in with their heavy building machinery and started their work, I received a threatening letter from the Brentwood architect. He wrote that he had visited the site and noticed that construction had started to build the units of a similar design as they had submitted. As the supervision was being done by another architect on the design they had submitted, therefore we had to pay them £10,000 fee as compensation. Failing that, the letter continued, they would take us to court to claim the fee with interest. I wrote back saying that the similar design was submitted by the other architects and they were not aware of your design as we had not disclosed them. Therefore, the designs had not been copied. Also, we believed that was the only optimal way to develop the site. If they had any argument for the design and the claim for their fee, then their fight should be with the present architects and not with us as we had not designed the buildings. So, we rejected their claim and refused to pay. I also sent them the name and address of the new architects and informed the new architect. They sent me another couple of threatening letters which I ignored. Then I heard nothing. Obviously, the matter ended there.

Construction started moving again. One day I was in my office and the father-in-law of the previous builder, who was also the builder's accountant, walked in. He paid a surprise visit to see what was happening at our place. A few days later, I had a letter claiming a few thousand pounds damages based on drummed-up claims. He also accused us that they should have been given preference to tender for the rest of the construction work. Obviously, he became jealous to see the progress being made in developing the rest of the factories. The builder had gone broke just before the completion of our first factory. According to our contract they had not concreted one side of the factory; some internal floors were left incomplete, and they had also not paid the supplier for the window grill. The supplier of the window grill came after we moved in and said that he should be paid £350 otherwise he would take the grill out of the wall. I told the supplier that it was already a part of our building and he could not remove it. His fight was with the builder who had gone broke and not with us. If he removed the grill I would call the police. He reminded me, with threatening behaviour, that the law was that if the material installed in the building was not paid for then the supplier had the right to take it away. I knew the supplier. He was my neighbour at my previous factory and I had a great respect for his bravery when one day F carelessly allowed the chip pan to catch fire. The supplier came rushing in to extinguish the fire, endangering his life. He was a trained firefighter, he later told me. Therefore, I did not wish to hold his money and I did not want any arguments with him. I paid him in full. I later discovered that legally he was right.

I took the builder's claim to a local solicitor and put a counter claim for the damages we suffered because of the incompletion of the work. We claimed the increased costs for the incomplete work, the damages for the shoddy workmanship inside the factory, the water leakage in the drainage system and the £350 we had paid for the grill. We submitted our claim with all the relevant documents to the solicitor. The builder was getting legal aid to fight the case. Our solicitor sent all the documents with details of the counter claim to the court. It never went further. They withdrew the case. The court could not understand how the same people who had struggled to construct the first building were now demanding a contract to construct the other five buildings.

The units were completed but a dispute arose with this builder too. He was asking another £30k. He said that the architect had failed to include the construction of the partition wall between us and the next-door neighbour. There were also some other services which were not covered in the contract, such as covering the channels dug by the water and the electricity boards. I checked with the architect and they agreed that it was the case. I think they had colluded to get more money from us. However, I went to my bank and got another £18k. The rest of the money I agreed to pay to the builder in instalments with interest within a year, which we did. The builder did cheat by using a wrong cement and sand mix. When questioned later, the builder put the blame on the architect - that he was a novice, inexperienced architect and had given that composition in the written contract. I don't know who was right and who was wrong, but these are the pitfalls of building projects. A lot of people had gone into difficulty with builders. My case was not a unique one.

Renting the units

As soon as the units were completed in the summer of 1990, we took over one unit thus leaving four more units to be rented. One was rented within weeks of the construction to a pattern maker, leaving us with three more to rent. Negotiations started on renting one more to a car body repair business, and it was rented in February 1991, thus leaving two more.

Hit a Rock

Hitting a rock and then surviving is no joke in business life. With every success in life there looms a danger of failure. The country faced a bad recession in its economic cycle. It is known in the city as the boom and bust cyclic period. We now owed to the bank nearly a ½ million. The interest rates were shooting up by the day. The chancellor lost control over the economy and in his desperation announced one evening an increase of the interest rate to 18%, a phenomenal rise. That meant finding £24k every quarter to meet bank re-payments. All the economic pundits were forecasting doom for the people like us. You as a businessman could devise no strategy to escape. It is beyond your control. The decision was made to borrow and construct the warehouses when the economy was running smoothly, and the environment was ripe for expansion. No one could look into a crystal ball and predict the gathering of the dark clouds. In those testing times one had to have nerves of steel. A little faltering in decisiveness and determination and you would be on the road on your bike, with every asset sold and nothing left in the kitty. I had turned 60 at the time, a very testing time of life. I had no experience in dealing with such critical situations.

Multiple Problems

One financial analyst asked me to give him my financial details to be analysed for free. They were looking for those companies which were going to struggle on borderlines and to whom they could give some financial help to survive, thus earning a commission for themselves. I knew the company and the guy who approached me. He looked at our financials and sent me his report without any comments. I waited for a few days to hear from him, but nothing came up. One day I went to his office to meet him. After a general chat, I casually asked his opinion of our financial position. I had not read his report. I was too scared in case it sent shivers down my spine and broke my resolve to face the music of the time. A lot of companies were in trouble and were hitting the rocks. In the business world everyone borrows to expand the business in good times, but to find the extra money to pay a sudden jump to 18% interest rates was beyond anyone's imagination. First, he hesitated but then reluctantly opened and said, 'In my opinion you should declare yourself bankrupt. I don't know how, with that kind of debt and interest rates of 18%, you can survive.' He further commented that that was the reason he did not write to me. He did not wish to add any more woes to the worries through which the whole country was now passing. A smack of an 'Iron Lady of not Turning Back' was out there to destroy the small businesses, the very fabric of the nation. I just could not believe what he said. I had never thought for a moment that I would not be able to repay my quarterly instalment. It just never crossed my mind. Rather I had some other difficult problems in hand to deal with.

The manipulative bank manager

As soon as the buildings were completed, the bank manager, who supported us in completing the factory constructions, died. He had a brain tumour. A new young, handsome, tall, very aggressive, and selfish manager took over the charge of the branch. He made an appointment with us and came to our home to introduce himself. We had a general chat about the present performance of our business, its progress, and its future. We discussed all those matters in the lounge and at the dining table. We assured him that we were generating enough income at the time and would be able to pay the bank instalments in time. But as the bankers are trained to be suspicious, to read the body language of the customers, and their psychology, he just did not believe what we were saying. We were not misleading him. We were also not putting a brave face in the difficult situation we were in. We were putting all our cards on the table without hiding a bit from him.

But the banker was not convinced in our ability to pay his instalments. We had a series of meetings after that. Some meetings took place at our home as he would just drop in without any appointment. On one meeting at home, he put a proposal that he would lend us a further £30k so that we could pay the bank's first instalment fixed for 23 December 91. I asked, 'What would I do with this money which we don't need? What is the catch in your offer?'

'You can do what you like with it. Buy a car, go on holiday, and spend on the house.'

'But we don't need it. We already must pay your bank ½ m. We do not wish to increase our borrowings.'

'Christmas is around the corner. Spend the money the way you want. Think about it.'

Obviously with interest rates at 18% he was out there to burden the solvent companies more to earn better profits for the bank. With those ideas of lending and spending the extra 30k he left. But he was not a quitter. He was a relentless pursuer for his cause. We were at a loss to understand that in this chaotic economic environment why he was pushing more money down our throats. Only a couple of weeks had gone by when he dropped in again. 'I was just in the vicinity and I thought I'd come in and say hello,' he said. 'No problem you can come in at any time.' We welcomed him with our Indian cultural background. We had learnt that the "Tahiti" (the one who drops in without giving a notice) is a god and hence must be respected as such. After a cup of tea and some general chat, he again asked what decision we had made regarding the loan he was offering us. He further assured us that he would transfer the money within a couple of days so that it was available to us in time before the first instalment was due. I again resisted and repeated the mantras we had been saying before, 'We have enough funds available to pay to the bank for the first instalment. Besides what are we going to do with this money? We don't need to buy any machines, go on holidays or spend £30k in casinos, what we would do with the money.'

'You can use it for what you want to use it for. The rest you may put in the bank deposit account and earn some interest on it,' he advised.

'That is a silly reason - to borrow the money on 18% and put it in the bank deposit to earn with a much-reduced interest rate. Which businessman would be that daft?'

He left that evening again a bit disappointed. He could not understand why a client to whom as a banker he was generously lending a further £30k, to round up the borrowing to ½ m, was so adamant to keep on refusing the offer. In those days of uncertainty, no one would refuse even a dime coming from any source. However, with only a couple of weeks left before the Christmas break, the banker knocked at the door again. We just did not understand what the need to come in now was. There were no issues to discuss. I knew the first payment was due within days but until we defaulted, the man cannot just conclude that the instalment would not be met. Besides, after meeting the first instalment with the borrowed money, what would happen when the time comes for the second instalment? The resources had to be created to pay the instalment every quarter. One cannot meet financial commitments by borrowing more money. It would lead to a bankruptcy court. We again refused to borrow 30k.

He dropped in once more a week later.

'Sorry I have come again. What I don't understand is why you are not taking the loan which I am ready to give you?'

'As I explained before we do not find any use for the money you are so kindly offering us.'

'You know I just don't understand it. As I suggested, whatever money you do not use, I will open a deposit account in my bank for you to keep the money there. Or you may deposit in the building society for a better interest rate.'

'I am sorry we would not like to borrow more money. You will get your £24k on 23rd December.'

We already had that money in the account and he knew it. That day he was getting quite upset and agitated. The truth is always blurted out when a person is angry and loses the grip on his mental faculties. His body language reflected his disappointment with anger. So, he shouted in a low tone but keeping within the norm of an Englishman.

'By lending you this money I was also making sure that the instalment would be met. Christmas being around the corner, I just wanted to earn a bit of commission from the insurance I was going to sell you. I don't understand why you are against my earning that commission.'

Oh, so that was the catch. So, all along his pretence of help was all farce. The concerns that we may not be able to pay our first instalment were false and selfish. He might be earning a few hundred £s in commission from the loan of 30k but he was throwing our future and wellbeing into the gutter by creating more debt on us. We had to service an added debt and the further cost of meeting insurance premiums. The tragedy is that the bankers first find out the health of the business from the management accounts provided. If the client is profitable they will then try to lend them more money. If the figures show that the client is a borderline case, they will increase their interest rates on the pretext of risk factor. Either way the client is a loser. It is a no-win situation. I responded to his admission of truth with some disappointment. With a heavy sigh, I said, 'I am not against your earning a commission. Good luck to you if you can earn a commission, but at the end of the day we must pay for the unwanted debt. Sorry, we do not wish to borrow more money.'

He looked at Mira but did not get much joy from her either. So, he left very disappointed, moaning and groaning as I walked with him to the door.

The day of reckoning 23rd December 91 came and it passed unceremoniously. There was £27k+ in our account on the day. The manager phoned to say, 'We are taking our first instalment of 24k today. You have sufficient funds available in your account. I don't know how you managed it.'

'I certainly have not raided a bank. I also have not borrowed from friends to pay you. That is what I have been saying to you all along that the company has enough income to meet its financial commitments. But the problem is that all the time you did not trust me.' My attitude was obviously clear - 'I told you so.'

We were happy that we had met our commitment. When the existence had provided so much commitment then it had also made sure the income was available to meet it. We were only listening to our inner voice and doing just what our being was saying to us. If I am talking fibs, then why would the divine send an uninvited angel onto the doorstep one day with an offer of a piece of land? Just to send me to a bankruptcy court?! No, the divine is not that cruel to those who have faith in it. It would just not make sense until and unless it was punishing me for some misdeeds.

The Christmas holidays arrived and went. The banker was a determined species, a man who would never accept defeat. Another meeting was arranged, just after we were back from the holidays in January, in his office at the bank.

He first congratulated us for meeting our repayment commitment to the bank in time. He still showed his astonishment at how we had managed to pay the money in time and had still enough left to meet the other commitments to wages and the suppliers, especially when the economic environment was so bad. I said, 'I believe in the philosophy that when the winds are blowing heavily, duck down like trees and let the storm pass over you with its destructive force. Once the calm returns, stand up, dust down, and resume your normality. The storms are never going to be there for ever.'

'Ah! So that is the eastern philosophy.'

'Well, that is the prescription for survival. Nature teaches us clearly from the branches of the trees which bend down to let the storm blow away. We humans only have to be wise enough to observe and learn.'

To me he was obviously being sarcastic to bring eastern culture into our discussion. Then he moved on to his favourite subject of the 30k loan. I was not expecting that matter to be discussed again. I thought he should have been satisfied by now after getting his first instalment in time. Christmas was also over and the reason of earning his commission did not hold water anymore. I must admit that when he brought up that issue again, I was annoyed. We had already said clearly that we did not wish to increase our borrowing. So, I said, 'I am really fed up with this issue being raised again and again. We have paid your instalment and we are also saying that our business is healthy, and we can meet our future payments in time too. I just don't know why you do not let this matter go.'

'I know but I would like you to have this money so that I can also earn some and you can use it for future requirements. I know you will need it. You say that you can meet your commitments, but I believe you will not be able to.'

To me this was insulting to our ability and integrity. He was thinking that what I was saying to him all along was nonsense. I had no clue about my business where it was going and he, an outsider, knew better than I did. I put my hand in my pocket, took out my factory keys and threw them in front of him.

'Here are my factory keys. If you think you are cleverer than I am, then you go and run the company. I am fed up with your patronising attitude and interference in my business policies.'

With that I got up to walk away. I was now angry, disappointed with his attitude, and his unnecessary pressure. He immediately pushed the keys towards me and asked me to sit down.

'Look I am not interfering in your business. The bank has no intention of running your business. You take your keys and go and run your company the way you want it.'

I sat down and allowed myself to cool down a bit. I felt bad about my silly reaction. Within minutes the ugly environment turned in to a normal working one. I had mellowed down so much that I said to him, 'You have been pressurising me so much in the last few months to lend me more money, ok I am ready to give up on you. I will accept your offer of a loan. I still don't know what I would do with it.'

Maybe the turnaround on my decision was because of the guilt I felt for my behaviour or because of some other unknown reasons but I relented. I don't exactly remember how I decided to reverse my stand, but it happened. We accepted his offer and walked away.

Shortly the money was transferred into our account and remained there and had probably found its route to other expenses. Money is like a water stream, it will always find its way to be spent somewhere. But till today, with divine's mercy, we have not faltered so far with our repayments to the bank. The loan was brought down to £110k and then we re-mortgaged with Nat-West with a base +1.5% as opposed to base + 3%.

The Other Bank Managers
This manager was unceremoniously transferred to another branch. We don't know why. However, another one, perhaps more experienced and a bit older, took over. Things went smoothly with us except that he would also aggressively follow the policy of earning more profits for the bank. He would pressurise to get more profits, not by providing a better service or funding us to expand the business, but by pushing us to take other financial services provided by the bank to boost its profits. He would ask on every visit for life insurances, car insurances, and house insurances. His approach, like any other bank managers, was to explore the opportunities where he could earn some commission for himself. His tactics were always heartless and manipulative. He never showed any interest for the benefit and welfare of the client company but how to grease his pockets and what was available for him in the deal, an unethical act. The boss of the local vegetable wholesaler once moaned that 'whenever my manager visits me, he talks nothing else but life insurances.' This manager pushed me into a lot of financial hassles by not renewing our overdraft facilities, not that our business had any problems, but for some other mean motive. He pushed us to open an account with the factoring arm of the bank where the interest rates were higher, and we ended up in financial slavery. Within months of opening the account, the factoring division was sold to an American company. I could now see why we were pushed into factoring. The bank was probably planning to sell that business. To achieve a better sale price for that business they wanted to increase its profits and people like us were used as fodder to achieve that goal, a despicable act. We lost a lot of money and we needed an uphill effort to find the money to pump into the business to maintain the cash flow and come out of the factoring.

This manager did not last very long and was booted out to another branch within a couple of years.

One of the bank managers asked for the life insurance for one of our young directors. We resisted because he already had cheaper insurance. We refused the offer three times in various meetings; the fourth time, when we refused again, the manager barged out angrily from the meeting, saying, 'What is wrong if I wish to earn some commission?' It was a terrible behaviour by a manager and we were shocked. However, in the next meeting we relented and took insurance to keep harmony in our relationship. Another manager talked me into paying £50/month 'to look into our accounts on monthly meetings'. It was a farce, a waste of time, a talking shop, and nothing used to come out of those meetings. How to stop these meetings without upsetting the manager became a problem. It took me three years to collect the courage and say to the manager that we did not wish to continue the meetings. No harm was done but by that time we had lost £1800 in fees.

The Turmoil and Tussle
The business had been moving forward from strength to strength.

1.   In 1991 just after moving into the second unit, we were packing more than a million packs a year for the airlines under contract

2.   We started packing all the fruits and nuts for a health whole-food company in London which was expanding its sale outlets. In addition to packing, we were also supplying Bombay Mixes and roasted cashews and peanuts. To distribute their products to their shops they also rented the next door unit thus paying us £14k rent.

3.   We were supplying Bombay Mixes to a company in London which was supplying them to a supermarket chain.

4.   We were supplying Bombay Mixes and the other associated products to two other wholesalers, about three tons a week.

5.   We had only one more unit left to rent. Our total rental income from the factories, rented to others, was now generating £27k per year without us paying any rent.

The income from them was good enough to pay back our loan to the bank in time even with high interest rates. However, the good days can never be forever. One can never keep on climbing without going down the hills. Ups and downs must follow each other. It is a law of nature. Nothing moves in this Universe in a straight line. Everything moves in an up and down movement. We were not then an exception to that rule. So, in 1994 a misfortune hit us with a vengeance.

Slide Down in 1994

A JOURNEY THROUGH PARTITION AND BEYOND

1.   A London company which was supplying two tons of our Bombay Mix every week to supermarkets sold its snack business to another company. That company was not that efficient. They bought our BM in bulk, packed it themselves, and sold to their outlets. After buying only two deliveries from us they stopped. The buyer phoned me to ask about our jewellery policy and asked, 'Do you allow the wearing of jewellery in your working areas?' I asked why he was asking that question. He replied, 'The supermarket has found a piece of jewellery in the BM.' I said, 'No but why do you ask? Don't you metal detect your products?' He did not reply but said that they were investigating. The order never came back from them. So, we lost that good order leaving a gap of £1800/ week in our revenue.

2.   The whole-food company was expanding and had plans to increase their outlets from five to eleven within two years. The business was funded by a venture capitalist. The company spent a lot of money on fitting a shop in Kent. That did not improve their sales as expected. The profitability was not improving as per their forecasts. The result was that the venture company got frustrated and refused to support the expansion any further. The company was sold to whole-food chain stores in the Midlands who decided to move the whole operation of packing and distribution up there. So, we lost all the revenue coming from selling BM, nuts, all the packing, and the rental income from the unit.

3.   One more wholesale buyer also folded shortly after that.

The loss of the above good regular orders was a real brutal shock. We had sixteen employees at the time. They started deserting. They thought the company would not survive very long, a thought which never crossed my mind until when, a few months later, I asked the driver who had left me why he had departed. He said, 'We left because we thought the company would never survive such a major loss in orders.' But I had been a good survivor. I never ever thought of losing that game. One can lose battles in life and it is a part of living, but it is the war which one must not lose. Also, if you don't lose battles you will never learn from your mistakes and you will never change your strategy to win the later wars of life.

We had only one wholesaler left who was buying the BM. He was packing it in his own brand name and minting money while we continued to lose it because he would refuse to give higher prices. We were losing nearly 15k a year because of the increased costs of raw materials and overheads. Wages were increasing, the rates and rents were increasing, and the raw materials were shooting up. It was a bad strategy to continue to serve this wholesaler with our exotic BM and roasted nuts but not develop our own brand. No one knew that it was our BM being eaten by so many in London. The wholesalers who sold it were improving their margins and sales by the day. Their sales were going up and up. They controlled our prices and left us to count pennies and lose pounds. It was an awful strategy with disastrous consequences. It had to be corrected and the pain that was going to be inflicted had to be taken, and soon.

The dark clouds were surrounding us once more from all directions. The vultures in the form of money lenders, the accountants, the suppliers were all hovering around to show their presence. We tried to see a ray of hope in the horizon, but it was not there. And when that happens to you, even your near and dear ones start deserting you too. They start criticising you. In that situation you are on your own. This is the way of life for the humans, fair-weather friends. Some employees left me, and a couple of others took me to tribunals to claim damages. In bad times you must bear them all. The life was hell at home and life was becoming hell on the outside too.

In that environment I continued to make a desperate effort to market my BM to other wholesalers but failed. The company which had bought the health food business refused to give any business to us. The two young employees of the buyer's company were so arrogant that they refused to meet to discuss the issues. The health food company had leased the unit for fifteen years. The buyer company cleared the unit of all the stock and walked away without any commitment to pay the rent for the rest of the eleven years left. When I offered to sell them some poppadums, one buyer made a derogatory remark (not pleasant words to say here) about India from where the raw discs were being imported. That financial year we lost £54,000. With that kind of balance sheet, I even could not sell my business. I was 63 at the time.

However, we continued to operate. The losses were reduced next year. The existing wholesaler would not let me increase their prices and they were the only one I had left. If we asked for payment on delivery, they would demand 2% discount, the ruthless exploiters. Life continued as such with struggles until Stansted airport became operational and sucked out all the labour force from the adjoining areas. That left me no option but to stop making BM as I had no staff available to make it. I wrote to the wholesaler that we were going to stop making BM and would not be supplying anymore. That was quite a bold decision, imposed by the circumstances but proved a blessing in disguise. The loss-making BM was gone out of the window, a big relief. It needed five people to produce three-quarters of a ton of BM per day. However, that put me into another difficulty. Overnight I lost £200k in sales from my books. But it reduced the wage bills, thus reducing the losses as well. The further advantage was that we were using no dusty flour; there was no steam pollution because of frying, and that resulted in a cleaner

A JOURNEY THROUGH PARTITION AND BEYOND

factory, fewer fire hazards, and less management time required in supervising the quality and the staff.

The banks were not giving any troubles. The loan which was negotiated for ten years on a repayment basis was now down to £110k. I went to NatWest and replaced the loan with base + 1.5% for five years with an option to borrow up to £250k if I wanted to. The repayment was so small that I could meet that with rental income alone. But the pressure from the family to sell both the businesses with the properties remained intense all the time.

The approach of my negative family

It is always very difficult and painful to write about one's own family with whom you have been sharing your life for decades. It is deception to tell only the beauty of roses but hide the sharpness of thorns which are part of the roses. Life never moves smoothly, and it has its pitfalls full with minefields and agonies. But if I don't, then I am not writing the book in honesty. I am deceiving the reader. I believe I should be an open book, transparent, and say what the truth is. Therefore, I have to say here all the truth, nothing but the whole truth as I see it and analyse it. Otherwise there is no point in writing it, is there? It is the reader who is to judge and decide.

When I was offered this piece of land, Mira was the first to tell me not to accept the offer. 'We don't have the money to develop' was the reason given. However, I went ahead and accepted the offer. As we moved through the maze of designing the factories, the architect problems, the builder problems, arranging of the loans, completion of the construction, renting of the factories, paying of the instalments, or whenever we hit a rock the comment had always been 'get rid of them', 'sell them we don't need them', 'I am fed up with them'. But there was never thankfulness to God for his merciful opportunity. No, 'just get rid of them', 'I am sick and tired of keeping them'.

I had explained many times that

- The rental income from them would be our future pension when we retired in ten years' time.
- The investment would also provide the income for the children and the grandchildren
- As the business was expanding, we needed a bigger place. If we were renting them we would be paying more rent to someone else than the mortgage repayment to the bank.
- The assets would increase in value every year with the time.
- We should be thankful to God that he had bestowed this gift on us. By rejecting His kindness, we were insulting Him.

365

But no, these explanations would hold water only for a few hours or a few days but then the mantra would be repeated again. These mantras continued for all these years. Came a certain day, we had already collected 400k rent and the borrowing was then down to 200k. We went to our daughter's flat. The issue of her usual mantra of 'get rid of the factories' was raised once again, forcefully, with raised voice and anger mixed with it. Both my children supported their mother's position that she was right, as it was too much financial pressure to keep the factories. Annoyed, I responded again with the usual arguments, but it was not taking me anywhere with them. I found myself all alone, isolated. Even grown-up children were favouring her negative attitude. It was getting too much for me. I had been taking that onslaught again and again for so many years. I felt enough was enough. If all of them don't want to have a secure future, then why was I bothered to carry on defending the status quo? I had no financial advantage either. All the income was being collected by Mira who was managing the finances of the company. I was not given a penny pocket money if I wanted some. Then why was I arguing for it? It was just stupid. So, emotionally and disgustedly I said, 'This vendetta has been going on for so many years now. Why on earth do I keep on saying that we are not selling? You are all shareholders in this property holding company. Let us vote and the majority decision will be taken. I will sell it if the majority vote says "sell."'

They all went quiet for a few moments. Then suddenly Vipul said, 'Dad we are not forcing you to sell it but what we are saying is that you should try and improve the business so that the family should be less under pressure.'

He was right there. We were under pressure because we had lost the packing contract of the health food company business which was bought out by a big company. They moved out of the unit, thus losing the rental income. They also stopped buying our roasted nuts and Bombay Mix, thus leaving a big hole in our revenue. We had sixteen full-time employees. Some full-time employees also left as they thought we as a company would not be able to survive as a business. However, this employee attitude has always been there throughout the industry. All employees run for cover to protect themselves when their company is in trouble, but when it is running in good shape they will fight tooth and nail to improve their wages. However, there was no suggestion coming from the shareholders about how to combat that situation. That was dad's problem. But one can never run away from life the moment you hit a rock. You must stand up and be counted. But there was no one to be counted.

When son took that attitude, daughter also mellowed down and did not comment further. So, the vote was to carry on maintaining the status quo at the

A JOURNEY THROUGH PARTITION AND BEYOND

time. But the pressure had never gone away. Till this day I still get the same mantra. Only the reasoning is changing.

What can you do when you are surrounded by negative people, even though they may belong to your family? Why don't they suggest a solution to improve the business to pay its way rather than be just critical?

A Ray of Hope

Then we saw a ray of light on the horizon. A sales fellow whom I knew was working for a company that went into receivership, and he was available to work. I offered him a job for £500/ week as a self-employed. He brought some good business; one of them was for £100k per year. The company was back on making good profits. In the meantime, my son decided to join us full-time to look after the business. But the salesperson who worked with us for nearly a year was poached by another competitor. Also, maybe he felt threatened because of my son joining the company. So, within a couple of months of my son's joining us, the salesperson left and took nearly all the businesses he brought. So, we were back to square one again. The business dived back into loss-making mode. When my son joined the company, our packing machinery was old and outdated; the BM manufacturing was discontinued; therefore, we decided to expand the business. We invested more than £300k into the next-door unit when it became empty. We built a mezzanine floor, clad the walls with wipe-to-clean boards, installed a false ceiling with plenty of lighting, and bought a computer-controlled multi-head packing machine to boost our packing capacity. We were now changing the whole strategy from processing foods to contract packing.

We also furnished the office with computers and new furnishings.

We were now ready to expand the business for contract packing for other companies. The old machines were literally scrapped. We tried to sell them but without much success. They'd had their day and eventually found their way into the scrap yard.

My son contributed a lot with his corporate experience by introducing computers for letter writing, creating sales brochures, for invoice generating software, and internet marketing for more business. He organised sales pitches at the national exhibition centres. He launched the poppadum's project, packing them in bags printed with our NF logo. I lacked in all those activities. Despite all those efforts, the business was not growing fast enough except that we added some packing work from a few companies. With all his hard work, when he found he was not getting anywhere and was not using his capabilities effectively, he got frustrated. He was a young energetic man and just wanted to get out and do something else which was more profitable and challenging to his ability.

The Hotel Venture

So, we started to look to the hotel industry. His mind was set to go for that. The children have dreams and the good parent should try to fulfil them. We looked around for two years for a suitable hotel. We missed one very badly that was only eight miles from home because our solicitor was dragging his feet to complete the deal within the eight weeks required by the vendor. The vendor was becoming frustrated and the agent was telephoning every other day to know the progress. He was using his high-pressure salesmanship. Maybe they do it in the hotel industry so that the buyer does not find out the truth about the performance of the hotel on sale. We were also short of collateral by 150k. We could have managed to find some answer to that shortage but because of the pressure from the vendor, I gave up. Finally, we found a countryside hotel in Suffolk and bought it on 10th September 2007. We had no cash to put down, but we had the collateral to meet the borrowing. That meant paying a lot of interest, thus putting a lot of pressure on the ingenuity of my son to meet the bank commitments. So far, he has done well with a lot of hard work and sacrifices. Of course, he does get irritated and frustrated sometimes but then it was his dream, and I as a parent helped him to fulfil it.

My son left the NF to run the hotel with his wife. Now I was back on the hot seat again. When my son was there, I was reduced to do-nothing. I did not mind that role because I wanted to give son a free hand to know the tricks of running a business and learn from his mistakes while I was still around. He is managing his hotel business very well though he does get frustrated when he hits some problems. This is the hard way of learning to run a business. But I am sure he would appreciate in future that these are part of a game in running a business. It is the responsibility of the manager to find how to run the business day-to-day. There is never an unlimited supply of money. When you grow your business, the liquid money would always be short, and a successful entrepreneur must learn to address those scenarios with his ability and experience. Some are born with that quality; others must acquire it with experience and hard slog. I believe that when the existence had put entrepreneurship and the opportunity in our way then he had also sorted out the resources we needed. And if we had the backing of the Existence and its vast resources to support us then why should we feel desperate. I always have a faith in my destiny.

Since 2007, I have endeavoured to find more business. Slowly I got there with some losses and then with some profits. It is part of a struggle. Some get it easy, but I find I must move mountains before achieving my goals.

In 2008, I got one business with sheer luck. I never made any effort for it, but God had just thrown it in my lap from nowhere. We have a car washing unit in front of our factory. All kinds of people come there with children to get their

A JOURNEY THROUGH PARTITION AND BEYOND

cars washed. I had a habit that whenever I would see a little child with parents, I would bring some chocolate buttons and give them to the children. One day a man walked in the office and said that he wanted to get some chocolate bars packed. I showed him the premises, gave him the price which he accepted, and we started packing. Soon we built up a good working relationship. In early 2009 he suggested that we should pack truffles for him. We agreed but because we wanted to have some more work and the recession was already hurting us, I gave some silly low prices. We got the job but as we started packing we found that we were losing money. We asked him to accept an increase in the prices; he refused and rather argued to decrease them. We knew that he was getting a lot more than he was paying us. I had the evidence that for a certain truffle box he was being paid 32p, but he would not pay us the 24p we asked but, rather, decreased it from 18p to 17p. However, we kept packing in thousands every week and as the year 2010 hit us, we found ourselves with cash flow problems. We lost the grating of chocolate and packing into tins. We also lost the flow-wrapping of the chocolate bars. But the truffles we were still packing. The VAT bill ran into thousands, the balance sheet showed a loss of thousands. Next year, 2011, we refused to pack any more when asked to continue. We gave our new prices on a 'take it or leave it' basis. He sat on it just to see if we would reduce them in desperation. However, in May 2011 he accepted our prices and asked us to be ready to start packing in September 2011. We did, and now we were earning to make up our losses.

CHAPTER 9: HEALTH ISSUES

<u>Keyhole Surgery – a Brief Brush with Death</u>

I had just turned 80 in February 2011. I was still healthy but noticing some physical changes in the body. A year earlier, I used to walk 5-6 rounds around our house. I could not do that anymore and gave up but continued my mild yoga exercises. The sheer load of work at that age was taking its toll. My knees were beginning to give pain. My legs were losing strength, and that was not a very good sign. The Chinese call the legs the root of the body and when they start showing deterioration in their function, it is the beginning of the rot setting in and for the body to prepare to go. I also felt some weakness creeping into my heart muscle. The old age was creeping in discreetly through the back door.

It all started in my right knee sometime in June 2011. That was quite sudden. One day as I came from the factory I found it difficult to walk after entering the house. I knew that the arrival of arthritis was now imminent. The pain would start in the knees after a few hundred yards walk in the morning. It was a battle between the two knees which one would go down first. So, it was the right knee which finally lost out.

Next day I made an appointment with my GP who checked it and made an appointment for an X-ray. The X-ray showed some sign of arthritis and some wear and tear in the joint. I was then sent a list of various hospitals near our residence to choose from, including a private one at Chelmsford, for further investigation. We chose the local Braintree Community Hospital (BCH) which had been recently rebuilt at the old site, with all kinds of modern facilities, free from hospital bugs and free from parking charges. The other hospitals are infested with such problems. Mira was also going there for her heart check-ups and was very happy with her treatment there. Therefore, it became a natural choice. All the consultants come there from the other big surrounding hospitals to cater to the needs of the local people.

BCH wrote to me on 5th July to attend the hospital to see the orthopaedic consultant and for X-rays on 19th July 2011. I was examined by the consultant after he'd looked at my X-rays. The X-rays department gave me a form to fill out which permitted the hospital to start the treatment. Effectively it was granting permission to the professionals to play with my body parts and if I died in that attempt, they would not be responsible for my death. That was a legal licence to get away with human errors or should I say, 'with murders'.

The consultant surgeon was very nice and friendly. He told me that he was a very experienced person and had already done around 6000 knee operations. I was happy to know that he did not give me a figure of 5999 operations. He asked me where I came from, how long I had been in the country, what did I do for a living, and so on. When I said I came from India, he asked, 'Is that where a well-known religious man has recently died?' I said yes.

He was referring to the well-known Sufi called Sai Baba who had millions of followers all over the world and had done a lot of charity work. He was also widely reported in the British press after his death because the tax authorities had found a lot of cash in the back room of his residence. The press never reported about the free hospitals, the free colleges, the free schools, and the roads he had constructed, but to defame the guru they had reported about some petty cash the authorities had found in his backyard. This cash might have come from the recent donations from his devotees to run his vast charitable organisations. This is how the British press operates – defame the charitable people of other countries by demeaning their contributions towards their followers while at the same time drumming up the small deeds of their own citizens to hide the corruption and rot in their own society. So, I gave him some views about the Baba and said some more things about OSHO, the author of the books which he saw in my hand. (OSHO, otherwise known as Rajnish, was a controversial spiritual leader and teacher who ultimately was evicted from USA and banned from many countries before returning to India.) This indulgence created some uneasiness among his nursing staff that were waiting to usher me out and get on with the care of the other patients waiting outside.

The consultant examined my knee, twisted and turned it with some force on the examining table and pronounced that I was a candidate for keyhole surgery. He said one option would be to inject the knee with a fluid which would only help me for 6-8 months and would cost £400. I would then be back for the keyhole surgery. So, the best solution he proposed was to go for the keyhole surgery now. This treatment would last about 4-5 years. If we didn't do anything, the knee would wear out soon from the rubbing between the bare bones. There would then be no choice but to replace the knee by major surgery with bolts and nuts. Obviously, I settled with the keyhole surgery option.

A week later I had a surgery date on 14th September 2011 to report at 7.30am at BCH. On the morning of the 13th I had a call changing the reporting time from 7.30am to 11.30am. I was not allowed to eat or drink after 7.30am.

I was getting great help from friends and family. G, my nephew, and his wife were also coming to give me company, take me to hospital, and stay with me there. As Vipul and his wife Amita had decided to take time off from the hotel, we thanked Gs' for their offer and asked them not to come. However, they decided to come home to stay with me when I would be off work. That so much goodwill is showered by the fellow beings in times of troubles is very encouraging.

V had taken three days off from the hotel to be with mother at the factory. A took me to the hospital. At the appointed hour we reported at the main reception desk who directed us to report at the receptionist desk on the first floor.

A had planned to stay in the waiting area until the operation was over. I suggested that she should go back home as it would be boring for her to stay in the waiting room. But she insisted on staying there.

We reported at the reception desk sharp at 11.30am. The receptionist, busy looking at her appointment register, as they normally do, announced without an eye contact, 'What can I do for you?'

'Here I am with my leg to change and chop for which I have an appointment to report at 11.30am.' She looked at me with an amused smile. And why not say that? We are passing through an era when women's legs are watched and admired as sexy and then why should not men's legs also be made popular? And who knows, my appointment for keyhole surgery may be just a pretext for altering my leg's appearance to look sexy to the liberated womenfolk of the day.

Smiling, she looked at her computer screen and said, 'What is your name?'

'Oh, I am Om Khurana.'

'Which knee is to be operated on?'

'It is the right knee which is troublesome.'

'Ok, have a seat there.' As I was turning, I remembered that I had brought some NF goodies for the staff. So, I opened my bag, took out the box with twelve bags of salted, spicy nuts, chocolates, and snacks, and offered them to her.

'Please do not misunderstand me. This is not a bribe to look after me more than others but an appreciation for the staff for how much they care and look after us, the citizens on the streets.'

'Oh, what is it?' I opened the box and showed her a bag of Wasabi Peanuts and chocolates. She was quite pleased to see those goodies and said, 'I will put them in my drawer to share with the other staff. They will be quite pleased. Thank you.'

Off I went to sit next to A.

About ten minutes later the nurse arrived to take me to the ward. She took my bag and I walked with her. Here was another inquisitive one to ask questions. My face had many question marks. It tempted the staff to ask more and know more about me. She first asked, 'Is your daughter-in-law staying all the time while you are in the ward?' I said yes.

'Well, what is she going to do there?' she asked.

'I think she is going to read a book.'

'No, she will be bored there. You might be here for 6-7 hours.'

'I have suggested to her to go back home but she is insisting to stay on.'

'Oh, then I will have a word with her.'

I waited there. The nurse went back and persuaded A to go back home. A agreed to leave and left her mobile number with the nurse to contact her in case of any emergency or as soon as I was ready to be picked up. In between times A called the hospital to know the progress of my operation. Mira also phoned the hospital a few times to know the progress.

The nurse came back, 'Your daughter has agreed to go back.'

'That is good. Looks like you have a good persuasive power.' I said, appreciating her efforts.

'How do you pronounce your name?'

'My name is OM, O M. Now I gave you a simple first name, easy to call and easy to pronounce OM.'

'Oh! Om! What is your last name?'

'See you are not happy with just my first name to call. You like to be more adventurous. Well, that is your choice. Ok, my second name is Khurana, K H U R A N A, and it is pronounced like BANANA.' She laughed and attempted to pronounce it and she perfected the pronunciation by saying it again and again. We were right there in front of the entrance to my cubicle where my hand-written name was on a billboard on the wall.

'Here we are; that is your bed. I am now going to fill up some forms before we move to other procedures.' So, she called out the questions to be completed. When it came to my date of birth, the year was 1932. I corrected her that it was 1931. The hospital records are wrong. I even filled up the form at my GP surgery and asked them to correct it but obviously they had taken no action.

'Ok let us do it now. I will go to the receptionist and get it done.' She disappeared for a few minutes and came back and said, 'It is all done now.' It was a big relief that these wrong records would not be confronted again. Some more interesting questions were thrown at me. Did I have false teeth, any loose teeth, did I have contact lenses, any hearing aids? And so on. She apologised for such questions. I could not figure out at that time but now I know why they were being asked. Once I would be in a coma there would be a risk of swallowing them. After the form-filling formality was over, she asked for my autograph on the declaration that in case of an emergency or misadventure during the treatment, the BCH would not be held responsible.

Now it was the time for action. The blood pressure and body temperature were monitored and recorded. Then she tried to find a vein to insert a needle to connect a drip on the right arm. Why did she select the right arm? I don't know. Maybe it was on the same side of the knee being operated on. She could not find the vein. I said, 'I think as the body is dehydrated since morning the veins are buried under the skin.' 'Maybe, let us close and open your hands a few times to improve the blood circulation.' I did, and it worked. Then she left.

Then followed a long waiting time of nearly an hour. No lunch and no drink. I had to bear it bravely. I had hiccups for a while that day. I believe the body was dehydrated.

After this long wait came the boss. 'Hello, how are you?' 'I am fine thank you,' I replied. He looked at the form and asked, 'Which knee are we operating on?' 'It is the right knee,' I said. He had an orange colour marking pen. He drew on my right leg a fat line with an upward arrow on one end and two crossed lines on the other and disappeared to the next cubicle. A few minutes later a lady anaesthetist arrived. 'Hello, I will be dispensing your anaesthesia before the surgery.' She glanced at the form. 'Which knee are we operating on?' 'It is the right knee.' She looked at the consultant's markings, 'Oh, so he has marked it already. Good.' Then she checked the vein feed connections and commented, 'Oh that is done as well. That is good. We will see you soon. We are ready for your operation.' 'Ok doc,' and she left.

Soon another nurse came in.

'I am your anaesthetist technician and I'll take you to the theatre where we will monitor your blood pressure and connect you to the drip as you have not eaten since morning. It's a glucose drip to give you energy as you go through the operation.'

'Ok, that is fine with me.'

'Which knee are we operating on, or is it your arm?'

'Here we go again. It is my right knee. Everyone is asking which knee. If I knew that so many people would be asking that question, I should have left my left leg at home so that it becomes beyond you people's reach. As you know it has happened in the past that some people have been operated on the wrong limbs.'

'Don't worry it is all marked on your leg, so you are alright.'

Then he asked me to remove all my clothes except the underwear, and to put on the hospital gown, leaving the back bare. I did. I lay down on my bed, and he wheeled me to the theatre room. As he wheeled me he asked, 'Which country do you come from?'

'That is a difficult question to answer. I have lived here for over fifty years, and this is my country now. I am as British as you are. Your question should be where I was born.'

A JOURNEY THROUGH PARTITION AND BEYOND

'Yes, that is right, where were you born?'

'I was born in India.'

'Which part of India?'

'New Delhi.'

'Oh, I went there in 1998. I was there for 7 months.'

A nurse at the reception desk, as we passed her on the way to the theatre, said, 'Don't you believe what he says,' and we all had a laugh.

'Oh, well, you know India more than I do. I went back to India first time in 1961 and again ten years ago in 2001.'

'Oh, wow that is a very long time before visiting your country.'

'Yeh! I know. That is life.' The conversation then turned to how to make curries and he said, 'I have never made curries so far. I do like the chili hot foods.'

I said it is very simple to make them if you know how to make the gravy base. The time for explaining how to make a curry base was abruptly ended when the tech said, 'Oh well it is time to connect the drip.' The tech connected a tube coming from the drip bag into the receiving end of the needle already pierced into my right hand. He also placed the oxygen mask on my nose to shut me up from further chatter. It was time to get on with the serious job for which I was there. As the tap from the glucose feeding bag was opened the liquid entered my vein with some tingling sensation. 'Did you get tingling in your arm?' he asked. 'Yes, I did,' I replied. 'Oh well, it is working then,' he confirmed.

Soon I noticed another tingling in the hand and I shook my arm. As I looked towards my right arm, the shadow of the woman anaesthetist appeared. She was administering the anaesthesia into the vein with the drip. 'It is me, administering the anaesthesia, don't get worried,' she pronounced. I knew I was now on my way to meet my maker. I wanted to experience death. What is it? Why is the whole of humanity, or nearly the whole except for a few adventurous Jihadis who bravely kiss death and never shirk back, so afraid of this monster phenomenon? Obviously there has to be the moment when my consciousness will be overpowered with no-mind, and that will be the moment when death would creep in. That is the goal of every life, to end there. To make sure when that situation would happen, I was now continuously monitoring the awareness in my active mind. I was slowly moving into a deep sleep just about then, when I noticed that someone jolted my right knee with a very heavy thumping force. I made a painful noise of 'Oh' as a protest, and then I had gone into the wonderland. I had lost the existence of this world. I had lost my touch with reality and did not know where I was, and the mind was totally dead and blank. This was the time I had no connection with the awareness. I had lost consciousness. I knew nothing of existence. Time had disappeared. It had to. When there was no-mind, the sense of time also had gone. Then I regained my consciousness. There seemed to be no

375

break in the awareness. It appeared as if I was conscious throughout this period. I heard a couple of words of someone talking, and then I began to hear the chattering sound between the wheels and the floor. That was the time I was being moved to my cubicle from the theatre. I lost my awareness momentarily again. Then I heard in my drowsy state of mind the nurse asking me, 'Would you like to drink tea or coffee?'

'No, I am not allowed to drink or eat anything,' I responded.

'No, it is all over. You had the operation. You have not eaten since morning. I can fetch you some coffee with biscuits.'

'Oh! Really! When did it happen? I did not know anything about the operation.'

As I answered, my attention went to my right leg and I noticed the tightness of the bandage there and I knew that I was being told the truth. Surprise, surprise, how come?! I had thought I would monitor the whole operation, but alas I missed it. So that was the gap in the consciousness when death takes place. Death is the lack of consciousness. It was so serene, peaceful, and disconnected from the whole material world. When the whole world cries for your physical loss, you have no idea where you are.

I now opened my eyes. The nurse had already brought a hot cup of coffee, a couple of packets of biscuits, and a cup of water.

'You must be dehydrated as you have not taken in anything since morning. If you want more coffee or water I can fetch some for you.'

'Oh, no thanks a lot. This will do just right. You are an angel. You nurses acted like goddesses to me. It reminds me of my early days when the chattering mind would not go quiet. I used to say to myself that this is where our Maker had gone wrong while creating us. He should have installed a switch on our head. When the mind is not needed we could just switch it off. But then I thought - once switched off, who would switch it back on? Society or your hating relatives would certainly love to see you remain switched off. Now you nurses had that power to do exactly that, but you were very kind to revive me back to life. Thanks a lot. You are real goddesses, nothing but dedicated goddesses.'

'Oh, we would not do that.'

'I know, and that is why I call you goddesses who have that power to control the life and death of the people on the streets.'

'You may get ready now. We have informed your daughter-in-law A, who will be here soon to pick you up.'

I had finished my coffee. The ladies went out of the cubicle, leaving me alone to dress myself to join back into the civilised world again. I collected my clothes which were tucked in a corner and started dressing. As I was about to pull on my socks, the two nurses reappeared.

A JOURNEY THROUGH PARTITION AND BEYOND

'Are you ok or do you need help?'

'No, I am just fine. I am nearly there to go home.'

'You said that it is the chattering mind that is a trouble in life, but it is very difficult to control. It just keeps on going,' one of the nurses said.

'It is very difficult but there are techniques to control it. It is the job of the mind to keep on chattering and keep on bringing the thoughts to your attention to dwell on. Now, when those thoughts are presented, you should let them pass. Just do not pay any attention to them. The thoughts will still come but they will go away as you are just ignoring them. Just do not be attentive to them but do not suppress them either otherwise they will find their way into the storage space of the un-conscious mind which is a lot more powerful than the conscious mind and is more destructive.'

'You know, all day when we are working, it is fine, but it is when we go to bed that thoughts start bothering you,' she pointed out.

'I know but there is a breathing technique to control the mind if it is really getting out of hand,' I suggested.

At that point I noticed that one of the two nurses was getting bored with my philosophical chatter and she left, and I also felt a bit embarrassed to keep harping on about eastern ideas to the unreceptive ears. So, I changed the topic. When I was ready, the nurse very kindly led me out of the ward into the lobby, giving me support as needed. A was there, waiting. The nurse handed me over and offered me a wheelchair to go to the car. I declined the offer as I was quite fit to walk the corridors of the hospital to the car. She again offered me the chair by saying that it was not because of the knee that might make it difficult, but it was also because of the influence of the anaesthesia which might make me dizzy and fall. I thanked her for her concerns and declined the offer again as I knew that I was quite fit to walk away on my God-given legs. She was very kind and caring and I thanked her for all that help she had given me during my brief experience of surgery on my knee. I then walked back with A all the way to the car.

So that was my brief encounter with the brush of the death which frightens nearly all humanity thus forcing them to kneel in temples, churches, and mosques and yet it does not spare them. It is the law of nature and the final destiny of every creation - what is created must be destroyed to make room anew. Otherwise the creativity of the creator would die too.

Appointment with the Physiotherapist

On the day of appointment, I presented myself at the reception desk of the Physiotherapy Department. The receptionist checked out my details and asked me to sit in the waiting room to be seen. I had just waited a few minutes when the physiotherapist appeared and after confirming my name, she asked me to follow her to the examining room. I have always believed that there are certain professionals with whom you deal in life who must be obeyed. Do always what you are told. The barber is one, the dentist, the doctors and nurses, and so many more like them. They are armed with sharp instruments and they have a power of life and death over you. It is advisable to obey them like a sheep. We entered a room, well equipped with beds, chairs, medical aids etc. She instructed me to sit down on a chair and remove all my clothes except my panties. I was shocked to undress before a lady and that too with only her being in the room. Just to confirm that her orders were right, I asked her again, 'Do you mean my shirt and vest only.' 'No, no remove all your clothes except your panties.' Oh my God what an order! As I said - you must obey them - therefore I duly obliged. I was blushing and feeling shy more than she was. She was used to all kinds of idiots like me every day. Some must be younger, stronger, older, infirm, fit, all kinds. When I was obeying her orders, she was reading my bio-data. She turned and said, 'You are eighty now.'

'Yes, I turned eighty in February this year.'

'You don't look eighty. You look younger than your age.'

'Thank you. Just luck I suppose.'

'Please lie down on that bed.'

I obeyed, but was fearful about what she was going to do next with me. She went around the bed. She inspected both my knees by twisting and turning.

'You've still got the surgical dressings. Have they not been removed yet?'

'No, I have the appointment to see the consultant. Maybe they will remove them at that time.'

'Have you got pain in the knee? Do you feel any improvement after the surgery?'

'Yes, I have pain when I get up and walk. In the beginning it felt as if I was going to fall. Maybe it will improve with time as it is only two weeks ago I had the operation.'

She then asked me to pull my toes towards my body, lift my leg about 300mm high while keeping the toes in that position, count five, bring the leg down, and relax the toes. I did and then she said exercise the other leg the same way. I obeyed.

She then instructed me to exercise both legs, one at a time five times a day. This will strengthen my muscles. I did one day but I was beginning to get cramps in my legs. So, I never attempted it again for a few days. But I got used to this exercise and do it regularly.

Finally, she asked me to sit down on the bed with my feet touching the floor. She came around to sit next to me. She first stroked my right thigh with her soft warm hands 3-4 times. Then she did the same to my left thigh and commented, 'Not very strong thighs.' What that meant I never dared ask. She was the first woman ever in my whole life that had the liberty to touch my thighs. The physiotherapy session was over. She ordered me to dress. I did and away I went to the reception desk to make another appointment if I needed it. I made the appointment but cancelled after a couple of days as I did not need any more attention.

Appointment with the Surgeon for a check-up

I reached there at the appointed time. After the nurse had seen me, she took me to the surgeon's office. I waited a few minutes.

'How is the knee?'

'I still have the pain', I replied.

'You will have to live with some pain but if it does not improve, I will have to attempt another surgery. Yours was the worst arthritis I have come across that day. It was quite bad.'

But I don't know why he said the 'worst arthritis'. When he examined my knee for the first time only 6 weeks before, he had said that the arthritis was just beginning in the inner side of the knee. Was he trying to hide his unsuccessful operation? I don't know. He never examined the knee. I just left with no instructions what to do in case the pain continued.

So that was the keyhole surgery to repair my knee and as at 2018 the knee is no better or worse.

The Heart Muscle and a Pill for the Old Age

The physical decline of the body had noticeably started. However, I took it as part of growing up.

One day I was at a party and a good lady came and asked me to go to the room where the ladies were chattering. A lady doctor, sitting with her stethoscope, asked, 'What is your blood pressure?'

'I have no idea.'

'Don't you get it checked up regularly at your age?'

'No, I never bothered. I think my blood pressure is normal as far as I am concerned.'

'Ok, let us find out.'

Reluctantly I rolled up my right sleeve and presented my arm for the check-up. She pronounced that my blood pressure was higher than it should be, and I should go and consult my GP for medication. Within seconds the boast of being a healthy pensioner disappeared. Under pressure from Mira, who is also under medication for higher BP, I went see the Doc. He tested my BP and confirmed it was high. He suggested that I should go on medication. I refused and said, 'Let me try my natural therapy to bring it down.' He warned me of the consequences of my refusal but accepted my freedom to decide for my health myself.

I started doing yoga regularly.

I also ventured to fast on one Saturday. I do not remember that I had ever fasted in my life before. It was a good experience. A, an alternative therapist, said that, when fasting, the body de-toxins itself as the energy which is used in digesting food is available for the body to cleanse its toxin. So, I decided to go ahead for the adventure.

Morning was fine. No hiccups except the tummy gave feelings of being full. By 10am I felt coldness in the body, no body fuel and no heat. By 11.30 I felt weakness but easiness in the tummy. I had a good rest and slept on the chair. It was 4pm and I felt a lot of chill in the body.

Now I realised for the first time how the people who are undernourished and go without food must feel. Previously it was a feeling without experience but that day I appreciated the pain of hunger much better. Is it a curse of God and his punishment, or the punishment inflicted by the bloody-minded society which is so selfish and self-centred that well-to-do individuals could not care less about those weak and poor in the society?

I broke my fast with rice and turnips curry at 6pm.

I did this twice and it helped, but not a great deal. A few months later I reported back to the Doc. He gave me tablets to reduce my blood pressure. My doctor persuaded me, and Mira agreed with him. But I refused to take them and left them alone. They were poison to me and I just could not persuade myself to swallow. I knew that once I started taking them, it would be impossible to lay them off. I refused to put that poison into my body. I still preferred yoga and believed in relaxation to keep the BP low. I am managing well but if I die early with that decision so be it.

A year went by and I went for a check-up again. The BP was on the move up. That worried me. The Doc gave me different tablets this time. I went to pick them up from a chemist who knew me. He came out and said, 'These are a new medication on the market for BP and I have to monitor your reactions to it.'

'Oh, but the doc said it has already been tested for more than a year now.'

'No, it is new. I have this form. Please sign it and if you find any adverse reaction to the medication, phone me.'

I felt very concerned that I was being used as a guinea pig for the drug company to test the medicine. However, I took them only for four days and I noticed swelling on my left foot. I also noticed pain on the left side of my leg and the ankle developed a painful weeping wound. I stopped the medication immediately despite my wife's repeated protests. I made an appointment to see the doc. He looked at it and took some photographs and advised that I should stop the medication and surprisingly added, 'I understand your concern. I am surprised that this reaction has happened. This medicine has been used for the last couple of years, without any side effects.'

'But the pharmacist told me that it is a new medicine and took my signature for no objection to monitor its side effects.'

He looked at the medicine book on his desk and announced his verdict, 'No, it has been used in the market for a couple of years and has been successful in treating BP in patients.'

'If it is true what the pharmacist has said then I am annoyed that I have been used as a guinea pig for trying this medicine on me. I came here to cure my BP if possible. Rather than getting help to do that, I have been given another illness to my healthy body. That is bad news.'

The Doc did not say anything, and we walked out. I have not taken any medication since for BP. I discovered that my BP was higher because I was taking a supplement.

CHAPTER 10: TWO BURGLARIES

Break-in Burglary

It was 1pm, on Monday, the 5th December, 2016. The business was busy as usual because of the Christmas rush. All the customers were chasing for their packing assignments to be finished as soon as possible and to be collected in time to be sent to their customers to cash in on the once-a-year shopping spree bonanza. Christmas, which is meant to be a religious celebration of the birth of Jesus, honoured by bowing down in front of the statue of Jesus Christ, the Messiah, Our Lord, the Apostle of Non-Violence, and Messenger of Love-Thy-Neighbour, has now been turned by clever businessmen into giving presents to near and dear ones in the name of Santa Claus. It is strange how the money-minded, crafty, clever businessmen have commandeered this religious day to hoodwink the common decent citizens of the world and turn it into a money-grabbing machine.

As I write this, in November 2018, I am eighty-seven, and I deliberate on what little I have in terms of material goods. I am also conscious that there is no way I will be taking any goodies with me in my box. What I have earned so far by hard slog will stay with this mother earth. Maybe I am not clever enough; but maybe some clever person might negotiate with their God and He might permit them to take their goodies with them.

Some of my customers may like to add an agenda item in a meeting to discuss the day of my retirement. I can easily tackle all the questions thrown at me, but how can I predict my retirement day? In fact, the implication is that, 'Oh man, look at your age and you are now slipping fast into the box.' But I cannot find the answer to what reply I should give to this tricky question. If my answer does not suit them, they would feel insecure and pull their good business from us and leave us cold. However, I have to answer this question. So, at a meeting, when they ask, I am ready for the expected question:

'Om, now finally, have you decided when you are going to retire?'

A JOURNEY THROUGH PARTITION AND BEYOND

'Yes! Last night I had a chat with my Maker and asked Him when he would be sending the angels of death to take me on my final journey. My Maker replied, "Om your box is not ready yet. So, keep going."'

So, obviously their faces drop after asking such a question. All mortals die at any time from birth to one hundred and eighty years plus. Then, why is this wishful question asked to a man of my age? How are the questioners so sure that they will survive me simply because they are younger to me?

It is not only the moneyed men but also thieves and burglars who think that what they are going to steal is going to go with them. Their thinking is very poor. Their vision of life only extends to the tip of their nose. They cannot see the other world, the inner world of super consciousness. They are happy to feed their precious, free, God-gifted body with stolen money. They might end up with a pretty woman and expensive wine in a posh hotel or restaurant. What they eat in that posh place would eventually end up in the morning in the toilet. I believe this free, gifted body, if cared for and fed with honestly earned money, can become a Temple of God. Otherwise it is a skin bag, full of rubbish. That is the greatest choice that has been given to all us humans by God, to become a sinner to a saint. No other living species has this choice even though they are a lot superior to us. If we look at the so-called animal kingdom, they do not rape, they do not steal, they do not fight wars, they live very harmoniously within their own kind, and they are not hoarders. Only one lion, the king of his area, keeps the peace. He has no army, no weapons, and he does not even allow the outsider of his territory to urinate in his territory. The humans call them a derogatory word, 'animals.' This is the only way you can declare yourself to be superior by derogating the opponent. The humans eat these simple creatures that beautify this planet; they butcher them, slaughter them, rear them by drugging them and restricting their movements, and they say bravely, 'God created them to be eaten.' I have no evidence to prove that they are meant to be eaten. What happens if a creature superior to man is created and they love to eat humans? How would humans feel when the same is said about them - that they are meant to be eaten?

Let us look at the vegetation on this planet. They are dumb looking but beautify the countryside and farmlands; they bloom in the seasons with colourful flowers and spread their scents and fragrance to the environment; they soothe us and touch our hearts when we are moody and pensive; we pluck them, destroy them and their beauty to decorate our homes and dead bodies; they extract nutrients from the soil of the mother earth so that our bodies are nourished and healthy; the trees show off their beautiful flowers, make us drunk with their fragrance, give shelter to millions of insects and shadow to humans; when they are laden with juicy fruits, they bend down to make it easy for us to pluck their nutritious nuts and fruits that prolong our life span; and finally we kill them, cut them, shape them to make beautiful houses and furniture. And what happens to this most destructive, war-mongering, exploiting, scheming body? Buried six feet under the ground to be eaten and become a great feast to the undertakers of God. What a tragedy for this human species, who had the chance to reach to heavens and paradise, to end up as a feast to the undertakers.

However, I like to carry on my story:

I Hurried Home with no Police in Sight
It was just after 1pm. The staff had already gone for their lunch break. We were discussing with our foreman the details of printing some labels. The telephone rang. Soon we saw Mira's happy face turning into a tense and pale one. As soon as she finished, she turned towards me and said, 'The burglar alarm has gone off at home and you have to go home right away. The alarm has confirmed that there is an entry into the house. The alarm centre has informed the police and they are on their way too.'

'What time did it happen?' I enquired.

'They said at 1pm.'

'Oh! Ok I am on my way then.'

I dashed down to my car and I was on my way home, hoping that it would be a false alarm. As I reached there, I first tried to see if there was any police presence around the house. There was none. I parked the car at my usual place in the front yard of our house. The alarm was bellowing its warning with a deafening, ear-piercing loud noise. I first checked the entrance door. It was locked. I then walked along the front and side of the house to check any damage to outside windows. They were all intact. I came back and opened the entrance door. I walked through the porch and I saw a handwritten note from our neighbour saying, 'Don't worry, Om, I have checked around and everything is OK.' With that reassurance, I walked through the utility room, and the kitchen. All the windows were intact. As I reached to the second door of the kitchen, I checked the lobby with the staircase that leads to the upstairs flat with two bedrooms, bathroom, and a lounge. I noticed to my horror a broken picture on the lobby floor. The picture should have been hanging on the staircase walls. Panic gripped my spine with a thought, 'Is there someone still up in the flat above?' I hurriedly dashed out the way I went in. I locked the entrance door and decided to go and see the neighbour to call the police. Then I thought, let me investigate the back of the house where we have a patio door that gives entry to the lounge on the ground floor. I walked through the garden. There were cars parked on the main road and the mothers had come to collect their children from the junior school that is a couple of minutes' walk from our house. I noticed the patio door was half opened. 'Oh well, that is the entry

A JOURNEY THROUGH PARTITION AND BEYOND

point for the burglars,' I thought. I retraced my steps and hurried back to my neighbour opposite.

He opened the door and said, 'Everything is OK, isn't it? I went around the house and there was nothing wrong.'

'No, there is a break-in in the house.'

'From where? I did not see any.'

'From the back of the house.'

'Oh, I did not go to the back of the house. What happened from the back?'

'I saw the patio door half-opened, got panicky, and hurried back. I first went inside the house and when I saw damage near the staircase, I rushed out of the house in case there was someone still inside who might attack me. In fact, the alarm people had informed the police and I thought the police would be here but there is no sign of them yet. It is possible they may be finding it difficult to locate our house but the alarm is still hooting and I am sure they could easily find it.'

So, he walked out of his house on to the road to see if there was any sign of the police car. There was none. I said, 'I also looked around before coming here in case they were late in coming. I think we should call the police again. Do you mind calling them for me please? It may be more effective than I if call them. In fact, if they had come in from Dunmow which is only five to seven minutes' drive, they would have caught the intruders red-handed thus saving themselves a lot more time in investigating the crime later.'

'No, there is no police station at Dunmow anymore.'

'Isn't there? What is that new building near the hotel?'

'Oh, that is a police administrative office.'

'Oh, damn!' I said disappointedly.

However, the neighbour called the police. While we were waiting for the police, he made me a cup of tea. He knew that I was in shock and needed some caffeine to boost my emotional drain. I also asked to use his phone to call my office to let my wife know the facts about the crime. It took nearly twenty minutes for the two officers to arrive. They could not find our house even with that alarm hooting. I walked down to the main road to guide them to my house. They met my neighbour who explained to them about his investigation outside our house after the alarm started bellowing. I then took the two officers to my house and opened the entrance door. They went in first and I timidly followed. They went in all the rooms downstairs and upstairs and declared, 'Yes, it is safe to go around the house now. All the bedrooms upstairs, downstairs, and the TV room have been ransacked. They are in a real state. You may cancel the alarm now.'

I went and cancelled the alarm.

I asked on my return, 'Can I go and see the damage done to the rooms?'

'Yes, you can only glance around but don't touch anything until the crime investigation officer comes later in the evening to inspect and gather some evidence for the burglary. Can we sit down somewhere to write a report?'

'Yeah.'

I showed them the lounge, and then, in the kitchen, the dining table with six chairs. They preferred to sit at the kitchen dining table.

Report Writing

The police officers introduced themselves and sat down to write a report to complete their final job of investigation. It was around 3pm. I narrated the incident, starting from the time of getting the call from the alarm call centre. Mira came back home and joined us. The report writing went on for another three hours. It is the irony of the situation that the victim first loses his precious goods and then has to go through the ordeal of hours in giving details of the burglary.

About 7.30pm, a police investigator arrived to gather evidence, if any, about the burglars. It is only a hope against hope in case the burglars have mistakenly left any evidence that would lead to them being caught. The burglars are very meticulous about not leaving any evidence. They have no intention to be caught and go to jail. After the investigator had finished, we were allowed to gather information from all those messed-up bedrooms about our losses. They had taken all our jewellery, much of which had a lot of sentimental value. As per Indian tradition, my mother and Mira's mother both gave some pieces of their jewellery to Mira which in turn, they had inherited from their parents. Mira in her turn, to keep her tradition, gave that jewellery to her daughter-in-law. The burglars also took all the cash they could find, lying around in cupboards and pockets.

Once the police were satisfied with their inquiry, they left around 9pm.

We managed to grab whatever we could and went to bed.

It was clear that in preventing burglary, new alarm technology is useless and a waste of money. Even if you have a dog, burglars will kill it first.

Finger prints! The modern thieves are cleverer than the police, the investigators, the security device installers, and the public. They wear gloves to avoid any sign of DNA from fingers and from their bodies. They wear face masks to avoid being identified by the public and to obscure the photo images recorded by the cameras. All the security services trail behind the burglars' activities. The burglars lead these services with their activities and by the time the services have invented new devices to stay with the tactics of the burglars, the burglars have devised some new tactics to beat the security industry. This leaves the police with the job of collecting data about the incidents from the victims; turning that data

A JOURNEY THROUGH PARTITION AND BEYOND

into an investigating report; and finally adding each incident into a statistical file. This leaves the victims to continue to shiver and lick their wounds in their residence, and insurance companies to foot the loss. The burglars and criminals are never caught.

Insurance Claim

At the weekend, our son and daughter-in-law arrived.

They started gathering evidence of the stolen jewellery and getting values from the on-line jewellers. They took pictures from their party pictures when they had worn that particular jewellery to send as evidence to the insurance company. It took them nearly two days to fill up the insurance claim with the evidence. They took another two days to put back all the scattered clothing in the wardrobes. It was literally a nightmare to manage all that mess.

The insurance company was great and paid our claims promptly without further questioning us.

Forced Break-In On Saturday 11th August 2018 9.30pm

The day rose with brilliant sunshine. The 2018 British summer had been excellent. It was just like an Indian summer and did not need weather predictions. Without worrying, one could say with confidence that every next day would be a clear, sunny day. As usual on Saturdays I got up a bit late at 6.30am to catch up the sleep lost in getting up at 4.30am during the week. I finished the usual chores of morning toilet, a bit of yoga, shower, and breakfast at 9am.

We were going to see our daughter at 2pm. We made our lunch at 12.30pm and some food to take for our daughter. We came back about 7pm, tired after driving through the London streets and the motorway. I just managed to eat a sandwich, had a hot mug of milk and settled down to watch an Indian Idol music programme on the Sony Indian Channel.

On the morning of the previous day, Friday, we had received tragic news of my sister-in-law who had died in Delhi with stomach cancer. Therefore, all Friday was busy with calls to and from India and with our two children. So, that Saturday our son and daughter were coming to see us at midnight. Mira wrote back to discourage them not to come as they both would be tired at that time of the night after working all day.

It just struck 9.30pm on the clock and we heard a thud sound from the front entrance end of our house. I walked down through the kitchen to the entrance door to see if our son had arrived. There was no sign of them. However, I took the opportunity to switch on the outside light. As I was coming through the kitchen and reached the door leading to the lobby and staircase, I met a slim young fellow with a face mask, coming from upstairs. In front of this fellow, I noticed one man walking straight into my wife's bedroom and another turned left in the corridor leading first to the TV room door on the right, where my wife was watching TV, and then to my bedroom. I was still not awake about these people's presence in our house. I was not fearful or shocked. I had lost all my senses and just could not comprehend how to react to their arrival inside our house. As I met this slim fellow at the kitchen door, I asked him, 'Who are you?'

'Don't worry I am here to help you. I am a policeman.'

'But our doors are locked. How did you manage to enter? If you are policemen, you would knock at the door to enter. And why are you wearing face masks?'

He now knew where his two colleagues had gone – into our two downstairs bedrooms. A fourth man was still upstairs. Seeing my wife in the TV room and the TV still running, he directed me to go in and sit next to my wife on the sofa. I obeyed. He was the 'in-charge' of our fate now. We had been enslaved in our own house. He sat down on the sofa next to us with a coffee table in front and started the dialogue.

'Who are you?' he said.

'What do you mean, who am I?' I asked.

'Are you Indian?'

'No, I am British.'

'Are you from India?' he asked again.

'Yes. I came to UK sixty years ago.'

'I am Indian too,' he said.

'But you don't seem to be an Indian. Your accent is different.'

'No, I am Indian.'

'Well I don't believe you, as I said before.'

'Where do you work?' he asked. It was the question that worried me the most as I did not wish to disclose that information in case they would take us there.

So, I replied, 'I work in a factory.'

'How old are you?' he asked.

'I am eighty-seven and my wife is eighty-two.' He paused for a moment and did not know how to react.

'Eighty-seven, you are looking good. Keep it up.' He further continued, 'You have a very nice house.'

'Not anymore, since you are here!' I said spontaneously, but later realised it could have been a mistake in case he reacted badly.

Now, he started fiddling with the contents on the table and asked my wife, 'Where is your jewellery?'

A JOURNEY THROUGH PARTITION AND BEYOND

'I haven't got any.' He looked fiercely at her face, hands, and fingers. She had none.

'We don't have any jewellery here. We had a burglary in December 2016. It was all stolen.' He fiercely looked around my neck and my fingers. I showed him all my empty fingers and told him I never wore jewellery.

'Are you sure? We will find out. If you are telling lies you will be in big trouble.'

'You can find out, no problem. You can ask the police or the insurance company, they know it.'

As he continued to fiddle at the coffee table and throw things on the floor, he found a small leather purse. He opened it and found a chain. He turned to Mira and said aggressively, 'You said you have no jewellery. What is this?'

'It is fake jewellery. You can have it if you wish.' Mira replied.

He examined it closely again and put it in his shirt pocket. Disappointed, he became more agitated. He started throwing the things from the table onto the floor more quickly. In between he would continue to say his mantra, 'Where is the gold jewellery, where is the big money?' I continued to repeat the same reply, 'No we do not have any.' Once the table was empty, he got up restlessly and went near the door and stood near the wall. He used his biro to fiddle with our daughter's small painting on the wall. Soon it dropped. He then started examining every item on top of the cupboard next to the TV box, throwing them on the floor. Then he opened the drawers and inspected all the goods and threw them on the floor. He was getting more aggressive as he was not getting the gold or money from anywhere. I was getting more worried as when these people do not get what they want, they become more violent and aggressive. At that point they start beating the victims. But victims have no control. If they do not have anything to give, what can they do? And we genuinely had nothing. Having ransacked the cupboard, his attention now diverted to the wall cupboard. He opened the door with his big screwdriver and examined the pockets of some old clothes and some other items in the boxes. He found nothing of interest there. The big boss came in, shouting his mantra, 'Where is the gold, where is the big money?' Having got the same reply from us he went back to continue ransacking my bedroom. Then our minder remembered something, dashed down to the kitchen and brought a couple of kitchen cleaning spray bottles. He started spraying on the metal frame of the ceiling light, again and again.

I asked, 'What are you doing? You will short-circuit the electricity. It may catch fire or it may blow the fuse and we will have no lights.'

But he continued to do that. He sprayed some liquid on the wall cupboard where he had touched it to open it. Then with a flash, he moved towards me on the sofa and sprayed some liquid on my left shoulder and then massaged it. Mira screamed, 'What are you doing this for?' He did not reply. Then he came back with a flash, pointed the screw driver towards me, and threatening me, he said, 'If you do anything wrong, I will sort you out with this.' Scared and frightened, we then stayed quiet and just watched him ransacking the room and spraying the liquid. (We asked police later why was he spraying the acidic spray? They said he was destroying all the DNA evidence even though he had a face mask and gloves on his hands.) So, the liquid he sprayed on my shoulder was to remove the evidence of pushing me from my left shoulder into the TV room. He was spraying the lights again and again as his head was touching the light's frame.

Finally, after ransacking all the three bedrooms, two on the ground floor and two upstairs and the lounge, the boss finally took the other robbers into the bathroom downstairs. We heard a lot of noise of throwing things on the floor but we did not know what they were doing there. After spending about twenty minutes, they escorted both of us into the bathroom. They had put there one chair and two mugs of water.

The boss thundered, 'We are going to lock you both here. You cannot escape as the window is locked and you cannot open it and you cannot open the door after we shut it.'

We screamed and begged them not to do this to us. 'How we can stay here all night and who will rescue us when nobody knows that you have locked us in?' They just did not bother about our plea for mercy. The boss pulled the door hard, slammed it shut, and removed the door handle. They then all disappeared through the thin air of the dark night, through the patio door in the lounge, we believed. It was around 10.40pm, the night was still young and neighbours must be busy in watching their favourite programmes on the TV.

Mira sat on the chair and I rested my bum on the edge of the old bath tub that needed to be replaced. Our attention now turned to how to raise the alarm to get out. There was no key in the sliding window to open half of the window. Breaking the glass was not a desirable option. Once the glass was broken it would have been a nightmare to get the window boarded next morning on Sunday. I looked at the door and tried to pull it open. It was jammed shut. I looked around for any tools, especially a screwdriver, but there were none. Disappointed, I sat down again. I had reached to my wits end. We just gave up. We thought of spending all night awake on one chair and on the bath edge. Thoughts are cruel, especially when they are being flooded with the negatives. What would we do in the morning? Shouting for help in the closed bathroom would have the same problem as it was at that time of the night. The nearest window of the neighbour's house is about two hundred feet away with hedges and the road in between. It was a totally hopeless situation that we were caught in.

A JOURNEY THROUGH PARTITION AND BEYOND

The clock was ticking, the heart beat was thumping in the chest, desperation was ruling our bodies and minds and we had finally given up hopes of being free. About fifteen minutes later, Mira had the urge to go to loo. I turned my face to give her privacy. As she lifted up the seat – lo! She saw two mobiles and two telephone handsets in the toilet bowl. After a little examination, we noticed an empty bottle of toilet bleach next to the toilet. We knew they had destroyed all the telephone system with that fluid. We flushed the pan twice and took all the telephone sets out. We washed them and found them lifeless. We had faced professional burglars and not cowboys. We knew the phones would not work, yet we tried in case luck favoured us. So, any hope of contacting the outside world, if any, was dashed again. The only option left was to pray to the Almighty for his forgiveness. This is what all the priests and saints tell us - that we must have done misdeeds in life to get this kind of punishment. To console the minds of the victims psychologically, it is the greatest invention of the priests. Having no other choice for the thinking mind and plenty of time at our disposal, I started putting the clock backwards to where and when I had attempted to harm anyone on the planet. To go through that exercise, I needed plenty of time and that was freely available.

Time passed on and we heard the sound of moving footsteps in the kitchen area. As I explained earlier, Mira had lost her sister to cancer in India the day before. Our son Vipul had said to Mira that he would be coming home late on Saturday to see her. Mira had discouraged him not to come that late and have rest, but now she was regretting giving that advice. But, with a bit of luck, he came anyway with his wife Amita. As Amita walked through the kitchen, she saw a number of kitchen bits, scattered on the floor. The dining tables and chairs were all in an unusual state. She was surprised and mildly shocked. She walked further and noticed the TV was on but no sign of us. We then knew that it must be our children who had come.

So, Mira screamed from the inside of the bathroom, 'Who is it? Is that Vipul?' Amita responded, 'Where are you Mum?'

'We are locked up in the bathroom. Can you please call the police to rescue us?'

In the meantime, Vipul also arrived inside after parking his car. He was surprised to see the unusual appearance of the house from the outside. All the inside lights were on, the garage lights were on, the porch and all the outside lights were on. He became suspicious and walked in the house to see more mess in the kitchen. Amita enlightened him with what she knew. He telephoned the police on 999 and explained the situation. About eight policemen arrived in force, with a trained first-aid policeman with all the necessary kit, and with the fire brigade on alert in case they were needed. A hefty well-built officer shouted, 'Please stay clear from the door in case it falls on you.' We followed the instructions. With a couple of big bangs on the door from the foot of a young officer, the door fell open. The first-aid officer walked in.

'Are you both ok? I am trained as a first-aid officer. You want me to give you a general check-up? I am well equipped to check your heartbeats and blood pressure. I am also equipped to check if you had a mild heart attack during this ordeal.'

'No thank you officer! I am just fine, I have none of those symptoms.'

He was surprised with my replies. Maybe he had a lot of other cases in which the victims had suffered such symptoms. Then he turned to Mira and asked the same questions, her answers were the same. He then further asked if we needed any help later to talk to some social workers for the shock we had had. We declined that too. It is not that we did not suffer the shock with the forced presence of those four thuggish young men who overpowered us by intruding into our peaceful lives. They had sent the shockwaves of grief into our healthy spines. Even now, whenever I talk about this subject to my friends and well-wishers, the tears roll down on my cheeks. It may take God to never give such experiences to anyone. But this is only wishful thinking. This world will never be saintly. The villains will always trot around on this globe to make waves of sorrows and pains to the law-abiding citizens. However, we were impressed with the police care and their response to help in the ordeal inflicted on two of us, not very young people.

The night was still young and it must have been around midnight. There must have been ten officers present with different roles to care, to investigate, and to write reports. More were coming to replace the ones whose duty was nearly ending. They even were equipped to extinguish fire if the thugs had started one somewhere in the house in desperation at not finding the 'gold' and 'big money'.

What a 'Caring' neighbourhood

I am really saddened to say this about the neighbourhood. It was not a discovery by me. It was our Lord Jesus who, two and a half millennia ago, coined the phrase 'LOVE THY NEIGHBOUR'. After living here in UK for more than sixty years I could not fathom why he chose to say this to the Western inhabitants. But now I know it and the message rings in my ears loud and clear. Previously, we always felt that it was something to do with their culture. The people here feel they ought to leave others alone to sort out their own problems. But nay, I now begin to believe that they are very selfish. They just like to mind their own business and are never bothered about what happens to others, even to their next-door neighbours. They are never very sociable. They hardly have parties. The television is their pastime gadget. They would neither invite anyone nor interact socially with others. It is not that they are indifferent to me because of my skin colour but they do not even interact socially with anyone. They just like to live a solitary life,

A JOURNEY THROUGH PARTITION AND BEYOND

minding their own business. They have only one festival of Christmas to celebrate. And even for that one celebration in a year, a lot of families moan about finding the money to give presents to their loved ones. I do not wish to humble their way of living, but this time when we were passing through such a rough time, there were none to come and share our ordeal.

However, the time was running fast that night. The clock does not care about the good or bad events. It just goes on clicking its seconds in our eardrums. Soon, it was 5am and 6am and then 7am. There was so much activity of the police on the silent night of our quiet street with many police cars coming and going; thumping of the road with the police officers' boots. Yet sadly, no neighbour woke up to find what was going on in their neighbourhood. They just could not care less. Their attitude was just 'I am alright Jack'.

It isn't that they did not know that we were not only burgled, but also were locked into a small bathroom. You see, three months later, on Friday 6th November 2018, when a milk float was put on fire just seven feet from our house and next to a gas control room, and when the whole street was outside, a couple of neighbours accepted that they knew of our ordeal. And yet they did not turn up to find out what happened and how we were coping. After the police had gone when their job had finished, we saw some neighbours busy in strengthening their garden fences. What kind of culture is this to leave their fellow beings to suffer alone? Have they no kind words to share the grief of those who suffer? I do not wish to compare, but when our friends came to know they came in droves to share our bad experience. They also brought food and we all ate together. Is that too much that Jesus had demanded from his followers?

Report Writing

About 7am of the morning after the burglary, the investigating officer arrived. He spent an hour and left. After all the other formalities were over the two officers stayed to write two separate reports. One officer stayed with Mira in the kitchen and the second one went with me in the lounge. Mira's report was of eleven pages and mine was of fifteen pages. The clock timed 11am. It was another ordeal of sleepiness. Amita and Vipul called for friends to come and help them to sort out the mess. The contents of every cupboard, every wardrobe, and every suitcase were thrown on the floor. All the beds, chairs, tables were turned upside down to find the valuables. They did not find any, except a couple of hundred pounds from our purses. We were worried that as they had not found much, they might hurt us or even kill us. But God saved us. They never harmed us and we are thankful for that. If they were really so desperate, they could have come to us, had dinners with us, and we would have given them whatever we had without creating such a big show. Maybe they will take all with them in their box, but for me I came here on

Meeting with our Local MP

The wakeup call never arrives; the penny never drops until it happens to you. I had been hearing the horrific stories of burglary and intrusion into our friends' million-plus bungalows and houses in the Chigwell and Woodford areas of London. A lot of our friends are doctors, dentists, professionals, and retired businessmen. They all have huge big gates and high metal fences and yet they were no deterrent to the intruders who climbed those fences and entered into bedrooms. I can give the details but it's no point in boring the readers.

Having gone through this ordeal of entry by four people into our own house, imprisoning us into a wet, dilapidated small bathroom, it was a wakeup call not to take it lying down but to knock at the doors of authorities whose duty it is to protect us in our so-called 'castles'. One of my knowledgeable, retired well-wishers who lives in Cyprus made some searches on Google and sent me the name of our new MP who was elected in 2017. Our previous MP, the Deputy Parliament Speaker whom I had met once in 2001 had retired. Armed with that info, I telephoned the MP's office at Saffron Walden. Having no joy from there I telephoned the Conservative office. The receptionist gave me the telephone number of the MP at Westminster and guidance about how to contact her. I first called her office in the morning on Friday 31st August 2018. Nobody answered the phone. I left a message. During the day, I made two more attempts without any contact. Next week, I called again on Monday 3rd September; again no reply. I tried again on Wednesday 5th and Thursday 6th leaving a message both times. I was now getting desperate and concerned about how these MP's work, what with all their office staff and telephones provided by the tax payers. I wanted to know more about their way of meeting their constituents. During this time, I also telephoned Conservative office again to know more about MP's procedures in meeting constituents. The receptionist was surprised that I had had no pleasure in contacting the MP's office. She took my details and the reasons for contacting my MP and said, 'I will pass on this info to the MP's staff whose office is next door to us.'

Luck finally smiled at me and I had the honour to have a call on Friday 7th at 3pm. The caller apologised for the delay in response. He asked my reasons for wanting to meet my MP. I gave him the brief history with tears in my eyes of the forced break-in, our ordeal of imprisonment, and the fear of living in our own house. After listening to my tale of woe, he assured me that he would call the Chief Inspector of Police immediately after our conversation ended and would ask him to increase the police patrol to our area immediately. And it happened.

A JOURNEY THROUGH PARTITION AND BEYOND

On Saturday 15th September as I drove to my factory at 9.30am I saw from a distance a policewoman patrolling the Stebbing Green area on her horse. Not believing my eyes, I slowed down my car to see the unbelievable scene that had not happened in the village for more years than I care to remember. Tears wallowed down my cheeks with joy. I overtook the horse and glanced at my car mirror. A compulsive urge came to get down from my car and bow my head to the officer and salute her. Then say, 'Oh Ma'am, thank you so much to show your reassuring face to the residents here. It was I whose house had an aggravated burglary.' But then on second thought I reluctantly drove on slowly in case my bowing down and saluting might be misunderstood by the officer. My actions might have been the gestures of appreciation and respect to the officer but its interpretation depended upon that lone policewoman and if she had misinterpreted wrongly, I might have ended up behind Her Majesty's walls. So, I drove off and wiped my tears of joy.

Meeting at Great Dunmow On Friday 28th September 2018

After so many attempts, I eventually had a call from the MP's office at Westminster that our MP would have time to see us at her Great Dunmow Surgery. We shut our office at 4pm to reach there in time. There were quite a few more people to see her. However, after a wait of nearly fifty minutes our turn came and we went into her small offices. In addition to the MP, there were two gents in attendance. The younger one was sitting with his laptop on his knees and the other, a bit older, greeted us with a smile. I and Mira both sat down on the two offered chairs. After the introduction by the MP, the dialogue started. I, as usual, became emotional. The tears were beginning to show up as soon as the MP said, 'I am sorry to know that you had a forced-burglary. What happened?'

'It was Saturday, 11th August 9.30pm when we were watching TV...' So, I narrated my ordeal. In between, Mira took over as I was choked with emotions.

'When I moved in this village there lived a Bobby in his office, about a couple of minutes' walk from our residence. Within a couple of years, he was gone. Then we had a police station at Dunmow. That was closed ten years ago. Now we have a police station in Saffron Walden with forty police officers. This station now looks after a huge area of the whole district. There is a rumour now that even this police station will be closed. The other nearest police station is Braintree which is manned by only six officers. I also hear that you are a member of the Justice Committee of the Parliament. That is most interesting to know and I am happy that I am talking to the right person about our ordeal.'

'Yes, I do belong to that committee and law and order is the issue I am interested in. I am taking a lot of interest in the law and order of the district and I want to improve the police services in this area. The success ratio of the police in this area is 24% and it is very good.'

'Sixty years ago, when I arrived in this country, an Englishman's house was his Castle. All gone. The politicians of all hue and colour have now turned the same house into rape houses, murder houses, shooting houses, drug houses. What an achievement of the present-day politicians,' I said.

Obviously, my remarks were not very congenial to hear. So, she got up and started saying what she was going to do. I got the message too that she wished me to leave. After a few seconds we also got up to leave. So that was the meeting that was.

The success ratio for the police in Essex is only 24%, yet the local police is congratulated by the local MP, thus sending a wrong message to the police to be inefficient and mindless; encouraging the burglars to continue their activities with impunity and without any possibility of being caught; without giving a damn to the other 76% victims by sending insulting messages. The burglars enjoy the tax-free loot and become more inventive to pursue their illegal activities, thus leaving the victims to lick their inflicted wounds for life. The criminals become more brazen to continue in their illegal activity of break-ins. They do not work as that is the time they use to continue in their research to find their new victims.

The police have no incentive to apprehend or catch these thugs. They are neither paid enough for the dangerous job they do to handle these criminals nor would they like to endanger their lives for the sake of victims. It is a very rare breed of men who would handle such duties. Therefore, the policemen are content with catching the law abiding, simple citizens who unfortunately erred once in life. Although no research is done on the subject, I guess there will be millions who have been punished and jailed for some petty crimes, but for the hard-core criminals who are quite smart, clever, and professional liars, it's easy to hoodwink the courts to get them off the hook.

The intruders gave me grief for life to live with. They gave me pain for life to keep on suffering from until I finally say good-bye to mother earth. They took away all the cash they could lay their hands on.

I have no regrets. They may be able to manage to take it with them in their box when they die. I wish them great luck in that endeavour, as I know I will leave this planet with my open hands with nothing in them. But one thing I am very grateful to them for is that they left us both physically fit and intact. They could not enter into our inner world. That is the most precious. They could not take away my talents and my inner being. They could not penetrate into my soul where only I could live and enjoy the fruits, gifted to me by my God. For this little mercy I am really grateful to them.

CHAPTER 11: THE CONCLUSION

The Life – The Final Circle in the Making

As I write this in 2018, we have been now running the business for more than 37 years. We never had a day off. It has been nothing but a hard slog. During these long years we had only four holidays. The first one was in 1991 when we went to Holland with my son and a couple friends. We were there for a week. It was fun, and we enjoyed the company we had. We had bought a new Honda Accord and we toured the country in that new car. We also went for a day to Belgium.

We had another holiday, a couple of years later and we went to Swansea, Wales for four days. The next one we took a week off to go to Belgium to stay with a young related family who worked there.

The final one was when we had a week off in October 2001 to get our son married in India with a young lady he met at Heathrow Airport after both were on a flight from Delhi. Since then no break except for ten, eleven days of extended shutdown of the factory at Christmas break in December. That too we started doing at Christmas 2003.

That has been the routine. That is the life and sometimes I wonder why. Why have I made a spider's web around me to suffer so? It is not only that I suffered, but my whole family also suffered. They had trusted that I would make the right decisions to make them happier. I had not taken such decisions purposely. My intentions were good to bring prosperity to all of us, but it is the ambitions of life that became the driving force to keep chasing the fruitless gains.

That web is now squeezing me and squeezing me hard with time.

Life is a very intricate journey, full of surprises and hurdles. It never moves smoothly. It has never known that route. It is like a stream, starting alone somewhere in the high mountains from its origin; moving through all kinds of terrains; negotiating its way through the mountains and valleys; hitting trees and rocks; and quenching the thirst of many living things on its way while at the same time collecting all kinds of garbage and rubbish. Then slowly and surely, by joining with other streams, it inches its way through the plains as a river to its destination – the ocean. Boats would be rowed on its water, piercing its heart with oars; propellers of motorboats would slice and dice its tranquillity, leaving its pure and serene water with polluted oils. If by stroke of luck it is declared to be a holy river, like the Ganges, it would attract a lot more savage treatment during its existence. Millions of people would bathe in its 'holy' waters to wash their sins and discharge their effluents. They would throw in beautiful, fragrant flowers which were created to beautify the landscapes and make the honeybees hover and dance around them and drink their nectar to get intoxicated. It is a slaughter of Nature's gifts to all living things. They would drink this 'holy' polluted water, bottle it, and take it as a souvenir to sip later. They would also discharge their excretions therein; throw in dead bodies to go to heavens that never exist. The 'holy' water is totally innocent. It would just like to move majestically to meet its source, the ocean. An individual life would like to move like a river, if permitted, in peace and tranquillity, but the other fellow travellers on this planet, with their dogmatic views, will just not let them. They just hate to let one live in peace and tranquillity.

I have reached a watershed of my life. As I write in 2018, I am now 87 and struggling to continue to inch my way through the mires of running a business in all kinds of environments. Man is weak, in fact very weak, emotionally and physically. The only way he wins is by using his mental faculties in which he is unique and unsurpassable by any in the universe we know about.

When Death Arrives

When I die, I will leave my past legacy to the surviving relations and friends, and also in my writing, provided it would continue to generate interest. The memories of my experiences, buried deep into this small miraculous brain, would all be destroyed and burnt by the sacred fires of the cremation. The mind would cease to exist with this body which nourishes it. The mind would be no more, the memories would be no more, and the past would be no more. What a great loss to the coming generations for the experiences of so many billions who had put their foot on this planet, especially of those with great brains and contributions to the civilisation. But this is what nature expects and this is how it is going to happen. It does not like the past of anyone to be a guide for another. It does not wish the old paths to be followed by the new generations. It wants everyone to search and make their own path with their own ingenuity and initiatives. It wants everyone to swim in this vast universal ocean where the path

A JOURNEY THROUGH PARTITION AND BEYOND

is destroyed as soon as it is made. Nature does not like copycats. It loves originals that create their own destiny.

I will then be moving to the future, the journey to the future that I will not be able to share with any. I do not know how the death of the body will arrive. Would I be conscious and aware, or would I just go into a coma and become a cabbage? This body is only a vehicle to express and share my phoney ideas with others. My real being which had made this body as a temporary abode would be on its way to join the source whence it came. The source is the energy of the consciousness that had put life into this body. I wish that on the day of my demise I could witness the arrival of the angel of death and then fly away with the angels to my abode of permanence where I came from. It would be the same experience as I had once before at the age of eleven when I lay on my bed and the angels were dancing and hovering around to bundle me into their delicate hands to make me fly away. Mercifully they had changed their minds to allow me to live on their planet for so many more years. I hope they are not regretting that decision. Again, I had the similar experience in July 2015 at 2 o'clock in the night when a couple of 'angels' were tearing me away from my body and I was fighting back to extricate myself from their clutches. I know the dreams are never true but who were they? Again, the same incident was repeated a couple of months later. So that is life.

It was my pleasure to share my life experiences with you. I hope you enjoyed its reading and presentation.

Have a great life and forgive me if I have offended your feelings anytime with my statements in this book.

APPENDIX 1: INSULTING CORRESPONDENCE

On 5th January 2012, I made an enquiry through Alibaba for a Stick Pack machine from Uflex in India. They replied to me by email, giving me a brief description of the machine. They also attached a machine picture with their terms and conditions. That picture, when viewed closely, caught my attention. It was an old rusted machine. Being a man of Indian origin, I was disturbed at how such a big reputable company could send such old pictures to their would-be buyers. I wrote a letter asking 'Is that the machine in the picture' you were selling me. From that letter, their Vice President got so much annoyed that he wrote me very rude and impertinent letters, accusing me of lack of integrity and disloyalty to the country I come from. Here is that correspondence.

January 2012

Hi **Om,**

Thanks for your mail. We value your opinion but will like to put our voice also as follows :-

1. We were equally disappointed when you again raised an enquiry asking for a **Moon in one machine**. We knew from the starting that the business is not going to happen.

A JOURNEY THROUGH PARTITION AND BEYOND

Om: Sorry I only gave my requirements. My experience is that whenever you buy a machine the supplier normally asks such questions and then comes back with a proposal to offer you the best solution with their existing machines. I was not in the market to buy a machine first time in life. So I don't know where 'moon' has landed from.

2. Still being an Indian we never wanted to leave our humbleness and tried to do justice as much as possible towards not only parting the information but also trying to educate the possibilities.

Om: Your language is piercing, it is not humble. Please do not bring all Indians in to it. This is your dialogue and you chose it that way to deal with the issue.

3. Once again it is to reiterate that probably there has to be a difference between a show piece and a working machine. We deliver working machines and not the show pieces, **which probably you need.**

Om: You took my comments on the brochure wrongly. I was only trying to help you improve the image of your company. You will appreciate that no suitor will choose a partner if sent with an ugly picture. I think I was only trying to help but then words are words and it depends how they are interpreted. I don't know why there is a hurt and why it is blown out of proportion. You should accept that that picture is wrong and should be replaced with a better one to tempt future buyers but what can you do with an ego. It does not bother me if you want to keep the same picture, does it.

4. We already have machines around the world, your country being one of them, with proven credentials, few of them are working with the biggest co-packers. Hence, may look forward to another appreciation but are not really thirsty for that.

Om: I do not dispute that and that is why a number of years ago I asked that let me have an agency to sell your machines in UK. I know you are not thirsty for more business as Sanjay mentioned that you have sale of 400 Crores. Mine was only a peanut contribution and nothing more. You might have heard Tesco's slogan 'Every little bit help's. Your reply reflects arrogance, making a buyer feel humble, reducing him to a dust.

5. You are right, you are not our foe but we know your organization for years and knew that kept aside buying, you will come across with some tiny points to went-out your feelings against your fellow Indians for reasons best known at your end.

Om: As I said before you have misinterpreted my words. I was only trying to help to insert some better picture, thus improving the image of your well-established company with so many good products at the market place. Surprisingly you do not comment on that but quite happy to attack my integrity without knowing me much.

6. Being a patriot, the finger towards my country has not been taken well and hence may like to point out that look at, where your empire was and what you are today. **Hardly being recognized in the global scene today** May we know who swallowed whom ?

A JOURNEY THROUGH PARTITION AND BEYOND

Om: (let this success not go to your head). By saying 'my country' and 'your empire' you are implying that I am a foreigner and you are an Indian - a very poor comparison. You found it so simple to write me off. What are the criteria that you are a better Indian than I am simply because you live there?

The truth is that you are lucky that you live and work now in well-developed India. The people of your calibre have jobs with good standard of living. I do not know your age but that does not matter. You must have read history in the high school/college.

Let us put the clock back to 1947, when my family lost everything with no fault of theirs and I am not asking you to sympathise with my plight. We (millions like us) were reduced to destitute, with no income to support or to educate. We lived in refugee camps, with a hand out from the government of the day. We picked up the crumbs to survive. Being young I and many like me left the country with Rs 14 in our pockets in search of some future abroad. In India there were no colleges, no factories and no jobs except the deprivation, death, and religious strife. When here we did all kinds of menial jobs to earn a few bob, lived as cattle in the crowded houses; supported our families in India who had no income (I still do it with remittances); educated ourselves with our savings; lived in the country which hated us, insulted us, called us black Bs and niggers. Lord Ram was only exiled for fourteen years and we still celebrate yearly his home coming but we so called NRI who are condemned to live abroad for life, and are now being questioned about their patriotism.

About 50 years ago when I met Hansa Mehta, the well-known social worker Gandhian and the wife of the Indian High Commissioner Jeev Raj Mehta in UK in those days, she said to me in her palatial house when we visited her that 'We wrote you Indians off who live abroad'. My crime was that I had just finished my degree in Engineering in London and during the introduction when she asked when I would go back to India, I said 'Give me a job now and I would be in the plane tomorrow to fly back to India'. With that arrogant remark I responded 'Who the hell you are to write me off. That country belongs to me as much as to you'. The meeting ended in the next two minutes. The tea served by her colonial servant stayed on the table and I with my wife was on my way home rather than to India. You are the 2nd one since then who has hurt my feelings that badly. Your language is typically British with sweet words in them but loaded with venom. It reminds me a slaughter house in which one recites the scriptures while slaughtering the innocent animals.

No one leaves home if he or she has a choice. I got all that above just for a small suggestion to change the old picture to improve your company's image. A very poor reward! It is very sad to know that you are hated by your own countrymen where you were born and you are also hated in the country of your adoption. What a world we live in?

We once again thank you for not placing an order. As otherwise your discontent on account of some or other reasons best known to you towards Indians may not have led relations to be very rosy.

Om: Let me give you the info about the machine being offered:

Offered: Single lane, computer controlled, with a printer, euro-hole, gas flushing, stainless steel,   Price $4,500 delivered

Can pack higher weights in bigger bags than yours, delivery within 4 weeks

Yours: Single lane, computer controlled,
Price £10.000 plus cost of packing
Delivery: 8-10 weeks
Cost of delivery, plus £2000 for the Printer and gas flushing

Let me know which one you would buy. If you wish I can send you the details and the offer letter for the machine. It is best to know your competitors.

With all humbleness, best regards and apologies, we request that at least spare the counting of origin if possible.

Om: I and many others like me do not live abroad by choice but because of the forced circumstances and that is why I went into a bit of my history to explain.

I do not expect and wish any response for this letter. Let us close this chapter for good. You won't hear from me anymore.

With best wishes

Om

APPENDIX 2: THE BABBLES

During this long journey, I was called upon to say a few words about my good friends and relations. I am neither a born writer nor a speaker. I shy away from such activities. I feel nervous and out of place when facing a more intelligent and learned crowd.

English is not my mother tongue. I have not a good command of it. I have acquired it by practicing it. I have learnt it mostly in the later years when writing business letters. I always left essays and critical analysis of the statements in my English examination papers. I never had the nag to say anything about such topics. They mostly carried about 40% of the marks. Therefore, I used to barely pass the English examinations. That would obviously reflect on my final grades.

However, with a bit of luck, I was only called upon four times in my whole life to say something. The following babbles are what I said. But how I said them in front of the crowd, only they can give their opinions. I cannot judge my performance.

A Party at a Friend K's House:

It was Saturday 26th January 2002, Republic Day of India. A good friend had invited a few friends whose children had married in the last few months. So, the scene was set to enjoy the party, given in the honour of the young newly married couples. The parents of these were there too. In addition to that there were some more friends. M came to ask that K wanted her to say a few words that evening at the party.

I said, 'Why don't you? Your d-in-l is there, you should say something.'

'No, I don't know what to say. You say it.'

She insisted. I persisted that in that case, she should ask her daughter R to say a few words.

'I asked her, but she also does not want to say anything either.'

'OK, let me think. I will say something if some ideas hit me. Have you any suggestions?'

'No, I haven't.'

So, I went into deep deliberations and lost the conversations which I was having with the assembled friends. I am not a public speaker. However, some ideas hit my brainwaves and I was ready to go into the battle.

After the cake-cutting ceremonies, I was called upon to say a few bits. I started as below.

'I have read that God created this world in seven days. The first four days he created matter, wind, water, light, insects, trees, universal laws etc. The fifth day he created a man. He investigated the crystal ball and visualised that He had created an arrogant monster; a cruel aggressive fighter with huge ego to dominate the world. He gave him brains to be inventive; to be compassionate, to be caring to mind His creation; to be free and yet be mindful of obedience. He had guessed it rightly that instead the man was going to use those energies to achieve his own destructive ends. By that evening he was not very happy with his creation. He was very disappointed and immediately retired to His solitary rooms to recoup his energies for the daunting task of His unique creation next day. Sixth day he created a woman. He corrected all his mistakes, which he had made in creating a man. He gave her everything superior he could think of. He gave her the beauty she

A JOURNEY THROUGH PARTITION AND BEYOND

deserved. He made her tender at heart, loving, and caring. He made her devout devotee of submissive nature. The most important part He assigned her the task of creating the next generation that is to be a mother of His on-going creation. Because He had put so much effort and energy in inventing a woman, that by the evening He was exhausted. So, the seventh day he took rest to recoup his energy to manage his creation. He is still reeling from the loss of that energy and the depression of creating an arrogant man. He is now searching frantically the ways to put that genie back into the jar but unsuccessful so far.

'So, we are lucky to have the women who are caring, loving, and guiding the destiny of a man. Without them we men would be lost. It is the greatest asset we have, and we are grateful to our womenfolk who do so much for us and get so little reward for it. We see here wide range of couples. C (my 1st D in law) has travelled from the other side of the planet India to adopt our home and our name in this country. She left all those loving parents and friends with whom she grew up to be with us. We are grateful for that and we welcome her in our folds. Take M's fiancée who has come from Italy to join up M to set up a home here. The only other couple I know with the Italian wife was Rajiv Gandhi who finally ended up as the Prime Minister of India. I would watch M with interest what he becomes in the days to come. Then we have some other couples too who have crossed the barriers of cast, country, and the religions. The whole world is now in a melting pot. It is a world where all kinds of nationalities, the religions, the colours, the beauties and beasts are mingling together. It would be a world where no casts and creeds would dominate the society. It would be a free world with paramount human rights.

'But, ladies & gentlemen, having said that I would be in dire trouble with those chauvinistic men sitting in that corner who would banish me amongst them (*mera hukka pani band kar dain gai*). So, I must hurriedly say that the God was no ordinary fool. With all his clever inventions on the sixth day, he also tried to equalise the genders He further gave some traits to a woman and they were to be submissive and the attention seeker. He put one seed deep into her head. She dies to have a fan, a follower, a lover, a chaser, a tiger. The man admiringly fulfilled that roll. She hankers for his chase. Only a few years ago, as you walked on these neighbourhood roads the young beauties, well dressed, and with dazzling make ups, eager to attract the opposite sex would stealthily look at you to discover whether you were looking at her or not. If not, she would go home and cry her eyes out that with all her efforts to attract men, no one was looking at her. But the times have changed. In my young age whenever we whistled at a girl in India, she would throw sandals at us (*jandon asan unhan te nazar setti, te unahn ne chappel kaddi*). But now-a-days, the woman must look straight on the road while driving. She cannot afford to divert her attention on the other drivers. However, the moment you wait at the red light, you will notice that the lady is looking sideways to find if any one is looking at her. So, the time might have changed but the nature of the ladies has not changed. Such was the craze in those days that without the admirers the ladies were going mentally sick.

'Years ago, when S's, G's, B's et al moved into this neighbourhood, the new generation of young lovers like S, S, V, R, A were now roaming the streets of Chigwell. The ladies of the area were again getting the attention. They seemed happier and contended. If you don't believe this, the proof is the closing down of the mental hospital next door to this house. That hospital area is now flourishing with housing developments.

'Finally, I would take courage to suggest to our next young generation that they should never be quitters in life. It does not matter what the odds are. The quitters never succeed. The struggle for life started at the time of conception. Our sperm ran faster through the thick fluid than the other millions injected and mated to its final prize – the egg. So, we are not going to give up now. As we call in Hindi that *yeh jeevan ek sangharsh hai* (this life is nothing but a battle ground). Bend down and let the storm blow over you rather than blow you away. Once the storm is over, get up and be ready for another fight on another day.

'In my tiny span of life, I have come across many people. But the bravest of them all is only one. I would like to bow my head to that person. (Bowed to K S who was suffering from cancer). K I apologise to have exposed my baldhead to you. You are the bravest. You have been even defying the will of God. In your fight to beat this cruel disease we are all with you. We might not have come to your prayer meeting that regularly, but our heart and mind has always been with you. We admire for your courage and your defiance to destiny. Ladies &

A JOURNEY THROUGH PARTITION AND BEYOND

gentlemen, I would now propose that we drink for her speedy recovery and our solidarity towards her. Now if you permit me and if I have the permission of my Guru whom I call the singing Sufi, I would like to sing a few beautiful words of a great poet. I would urge you not worry about my silly singing but pay special attention to the beautiful words of the song. As you know in life we all bleed inside one time and another. These words help me to see the daylight.

'*Ek andhera lakh sitare*, (there is only one darkness but millions of twinkling stars)

'*Ek nirasha lakh sahare*. (there is only one grief but millions of supporting hands)

'And so on.

'So not ending up into a big speech, I am grateful to K who invited us and gave us this opportunity to enjoy the good company of our friends with tasty and well served food.'

There I ended to keep it 'short and sweet' as C said later.

Om Khurana

Tribute to my cousin on his cremation

Date: 11th February 1999
Tribute to Brother D. C. Gulati, retired Army officer at his Cremation Ceremony

Born on 11th August 1917, Died on 9th February 1999, Cremation on Friday, 12th February 1999.

At the cremation assembly I was sitting next to the deceased's son G. The priest was busy in reading his last rites to the departed soul from the Hindu scriptures. Before announcing the body to be moved through that little door for the cremation he asked G if there is anyone who would like to pay some tribute to the deceased, G looked towards me and said, 'Om Ji can you say something?' With a bit of luck, I had written something the evening before about what I was going to say. So, I took out the rough draft from my pocket and walked towards the speaker's table to say the following:

'Public speaking is the domain of politicians. Engineers don't make good orators. However, I will try. It is an emotional moment. If I do get into emotional outbursts and I inflict pain on you. Please forgive.

'We are all travellers on the back of this mother earth. My brother travelled nearly 82 times around the sun and another about 1/2 million miles on other transports on its surface. A huge journey by a tiny creature! Some of us are travelling as brothers and sisters; others as husbands and wives, friends, or as sons and daughter-in -law, grandson and grand daughter. I travelled with him on this planet as a brother. According to an Indian tradition, being younger I knew him only a little because it depended how much time he could spare for me, the younger one. But whenever he had time, I sat with him and asked him questions about his adventures in the Indian Army. I even sometimes begged him to write about his experiences. He was a great soldier. He fought in Europe in the 2nd World War. After Independence, he was on the front line when Hyderabad was attacked. He also saw action in Jammu & Kashmir. He fought for the country whenever and wherever the country needed his services. He put his life in danger so that we civilians can live free and in peace and harmony. His narration of army actions in different battles was very fascinating and exciting to me.

'He grew up like any other kid. My eldest brother and he were good chums. In their spare time they did what any young people do - hunt girls. He worked very hard. He educated, married and well settled his son, Gullu ji. Age was catching up with him. The demands of life were making him to struggle harder and harder to keep up. In this life race he was now beginning to feel tired, weaker, and eventually fell. Fallen, tired & underperformers are never liked by the mother earth. So, it eventually pulled the plug.

'I look towards the sky and I see river of tears in his mother's eyes. She is justified to cry. She had gone through hell to bear her beloved son and brought him up to be a good citizen of the world. Today he lay dead, there in that box, helpless, motionless, and speechless. You hit him, hurt him, cuddle him, kiss him, he does not respond. He is gone cold. All she had done lay on waste heap now. What a tragic waste of a person who ceaselessly fought for the honour of his countrymen? But sadly, she forgot that the same cruel mother earth had pulled one day her plug too when it found that she was old, infirm and unable to play by the rigid rules, laid down by the mother earth to carry on its own grand design of Creation (SRISHTI).

'Pandit Ji- what I am going to say now may not be so pleasant for you to hear. Therefore, forgive me for that.

'Death is a disease. Sceptics will disagree, but we always die with a cause or a disease. It is time that we defy death. It has humiliated and insulted the imagination and intelligence of us humans for millions of years. It inflicts unbearable pain for this permanent separation of the loved ones. Let us not despair any more. One day we will win it and disband it from our lives. Win we must, if not for ourselves, then for our children and grand children who will have the right to live forever without a hanging threat of death on them. They will die when they choose to die as Bisham Pitamah did in Mahabharat. That day I foresee is not very far when we would decide to die the age we wish to. I would like to live to the healthy age of 140 and more rather than being condemned into a box at a younger age of seventies. However, it would not be brought about by Indians. Never! They are too dogmatic in their approach. They worship those who threaten their existence. They worship snakes; the mighty rivers of Ganga and Brahmaputra; and diseases such as measles, typhoid etc. which kills them. They have carved out stones to turn them up into imaginative gods. So, the solution must come from others. Until then, let us keep living and enjoying the best of our lives.

'Now he is gone forever, and we finally say our goodbye to him. We will miss him forever. We will always cherish the unwritten history of his life which he left behind for us. We will talk about his both naughty habits and good habits because he was a human and not God. That is how he will continue to remain a part and parcel of our lives. Having now known the bleeding pain which is inflicted by the permanent separation of the loved ones, I would like to run away from you all to die in some remote corners of this planet, where no one will know me. They will ditch or dispose of this body the way they will feel fit, so that I do not inflict the grief and pain to those whom I love and admire and together made a journey of my life time.

'Thank you for coming and supporting the Gulati family in their hour of need. Please do not forget to attend the religious ceremony at their residence.

'God Bless you all.'

OPK

Some comments: -

Friend's wife: As soon as we came out, "True and well said."

On the way back in the car I said to my cousin's son, "I hope you are not upset by my saying that your father was hunting girls when he was young."
"Why would I get upset? He was your brother and it is between you and him. But what you said was said very well."

A JOURNEY THROUGH PARTITION AND BEYOND

With a friend's sister I had a long discussion. I gathered that she is very religious. Objected and questioned what I said about living forever because it was against the will of God.

A friend - laughing and in a bit of sarcastic tone, "I should have born 40 years later to qualify to live 140+ years."

His wife: "I have no desire to live longer. I believe I have nothing more to do and am ready to go whenever." I said, "You are quite right what you said. You have fulfilled a female's roll assigned by our maker and that is that you have given birth to children and so you are now contented that your job on this planet is over. But there are others whose ambitions to achieve are limitless and therefore they would like to live much longer."

Friend's wife: "I have been hearing that you spoke on the funeral. I have missed it."

My son a couple of days later the phone- "Dad, whatever you said on (the funeral on that day) was very well said."

My daughter said after reading my text, "It is very well written. But did you then say it there properly as well?" "I hope so but other can judge it better." My wife butted in and said, "Oh yes, he said it very well. Everyone was impressed." Surprisingly she was also quite impressed, and I could see for first time in life that she was a bit proud and respectful to me. She never expected that I was capable enough to write and say what I said. She thought that I am only good enough in washing dishes at home and, therefore, respect I should be accorded is to be fitting to that type of person. After the speech, she said "So that is what you had been writing last night on the computer. I wondered what you were doing at such late hours." I had finished my text around midnight. There was no time to polish it. When I spoke, I was in real anguish and the grief was not only visible in my voice, but it was inside too. Someone said to me later that nearly 70-80% were in tears as I spoke. The biggest advantage was that I could say whatever I wanted to, without being haggled and interrupted by others.

415

Friend: "We will talk about what you said when we meet," said on the phone. We met, and he was sceptical that we humans can ever live that long and even if we can there will be a population explosion. Besides what are you going to achieve by living longer. I said, "We are commoners and perhaps our contribution to the civilisation is zero but there are others such as eminent scientists, artists, singers, painters etc. for whom the life is not long enough to contribute more of their talents for the betterment of the world. Besides I might like to experiment a few years of my life to try other professions or to explore other planets but if the life span is so short, I would not be able to venture out to do it." Obviously, we differed.

SURPRISE! SURPRISE! On next Sunday, 14th February 99, The Sunday Times had headlines on the front page that the children born now can expect to live 140-150 years with the modern technology, medicine, and availability of human spare parts produced with our own cells to avoid rejection. It ran special magazines on the future living for six weeks. So, it vindicated what I had said.

Friend's son at a birthday party: "What you said at the funeral came out true, especially by the article in the Sunday Times. It was a really surprising to read that how your forecast came out so right."

A friend: "I did not know DC was your cousin. I asked someone next to me what the hell he is doing up there (when you were asked to speak by the priest), then he told me that DC was your cousin."

MY 70th BIRTHDAY:

It was Saturday 18th February 2001

I normally celebrate my birthday on 13th February of the year. There are a few other friends whose birthdays also fall around the same time. A few years ago, it became a tradition to celebrate the birthdays together. We did for a few years and then it faded away. It always happens that way in life. New ways and means are found to enjoy the life together and after a while such occasions become boring and are then replaced with some other reasons and excuses. Now we all celebrate on our own. This year A celebrated by having a Kirtan on last Saturday on 10th and G went out with his family on Monday. My birthday was being celebrated on Saturday 17th at home.

My 65th birthday was celebrated by my friends. They came to our home and gave us a big surprise. They brought us dinner and presents. Therefore, on 70th birthday I had decided to celebrate it by inviting the friends at our home.

Birthday Wishes to a friend's daughter: MALINI

To whosoever it may Interest:

Malini is a multi-dimensional, multi-talented, simple, down-to earth, inspiring, beautiful, attractive young lady. She has so many qualities that perhaps, given a chance and a bit of research, I may manage to write a book on her. I have seen her growing up right from her early childhood and yet I have only a very limited knowledge of her. And that I gathered during my meetings with her, now and then, in small parties. I would not be exaggerating if I say that it was my privilege to know such a lovely girl from a distant and yet so closely.

Some of her best qualities are that she is very caring, determined, and single minded to achieve her goal on which she sets her mind on. This quality was shown so clearly when her dad got into some serious medical problems of survival. I always believed that it was her devotion and love for her father that she refused to allow every visitor to see him, even though they were all his good friends of many years and they all had the goodwill for her father, but she just did not budge from her main aim of protecting his health. When we went there, her mother apologised that there was no chance of bypassing Malini who was sitting as vigilante next to her father. It is because of her strictness on all the visitors, her coaxing of the doctors in attendance to bring out their best talents, and to prescribe the best medicines, that her father came out so well from his ordeal.

She is also an easy going, co-operative, and courageous girl. She is a very good friend and would always be willing to share and participate in the happiness and sorrows of those whom she happens to know. She travelled all the way to India to attend Vipul's marriage in 2001. That was the time when the timid were cancelling their travel arrangements by air because of the 9/11 attack in America. Americans were the first to do that and yet in that uncertainty of flying, she was in Delhi to support her friend's marriage. Not only that, when there were no spare rooms left to share, she volunteered to sleep in the hall on the floor. So far, I have never heard even once her moaning to any one that Om uncle failed in his duty to provide her a decent bed with all the travels, the hassles she had gone through in attending Vipul's marriage. But to me, I still cannot forgive myself for not been able to provide a comfortable stay in Delhi. I just would not forget it.

I may now like to go very deep into my memory lane. I see a video playing in my head. That video is running from that very first day when we went

A JOURNEY THROUGH PARTITION AND BEYOND

to meet her family at Basildon. Guess what I saw. A little girl, very confident, very curious, standing in the corner of her lounge with a smiling face, and watching the strangers entering the lounge for the first time in her house. That smiling faces – the unforgettably smiling face on that day and as well as today - has become her trade mark. That is how she is, a happy smiling girl. And that is how I see her in my memory lane. But before she gets into some ego trip, I may also hasten to add that I have also seen a couple of times for snapping at her mother. Sorry! But then she is a human and she is not a god. Even gods can be very angry at times, then why not humans.

Number of times I had the opportunity to debate and discuss some issues of the day with Malini. We discussed religions, politics, social and economic problems, poverty and many more subjects. She always debated those issues in a cool, calm, and informative manner. These debating traits perhaps she inherited from her dad who is also willing to talk on any subject under the sun. She always had the originality of the ideas – always. Not repeating anything from scriptures or texts. She never has fixed ideology to cling to. As the life evolves, she evolves with it. She is never a copycat. These are the qualities which impress you when you debate with her. She is true picture of a changing life in her. As we all know that the life never repeats itself. It is always fresh and changing all the time. So, does Malini – fresh and vibrant. These qualities come only to those who are gifted and talented and she is one of them.

I have watched her to play with children. She is quite comfortable to become a child again, very innocent, and very friendly with them.

Finally, and very reluctantly I would like to dwell on something about her personal life from the society's point of view. The society is brutal, ignorant, selfish, and look at its members in a very strange way. Humans can neither discard it nor can live with this evil. The society wants you have a partner, have the children, and then spend rest of your life to build their future. Once that is achieved, the society just wants you to wither away into wilderness. Is that the meaning of the life? I believe - no certainly not.

Malini tried her best to find someone who could match to even a few of her qualities. Has she failed in her quest? No. It is not the case. She is not lacking in the charm, in beauty, in talents, in qualities of a good mother, in caring for a partner (I hate to say wife as it sounds possessing or subservient to the other). But it is those unfortunates who met her but failed to recognise and distinguish between a diamond and a stone. If the jeweller goes blind with the reflecting rays of the sun coming from the diamond, it is not the fault of the diamond, is it? The diamond cannot change its nature just to please the jeweller. It is the jeweller who should be aware that how much its own value would enhance by acquiring that diamond. Diamond does not become poorer. It is the jeweller who suffers. He lost the opportunity to become a part of that priceless diamond.

The suitors are looking at her with their small mind. They were not that much gifted. This world is abounded with (99%) of such incapable, ill-equipped people. She belongs to that 1% category. The vision of that 99% is very limited and narrow. It only reaches to the tip of their nose. It is they who are unlucky. It is they who are missing a gem. The rose never changes its fragrance and its beauty simply to please the dangling bees.

But then marrying and breeding the children – although desirable and a great ambition of every woman – should not be the sole purpose and the only goal of life of any individual. The purpose of life and why we are here is more important to investigate than to bog down in meeting the demands of the society. However, these are very much personal matters, and everyone must find the answer to such questions for themselves. I am no one to give directions.

Finally, I am honoured to be asked to say few words about Malini. If I have said anything wrong to some one's taste, I beg to be forgiven. I wish Malini a great life, with many pleasant surprises to come, and to live the life she likes to live, not dictated by anyone, including the Divine.

I remain her uncle

OM

A JOURNEY THROUGH PARTITION AND BEYOND

* * * * * * * * * * * * *

Mira Auntie Writes:

Dear Malu

Hurray! You are going to be '40'in a few days time. Congratulations.

We can't imagine, you just look like sweet 16. We have always known you very polite, patient, and ready-to-help, even tempered, lovely, and recently discovered very wise, philosophical, and down to earth.

While we sit down and talk to you, we feel very elated and proud of you. We feel that you discuss matters with great maturity. Your Mum is always full of praise of as well.

May God bless you in all walks of life? May all your dreams be fulfilled?

Much Love

Om Khurana

The Marriage Anniversary of a Great Friend turned into a Relation:

A message came through my wife to say something on the occasion. As a novice on the speaking game at special occasions, I was surprised to be asked as there are very many good orators in the circle. However, I sat down to write the following and spoke when I was called to do so. The whole show was being managed by the two well-settled daughters, the elder one as doctor in Paris and the younger as ophthalmologist in America.

Jolly's 50th Anniversary

At

Kanchan's

29.07.12

Hello All

A loving, dedicated daughter rushed to the family priest to ask him to say a few words about her parents in the evening party. She requested,

'You know him so well. He comes to your congregation every Sunday. Would you please say some good words about my husband in the evening party today?'

'Yes, I would be very pleased to, but I normally charge £200 but for you I would charge £100'

'£100! That is a lot of money priest? I have not got that much money. I cannot break the bank to pay you that much. (Besides I have not got the Pounds. I can give you Francs. If that is any help).'

(No, I don't handle Francs.)

(How about US Dollars? I can ask my sister to pay in Dollars if you like.)

(No, I don't accept that currency either.)

(Ok let me pay you in Indian Rupees. You come from India. Spend that there when on holiday next time.)

A JOURNEY THROUGH PARTITION AND BEYOND

(Look madam you are now getting awkward. If you want me to speak pay me in Pounds or let us forget it)

(Ok, ok don't get upset. I will have to dip my hands into my dad's pocket.)

'Ok I will settle for £50 but no less and that too because he regularly attends my Sunday mass.'

'Sorry priest, I cannot afford that, and I am not going to dip my hands deeper into my dad's pocket.'

So, they haggled on and eventually the priest said,

'Ok, you offer, how much you can pay me?'

'£15 is the maximum I will pay, take it or leave it'

'Oh, for that money then I will have to tell the truth about your parents.'

So, ladies and gentlemen I am not even paid a dime by the family. I have no choice but to tell the truth, nothing but the whole truth.

Having said that may I please have a bodyguard in case I am attacked by J who is closely standing next to me?

Mystery at Fancy Party

Welcome to Jolly party and enjoy. Their parties always have a theme like Raj Kapoor films. I remember a fancy-dress party a few years ago here in this place. A young lady dressed in such a manner that all the Jolly family were going around and round her for fifteen minutes. They were at their wit's end to discover who she was? I was next to them watching the mystery show and they kept asking me 'Khurana Ji, do you know who she is?' It was not my job to disclose the secret. Finally, Jolly offered bribe to the lady – first prize with a bottle of antique red wine. She coughed up and the mystery was solved.

Today they have theme of a casino. So, if you have spare cash, lose it or win it

SALA (brother-in-law)

One fine morning I had a call from Jito.

'Khurana Ji, I would like to change our friendship into a relationship. I would like to make you my SALA'.

SALA a great relationship, but the terminology has been turned into a derogatory expression. I thought for a moment - a brother to a lovely, pleasant, cheerful, and smiling lady; Mama to two young very talented ladies Mini and Delia. What else one needs in a relation? I consented, and, on that day, I became a S A L A, S A L A to Jito, a very clever move I thought to bring me down to earth.

A few Words for Jolly:

I hate to praise people on their face in case I boost their false egos. I might even influence their natural character or personality, but I have no choice here. I must tell the truth.

Jito is a great friend. I would not like to talk about his trivial traits such as honesty, decency, loving, affectionate etc. I would also not talk about his yawning in the morning wake up or his walking in style to the bathroom to ease himself for his daily chores. I have not seen him doing that, so no comment on that.

But I would like to say that he is a great friend with all the best qualities a good friend should have. He will stand by you like a rock, like a steel tower. Once you know that he is behind you, you can take on the world fearlessly. If you wish to know him truly then go deep into his inner being, into his soul and you will find nothing but the heart full of diamonds. You must penetrate his mysterious heart to know him. But if you look on his outer world, on his fleshy body, you will miss him. Because there, under the fleshy garment, you will find nothing else, but the smelly flesh, covered with millions of hairs. We all have an ugly body, made it into a beautiful and handsome flesh by decorating it with various designer's colourful attires. I suggest that you just stand in front of the mirror and examine the various curves of your naked body.

A JOURNEY THROUGH PARTITION AND BEYOND

The human body is the ugliest looking. That is why God would never dare come on this planet. He is ashamed of himself for the creation of the human body and he knows it. He knows that He would be the first one to be shot. His son was crucified, and his prophet was tortured. If you have time to ponder on, think about an imaginary world of humans walking around naked all over the streets. I bet the sex will disappear from the human thinking. The pills for the contraceptives and the morning after would disappear. The monks and nuns will join back to the society.

But look at the animal world; the peacocks, the pigeons, the fish, the cows, the monkeys, they are the most beautiful creations of the Divine. It is they which were used by the Nature as guinea pigs to perfect all our limbs, the bones, and the organs. Most of you eat them – disgusting - our predecessors who helped to make our body.

Forgive me I was carried away.

My simple advice to you all is

Only strive to seek his friendship. He is a great friend and would never let you down.

Do not offend his religion because he is proud Sikh and its heritage.
Do not give grief to his friends either because he would not spare you
Equally do not ever try to step on his tail; his growl could be equally bad.

Finally – Talking Time

Finally, before I finish, Mini was generous to allot me 10 minutes. Thank you, Mini. My wife of 50 years had cut it down to five minutes because she knows that I am a bore.

That reminds me a story.

A minister was installed in a newly created ministry. He wanted to impress the public with his speeches. One day when speaking, he noticed the audience was getting bored. They were yawning, scratching, and dosing off. After the event, he called his press agent and asked that in future he writes very brief speeches for him to read. On another occasion as he was speaking he noticed the people were getting bored. He was very much annoyed with the agent. He was worried that he would lose election if that continues. So, he asked for the agent to come to his office immediately. He demanded to know why he failed to follow his instructions for a short and to the point speech. He replied,

'Sir, the speech was short, but nobody asked you to read all the three copies you were given'

[Really, final, I know you must be bored and hate me for my intrusion into your enjoying the evening:

Please forgive J whatever is said here. He is poking a gun (is that gun or fingers, oh I thought it was a gun) at me and I have repeated whatever he asked me to say here. I was only saying whatever he was whispering into my ears. I was scared, and I had no choice.

Ladies and gentlemen, so far you have come across surrogate mothers but today you have witnessed a surrogate speaker]

Thank you for listening to my babble. God bless you all and very HAPPY 50th ANNYVERSARY to Jolly's and their family.

Note: The sentences in bracket were not said because of lack of time and, I spoke the text from memory and not by reading it.

Printed in Poland
by Amazon Fulfillment
Poland Sp. z o.o., Wrocław